1978

REMINISCENCE, MOTIVATION, AND PERSONALITY

A Case Study in Experimental Psychology

REMINISCENCE, MOTIVATION, AND PERSONALITY

A Case Study in Experimental Psychology

H. J. Eysenck and C. D. Frith

University of London
London, England

PLENUM PRESS · NEW YORK AND LONDON

Library of Congress Cataloging in Publication Data

Eysenck, Hans Jurgen, 1916-
  Reminiscence, motivation, and personality.

  Bibliography: p.
  Includes index.
  1. Memory, 2. Motivation (Psychology) 3. Personality. I. Frith, C. D., joint
author. II. Title.
BF371.E94   152.3'34   76-40136
ISBN 0-306-30924-6

© 1977 Plenum Press, New York
A Division of Plenum Publishing Corporation
227 West 17th Street, New York, N.Y. 10011

Printed in the United States of America

Although the invention of plausible hypotheses, independent of any connection with experimental observations, can be of very little promotion of natural knowledge; yet the discovery of simple and uniform principles, by which a great number of apparently heterogeneous phenomena are reduced to coherent and universal laws, must ever be allowed to be of considerable importance toward the improvement of the human intellect.

THOMAS YOUNG: *First Bakerian Lecture,* 1801

This book is dedicated to the many friends, colleagues,and students whose work in this department contributed to our final formulations:

A. Broadhurst	J. Germain	R. Kessell	K. H. Star
P. Broadhurst	J. Grassi	P. Ley	K. Sterky
G. Claridge	M. Garg	A. E. Maxwell	C. Stroh
A. M. Clark	J. E. Gray	P. D. McLean	J. Tizard
D. Cookson	H. C. Holland	N. O'Connor	E. Treadwell
C. G. Costello	E. Howarth	J. Pinillos	W. Thompson
J. Das	A. Iseler	S. Rachman	O. Tunstall
W. DiScipio	A. Jensen	G. E. Sartory	P. H. Venables
S. B. G. Eysenck	H. Gwynne Jones	O. H. M. Seunath	K. M. Warwick
F. H. Farley	J. Jones	P. A. Slater	O. White
M. P. Feldman	D. C. Kendrick	I. Spielman	G. Wilson

Contents

Introduction

This is a book on reminiscence, or more modestly a book on reminiscence in motor tasks, or more modestly still on reminiscence in pursuit rotor learning, with occasional references to other types of reminiscence. The vast majority of experiments investigating reminiscence with the pursuit rotor have been carried out within the framework of Hullian learning theory. Thus, of necessity, this book also will be much concerned with that theory. Some readers may feel that so much detailed attention paid to one piece of apparatus and one now rather discredited theory, is overdone; we could not agree with such an evaluation.

There are several features of pursuit-rotor performance which make it particularly worthy of attention. One of the more important of these features is the easy replicability of many of the phenomena found in performance of this task; this is our first point. Replicability is the life blood of science; what cannot be replicated by any well-trained observer is of doubtful status in science, and on this score pursuit-rotor work certainly emerges as perhaps the most reliable set of observations in experimental psychology. The effects of massing and spacing; of rest pauses of different length; of switching from massed to spaced learning, or vice versa; of interpolating different activities; of introducing distracting stimuli; of switching from right to left hand, or vice versa; of changing the speed of rotation, or the diameter of the target disk— these are clear-cut and replicable as few phenomena in psychology are. There are few other examples where a young student can be told to carry out an experiment on a few subjects with the absolute certainty that the results will be predictable and precisely in line with what the literature says they ought to be; we should cherish such experiments, and hope that in due course there will be more of them!

It may seem to some readers that we lay too much stress on reliability of findings, and their replicability. We do not believe this to be a fault, but rather a virtue. Having both had some training in the physical sciences, we are astonished that replication of important findings is so rare in psychology; in the hard sciences replication is regarded as an essential feature of advance. Even when attempts are made at replication in psychology, there are usually so many changes in apparatus, choice of subjects, and parameter values that what is regarded as a "replication" is in fact equivalent to a change in virtually all the important properties from the original study. Psychologists, to put it bluntly, lack only too frequently the essential research discipline which has been responsible for the great advances in physics and chemistry; the failure to agree on the physical dimensions and properties of the pursuit rotor, to which Ammons (1955) has drawn attention, is only one example of this defect. Where no two studies are alike in such properties of the apparatus as speed of rotation, size of target, height of working surface, length of stylus, material properties of rotating disk and target, maintenance, lighting, and many more, it is surprising, and speaks highly for the indestructibility of the main phenomena observed, that so much agreement has in fact been found. Where outcomes are less robust, as in verbal learning, these faults emerge with even greater clarity. Changes in research parameters which are intended, and made for theoretical reasons are of course acceptable and welcome; most changes found in the literature, however, are simply capricious or motivated by a vain desire to be different and "original." We have tried to follow our own advice; in important areas, such as the influence of personality or motivation on reminiscence, we have replicated our findings five or more times before accepting the conclusions as representative.

Of course it is possible that even such replicable phenomena may be of little theoretical importance; this is our second point. We feel that there is a regularity and a precision about these phenomena which suggest that nature is trying to tell us something; that these phenomena carry with them secrets about an understanding of learning, of memory, of the very way the brain behaves in processing and making use of new knowledge and skill. We believe that had we only the *nous* to read this coded message aright, we would be so much nearer an understanding of some of the central problems of psychology. Others may not share our enthusiasm, but we would beg them to stay with us to the end before making up their minds on this point.

Our third point reinforces this belief in the importance of pursuit-rotor reminiscence and its attendant phenomena. Reminiscence interacts with other important areas of psychology in a precise, quantifiable, and theoretically meaningful manner. Motivation has important effects on reminiscence; high drive produces large reminiscence effects, low drive produces small ones. Yet, contrary to Hull's theory, high drive does not produce better pre-rest performance than low drive; such a finding is of great importance for any motivational theory. Personality, too, interacts with pursuit-rotor reminiscence; many studies agree in showing that extroverts demonstrate greater reminiscence than do introverts, although the two personality types do not show any difference in pre-rest practice. Even abnormal personality interacts with reminiscence, as Kraepelin (1895) posited long ago; schizophrenics show much less reminiscence than do normal or neurotic subjects. Lawful interactions such as these reinforce our belief that the whole set of phenomena (including also direct measures of arousal, and their interaction with reminiscence) is of great scientific importance, and cries out for a theoretical understanding which will serve to explain the observed facts in a parsimonious fashion.

We have chosen to discuss pursuit-rotor reminiscence because the various phenomena associated with this task can be demonstrated with great reliability and show regular and clear-cut relationships with basic task parameters, such as length of rest, and also important psychological concepts such as motivation and personality. Could we not, for similar reasons, pay more attention to reminiscence in other tasks as well? If by reminiscence we mean simply improvement in performance after rest, then we would seem to cast our net so wide that many heterogeneous phenomena would be thrown together; such improvement is seen in vigilance tasks (Stroh, 1972), in spiral after-effect (Holland, 1965), in eye-blink conditioning (Jones, 1974), in ergograph performance (Weiler, 1910), in work on Kraepelin's *Rechenheft* (Oehrn, 1895), in inverted alphabet printing (Kientzle, 1946), on the pathways test (C. H. Ammons, 1960), on a variety of motor skills tasks (Melton, 1947), and of course on verbal learning tasks as well (McGeoch & Irion, 1952). We shall suggest that there are at least three different kinds of "reminiscence" involved in these various tasks, caused by quite different mechanisms. Ergograph-type tasks show "reminiscence" due to *recovery from fatigue;* vigilance-type tasks show "reminiscence" due to *dissipation of inhibition;* pursuit-rotor type tasks show "reminiscence" due to *consolidation of learning.* It would not be sensible to treat all these theoretically quite distinct effects of rest periods interpolated among periods of massed practice in the same book, or use the same term to characterize them; historically there has always been some confusion in the definition of the term "reminiscence," and we would suggest that there are good reasons to restrict its use to tasks involving only or mainly consolidation-type processes in its causation. This means that the study of reminiscence would be concerned with the effects of rest on learning, rather than on performance; this is an important restriction which has in the past been followed by some writers, but not by others.

It will now be clearer why we have concentrated so much on just one of the many tasks which have been used in the study of reminiscence. As we shall argue, pursuit-rotor work is concerned in a relatively pure way with reminiscence as above conceived; there is little or no "fatigue" and little or no "inhibition" (in the sense of the word popularized by Ammons and Kimble in their classical studies of reminiscence). We started our work originally within the Hullian tradition, according to which pursuit-rotor reminiscence was explained in terms of dissipation of inhibition; after twenty years of experimental studies along these lines we feel that this explanation is definitely and definitively disconfirmed, and that some such explanation as have advanced in terms of consolidation is much nearer to the experimental facts. Whether this is so or not, the reader will be able to judge after perusing the pages of this book; we find it rather paradoxical that the one task which more than any other has been used to study, and to explicate hypotheses about, "reactive inhibition" and its dissipation, should be the one task which more than any other is completely free of any trace of inhibition and dissipation of inhibition.

We also believe that psychology may be able to learn an important lesson from the development of these theories, the changes that took place in them, and the final replacement of the inhibition theory by the consolidation theory; we hope to discuss these lessons in more detail in our last chapter. By tracing the development of investigations of a particular phenomenon over many years and also the rise and fall of the various theories devised to explain that phenomenon we hope that this book will be of interest not only to the student of motor skill learning, but also to all those actively engaged in practicing the art of experimental psychology.

It is considerations such as these which are responsible for the way this book was conceived and organized. Scientists are not usually very much interested in the history of their science; yet our theory would be difficult to understand without some rather detailed discussion of the development of the various conceptions which have been put forward to explain "reminiscence" and learning. As Medawar (1972, p. 105) has pointed out, "a scientist's present thoughts and actions are of necessity shaped by what others have done and thought before him; they are the wavefront of a continuous secular process in which The Past does not have a dignified independent existence of its own. Scientific understanding is the integral of a curve of learning; science therefore in some sense comprehends its history within itself." It seemed worthwhile to make the debt we owe to those who went before us more explicit—particularly as most textbooks fail to acknowledge the earliest experiments and theories in this field, which go back to Kraepelin and his students in the closing years of the last century. It is they who first discovered (explicitly) the phenomena of reminiscence, who advanced theories of inhibition and dissipation of inhibition to account for the fact, who discovered the phenomena of "blocking" (involuntary rest pauses) long before Bills, and who quantified many of the phenomena associated with reminiscence. It would be an interesting task for an historian to discover why their pioneering work was never given the recognition which it so richly deserves.

In line with our belief that history is important, and gives ballast to an otherwise purely factual and experimental account, we have given a somewhat detailed description, along historical lines, of the development of the experimental methods, and the apparatus, which eventually produced the classical work of Ammons and also of the theories which were developed to account for the facts discovered. Initially these theories were based on the concept of inhibition, but later this was abandoned in favor of consolidation.

The work of our Department mirrors clearly the change from inhibition to consolidation theory. We started out from the premises of Hullian theory, very much impressed by the apparent success of Ammons and Kimble to construct a theoretical system which appeared to cover all the observed phenomena. We tried to fit our own research findings into this system, and at first this process seemed to support the system in every detail. Predictions that extroverts would show greater reminiscence than introverts, or that high motivation would lead to greater reminiscence, were triumphantly verified. However, the worm was in the bud; there were many anomalous details, as we shall see in the course of this book, and attempts to shore up the leaning tower were of indifferent success. Finally it became clear that the whole system was becoming so complex and unwieldy, necessitating so many ad hoc hypotheses, that it ceased to be of any value in making predictions; it became like the Freudian opus, in that it could explain everything, and predict nothing—nothing, that is, that was not already known! Radical surgery was clearly required, and the consolidation theory was put forward as an alternative and less involved and complex hypothesis (Eysenck, 1965). This theory required much revamping and rethinking before it could be accepted as accounting for all the well-established research findings, and even the form presented here is still held only tentatively; we believe that it possesses the main advantage of a good theory in that it points to new and different types of research to those which we have become accustomed to. Whether the predictions which can be made from this new theory will continue to be borne out is of course a question for the future; it would be unwise to put too much faith in such a happy outcome. Indeed we are already aware of certain phenomena concerning the precise details of pursuit tracking performance which this theory cannot successfully account for. These are discussed in our chapter on "strategies."

Having outgrown our first love for inhibition theory, we still have lingering feelings of affection and regard for it. Although we have no doubt that it was completely inappropriate to pursuit-rotor learning and reminiscence, nevertheless it was a good theory in the proper scientific sense. For a time it accounted for the main facts in a satisfactory manner; it meshed with "big time theory" very adequately; and it made interesting and important predictions which could be experimentally tested and disproved. More than that no theory can be required to do, and it would be foolish to heap obloquy upon its remains, as many anti-Hullian theorists are apt to do. In retrospect, it is surprising how well an erroneous theory fitted the facts; how we seemed to be able to measure variables, such as I_R and sI_R, which in fact do not enter the picture at all—certainly as far as pursuit-rotor learning is concerned. Such an experience must make one suspicious—when consolidation is evoked as an explanatory concept, are we fooling ourselves in a similar manner, only to find that thirty years later some new and untried concept will be advanced with equally high claims, and consolidation contemptuously dismissed? When such has been the fate even of apparently invincible concepts like Newton's universal gravitation, this seems only too likely. However, we cannot predict what kind of concept will take over in due course, and until anomalies accumulate and make such a change-over imperative, this is the best theory we have, and we suggest that it might be worthwhile trying it out to see how far it will get us.

It is the failure of the inhibition-type theories to produce an explanation of reminiscence which provided a major motivation for writing this book. We believe that pursuit-rotor learning was an ideal stamping ground on which to test conflicting theories about learning and memory. Our own theory grew as a reaction to the ever greater complexity of Hullian formulations, in their efforts to encompass the many findings which clearly did not fit in with the original hypotheses. The fifties and sixties provided a classical example of the picture given by Kuhn (1962) of the state of affairs preceding the scientific revolutions which he believes to occur whenever an existing theory (or paradigm) is encountering too many anomolies which cannot be explained (or explained away) by modifications of the existing theory. In Lakatos's terms, a once *progressive* research programme shift has become *regressive*, more concerned with defence than with extension (Lakatos & Musgrave, 1970), and it was time for a new research program to take its place. This was attempted in a programmatic fashion by Eysenck (1965), and we have tried to do so in a much more extensive and (we hope) successful manner in this book.

The need for such a venture, and an empirical analogy to the Kuhn and Lakatos interpretations of the history of scientific theory building, can be found in an interesting paper by Krantz (1965). He takes his departure from the results of counting the number of articles appearing each year in *Physics and Chemistry Abstracts* (Price, 1963); the yearly increase can be described by an exponential function. He then argues that a plotting of research activity in particular research areas within a science would show a large variety of curve forms, and asks the question "Can any consistency be found in the curve forms for research activity on this more molecular level of analysis?" Taking his cue from Kuhn, he argues that in the course of delineating the paradigm which constitutes current orthodoxy, research findings are obtained which violate the paradigm-induced expectations. "The course of 'anomalous' research is a more or less extended exploration of the area of the finding and ends when the anomaly has been shown to be either an unreliable event, assimilable into the current paradigm, or, least probably, produces a paradigm change where the finding is no longer perceived as contrary to expectation (scientific revolution). It would follow from this position that research in an 'anomalous' area should show a period of concentrated research, directed toward evaluating the finding, with a subsequent marked change in activity. The nature of this change would be dependent upon the outcome of the concentrated exploration; if the finding is shown to be unreliable or assimilable there should be a relatively rapid decrease in research with little probability of recovery of interest. However, if the findings eventuate in a paradigm change, the course of activity in the 'anomalous' area would show a continued and perhaps more accelerated increase in research. In short, it is hypothesized that a comparison between research activity in 'normal' vs. 'anomalous' areas should show differences primarily in the eventuation of research; in 'normal' science, activity should be generally continuous while 'anomalous' science should show either a marked decline with no recovery of interest, or a continuation of research." (Price, 1963, p. 39.)

In order to test this hypothesis, Krantz selected two cases of 'nor-

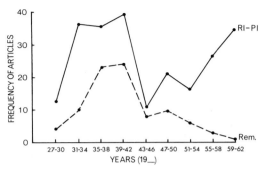

Figure 1. Research activity in verbal reminiscence and retroactive–proactive inhibition.

mal' and 'anomalous' research in psychology; "the 'anomalous' area is matched with a 'normal' area in that they represent explorations of similar viewpoints." One comparison was made between research activity in latent learning and secondary reinforcement; the other between activity in verbal reminiscence and retroactive–proactive inhibition. The frequency of articles, from 1927 to 1962, was found from consultation of the *Psychological Abstracts,* and the data for verbal reminiscence and retroactive–proactive inhibition are plotted in Figure 1. (A similar figure is plotted in Krantz's paper for latent learning and secondary reinforcement, showing latent learning research to have a similar course to verbal reminiscence, while secondary reinforcement had a similar course to retroactive and proactive inhibition.) "The research activity forms for the anomalous areas of latent learning and verbal reminiscence show very similar shapes; a rise in the frequency of research, followed by a period of high productivity, concentration or peaking and then a marked decline. The level of activity in the postdecline period is less than, or equal to, that prior to rise and concentration with no indication of subsequent recovery. It is clear, from the graphs and an analysis of the research findings in these 'anomalous' areas that a scientific revolution did not occur. Although it is difficult to pinpoint the factors contributing to decline in these two areas, an analysis of the literature indicates that latent learning was partially assimilated into the then current learning position (Hull, 1952) and for verbal reminiscence, accumulating evidence indicated that the phenomenon was unreliable (Hovland & Kurtz, 1951)." (Krantz, 1965, p. 41.) "In contrast to the decline and lack of recovery in the 'anomalous' research curves, the activity in the 'normal' science areas shows a continual increase; secondary reinforcement presently in a period of increasing activity and retroactive-proactive inhibition recovering to its previous level after the

World War II slump (the 1943–1946 point on the graph). In both areas a diminishing point in research is not yet apparent." (Krantz, 1965, p. 42.)

The data presented by Krantz are interesting, but his interpretation is somewhat doubtful. Motor reminiscence is one of the most reliable phenomena in experimental psychology, yet its course of research activity is not dissimilar to that of verbal reminiscence; here too we observe a period of high productivity following the work of Ammons and Kimble, to be replaced in recent years by a marked decline in the number of articles written. (The peak in research activity for motor reminiscence is some 10 to 15 years later than that for verbal reminiscence.) It is certainly true that verbal reminiscence is unreliable; Buxton (1943) called it the "now you see it, now you don't" phenomenon. But that may not be the only, or even the main reason for its decline; it may be as in the case of motor reminiscence, that the observed anomalies could not find an explanation within the context of Hullian learning theory. Unreliability undoubtedly aggravated the position, but it was itself probably produced by a failure to take into account variables which played no part in the traditional theoretical explanatory system of experimental psychology of the time (Eysenck, 1973). Clearly a "new look" was needed to replace a theoretical system which had run out of steam and could not account for the numerous anomalies which arose in the course of empirical work. We have attempted to provide such a "new look"; it will be interesting to see whether Krantz's prediction of a new rise in interest in the topic, following such a theoretical refurbishing, will be fulfilled.

It will be clear, from what has just been said, why we have concentrated on motor reminiscence, to the exclusion of most of the work that has been done on verbal reminiscence. Unreliable results make summary of findings meaningless, and do not lend themselves to theoretical conclusion; we have simply quoted in passing some studies indicating the importance of personality and motivation variables for a proper understanding of verbal reminiscence phenomena, and for their experimental control; beyond that it seemed inadvisable to go. A much more detailed treatment can be found in Eysenck (1973).

Another advantage of the broad historical approach we have chosen for our study of a rather specific phenomenon is that it enables us to discuss the advantages and disadvantages of various theoretical attitudes that psychologists have adopted.

Some critics will almost always oppose any kind of "conceptual nervous system" concept; they argue that such concepts are unnecessary, and that we should be contented with a set of differential equations to describe our findings. Our theory can certainly be considered "dynamic" in the usual sense in which physicists use this term, i.e., expressible in terms of differential equations; we still believe, however, that psychological or physiological concepts, such as "consolidation" and "arousal," have an important part to play in such a theory. Similar arguments have of course gone on in physics too; as we shall see in the last chapter, the thermodynamic and kinetic theories of heat present a similar confrontation, the former dealing with unimaginable concepts of a purely quantitative kind, the latter giving us an eminently "visualizable" picture of what is going on when small particles in constant motion are colliding with each other (Eysenck, 1970). Perhaps a scientist's preference for one or other type of theory is determined by his extraverted or introverted tendencies; where physicists are still undecided about the respective value of these two ways of regarding nature, we would be hesitant to suggest any final conclusion.

Neither would we like to be dogmatic about another controversy which has frequently engaged experimental and theoretical psychologists, namely the debate about the relative usefulness of "big theory" or "small theory." Is it useful at the present time to try and put forward large-scale theories of the Hullian type, or should we rather occupy ourselves with "miniature theories," relating to a particular phenomenon, or even a particular phenomenon as demonstrated on a particular piece of apparatus? To ask the question is to realize that fundamentally it is meaningless. The reaction to Hull's great system, and its relative failure, has been exaggerated; we need fundamental concepts, and general theories, just as much as we need specific applications, in great detail, to selected areas. Our book deals with a very limited area, reminiscence in pursuit-rotor learning, but the concepts we find necessary (consolidation, extraversion–introversion, motivation) are obviously of much greater latitude, and would apply to many other areas. We find this whole discussion unreal; Hull's theories resembled the curate's egg, which means that they were neither wholly good nor wholly bad, although the rapid swing of opinion would suggest that they were the former at one time, and are the latter now. This is an unrealistic way of looking at theories as if they were modish changes in skirt length. What Hull tried to do will have to be done sometime; it seems slightly absurd to throw out the baby with the bath water. But of course if theories *au grand* do not fit the facts, even in a small backwater like pursuit-rotor reminiscence, they have to go; there is a reciprocal relation between "big theory" and "small theory" which advocates of either may not always recognize.

As expressed in our dedication of this book to the large number of students and colleagues who have worked in this Department, on problems associated with reminiscence, we have based ourselves very much on the principles expressed in some detail in an article on "Programme research and training in research methodology" (Eysenck, 1970). Seeing a problem in science from a broad, historical perspective is of importance not only for understanding particular theories and how they have developed, but also for discerning the line of future research that is likely to be productive. It follows from this belief that training in research can best be accomplished by having the student work on a kind of apprenticeship level with an experienced research worker, on problems which have engaged the Department for a long time. Participation in such a program eliminates the "one off" type of research so familiar in psychology; research which is inherently unlikely to produce worthwhile results, which ends just when the student is in a position to make a proper start, and which is never followed up by anyone else—in spite of the traditional last words about further research being required. Program research shows the student the value of continued work on a particular set of problems, it makes certain that his work and results will indeed be followed up by the next generation of students, and it shows him how his own work is based intimately on that of his predecessors. These are important insights for a research worker to gain; he is more likely to make them his own when experience shows their value, rather than when he simply reads about them in some text book or other. Our experience suggests that these theoretical propositions possess some value for the training of research workers in psychology; whether the accumulated work done by generations of students on the problems discussed in this book has been worth the trouble must be left to the reader to judge.

H. J. EYSENCK

Institute of Psychiatry
University of London

C. D. FRITH

PART I

The Origin of the Grand Design

CHAPTER 1

Kraepelin and the Age of Innocence

DEFINITION OF REMINISCENCE

Reminiscence is a technical term, coined by Ballard in 1913, denoting improvement in the performance of a partially learned act that occurs while the subject is resting, i.e., not performing the act in question. He may be performing other types of activity, so that the term "resting" may seem inappropriate; similarly, the term "reminiscence" does not seem too well chosen in view of its everyday meaning to convey the substance of "improvement over rest." The reality of the phenomenon was of course widely known before Oehrn (1895) first explicitly demonstrated it experimentally; William James, in his typically paradoxical style, referred to our learning to skate in the summer and to play tennis in the winter. Actually this is not so; tennis players and skaters, as well as learners of other sportive activities, need several weeks to recover from the effects of a lengthy rest. If anything, there is a loss of performance during long rest, and even in laboratory tasks quite short rest periods can produce forgetting, i.e., a decrement in performance. Possibly the point James alluded to was the relatively quick recovery of "form" after lengthy rest; this may subjectively feel like improvement over rest.

   Definitions of reminiscence abound, but they are not altogether satisfactory. Hovland (1951, p. 653) defines it in terms of increments in *learning* which occur during a rest period; he warns that before reminiscence "can be considered a fundamental *learning* phenomenon, expla-

3

nations of it in terms of fatigue, motivation, and artifacts of measurement must be eliminated." Osgood (1953, p. 509), on the other hand, defines reminiscence as "a temporary improvement in *performance*, without practice," and says that "the term . . . refers to the objective fact of improved performance" (our italics). It is true that learning is usually indexed in terms of performance, and to that extent the two definitions may be considered equivalent, but it is also true that modern learning theory makes a radical distinction between learning and performance; learning may or may not issue in performance, depending on various conditions which require careful investigation. Some of these conditions are indeed mentioned by Hovland in the sentence quoted above, but the terms used are not precise enough to carry much meaning. Would Hull's concept of "reactive inhibition" be considered equivalent to "fatigue," or would it be considered as "negative motivation?" As long as we have no agreed upon definition of terms such as these, there might be difficulties in unambiguously demonstrating the phenomenon under investigation. Furthermore, to recognize artifacts of measurement implies knowledge of the *true* principles of measurement; there is no agreement on just how measurement ought to proceed.

To show how different the two definitions really are, let us consider two sets of experimental results. The first comes from a report by Denny (1951), who administered a pursuit-rotor task to two groups of 18 subjects each; one group worked continuously for 16 min, the other group worked continuously for 5 min, received 5 min of rest and then worked continuously for 12 min more. We shall later discuss the nature of the task, which involved following a small metal disk, embedded in a large bakelite turntable rotating at a speed usually of some 60 rpm, with a metal stylus; time on target was registered electrically on a suitable clock. For the present let us look merely at the results shown in Figure 1-1. It will be obvious that the two groups pursue quite divergent courses after the rest pause; the experimental group shows an increase from the 10th to the 11th 30-sec trial of 8%, i.e., from 14% to 22%, while the control group shows no change of any kind from the 10th to the 11th trial; this is an instance of "reminiscence."

It will also be seen that there are other differences between the two curves, subsequent to the imposition of a rest pause. First there is a sharp rise immediately after rest; this we shall call post-rest upswing (PRU). This is sometimes attributed to reinstatement of the set to perform the task in question, or "warm-up"; this notion was introduced in this connection by Hoch and Kraepelin (1895), and widely popularized by Thorndike (1914) in the English-speaking countries.

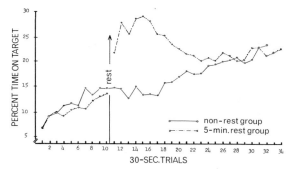

Figure 1-1. Reminiscence on the pursuit rotor, also showing post-rest upswing, post-rest downswing, and the eventual meeting of the rest and control groups. Taken with permission from Denny (1951).

Ammons (1947) refers to "warm-up decrement" to describe the fact that without the need for warm-up performance would be higher on the first post-rest trial. We prefer the term "post-rest upswing" because it does not incorporate a questionable hypothesis, which may or may not be an accurate account of what is in fact happening, in the description. In any case, PRU is followed by a leveling off of performance, followed in turn by a gradual decline; this may, by analogy, be called post-rest down-swing (PRD). Finally, this decline is arrested and a slow, regular up-swing is resumed which seems to run at roughly the slope and level of the control group, which has continued to improve slowly with a roughly linear slope throughout. We shall be concerned with theoretical interpretations of these and other facts later on; here let us simply note the facts, and note also that a theory of reminiscence must do more than account for the reminiscence effect itself. PRU and PRD are equally clear-cut consequences of the interpolation of a rest pause, and any worthwhile theory of reminiscence must also cover these effects.

Consider now an experiment reported by Holland (1963, p. 265) in which 14 subjects were administered 20 massed trials on the rotating spiral, subjects reporting on the length of after-effect experienced. Immediately upon the after-effect's cessation, the next presentation of the rotating spiral was commenced. A 15-min rest pause was intro-duced after the 20th trial, and a further 10 trials followed the rest pause. It is seen in Figure 1-2 that the length of the after-effect declines from a maximum of 14 sec on the 2nd trial to 11.2 sec on the two trials preceding the rest. After rest there is recovery to 14.3 sec, which is not significantly in excess of the highest pre-rest score; this recovery is short lived, and followed by a decline to a minimum of 10.8 sec. The question that arises is of course whether these findings should be

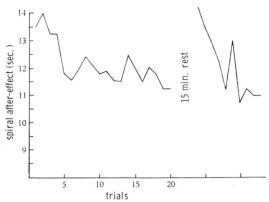

Figure 1-2. Reminiscence on the spiral after-effect test, showing recovery of the effect after decrement during massed practice. Taken with permission from Holland (1963).

discussed under the heading of "reminiscence"; there is improvement of performance, as demanded by Osgood, but no evidence of learning, as required by Hovland. At first sight it might be argued that this is a fatigue effect and hence not properly admissible, but this argument is not very strong; Holland explains the phenomenon in terms of "reactive inhibition," which dissipates during rest, and Denny offers a precisely similar explanation to account for his pursuit-rotor experiment. If there is a possibility that identical causes are responsible for the superficially similar effects, then it would be unwise to exclude on *a priori* grounds experiments of the second kind from consideration. It might turn out on careful consideration that the observed similarities were little more than analogies, but such a theoretical issue should not be prejudged and consequently we shall consider all phenomena which might reasonably be subsumed under the heading of "reminiscence" in its widest meaning in this book.

THE SPECIFICITY OF REMINISCENCE

Our example will serve another purpose, namely to illustrate how task tied some of the phenomena we are considering are. In the Denny experiment the pre-rest trend is upward, reminiscence produces scores very much in excess of starting scores, and there is both PRU and PRD. In the Holland experiment the pre-rest trend is downward, reminiscence just manages to bring scores back to the starting point and there is

no PRU, only PRD. Nevertheless, both experiments do show reminiscence, i.e., improvement in performance over rest.

Results very similar to those of the Holland experiment are shown
in the typical vigilance-type experiment (Davies & Tune, 1970); here too
there is a regular performance decrement during massed practice, but
when a rest pause is given, performance rises again to the initial level,
without PRU. This phenomenon is not usually thought of under the
name of reminiscence, but Osgood's definition would clearly embrace it
comfortably. We may with advantage regard reminiscence phenomena
as being positioned along a continuum, the lower and upper extremes
of which are defined by the Osgood and the Hovland definitions,
respectively. Tasks resembling pursuit-rotor learning involve learning,
as shown by the fact that post-rest performance is greatly superior to
starting level or pre-rest level, and that there is no pre-rest deterioration in performance. Tasks resembling vigilance tests typically do not
involve learning (although some of them may involve a modicum of
learning); there is deterioration of performance during pre-rest practice, and a post-rest return to the starting level, but without improvement over that level. We shall suggest that an appropriate explanation
of pursuit-rotor tasks may be in terms of *consolidation* of the traces laid
down by the practice pre-rest, while an explanation of performance-
decrement tasks may be in terms of some *inhibition* concept, involving
dissipation of inhibition to account for the post-rest improvement. One
of the paradoxes of learning theory, particularly of the Hullian variety,
is that it has attempted with great determination to apply inhibition
theory to pursuit-rotor learning; indeed, pursuit-rotor learning is probably the area most closely investigated by learning theorists interested
in Hull's system generally, and inhibition concepts in particular.

Postulation of a continuum from one type of task to the other
demands that there should be tasks involving both learning consolidation and decrement inhibition. One such task may be the inverted-
alphabet printing test (Kientzle, 1946), in which the subject is required
to print the letters of the alphabet upside down. In one experiment,
Eysenck and Cookson (1974) administered the test to 2560 boys and
2679 girls, aged between 10 and 11 years; twelve 1-min periods of
massed practice were followed by a variable rest (0, 1, 5, 10, and 60 min,
respectively), and the rest was in turn followed by another 5 min of
massed practice. The results are shown in Figure 1-3a and b. There is
clearly some learning pre-rest, as shown in the first 3 trials, but then
there is performance decrement, bringing the terminal score almost
down to the initial level. The rest produces a marked reminiscence

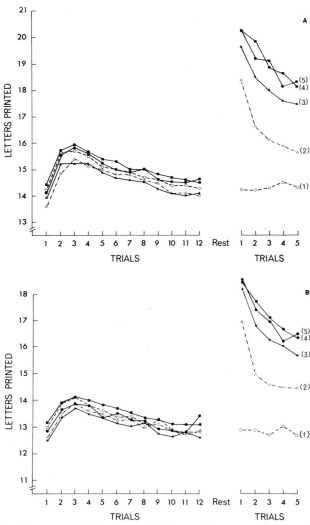

Figure 1-3. Reminiscence on the inverted alphabet printing task, showing effect after rest pauses of 0, 1, 5, 10, and 60 min, respectively. Data are for boys (a) and girls (b). Taken with permission from Eysenck and Cookson (1974).

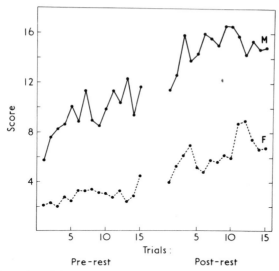

Figure 1-4. Failure of reminiscence to appear in a two-hand coordinator task. Taken with permission from Quarrington and White (1958).

effect, again showing learning effects (initial post-rest performance is well above the highest level reached during pre-rest); however, there is no PRU, but only PRD. Thus alphabet printing clearly lies intermediate between our two extremes, and its explanation may have to partake of both consolidation and inhibition hypotheses.

Not all experiments using perceptual-motor tasks show reminiscence. As an example, consider the work of Quarrington and White (1958), who used a task superficially rather similar to the pursuit rotor. A two-hand coordinator was used; this device presents the operator with a tracking task which requires him to keep a cursor on top of a target by means of two lathe-type cranks. The right hand moves the cursor in a left–right direction, while the left-hand crank moves the cursor toward or away from the operator. Success is measured in terms of time-on target. 15 males and 15 females were given 15 consecutive 30-sec periods of practice, allowed to rest for 24 hr, and then given another 15 consecutive 30-sec periods of practice. Results are shown in Figure 1-4; they illustrate that learning is clearly taking place in males and females, but also that there is no trace of reminiscence. (The superiority of men over women on this task is of no interest here; sex differences are common in this type of motor task.)

It is possible that the superficial similarities between the two-hand coordinator and the pursuit-rotor (pursuit task) are less important than

the less obvious differences. Thus on the pursuit-rotor work is continuous, and attention is centered on the same type of movement throughout. On the coordinator there are essentially two tasks differing in
nature and related to right-hand and left-hand practice; it is possible for
the subject to switch attention and concentrate on one or other of these
two tasks, thus allowing the brain cells associated with practice on the
other task to rest. Thus this task might be thought of rather as two
alternating tasks, neither providing the conditions of massing thought
to be favorable to the development of reminiscence. It is of course not
necessary to accept this very tentative theory in order to see that task
conditions very much determine the shape of the work curve and the
presence or absence of reminiscence. It is for this reason that we have
concentrated on pursuit-rotor work in this book; no other task has
received even a fraction of the amount of attention that pursuit-rotor
work has received, and any hopes of arriving at an even partly quantitative theory of the phenomena associated with reminiscence must rest
on this rich treasure house of experimental findings. Other tests are also
covered in part, but mainly in relation to questions arising from the
problem of similarities and differences to pursuit-rotor learning; no
thorough coverage is intended of verbal learning, animal learning, or
perceptual reminiscence.

If task differences are so important, then surely a classification or
typology of tasks would seem desirable. Unfortunately there is at
present no satisfactory approach to such a typology, although beginnings of at least a taxonomy of perceptual-motor skills have been made
(Fleishman, 1967). Experimentally, there is a heuristic distinction
between motor skills learning and verbal learning; this coincides very
nicely with marked differences in reminiscence phenomena discovered
in these two fields (although there are also certain similarities, as we
shall see). When we look at extreme cases this distinction seems quite
clear-cut; pursuit-rotor learning is an example of the former, nonsense-
syllable learning an example of the latter. But what about the tasks
which were used in the first groping days of Kraepelin, when the
foundations were being laid for so much that we now take for granted?
Does routine mental arithmetic (single-digit addition, under conditions of massed practice) qualify under motor skills or verbal learning?
Does the more modern pathways test, in which a path has to be traced
from one number to the next, randomly spread over the page, resemble
the one group or the other? Or do they require a separate niche, or
perhaps several separate niches?

We have considered these two types of learning as belonging more
properly with motor learning than with verbal learning; what is learned

is not, after all, the act of addition or the sequence of numbers—these must be known, and may be supposed to be overlearned, before the beginning of the experiment (at least, with the type of subject used). What is learned, then, is more likely to be motor skills of writing and tracing, perceptual skills in spotting and connecting numbers, and other such nonverbal abilities. But there is of course no reason why certain tasks should not combine features from both camps, and involve both motor and verbal elements; the taxonomy does admit whales and porpoises to be both fish and mammals. It is used here mainly for the sake of classifying together what appear to be similar experiments; no ultimate validity is claimed for it. Furthermore, we shall be particularly interested in seeing to what extent generalizations are possible from one field to the other, and to what extent such generalizations break down (Underwood, 1966).

MUSCULAR FATIGUE AND REMINISCENCE

One type of reminiscence, however, has been firmly excluded from our survey; that associated with recovery from muscular fatigue (Schmidtke, 1965). Kraepelin (1895) stimulated much work on the dynamometer (Weiler, 1910, Oseretzkowsky & Kraepelin, 1901) and used the different work curves produced by schizophrenic or manic–depressive patients as a diagnostic device, as did Hoch (1901) and Lefman (1904); he also used mental work, notably arithmetic (as in his Rechenheft), and the work curves resulting therefrom in a similar manner. In doing this work, he was thinking that the observed similarities, e.g., in reminiscence, work decrement, and fatigue effects, were more than mere analogies; he tried to account for mental events (decrement in attention) along the lines of metabolic waste products interfering with performance, very much as he did in connection with physical work. There is no doubt that ergograph work produces work decrement, and that pauses introduced during the course of this massed type of practice produce reminiscence. Figure 1-5 is taken from Weiler's paper and shows the regular decrease in output on the ergograph (solid line), as compared with the restitution produced by a rest pause. Six pulls are averaged to produce the mean effect for each of 10 recorded trials; the work done by one experimental subject is totaled over 10 days. (i.e., 5 days with, 5 days without rest periods.) Pulls were synchronized by means of a metronome; the rest was of 2-min duration.

However, Kraepelin's notion that there might be more than an anology to mental work in physical work is almost certainly mistaken.

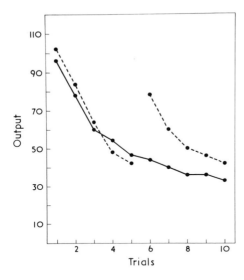

Figure 1-5. Reminiscence of a dynamometer task, showing performance of a rest and a control group. Taken from Weiler (1910).

What happens in physical work to produce temporary and semipermanent work decrement is the following. Hemoglobin is a compound containing iron which is found in the red blood cells, and whose function is to carry oxygen in a loose combination from the lungs to the tissues. By means of hemoglobin the blood can transport 100 times as much oxygen as it could if the oxygen were simply dissolved in the fluid plasma of the blood. During exercise, hemoglobin gives up more oxygen than normal, and the venous blood level can drop to as low as 3%, compared with the normal 12%. During exercise the active muscles require up to 3000 ml of oxygen per minute, 50 times their resting need. Most of this extra oxygen comes from the increased rate and depth of breathing, and is transported by the increased heart output, but about ⅙th of it comes as a result of blood being shunted away from other organs. This added oxygen supply contributes energy to the muscle cell, which uses it to interdigitate the filamentous molecular racks inside each muscle cell, thus causing the cell to shorten and, ultimately, the whole muscle to contract. Muscle cells are relatively tolerant of lack of oxygen, largely because of the myoglobin which they contain. This substance is similar to hemoglobin but does not release its oxygen nearly so easily; it keeps it until marked oxygen lack has set in. Once the myoglobin has exhausted its oxygen it recharges avidly with oxygen diffusing into the muscle cell.

This is the first of two principal energy-releasing pathways in muscle cells. Sometimes called the Krebs citric acid cycle, it requires oxygen and glucose as fuel, and forms carbon dioxide and water as waste products (after many stages). The other pathway (anaerobic glycolysis) is only 5% as efficient in extracting energy from glucose, but it can do so *without* oxygen; however, it does produce as a waste product the harmful lactic acid. It is the myoglobin recharging—storage mechanism which accounts for the efficiency of brief rest pauses in mammals, i.e., intermittent contracting and relaxing of muscles. These brief rest pauses allow the myoglobin to recharge, and the existence of the myoglobin in the first place is of course responsible for the ability of the animal to incur an oxygen debt at all! Continuous work, however, leads to severe oxygen lack, and the organism has to fall back on anaerobic glycolysis but does produce a concentration of lactic acid in blood and muscles, thus leading to fatigue and ultimately enforcing a cessation of the activity in question.

Lactic acid is removed from the body of the liver and kidneys, where lactic acid is converted back to glucose (the Cori cycle). Lactic acid fatigue is long lasting (comparatively speaking); aerobic exercise is maintained by numerous short "micropauses" during which myoglobin is recharged. Thus there is a good physiological reason for differentiating "short-term fatigue" leading to micropauses and restitution almost immediately, and "long-term fatigue" leading to excretion of lactic acid over a relatively long period of time.

Work on a bicycle ergometer, following a standard rate of pedaling, clearly shows how the spacing of practice determines long-term fatigue even though the work/rest ratio remains constant. During a half-hour period, trained subjects practised for 10 sec, rested for 20 sec; practised for 30 sec, rested for 60 sec; or practised for 60 sec, rested for 120 sec. Blood lactate at the end of the half-hour was 20 mg/100 ml (near resting level) for the first group, with no subjective fatigue; 70 mg/100 ml for the second group, with marked subjective fatigue; and 140 mg/100 ml for the last group, with total collapse supervening before termination of the half-hour period.

Figure 1-6, taken from Åstrand *et al.* (1960), shows the effect of various lengths of work period on blood lactate level when work/rest ratios are kept equal; it will be seen that short bursts of work, followed by short periods of rest, preserve a low lactate level, whereas longer bursts of work, followed by long periods of rest, lead to high lactate levels. The load in this bicycle ergometer task was 2530 kg-m/min in all cases during the active periods, and the total work output in all cases 15,120 kg-m. Similarly, Christensen *et al.* (1960) found that subjects could run at a speed of 20 km/hr in short spells of 5–10 sec, with interspersed pauses of the same duration, for 20 active minutes and

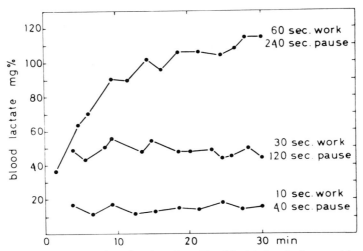

Figure 1-6. Effect of various lengths of work on blood lactate level when work/rest ratios are kept equal. Taken with permission from Åstrand *et al.* (1960).

have only a slight increase in blood lactate, while the same subject running continuously at the same speed was exhausted after 4 min, with blood lactate reaching maximal levels. Mental work shows nothing similar to this, possibly because the brain cells are better protected against over exertion and collapse. In any case, modern psysiology does not consider that oxygen lack is associated with mental work, or its deterioration (Asmussen, 1965).

The relations between strength exerted (as a fraction of maximum strength), duration of exertion, and length of rest pauses have been studied in detail by Müller (1965) and by Rohmert (1960); the latter has put forward a formula for calculating the rest allowance required to continue static work for t hours without fatigue:

$$R.A. = 18(t/T)^{1.4} \quad (k/K - 0.15)^{0.5} \times 100\%$$

where *R.A.* is the rest allowance in % of t, T is the maximum holding time, t the holding time, K the maximum force, and k the holding force.

KRAEPELIN'S STUDIES OF REMINISCENCE

Verbal and motor reminiscence, and the associated phenomena of distribution of practice (massed vs spaced) developed along rather independent paths for quite a long time. Ebbinghaus (1885) is credited with the discovery of the superiority of spaced over massed practice in verbal learning, and Jost (1897) demonstrated the failure of theories involving fatigue and boredom to account for the findings. Reminiscence as a separate phenomenon was, however, not isolated in verbal learning until Ballard's work in 1913, and Huguenin's 1914 study. Thus verbal reminiscence appeared on the scene almost 20 years later than motor reminiscence, an indication of how separated the two disciplines had become.[1] We shall return to the development of work on verbal reminiscence in a later chapter; here we shall be concerned rather with the story of motor reminiscence. This story may be told in some detail, partly because it is of interest and importance to what follows, but also because it seems largely unknown; thus McGeoch and Irion's scholarly work (1952) makes no mention of Kraepelin and his many associates who may be said to have created this branch of study, very much as Ebbinghaus created the experimental study of memory. Bilodeau (1966) is similarly remiss, and so are Osgood (1953) and Hall (1966). Even Boring (1950) fails to recognize the outstanding importance, originality, and thoroughness of the many studies reported in Kraepelin's *Psychologische Arbeiten*.

The systematic study of reminiscence, the effects of rest pauses of variable duration on learning, the phenomena of "set" and "warm-up," the effects of distribution of practice, the influence of motivation on learning, and the pervasive determination of all these variables by personality differences were pioneered by E. Kraepelin and his students. Most of this work was published between 1895 and 1910 in Kraepelin's *Psychologische Arbeiten;* the studies were begun during his stay in Dorpat, and completed during his tenure on the chair of Psychiatry in Heidelberg. Both the experimental work and the theoretical interpretation bear the stamp of W. Wundt, under whom he studied in Leipzig, but there can be no doubt that he extended these methods and interpretations to an essentially new field, and in so doing became the founding father of a large and still growing field of psychology. His parentage, although equally clear and indisputable as that of Ebbinghaus in the field of memory investigation, has been obscured by

---

[1] Other early investigators of reminiscence phenomena anticipating Ballard, were Henderson (1903) in the U.S.A., Lobsien (1904) in Germany, and Binet (1904) in France. McGeoch (1935) gives a long list of other early workers in this field. Binet points out how widespread was the realization that incompletely learned material would show improvement in recall after an interval of time, even around the turn of the century: "Cette sorte d'amélioration de la memoire pars le temps, sans être générale, a été observée si fréquement qu'il a paru difficile de la mettre en doute, de l'attribuer a quelque cause d'erreur."

historical accidents; in part his growing fame in the field of psychiatry, and in part the fact that his work was never pulled together and published in book form, but remains scattered over a large number of students' theses. The growing inability of Anglo-American students (and teachers) of psychology to read German, and the failure of his contributions to be translated into English, have made a proper appreciation of his work difficult. This is regrettable; a reading of his extensive studies makes one realize how modern his approach was in many ways, and how prescient his theorizing. There are few modern notions which he did not anticipate, and few fundamental findings which are not adumbrated in his writings. Even now he has much to teach us, and we may well start with a detailed, if brief, consideration of just what he was trying to do, and what he discovered.

Kraepelin (1895) considered that prolonged work, whether muscular, as on the dynamometer, or mental, as in adding single digit figures, produced certain effects, such as fatigue, and was in turn affected by certain variables, such as motivation; these variables and effects were a function, in part, of the personality, normal or abnormal, of the experimental subject, and could in turn be used to throw some light on aspects of his personality. Hence the painstaking analysis of the work curve was to him one important method of gaining a better understanding of the dynamics of behavior, and of individual differences. He was also concerned with modifying behavior through drugs and using his experiments to study the effects of drugs, but this line of approach will not be dealt with here (Aschaffenberg, 1895; Loewald, 1895; Hoch & Kraepelin, 1895; Haenel, 1899; Kürz & Kraepelin, 1901; Ach, 1901; Rüdig, 1904). He was aware of the fact that a better understanding of fatigue, motivation, set, reminiscence, and learning might have far-reaching practical consequences in the clinic, the classroom, and in industry, but he did not personally concern himself very much with the application of such factual and theoretical results as were produced by his school; his concern was first and foremost the clarification of the scientific and academic problems thrown up by his work.

Readers of the articles referred to below will undoubtedly experience a curious sensation of disbelief when they are confronted with table after table giving detailed results achieved by one person, on one occasion; only occasionally are these results averaged over occasions, hardly ever over persons. In any case, the number of cases is usually very small; in the early studies three to five subjects seems to constitute the norm, and even in the latest studies the number never seems to rise above twenty. The reader looking for statistical treatment of data will be sorely disappointed; what little statistics there are, are of a very mundane and elementary kind. In this method of working Kraepelin is very close to Ebbinghaus, whose monumental work on memory was of course carried out with the aid of just one subject—himself; there is also a close correspondence to Pavlov, whose great book constantly gives detailed data for just one or two animals to demonstrate the most far-reaching generalizations. Both Pavlov and Ebbinghaus showed that such reliance on extremely careful control and very thorough study of a few selected cases can lead to conclusions which may stand up to the most varied replication, and Kraepelin, too, will be seen to have been led to conclusions which are not contradicted by more modern, statistical methods of research. There is a curious tendency for the wheel to come full circle; Skinner's studies, in their reliance on single case histories and their abhorrence of averages and other statistical devices, strike one as a partial return to the type of research current around the turn of the century.

To say this is not to suggest that Kraepelin's methods are necessarily superior to those of modern psychologists, just as it would be right to say that insistence on complex statistical methods is inevitably superior to the simple approach of Pavlov, Ebbinghaus, and Kraepelin. There are advantages and disadvantages attending both approaches, and both are needed in reaching a proper evaluation of the confusing and contradictory evidence. Means, variances, and covariances can give us important information when their use is appropriate and permissible; but they can also hide important dissimilarities between subjects which only become apparent when other methods of analysis are employed. Kraepelin's results suggested that some people benefit more by short, others by long rest pauses; averaging would completely destroy the possibility of finding such important differences. Modern psychology has not yet found a statistical approach which reconciles the divergent needs indicated in this example; until it is found we would be well advised not to smile at methods which after all produced more fundamental knowledge in the hands of such masters of research as Pavlov, Ebbinghaus, and Kraepelin than have all the complex statistics which we so confidently apply to problems which quite often are inappropriate for their use.

The first study which is relevant to our topic is one published by Oehrn (1895), in which he employed the sensationally large number of 10 subjects (Ss); he used a variety of tasks including letter counting, letter search, proofreading, nonsense syllable learning, number learning, various motor functions such as writing, and finally the one most important from our point of view, addition of single numbers in Kraepelin's *Rechenheft*,[2] timed over consecutive 5-min periods. Work continued over periods of 2–4 hr. Oehrn clearly states Kraepelin's fundamental belief that practice and fatigue are the two most important influences which between them determine the major portion of an individual's performance at any one point; "Uebung und Ermüdung stehen in Bezug auf ihre Wirkung in geradem Gegensatz zu einander. Während erstere die Leistungsfähigkeit sowohl quantitativ als auch qualitativ erhöht, wird durch die Ermüdung sowohl die Quantität der in einer gewissen Zeit geleisteten Arbeit, als auch ihre Qualität herabgesetzt." Fatigue is conceived as partly a peripheral, physiological effect associated with specific end organs, but also as a decline in attention; Oehrn quotes Wundt's *Physiologische Psychologie* as saying that this decline in performance "zum Theil in einer physiologischen Abstampfung des betreffenden Organes, namentlich aber in der Abnahme der Aufmerksamkeit zu bestehen pflegt."

The effects of practice are semipermanent, those of fatigue are transitory. It is here that rest pauses (of 24 hr or more) are important; they allow fatigue to dissipate, while the effects of practice remain. Figure 1-7 has been drawn after results reported by Oehrn (1895, p. 132); representing the mean duration, in 1/1000 sec, of adding a single number during a 30-min practice period. The figures are averaged over 5-min periods, of which there are 6 in each half hour, and 10-min rest pauses are introduced between successive half-hour periods. It will be noted that there is an overall learning effect: addition becomes quicker with practice. It will also be seen that there is a clear reminiscence effect: improvement takes place during the rest period, and is shown most clearly by comparing the terminal pre-rest period with the initial post-rest period. This effect is obvious for each of the 3 rest periods. These results are for one person, on one occasion, but we are told that they are quite universal: "Also nach der Pause wird mit einer Geschwindigkeit begonnen, die *grösser ist, als sie vor derselben erreicht war*. Ganz dasselbe Verhalten beobachten wir bei Versuchen, die durch 24 Stunden oder noch längere Pausen von einander getrennt sind." (Oehrn's italics.)

---

[2]The Kraepelin *Rechenheft* never became very popular in the Anglo-American circle, but it was widely used in Germany, particularly in the form given the test by Pauli (1921, 1936). A detailed account of work with this test is given by Pauli and Arnold (1951). In English, Reuning (1957) has discussed some of the results, and has shown how the test can be analyzed into its component factors. All this work is in the tradition of Kraepelin, but is of no direct relevance to the study of reminiscence.

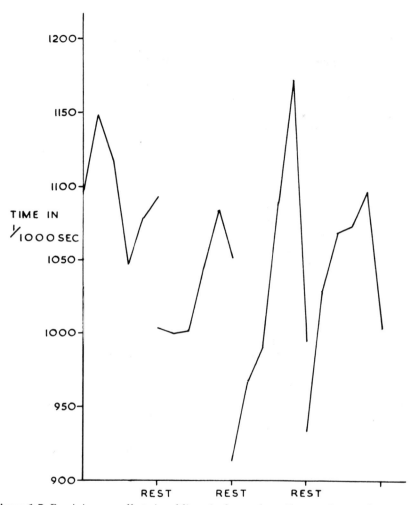

Figure 1-7. Reminiscence effects in adding single numbers. Drawn after results given by Oehrn (1895).

Oehrn's explanation of this phenomenon is not a model of clarity; he maintains that "die Uebung . . . in einer Erleichterung des psychischen Vorganges besteht, dass also auch wahrend jedes einzelnen Versuches der dauernde Einfluss der Uebung zur Geltung kommt" (1895, p. 133). This is difficult to translate without suggesting concepts which may not have been present in the author's mind; he seems to suggest that practice consists in a facilitation of psychic processes, and that the continuing influence of practice is apparent in every single experimental determination. This may suggest a consolidation rather than an inhibition theory of reminiscence but it is doubtful that Oehrn was really conscious of the dichotomy when he wrote the above sentence, or had any very definite notion of how the phenomenon he had discovered came about. Nevertheless, this would appear to have been the first experimental demonstration of reminiscence, and as such the paper constitutes a landmark in the history of the subject.

Oehrn also observed marked *fluctuations* of speed in adding single numbers; it must be remembered that these were obtained by averaging results obtained over 5-min periods of work; we will later review what another student of Kraepelin's was able to deduce from a more detailed study of fluctuation phenomena. The observed fluctuations were interpreted as "Ermüdungserscheinungen"; the dependence of these phenomena on fatigue was demonstrated by showing that fluctuations tended to appear late in performance, usually after the point of maximum performance, and when performance was beginning to decline. Oehrn notes marked differences in the size of fluctuations between individuals, and also between tasks; this effect, as well as the others discussed, assumes different importance in different individuals, and in different tasks. Particularly impressive are the individual differences in ability: the best subject in this highly educated group scored over twice as many additions as did the worst. Variability, too, showed marked differences, but these were unrelated to ability. This variability, which is of course a function of the number and size of fluctuations observed, was considered by Oehrn to be "ein Dynamometer der Aufmerksamkeit." He supported this notion that variability in performance could be used as a measure of attention by showing that simpler, more reflex types of task showed less variability. This, in turn, is of course a function of the degree of learning; variability is lessened, the more a task has been practiced.

Oehrn ends by saying that work curves are always the product of two influences, practice and fatigue; hence no pure measure of either can be obtained directly. He suggests that to study pure learning one must eliminate fatigue; this can be done by introducing lengthy rest pauses (spacing of practice). If we want to study pure fatigue, then we must practice until no further improvement in performance is observed (asymptotic performance). The suggestions contained in this paper were taken up by other students of Kraepelin, as we shall see.

Hoch and Kraepelin (1895) investigated the effect of rest pauses of different length (5 and 15 min) after different lengths of practice (1 and 2 hr), the task being again that of adding single-digit numbers. They found that after 1-hr work the 5-min pause facilitated later work, while the 15-min pause had a decremental effect; conversely, after 2 hr work the 15-min pause also had a facilitating effect. (In learning tasks they found that the 15-min pause had a facilitating effect even after 1-hr work.) They concluded "dass die Wirkung der Pause nicht eine an und für sich feststehende ist, sondern dass sie wesentlich abhängt von dem Zustande, in welchem sich der Arbeitende in den verschiedenen Abschnitten seiner Thätigkeit befindet" (1895, p. 372). This firm statement that the effects of rest pauses are not absolute but depend on the particular state in which the worker finds himself during the various phases of his activities may seem little more than common sense, but much experimental work has since been done which has neglected this salutary warning. In particular, Hoch and Kraepelin insist that pauses are more likely to facilitate future work if the subject has accumulated a considerable amount of fatigue; little fatigue gives the rest pause little chance to have a positive influence. Again an obvious conclusion, but one which suggests new methods of quantitatively investigating the amount of fatigue which has been accumulated. In a similar manner Hoch and Kraepelin explain the difference observed between work on simple addition, and work on rote learning; the facilitating effect of the 15-min pause for the latter, but not the former task after 1-hr work is due to the greater fatigue induced by the more demanding learning task, compared with the more automatic adding task. Thus we have here the beginnings of a taxonomy of tasks, indexed according to the degree of "fatigue" induced.

But all this does not explain why the 15-min pause actually had a decrementing effect on further work after 1-hr addition. Uebungsverlust (forgetting) is pretty well ruled out because after the 5-min rest there is an actual gain; Ebbinghaus already showed that most forgetting follows the general rule of showing a steep decline during the first few minutes, leveling off afterwards. Hoch and Kraepelin suggest quite a different hypothesis, namely "dass während der Arbeit sich *unabhängig von der Uebungswirkung* Einflüsse entwickeln, die eine bedeutende Steigerung der Leistungsfähigkeit bedingen, nach dem Aufhören der Thätigkeit jedoch ungemein rasch wieder verschwinden" (1895, p. 374). These influences which are independent of learning, which facilitate performance, and which dissipate during rest they call "Anregung," a term which might literally be translated as "suggestion" or "excitation," but which would today be called "set." (The proper German term for set is of course Einstellung, as used for instance by the Würzburg school; Kraepelin's choice of term is curious and inexplicable.[3] However, the description given by Hoch and Kraepelin of the way *Anregung* is supposed to work leaves little doubt about the interpretation given above.) Discussing this concept of *Anregung*, Hoch and Kraepelin say "dass beim thätlichen Aufhören unseres Versuches unser psycho-physischer Mechanismus noch eine kurze Zeit auf die betreffende Arbeitsleistung eingestellt bleibt, dass sich erst allmählich die besondere, durch die Arbeit hervorgerufene Disposition zum Lernen, Addiren u. derg. verliert" (1895, p. 375). Thus *Anregung* is a disposition favoring work in progress, a disposition or set which is gradually lost after cessation of the activity in question. This loss is great enough after 15 min to more than counterbalance the facilitating effect of recovery from fatigue when the amount of fatigue is relatively small; when a lot of fatigue is present, as after 2 hr of addition, then recovery from fatigue produces a greater positive effect than the negative effect of loss of set can balance. Loss of set is explicitly related to duration of the rest pause; the longer the rest, the greater the loss: "Es ist uns bekannt, dass solche Unterbrechungen uns um so stärker beeinflussen, je länger sie andauern" (1895, p. 376). Here then we have another concept to account for some of the phenomena of the work curve, and another quantitative law to help in the measurement of these phenomena.

Rivers and Kraepelin (1895) add another concept, that of permanent work decrement. Hitherto we have dealt with fatigue, which was supposed to dissipate completely during sufficiently prolonged rest pauses; this fatigue, which was essentially mental and related to loss of attention, thus produced a temporary work decrement. (In order to distinguish this mental fatigue from the physical kind induced through work on the dynamometer, also pioneered by Kraepelin, it might be useful to introduce a term such as "inhibition" which is purely descriptive of the temporary decrement produced, and does not lend itself to confusion with physical fatigue. From here on we will use the terms "mental fatigue" and "inhibition" interchangeably.) In long-continued work on simple addition, these authors found that rest pauses of equal or even greater length sufficed during the first day or two to produce complete restitution from the effects of fatigue; "späterhin entwickelte sich eine rasch wachsende Abnahme der Leistungsfähigkeit, die durch einfaches Ausruhen wahrscheinlich nicht mehr völlig ausgeglichen werden konnte" (Rivers & Kraepelin, 1895, p. 677). A similar effect had

---

[3] "Gerichtetheit" is the current translation of set in the present sense of that term.

already been noted by Hoch and Kraepelin (1895) in dynamometer work; now they state: "Es liegt nahe, auch für die geistige Arbeit ähnlichen Vorstellungen nachzugehen." The observed similarities, however, obscure certain important differences; fatigue in mental work arises more slowly, dissipates more slowly, and produces semipermanent effects which also persevere longer. Kraepelin does not really produce an explanation of this new phenomenon of permanent work decrement; such physiological speculations as he offers do not seem to have much value for us.

This paper also discusses another concept which Kraepelin was forced to introduce in order to account for certain empirical findings: that of *Antrieb* (drive, motivation). This factor was considered particularly important "weil es das Eingreifen des Willens in die geistige Arbeit anzeight" (Rivers & Kraepelin, 1895, p. 675). Drive, it was thought, produced its effect through voluntary effort; this was most noticeable at the beginning and the end of the practice period. These effects, however, were of short duration. Degree of motivation was found to be a function of personality; "Häufigkeit und Grösse der Antriebswirkungen hängen in erster Linie von den persönlichen Eigenschaften, dann aber von der jeweiligen Disposition ab" (Rivers & Kraepelin, 1895, p. 677).[4] Kraepelin does not really make much of this concept; he uses it merely to explain the spurts which under certain conditions appear at the beginning and end of prolonged activity, but this *ex post facto* explanation does not carry us very far. In particular, Kraepelin fails to consider the overall effects of drive on performance and reminiscence.

Kraepelin introduces here also the concept of forgetting (*Uebungsverlust*); "ohne Zweifel geht . . . von einem Tage zum anderen bereits ein beträchtlicher Theil der gewonnenen Uebung wieder verloren" (Rivers & Kraepelin, 1895, p. 647). This loss of performance through forgetting requires us to introduce correction factors, and in order to do that we must measure its extent (which Rivers and Kraepelin proceed to do). No alternative explanations to forgetting are considered, such as retroactive or proactive inhibition, and the discussion here is not on a very high level; nevertheless, most modern workers still measure reminiscence without correcting for any "forgetting" that may have

---

[4] The distinction between "Eigenschaften" and "Dispositionen"' is similar to that between "state" and "trait," i.e., semipermanent traits predisposing subjects to react in a certain manner, and momentary dispostions largely produced by the circumstances of the test situation. The distinction dates back at least as far as Cicero (45 B.C.), who distinguishes clearly between "trait anxiety" (*anxietas*) and "state anxiety" (*angor*).

taken place, whatever theoretical explanation may finally be found acceptable for this forgetting. In this respect, therefore, Kraepelin was well ahead of his time and perhaps of ours, too.

In their paper, Rivers and Kraepelin say that "die Ermüdung beginnt ohne Zweifel mit der Thätigkeit selbst" (1895, p. 669). This stress on the nature of the activity itself in producing inhibition was taken up by Weygandt (1899), who tried to discover what it was in the activity that caused it to produce a given amount of inhibition. The approach and the problem are similar to those of Hull in his discussion of the "work hypothesis" of inhibition, but instead of calling upon the amount of physical work done in ft-lb/sec, Weygandt stresses the fact that we are dealing with mental work, and concludes from his investigation that different tasks produce inhibition to different degrees in different people (postulate of individual differences), and also that the same task may change its character and become easier (produce less inhibition) with practice. Difficulty of mental work (and hence inhibition produced) is a function of the demands made upon attention; the more practiced we become, the less attention we need to pay to the work, and the less fatiguing (inhibition producing) it becomes. This inhibition can transfer from one task to another; it is by no means task specific. "Als das Ausschlaggebende haben wir lediglich die *Schwere der Arbeiten* in ihrem gegenseitigen Verhältniss gefunden. Eine Arbeit, durch eine schwerere unterbrochen, wird nachher geringere als die erwarteten Ergebnisse liefern, eine durch leichtere Arbeit unterbrochene dagegen bessere" (Rivers & Kraepelin, 1895, p. 201). This discovery that if work on A is interrupted by work on a more difficult task, then later work on A is decremented, while if the interruption is by easier work, then later work on A is incremented, is probably highly task specific; it almost certainly does not apply to pursuit-rotor learning.

Voss (1899) made a more analytic investigation of the fluctuations of performance already noted by his predecessors; he constructed an instrument which enabled him to measure the length of each single addition in 1/1000 of a second. He studied fluctuation of attention by plotting fluctuations of addition times from one maximum to another. Individual data were plotted in terms of the percentage of various duration times over 5-min periods; there are of course 12 such periods in the 1-hr long experiments. A typical table, slightly condensed, is given below (Table 1-1); it is seen that the majority of solution times fall into the 0.6-in band, but that an unusually large percentage of solutions also fall into the 1.2-in band, i.e., they are twice as long as the modal solutions. As he said, "die Ermüdung bewirkt das Auftreten sehr langer Additionszeiten" (Voss, 1899, p. 448). Altogether he concludes

TABLE 1-1. Percentage of Durations in Each Five-Minute Period [a]

Duration of addition in sec.	1	2	3	4	5	6	7	8	9	10	11	12
0.4	2.0	4.7	7.0	4.0	5.0	4.0	10.0	7.5	10.5	4.5	5.0	4.5
0.6	68.0	71.5	68.0	67.0	69.0	72.5	63.5	63.5	61.5	61.5	61.5	60.5
0.8	12.0	11.5	8.5	13.4	13.5	12.5	12.5	11.5	14.0	16.0	10.0	13.0
1.0	6.0	4.5	5.5	4.0	4.0	4.5	5.0	7.5	3.5	5.0	6.0	7.0
1.2+	12.0	7.8	11.0	11.6	8.5	6.5	9.0	10.5	10.5	13.0	17.5	15.0

[a] Taken from Voss (1896).

that in the course of work there appear numerous shorter or longer fluctuations, these tend to occur in multiples of the time needed to produce a single addition. The cause of the fluctuations in attention is to be found in central mechanisms, not in peripheral ones; "die *Ursache* der Arbeits—und damit auch der Aufmerksamkeits-schwankungen überhaupt ist in *centralen Vorgängen* zu suchen" (Voss, 1899, p. 449). These long addition times correspond to what Bills was much later to call "blocking," and what we will call IRPs (involuntary rest pauses).

Voss adds that drive acts not only at the beginning and end of the work period, but also often during practice; "der Antrieb bewirkt das Auftreten einzelner ganz kurzer Additionszeiten unc macht dadurch die Arbeitsweise ungleich-mässiger" (1899, p. 448). This appeal to changes in drive is gratuitous; there is the alternative possibility that long addition times permit the subject to rest, and thus emerge refreshed and able to respond quickly. Here, as elsewhere in Kraepelin's work, drive appears as something of a *deus ex machina* to explain, after a fashion, phenomena otherwise unclear. Motivation is the weakest part of Kraepelin's system.

Lindley (1901) restates, on the basis of his extensive work, the experimentally ascertained effects of introducing a rest pause into a period of massed practice: "Die Wirkung jeder Arbeitspause ist eine dreifache: die Ermüdung gleicht sich aus, die Anregung geht verloren, und die Uebung schwindet" (1901, p. 534). Inhibition dissipates, set is lost, and forgetting sets in. The mutual interaction of these three factors determines the optimal length of rest periods. However, he found that individual differences are very marked in determining the optimal length of rest periods; in educated, highly motivated adults the optimal length of rest between two half-hour periods of simple addition lay between 15 and over 60 min. He even found that "unter Umständen, bei geringer Ermüdbarkeit und grosser Anregbarkeit, kann das ununterbrochene Fortarbeiten bei den angeführten Bedingungen vortheilhafter sein als jede Pause" (Lindley, 1901, p. 534). Gradually this and similar findings led Kraepelin to introduce the notion of individual differences into his terminology: *Ermüdbarkeit,* as above (liability to develop fatigue or inhibition quickly and strongly), *Anregbarkeit,* as above (ability to develop set strongly and quickly), *Uebungsfähigkeit* (ability to learn quickly on a particular task), *Leistungsfähigkeit* (ability to perform a given task), and others. This recognition of the need for introducing personal constants into general equations of performance curves preceded Hull's (1945) programmatic statement by some 50 years, and issued in far more experimental attempts to put the program into practice than did Hull's; its neglect by experimentalists has vitiated

all too many empirical investigations. Attempts to find optimal durations of rest pauses in general, or to compare the effects of different rest
pauses, relies on averaging inherently distinct values and thus obscures
the underlying reality; averaging should only be used when homogeneity is assured.

Several other authors took up the investigation of massed and
spaced practice, and the effects of different lengths of rest pauses.
Hylan and Kraepelin (1904) used short work periods (5 min of adding)
and found that on the whole improvement in performance was a direct
function of duration of rest pause, at least up to the half-hour period
which was the longest rest pause used. "Die fortschreitende Besserung
der Leistung mit Verlängerung der Ruhepause ist im allgemeinen, den
Erwartungen entsprechend, eingetroffen" (Hylan & Kraepelin, 1904, p.
489). This conclusion suggests that even with individual differences to
obscure the picture, certain generalizations may still be feasible.
Heüman (1904) also arrives at certain generalizations which are only
partly obscured by individual differences. Dissipation of inhibition
during rest is a function of the length of the rest pause and of the
duration of pre-rest practice: "In der Wirkung einer Pause überwiegt
die Erholung im allgemeinen um so mehr, je langer sie selbst ist und je
langer die Arbeit vorher gedauert hat" (Heuman, 1904, p. 602). This
conclusion has of course been tested time and time again in later work
with the pursuit rotor, always with results which support Heüman.
Miesemer (1904, p. 433) suggested, on the basis of his work, that mental
and physical work may interact; "körperliche und geistige Arbeit
beeintrachtigen beide die Auffassungsfähigkeit." This may serve as a
precursor of Hull's adoption of the Mowrer–Miller work hypothesis,
but it only partly justifies it. Miesemer suggests that physical work may
have an inhibitory influence on attention, but not that *only* physical
work has such an influence; other factors are also allowed for. Hull's
hypothesis overgeneralizes a perfectly sound notion.

Kraepelin (1913) used results from work curve studies to assess the
mental state of psychotic patients, and also tried to throw light on the
nature of the disorder in question. Thus he presents data on adding
from a dementia praecox case (1913, p. 692), comparing massed practice
during a 10-min period with the effects of introducing a 5-min rest
pause after the first 5 min. (Figure 1-8 is redrawn from Kraepelin's
original.) There is a clear-cut reminiscence effect, i.e., after the rest
pause performance is markedly better, but this effect only lasts for 1
min and is then soon lost; "Der Vergleich mit den Kurven der Gesunden . . . zeigt den Unterschied in der Pausenwirkung mit voller Deut-
lichdeit." Hutt (1910) has published similar, more systematic studies

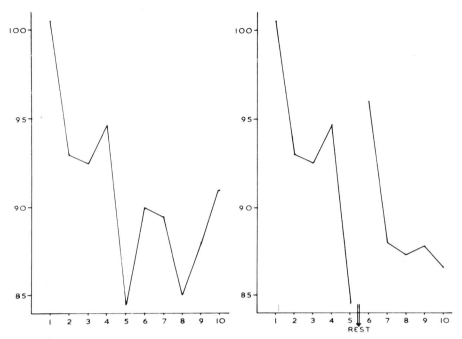

Figure 1-8. Reminiscence in the adding performance of a schizophrenic patient. Drawn after results given by Kraepelin (1913).

with manic-depressive patients, carefully selected and tested in a typical manic or depressive state. Reminiscence was markedly less in psychotics than in normals; "die unmittelbare Pausenwirkung bei unseren Kranken ist durchschnittlich erheblich geringer als bei den Gesunden" (Hutt, 1910, p. 361). Other differences were also noted, but we are not concerned with these detailed findings here; suffice it to say that later work, as we shall see, supports the discovery that psychotics in general have lower reminiscence scores over relatively short rest periods.

So much for a brief summary of some of the studies carried out by Kraepelin and his students. Heüman (1904, p. 577) sums up the main conclusions: "Der Arbeitswerth in jedem Punkte der Arbeitscurve wird . . . wesentlich durch vier verschiedene Einflüsse—den Antrieb, die Anregung, die Uebung und die Ermüdung bestimmt. . . . Die Pause unterbricht die Wirkung aller der aufgeführten Einflüsse. Sie schwinden, aber mit sehr verschiedener Schnelligkeit, so dass der Arbeitswerth nach der Pause in jedem Augenblicke durch die noch fortbestehenden Reste jener Einflüsse bestimmt wird." Most of the rest of this book deals with the experimental solution of the problems arising from the further implementation of this general scheme, and the quantification of the various determinants of the work curve, both before and after a rest pause.

There are of course hints of quantitative laws in Kraepelin's work, although these are not worked through very thoroughly. Thus, for instance, it is suggested that dissipation of inhibition follows a negatively accelerated time course (Hylan & Kraepelin, 1904, p. 490); this agrees with more recent findings. There is also the suggestion that set is acquired more readily after later rest pauses than after earlier ones (Lindley, 1901, p. 491). The same author argues that great gains in performance are accompanied by a considerable build-up of inhibition (1901, p. 534); there may very well be a causal connection here. But a final synthesis, either qualitative or quantitative, is missing; Kraepelin never built up a systematic theory of the kind with which Hull has made us familiar. This has the disadvantage that the reviewer has to piece together the various building stones for himself, and discard those which Kraepelin later found useless. Thus an element of subjectivity may be introduced which is strengthened by the need to translate German terms, often specially coined for the purpose, into English. Such translation may very easily slant the meaning in a direction not intended by the original author; it is for this reason that in many cases the German original has been quoted. But ultimately the work of the Kraepelin school can only be judged by careful perusal of the original documents; nothing less will do.

For Kraepelin, distribution of practice and reminiscence (although not so called by him) formed part of one and the same research program, and were subject to explanation in terms of much the same factors. With respect to verbal reminiscence, there was an early period of separation, in which both theories and research designs related to these phenomena differed; it was not until the work of Ward (1937) formally identified the experimental operations of these hitherto somewhat distinct sets of experiments that both were universally recognized as being the same kind of phenomenon. Distributed practice had been studied by comparisons between groups receiving differently spaced practice; reminiscence had been studied by comparing pre-rest and post-rest level in one and the same group.[5] In this latter procedure the

---

[5] The design of the early reminiscence studies was as follows:

Original learning   1st retention test   Rest   2nd retention test

The Ward-type design, taken over from distribution of practice studies, was as follows:

Experimental group:	Original learning	Rest	Relearning
Control group:	Original learning	No rest	Relearning

amount of practice produced by the initial test of retention remained uncontrolled, and Brown (1923) showed that this lack of control could be of considerable importance; authors like Gray (1940), Ammons and Irion (1954), and Bunch (1938) have suggested, on the basis of experimental data, that much if not all of the reminiscence observed might be due to this experimental artifact. Ward, by using two groups for the reminiscence type of study, removed this source of confusion and made the experiment formally identical with the distribution of practice kind of experiment. It should be noted that in motor learning this problem hardly arises. Typically a single presentation of verbal material adds significantly to the sum total of learning, so that the problem of the initial test of retention after learning is serious. In motor learning, however, a single presentation, or a 10-sec run, adds very little to the amount learned, so that no correction is required. Hence, Kraepelin did not encounter this particular problem which is more or less exclusive to verbal learning.

It would be more in line with Kraepelin's expressed suggestion if we made it a habit to introduce the spaced group shown in Figure 1-9 as a control group, i.e., a group where we could be reasonably sure that no fatigue/inhibition had been allowed to arise, and which therefore gave as accurate a measure of learning as could be devised. As Rivers and Kraepelin (1895, p. 643) put it, "am wünschenswerthesten wäre es villeicht, von dem *reinen* Uebungswachs auszugehen, wie er sich ohne Ermüdungswirkungen und ohne Uebungsverlust gestalten würde. Dazu würden Versuche gehören, in denen einerseits die Ermüdung vollkommen ausgeglichen wäre, während andererseits der Uebungsverlust noch keinen nennenswerthen Einfluss ausgeübt hätte." Such an experimental arrangement would thus add considerably more to our knowledge in any particular case than would a control group with massed trials throughout; in particular, we would be able to obtain information regarding the permanent (or semipermanent) amount of inhibition ($_sI_R$) at every point of the practice curve. The lack of either reminiscence or forgetting shown in Figure 1-9 (to be discussed in detail presently) suggests that for pursuit-rotor practice at least the distribution used may be optimal for the purpose suggested; it does seem to fulfill the requirements stated by Kraepelin. [10-sec trials were separated by 30-sec rest pauses (Eysenck, 1956). The lower curves show marked practice effects, with two rest pauses of 10 min each.]

Kraepelin expressly rejected the concept of *inhibition,* preferring that of *fatigue.* Other psychologists working around the turn of the century did not share this preference, and Ranschburg (1902, 1905) in particular, may be credited with working out the basic nature of the concept along lines which still sound modern and acceptable. His

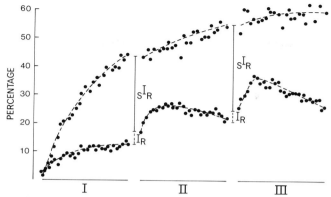

Figure 1-9. Pursuit-rotor scores obtained during massed (lower curves) and spaced (upper curves) practice. Taken with permission from Eysenck (1956b).

experiments were very simple: series of from 2 to 6 digits were exposed tachistoscopically and had to be reproduced by the subject. Ranschburg noted that certain arrangements of digits produced large numbers of errors, and he particularly singled out the presence of "homogeneous elements," by which he understood two identical or similar numbers in close proximity. He expressed this fact as a general law: "Heterogeneous stimuli which are presented simultaneously or in quick succession have a lower threshold than do homogeneous stimuli." This is not too dissimilar to Hull's (1934) statement of the law of inhibition: "Whenever any reaction is evoked in an organism there is left a condition or state which acts as a primary, negative motivation in that it has an innate capacity to produce a cessation of the activity which produced the state. . . . We shall call this state or condition *reactive inhibition*. . . . The reaction decrements which have been attributed to reactive inhibition obviously bear a striking resemblance to the decrements which are ordinarily attributed to 'fatigue.' It is important to note that 'fatigue' is to be understood in the present context as denoting a decrement in action evocation potentiality, rather than an exhaustion of the energy available to the reacting organ." Except for the link with motivation (which is of doubtful value, and which has little experimental support) Hull's definition and Ranschburg's are formally identical, although the expression of this identity follows slightly different lines.[6] And consid-

[6] Even the motivational nature of reactive inhibition finds an echo in Rivers and Kraepelin (1895, p. 639), who write that "wenn man will, kann man in dem Schwinden des Antriebes ein Kennzeichen für das Auftreten der *Langenweile* (sic!) sehen"; thus boredom, which is considered the subjective aspect of reactive inhibition, is here connected with a lowering of drive or motivation. Kraepelin knew of course that boredom was far

ering the homogeneity of the material used in his experiments, Kraepelin too might have considered this "inhibition" analogous to his "fatigue" in important ways.

Let us now consider a typical modern experiment, already mentioned above, contrasting spaced and massed learning on the pursuit rotor (Eysenck, 1956). Figure 1-9 shows the results of this experiment in which the lower set of curves presents the mean time-on-target scores during successive 10-sec intervals of 50 Ss; 3 sets of 30 massed trials are separated by 10-min rest pauses. The upper set of curves consists of 10-sec trials separated by 30-sec rest pauses; after 300 and again after 600 sec this group was also given 10-min rest pauses. How would Kraepelin have explained the findings, using only concepts expressly put forward by him and his students?

The very marked improvement in performance of the distributed group he would have considered due to practice (learning); the failure of the massed group to achieve equally good performance he would have considered due to fatigue (inhibition). This fatigue dissipates during rest, thus producing the reminiscence effect, denoted I_R in the figure after Hull's symbolic representation of reactive inhibition. The failure of the lower curve to reach the upper curve even after rest Kraepelin would have explained in terms of his semi-permanent fatigue (inhibition); this effect is denoted $_sI_R$ in the diagram after Hull's symbolic representation of conditioned inhibition, which is also supposed to be permanent (unless extinguished by suitable experimental manipulation). The rapid post-rest rise (PRU) Kraepelin would have attributed to the regaining of set lost during rest (warm-up); PRD he would have attributed to the rapid accumulation of fatigue, possibly adding semi-permanent fatigue to that due to the resumption of practice. The failure of reminiscence to appear in the distributed group would not have surprised him, in view of the lack of fatigue accumulated by that group, with its frequent long rests.

The upper curve in Figure 1-9 corresponds reasonably well to Kraepelin's requirements for a "pure" learning curve, i.e., one in which the influence of fatigue has been eliminated through mixing short practice periods with long rest periods. The difference between the curves at any point would serve him as a measure of fatigue, except

---

from being an infallible sign of poor performance; his experiments showed "dass die Leistungsfähigkeit durch die Langeweile, wenn überhaupt, so doch in weit geringerem Masse beeinflusst worden ist, als durch das Verhältniss zwischen Arbeit und Erholung." (1895, p. 632.) In other words, boredom is effect, not cause, of performance; work produces a lowering of drive, and this is (sometimes) felt as boredom.

where "warm up decrement" added its effect to those of fatigure. How does fatigue produce work decrement? Kraepelin would have appealed to metabolic factors (probably erroneously, as we have pointed out above), and he might also have drawn on the work of Voss to explain that frequent "blocks" or involuntary rest pauses produced by fatigue would reduce the total work output. These rest pauses themselves, he might have argued, were very likely the product of metabolic waste products. This general theory, here only sketched in lightly, is not very dissimilar to that offered 50 years later by Ammons (1947), or by other writers of that period who followed Hull in his general theoretical point of view (Kimble, 1949). Was there any viable alternative theory in existence around the turn of the century?

AN EARLY CONSOLIDATION THEORY

Müller and Pilzecker (1900) advanced the hypothesis, based on their extensive work in nonsense-syllable learning, that "Jede Vorstellung besitzt nach ihrem Auftreten im Bewusstsein eine *Perseverationsten-denz*, d.h. eine im Allgemeinen schnell abklingende Tendenz, frei ins Bewusstsein zu steigen" (1900, p. 58). This perseverative tendency, which was assumed to pertain to any image, idea, or other content of consciousness, had a physiological basis and served to strengthen any associations formed during learning. "Nach dem Lesen einer Silben-reihe dauern gewisse physiologische Vorgänge, welche zur Verstär-kung der beim Lesen der Reihe gestifteten Associationen dienen, mit allmählich abnehmender Stärke eine gewisse Zeit hindurch nach" (Müller & Pilzecker, 1900, p. 196; sentence slightly rearranged). This process of perseveration interferes with the learning or reproduction of other material originally learned. The authors specifically use the term "consolidation" ("consolidirung"; 1900, p. 97), and spell out the hypothetical interference effects mentioned above. They also explicitly mention the possibility that this process of consolidation might lead to some form of reminiscence, and conclude that while this is possible it it not always and under all conditions essential that such reminiscence should be found. "Die durch das Lesen einer Silbenreihe bewirkten physiologischen Effecte, welche den Associationen der Silben zu Grunde liegen, haben eine Tendenz, nach Beendigung des Lesens schnell zurückzugehen. Diesem Rückgange wirken die Persevera-tion-stendenzen entgegen; sie verlangsamen ihn, sie brauchen ihn aber nicht in sein Gegentheil umzuwandeln." (1900, p. 197.) Thus Müller and Pilzecker put their finger on the precise point which has led to so much difficulty in demonstrating reminiscence in verbal learning; forgetting (interference?) is so rapid that consolidation can often only retard it, but cannot overcome it and produce positive reminiscence effects. The authors did not attempt to apply their notions to motor learning, but here, of course, forgetting (interference?) is so much less marked that the theory could be used to predict strong reminiscence effects. However, no such use was in fact made of consolidation theory until much later, and there would be little point in entering into a more prolonged discussion of this theory here.

It may be worth while at this point to mention the possibility that inhibition and consolidation theories can explain different aspects of the reminiscence phenomenon along their different lines. As we have seen in Figures 1-1 and 1-2, reminiscence may refer to the *restitution* of performance to its previous level, from whence it has dropped during the course of massed practice, or it can refer to an *increment* in performance above the highest level previously reached. Possibly fatigue/ inhibition, and its dissipation, lie at the base of the former phenomenon, and perseveration/consolidation at the base of the latter. In many cases, as already pointed out, both phenomena may be at work, and hence both explanatory concepts may be needed. Later discussion will attempt to clarify the points here raised.

The theoretical concepts used by Müller and Pilzecker sometimes read as if they had been cribbed from such writers as Walker (1958), just as Kraepelin's discussions sometimes sound as if he had been a disciple of Hull. There is one further point in Müller and Pilzecker's work which has proved of great and prophetic importance: their stress on individual differences. Like Kraepelin, Binet, Pavlov, and other writers at the time, Müller too had not yet succumbed to the schizophrenic modern tendency of making a water-tight boundary between "Experimental" psychology (figuratively spelled with a capital E) and personality study, as if the phenomena studied under varied experimental conditions could ever be divorced from the personality of the individuals exposed to the experimental stimuli. Hence many cogent and interesting observations of such individual differences are recorded, and Müller and Pilzecker conclude that "da die Perseveration bei verschiedenen Individuen verschieden stark ist, so zeigen sich erfahrungsgemäss auch diejenigen Seiten des geistigen Lebens, denen die Perseveration dient, bei verschiedenen Menschen verschieden entwickelt . . . Es ist leicht zu erkennen, dass Individuen mit starker Perseveration in einem Berufe, welcher einen schnellen und häufigen Wechsel der Richtung der Aufmerksamkeit, eine schnelle Erledigung zahlreicher ganz verschiedener Geschäfte verlangt, mit ihren Fähigkeiten nicht am rechten Platze sind." (1900, p.77.) Elsewhere our authors point out "dass eine starke Perseveration auch für den Charakter von gewissem Einflusse sein muss," (1900, p. 73) and that "starke Perseveration schliesst die Fähigkeit aus, die Aufmerksamkeit schnell von einem Gedanken- oder Beschäftigungs-kreise gänzlich zu einem anderen übergehen zu lassen" (1900, p. 72). Several examples of these generalizations are given by reference to everyday behavior patterns of experimental subjects showing strong or weak perseveration in the experimental situation.

These suggestions were later taken up by Gross (1902, 1908) of Vienna, and by Heymans (1908) of Holland, who constructed a theory of personality on this basis; Spearman (1927) introduced these notions into England and designed various measures of "perseveration" as tests of personality. The theory of individual differences in perseveration also links up with Wundt's theory of personality, in which the dimension of "changeable–unchangeable" plays an important part; as Eysenck (1967) has pointed out, this dimension is descriptively very similar to that of extraversion–introversion. The intimate historical link-up between this concept and the notion of perseveration has been traced in some detail by Eysenck (1970). We shall come back to these notions in a later chapter, and see that much of what Müller and Pilzecker had to say on the relation between learning, memory, perseveration, and personality has in fact been verified by modern methods of research.

One further point may deserve mention. Müller and Pilzecker attempted to locate the seat of the perseveration/consolidation phenomenon by pointing out its similarity to the steretoyped, repetitious behavior resulting from the varied disorders of the subcortical motor centers; it was with these, therefore, that they associated perseverative tendencies. More recent work suggests that consolidation is intimately connected with the activity of the ascending reticular activating system, which also provides the physiological background for the phenomena of "attention" playing such a large part in the explanatory and descriptive writings of Kraepelin and his followers. A more detailed discussion of these points will also be given later on.

CHAPTER 2

The Pursuit Rotor: An Apparatus for All Occasions

Much if not most of the work on motor reminiscence has been done on the pursuit rotor, and in fact our account in this book is very much concentrated on this particular apparatus. This choice may seem somewhat paradoxical; is not verbal learning of more interest than motor learning, and is not concentration on one type of apparatus lacking in generality? The obvious answer would be that motor learning results in replicable, clear-cut, and coherent findings which are of obvious interest and relevance to psychology, results which furthermore can be integrated theoretically with findings from many other areas such as conditioning studies. Reminiscence in verbal learning is much less reliable, as we shall see, and, although of course no less worthy of attention for that reason, may be just a little too complex and obscure to form the basis for a proper quantitative treatment. It is possible that the general laws and theories of motor learning may be capable of extension to the more complex field, possible with certain modifications or additions; if so the preference for starting with the simple, rather than with the complex, is probably justified. Even should this hope not be justified, and should reminiscence and other learning phenomena follow quite different laws when verbal rather than motor behavior is at issue, the choice of preferring the simple over the complex would still be justified; it would give us a secure starting point from which to evaluate similarities and differences. Arguments such as these cannot of course prove our choice to have been correct; they are offered rather to make it more acceptable.

As regards concentration on one particular piece of apparatus within the field of motor reminiscence, it might be said that the choice has been forced upon us by the fact that published work has (wisely) concentrated on the pursuit rotor. It is not always realized how advances in science can be speeded up or retarded by suitable or unsuitable choice of experimental paradigm, apparatus, or animal. Pavlov would almost certainly not have succeeded as well as he did had he concentrated on cats, or rats, rather than on dogs; much of current American animal work would probably be much more relevant to human psychology if laboratories had concentrated more on dogs than on the cheap and ubiquitous rat! A clear-cut example of the superiority of one and the inferiority of another experimental choice comes from the work of Gregor Mendel, who is credited with discovering the mechanism of heredity, and who laid the foundations of modern genetics. Mendel concentrated exclusively on *Pisum,* and in particular he studied two clear-cut characteristics of his plants: Tall vs dwarf, and smooth vs wrinkled. (He actually studied seven pairs of characters, including in addition to those mentioned differences in the color of the cotyledons, the tint of the seed coat, the shape of the ripe pods, the tint of the unripe pods, and the difference in the position of the flowers— axial or terminal.) *Pisum* is ideal from the point of view of Mendel's objective, and his clear-cut results owe much to this inspired choice.

Mendel was much impressed with the fame and authority of C. Nägeli, to whom he sent a copy of his published work on *Pisum;* Nägeli, in his letter of 25 February 1867, recommended Mendel to work on *Hieracium* instead, which Mendel proceded to do (Iltis, 1966). Unfortunately *Hieracium* was an extremely bad choice from Mendel's point of view, because of the apogamous development of its ovules; Mendel never really got anywhere with his breeding studies and his analyses. Had he started out with *Hieracium* rather than *Pisum,* it is safe to say he would never have discovered the laws which bear his name. Neither he nor Nägeli could have known at the time how complex *Hieracium* really was; the suggestion for research workers which emanates from this story is surely that when a particular apparatus, design, or animal (or plant!) gives good, clear-cut, replicable results, then it is wise to persist with this particular choice and not depart from it except for a very good reason. This is not to say that at some stage efforts should not be made to advance beyond the original type of study and extend the laws found there to other designs, organisms, and pieces of apparatus; all this should be done, but preferably from the safety of an impregnable, assured position, and in full knowledge of the elementary laws pertaining to one's original choice. Note will be taken throughout this book of work on reminiscence not using the pursuit rotor, but our main effort will be directed towards the construction of a quantitative theory of pursuit-rotor reminiscence.

The insistence on a *quantitative* theory is important; it derives from the impatience which one must feel with the purely qualitative type of argument which has pervaded the field since Kraepelin's pioneering work. Given concepts like fatigue/inhibition, drive, practice/learning, and warm-up it is possible to account for any observed (or imagined!) work curve by reference to certain combinations of these. When everything can be explained, nothing can be predicted; it is only when we begin to fit constants to our equations, and specify precisely the conditions under which our theoretical concepts may be presumed to work, that we are advancing beyond a purely verbal type of explanatory stage.

The pursuit rotor appears to have originated with the "pursuit pendulum" of W.R. Miles (1920), which was constructed in response to aviation student selection needs during the first World War. In the spring of 1917, working at the Nutrition Laboratory, Miles tested aviation candidates by means of a pendulum which subjects, head secured in a head rest and left eye covered, were instructed to follow with their eyes; "six or more successive trials by a subject were photographed side by side on one plate" (Miles, 1920, p. 361.) Miles comments that it was not easy to score these records, but found it "convenient to rank these photographic records showing the reaction time occurring at the start of the pendulum's swing, together with the number and size of abrupt horizontal movements by which the subject supplements his inadequate pursuit, into five grades or groups of excellence. Such grouping gave a positive correlation of 0.40 with the subsequent progress of these men in learning to fly" (1920, p. 361.) The apparatus was much too laboratory-bound to be of practical use, and Miles constructed a more robust, nonphotographic version in which the pendulum dispensed a stream of water through a nozzle during its swing; this the subject attempted to catch in a metal "cup of limited diameter." The water came from a large reservoir, containing sufficient fluid to make the change in position of the center of gravity which occurred with the outflow of water rather unimportant. The score was the amount of water caught in the cup during one 2-sec swing of the pendulum, back to its starting point; the next swing was started when the subject had put down the cup, had taken an empty one and had signaled his readiness. Miles gives a figure which shows average results for 10 women and 8 men tested on 35 days with 20 catches per day's practice, as well as the variability of the group (standard deviation divided by mean); as mean performance rises to 75% of the possible catch, variability falls.

Miles notes the extreme individual differences in ability to perform on his pendulum. Since Hilgard introduced Freud as an outstanding learning theorist in his well-known book, *Theories of Learning*, the temptation has been irresistible to subject the pursuit pendulum to a dynamic analysis. The extremely symbolic nature of the test springs to the eye without prompting; a rigid, elongated instrument ejaculates a fluid into a cup-shaped container. Clearly performance would be interfered with by castration anxiety in men and penis envy in women; thus the unresolved Oedipus complex must be assumed to lie at the basis of poor performance on this test. (Alternative theories will be considered later.) Conversely, it may be argued that clinical psychology has lost a valuable measure of dynamic personality characteristics by throwing in its lot with the Rorschach; the pursuit pendulum would seem to offer far greater possibilities. Possibly the rejection of the pendulum in favor of the pursuit rotor (to which we shall turn next) is also due to dynamic resistances on the part of the censor; the sexual nature of the test is too overt to go by unnoticed. In the pursuit rotor too, of course, we have a pointed, rigid instrument homing on a round, fleeing target; in addition there is the grinding and bumping movement of the subject as he bends to the task, reminiscent of the expert stripper at work. (Interesting possibilities of the pursuit rotor as a selection test are raised in this connection.) Altogether, this side of experimental work has unfortunately been investigated too little to permit any longer discussion; it is hoped that these suggestions may be taken up by others more competent to judge them, and carry out the needed experimental work.

Miles mentions in a footnote (1920, p. 366) that "Professor Carl E. Seashore informs me that, after trying the original test at the Nutrition Laboratory, he has arranged a very successful combination for testing motor ability to perform circular movements, but using a phonograph motor, a time-interrupted circuit, and an electric counter." This instrument is described in detail by Wilhelmina Koerth (1922), whose short paper is the first to show the apparatus as we now know it (if with certain rather primitive measurement characteristics). Figure 2-1 is taken from her paper; "the apparatus consists of a rotating wooden disc carrying a polished target and commutator with flexible contact, a Veeder counter operated by magnets, a control key, a hinged pointer, a storage battery, and a small phonograph. The wooden disc, 17.5 cm in diameter, and 2.2 cm thick, rests firmly on the phonograph plate, revolving with it. The brass target, 1.9 cm in diameter, is sunk flush with the surface of the disc 8 cm from the centre. A commutator to govern the counter is provided by ten brass plates sunk in the edge of the disc in such a way as to present a smooth surface of alternating

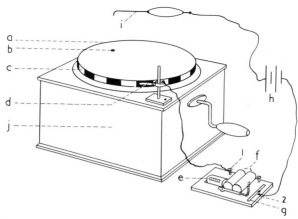

Figure 2-1. Original Koerth pursuit rotor, redrawn after picture in Koerth (1922). (a) Wooden disk; (b) brass target; (c) commutator; (d) flexible contact; (e) Veeder counter; (f) magnets; (g) control key; (h) battery; (i) hinged pointer; (j) phonograph; 1 and 2: binding posts.

metal and wood to a flexible contact. The plate and target are connected by concealed wires. The disc is stained dull black and all metal parts are highly polished." (Koerth, 1922, p. 288.) The pointer is hinged to avoid the possibility of the subject slowing down the rotating disk by pressing down on it.

Administration and scoring are rather cumbersome and lacking in refinement. The subject is shown the apparatus, practices on it for a couple of minutes in a rather uncontrolled manner, and finally begins practice proper when given the starting signal; this coincides with the closing of the control key. The key is kept closed for 20 sec, then the order "stop" is given and the key is released. The number on the Veeder counter is recorded pre- and post-practice. Five trials are given as rapidly as possible; then a 2-min rest is allowed, followed by another 5 trials, etc., until 20 trials have been given. This "number of Veeder counts per rotation" is not a recommended method of scoring; it clearly makes proper massing of trials (zero distribution) impossible if we wish to have scores integrated over smaller units of time. Renshaw and Weiss (1926) introduced the more familiar continuous time-on-target type of score, and this has been used almost exclusively ever since. Only quite recently have attempts been made to record number and length of hits and misses in addition to time-on-target integrated over 10-sec periods (Frith, 1968).

Humphreys (1936), Travis (1936), and Bell (1942) were among the early workers who used pursuit rotors similar to the one used by

Koerth; in addition there were a number of alternative versions. Thus Renshaw and Weiss (1926) and Renshaw and Schwarzbeck (1938) used a pursuit meter; "its essential features consist in a cam and gear mechanism which drives a small electrode in a complicated pattern of changing directions and rates. The path of this target electrode covers an area of about 6 by 8 cm. The subject contacts this electrode with a similar one held as a stylus in his hand. The handle of the stylus is rigid. Each of the electrodes is so rounded that about nine degrees tilt of the handle in any direction breaks the contact. If the subject fails to maintain contact accurately, the mechanism which drives the electrode stops and an error is recorded. The subject's task consists in keeping the electrode constantly in motion." (Renshaw & Schwarzbeck, 1938, p. 7.) Practice was in terms of cycles, identical with each other in terms of movement of the electrode; each cycle contained 63 revolutions of one of the driver pinions, resulting in nonduplicated patterns of movement of the target electrode.

Independently of Koerth, Wishart (1923) in Scotland designed a linear type of pursuit rotor in which an irregular movement of the target along a single dimension is produced by an irregularly cut cam which activates a rocker; tracking is by means of a pressure-activated lever system. Measurement of time-on-target is rather ingenious; contact with the target causes a current to flow through an electromagnet whose cylindrical armature is held clear of a rubber tube, thus allowing water to flow from a container to a graduated vessel. Disruption of contact closes the rubber tube, and the flow of water is stopped. Hence the amount of water collected in the vessel during unit time provides an accurate measure of time-on-target. Buxton and Henry (1939) appear to have been the only psychologists to have used this type of pursuit meter.

Travis (1936) used a pursuit oscillator of his own design. "A small platform (15 cm by 20 cm), carrying a silver target (11 mm in diameter) sunk flush with the surface of the platform, was mounted on a pivoted support to permit the platform to oscillate through an arc. In the present study the platform was oscillated through an arc of 13 degrees by a synchronous motor attached to a pulley and crank at the constant rate of one complete oscillation per second. . . . The task of the subject was to stand before the oscillating platform which was about wasit high and to hold a gravity-stylus on the oscillating target. . . . If the subject held the gravity-stylus on the oscillating target continuously the electric marker made ten deviations per second on the smoked drum by virtue of the electric circuit through synchronous motor timers which permitted ten electrical contacts per second. A continuous record of the subject's performance was made on a spiral kymograph."

Many other variations were tried, but only those which resulted in work relevant to various theoretical points will be noted as they occur naturally in the course of our inquiry; no attempt will here be made to trace the history of perceptual-motor skills apparatus. Most of the work to be discussed was done with pursuit rotors having a bakelite top, with inset metal disk, rotating at sixty revolutions per minute; contact was made with the aid of a hinged metal stylus, and recorded on some form of electric chronoscope which was activated while the touch of stylus on disk made the electric circuit, and disactivated when contact was lost and the circuit was broken. Usually two clocks were used in turn, being thrown into circuit and out of circuit every 10 sec, thus allowing the experimenter to read off the score from the clock not in use, and zero it (or have it automatically zeroed). Details of how this recording was accomplished in each case are of no great interest, except that in many cases when only one clock was used this imposed certain restrictions and inaccuracies on recording. In any case, as Ammons (1955a, p. 73) has pointed out, "no experimental article specifies the components of the scoring unit sufficiently exactly to allow reproduction." Apparatus articles, like those of Eckles (1951), Melton (1947), and Seashore (1928) do give adequate information.

Altogether, Ammons (1955a, p. 74) is undoubtedly right in saying that reporting of apparatus details in work with the pursuit rotor has been seriously deficient; he made a survey of the handling of 18 variables in each of 28 pursuit studies, and found that "at the most, the handling of 9 variables was adequately described, while two articles failed to specify handling of any of the variables." Among the variables he considered are target size [shown by Helmick (1951) to be relevant to performance], direction of target rotation, rate of target rotation [also found by Helmick (1951) to be relevant], target distance from center, target material, target surfacing, target–turntable articulation, stylus handle (size, shape, and material), stylus arm (size, shape, and material), stylus tip (shape and composition), weight of stylus tip on turntable, total weight of stylus, size of turntable, its material and surfacing, scoring unit, and height of turntable surface. Some of these are unlikely to be very important; stylus length for instance seems largely irrelevant (Ammons, 1955b). But until standardization has eliminated the need for accurate reporting, it remains true that duplication of experimental work is impossible unless much greater care is taken by authors to report details of their apparatus and experimental setup, and unless editors become resigned to give up more space for the purpose. Psychology falls far short of, for example, physics in its concern with replicability in this respect.

Much the same may be said with respect to maintenance. Speed of rotation should be checked daily, as quite marked changes may and do take place unless care is taken. The surface of the turntable becomes pitted, as does the disk itself; furthermore the alignment of the two can easily be upset, so that the transition from one to the other is anything but smooth. The tip of the stylus can become abraded, making continuous contact hazardous and uncertain. Connections from the target disk internally are difficult, and may deteriorate with time; they are at all times subject to disturbances and minute interruptions. The contacts between stylus and disk are also easily disturbed; dust and dirt from the surface of the turntable are easily picked up by the stylus and may interfere with the electric contact. Frequent cleaning with carbon tetrachloride is indicated. Published work does not always indicate whether all these precautions have been taken, and frequently appearances suggest that they have not. As much of the work reported in subsequent chapters comes from our own laboratories, our standard practice may be worth stating.

The apparatus consists of a brown turntable of 10 in diameter, rotating in a clockwise direction at 60 rev/min. A "target" 7/10 in in diameter is set with its center 3 1/4 in from the center of the turntable, and flush with its surface. The subject is required to keep the tip of an articulated stylus in contact with the target while the turntable rotates. The stylus, of total weight 2 oz, consists of a circular plastic handle 4 1/2-in long, with a guard set 1 in from the end of the handle. An extension rod (6 in long, 1/10 in in diameter and with an 85° bend 1 in from its end), hinged so that only its weight rests on the turntable, projects from the guard. The steady contact between stylus tip and target closes a circuit to two recording chronotrons. Time-on-target is integrated over 10-sec periods, each period being termed a trial, and is registered alternately on one of the chronotrons, an automatic switching device bringing the other into action at the end of every trial. Height above the ground of the turntable is 35 in, and light is either natural (but not direct sunshine) or nonglare artificial light; it is not our impression that height of surface or amount of light are, within reasonable limits, very crucial parameters of performance. Apparatus is checked daily, and cleaned at regular intervals. Minor deviations from these specifications, when they occur, are described in the relevant research reports.

Two important improvements have taken place in the construction of pursuit-rotor apparatus in recent years, and may be noted here briefly. The first is the introduction of multiple-target disks, and the second is the introduction of light-sensitive cells as recording devices, coupled with moving light sources as targets. Multiple-target disks consist of the central metal disk, surrounded by metal annuli, circular in shape and insulated from the central disk and from each other; disk and each ring are separately connected to recording chronotrons so that it becomes possible to read off time-on-target for each of the targets (disk and rings) separately. The number of such rings may be small, as in the case of the Maudsley Multiple Pursuit Rotor (e.g., Gray, 1968), or it may be quite large, up to 19 concentric bands, as in the case of the Humphries' (1961) apparatus. The reasons for having these additional targets are associated with measurement theory, and will be discussed later in this chapter. There are obvious advantages associated with the more analytic recording made possible by multiple targets, but the labor involved in analysis rises proportionately.

One of the most unsatisfactory features of the orthodox metal-stylus—metal-disk contacts is the failure of the contact to be truly continuous. The stylus, being rather light, is easily made to bounce and jump by slight departures from perfect flatness in the disk, or by slight differences in height between the disk and the turntable; in addition, dirt collected by the stylus may prevent perfect contact. The inaccuracies introduced in this manner are not, in all probability, very large when all we want to record is the mean time-on-target over a specified period (although even here little seems to have been done to ascertain the actual error introduced by mechanical imperfections of this kind). However, as we shall see later, it may be of interest to measure the duration and number of hits and misses somewhat more analytically; for many theoretical problems this additonal information can be vital. Errors introduced through faulty recording may completely vitiate records so obtained, and thus make testing of theoretical predictions impossible. This is particularly true when information from the rotor is fed directly into a computer, as in our later studies; the very fact that the on-line computer works at a very high level of accuracy makes it extremely sensitive to errors and deviations in recording which the rather insensitive chronotron would have disregarded. Consequently, it has become useful to substitute a glass-covered light bulb for the disk, and a light-sensitive cell mounted at the end of a traditional stylus for the metal-tip used in the past; this connection in our experience is not subject to the criticisms made above of the metal-to-metal contact.

For on-line computer recording this new method is almost mandatory if useful results are to be obtained.

This method also has the advantage that different targets and target paths can be easily prepared, as in the commercially available "polar-pursuit trackers" (Research Media, Inc., 163 Eileen Way, Syosset, New York 11791). In these, the light source for generating the target is a twin circular fluorescent lamp. Mounted over the lamp is an opaque disk which contains a radial slit which is rotated at an adjustable speed; the disk blocks all light but that which passes through the slit, creating a constantly rotating light source. A glass, covered with opaque tape, is located immediately above the disk. The target path or pattern is made by cutting and removing the tape as desired. The intersection between the slit and the pattern on the glass forms a "window" through which the light can pass as the disk rotates. (If the target path is other than circular, the resultant target velocity will be nonlinear, and the target shape changeable.) Detailed studies using this apparatus have been reported by Frith (1969); we will return to this work in a later chapter.

The actual reminiscence score often used by workers is the difference between the last pre-rest trial and the first post-rest trial. This practice gives rise to many problems. When trials are short (e.g., 10 sec) they are also rather unreliable, i.e., subject to many chance factors, and the taking of a difference between two such unreliable scores results in a measure even more unreliable. If longer trials are used (30 or 60 sec) then reminiscence and PRU are mixed up to such an extent that it becomes very difficult to sort out which is which. This difficulty is also attached to 10- sec trials, of course; even during such a short period one must admit at least the possibility that PRU is taking place, a point which could easily be proved by separately scoring the first and the second 5-sec periods of the 10-sec trial. But the amount of PRU involved is minimal with short trials, and individual differences in PRU will not exert too much influence; with longer trials this is no longer true. On the whole it seems preferable to record and plot 10-sec trials to indicate the trend of results; if desired, it is then always possible to combine these trials into longer ones, while it is not possible to chop longer trials up into smaller pieces. Longer trials are admissible for the pre-rest portion of the difference score, as this usually shows little in the way of dramatic change; it has been our practice to use the difference between the average of the last 3 pre-rest 10-sec trials and the first post-rest 10-sec trial in our work, with occasional exceptions which are duly noted. Other methods of scoring derive from theoretical notions about the nature of PRU and will be dealt with in a later chapter; altogether, measurement is obviously dependent on theory, good theories give rise to proper measurement. Equally, we cannot formulate good theories before having some measures to guide us, if only in a rough and ready way. Theory and measurement go hand in hand, and improvement in one leads to improvement in the other.

One additional point of technique should be mentioned here, as it affects the measurement of reminiscence. In comparing the terminal pre-rest and the initial post-rest trials, we are strictly in error because the last pre-rest trials starts with S already moving with the target, and possibly actually on target; in the first post-rest trial he starts by standing still, and cannot possibly be on target. To make conditions more properly comparable it has become customary to precede the first 10-sec post-rest trial by 2 sec of (unscored) practice, so that the commencement of the first trial post-rest finds S already moving properly with the target, and possibly on target, i.e., in a condition identical with that found on the last pre-rest trial. Two seconds of unscored practice means 2 rotations of the turntable, and seems to be sufficient for our purpose.

With pursuit-rotor apparatus as described, learning curves are obtained which usually include a pre-rest period of massed practice, a rest period, and a post-rest period; these may conveniently be referred to as P_1, R, and P_2. Conventionally the lengths of these periods are indicated by writing them in this fashion: 5 - 10 - 5, meaning that a pre-rest period of 5-min practice was followed by 10 min of rest and then another period of 5-min practice. The main alternative to the practice-rest-practice paradigm, which is of course the classic one for reminiscence, is the distributed practice paradigm, in which a number of practice periods are separated by a number of rest periods; differences in distribution (i.e., in the length of the rest periods) throw much light on theories of reminiscence, and are treated in detail in another chapter. Both paradigms are illustrated in Figure 1-9. Typically the results in that figure are given in the form of *means*; this is perhaps inevitable but it has certain dangers which may be noted with advantage as they impose certain restrictions on the conclusions which may be drawn from such data.

It is of course well known that the average curve of learning, or performance, may be quite unlike any of the averaged individual curves; if learning is of the single trial kind, and if the trial on which learning occurs differs from person to person, then the mean curve will assume a regular, negatively accelerated shape which bears no relation to the shape of the individual curves. Fortunately this is not the position in pursuit-rotor learning; individual curves, although of course rather irregular, tend to be similar to each other, and to show the same features as mean curves. Up to a point, then, we may be justified in reporting mean scores, and relegate individual differences from this average to the error variance.

Experience suggests that performance scores on the pursuit rotor are reasonably reliable, and the literature bears this out; reliabilities are usually above .90 when practice is continued over more than a few minutes, and even higher values are often reported, as we shall see later. Thus, there are marked differences in ability on the test, using this term to mean differences in performance level, and these differences in performance level are maintained from the beginning to the end of learning (at least, as long as learning does not reach asymptotic values; what happens then is not really known). It is possible that persons of lower ability, as defined by scores achieved during the first few minutes, have lower asymptotes than persons of higher ability, and some observations by S. B. G. Eysenck (1960) suggest that this may be so. However, the possibility that asymptotes may converge is not absolutely ruled out; this is still a fairly open question on which information would be useful. Up to the time that asymptotic values are reached, however, Ss preserve their rank order, and hence it is useful to talk about individual differences in ability, and to wonder whether these differences are entirely due to learning previous to the first trial on the rotor, or whether hereditary differences play an important part in producing these individual differences. Two studies are available which strongly suggest that hereditary factors play an overwhelmingly strong part in phenotypic performance.

In a classic study, McNemar (1933) used the Koerth pursuit rotor, the Whipple steadiness tester, the Miles speed drill, the Brown spool packer, and a card sorting task on 44 pairs of male high-school fraternal twins and 46 pairs of male high-school identical twins. The main results of his study are brought together in Table 2-1, which gives the intraclass correlations for monozygotic and dizygotic twins, Holzinger's heritability measure, the test reliabilities, and the observed correlations of each test with age. It will be seen that the pursuit rotor has an extremely high reliability, falling short of unity only by an insignificant amount ($r = 0.99$); all the other tests are also highly reliable. All correlations with age are positive, but not very high, averaging around .3 for the pursuit rotor; thus performance increases with age in high-school students, as one might have expected. Monozygotic twins correlate .96, dizygotic ones .51; this gives a heritability estimate of .90; in other words, the within-family variance is determined by heredity to the extent of 90%. This figure is far higher than those calculated for the other tests; the reason for these gross differences in heritability is not

TABLE 2-1. Interclass Correlations and Holzinger Heritabilities, Reliabilities, and Correlations with Age for Five Motor Tests [a]

Task	r_m	r_D	h^2	Reliabilities M[b]	D[c]	Correlations with age M	D
Pursuit rotor	.96	.51	.90	.99	.99	.27	.34
Steadiness	.87	.25	.80	.99	.97	.27	.25
Speed drill	.84	.45	.69	.98	.97	.20	.51
Spool packing	.64	.51	.25	.96	.96	.02	.24
Card sorting	.77	.51	.46	.95	.97	.41	.37

[a] Taken with permission from McNemar (1932).
[b] Monozygotic twins.
[c] Dizygotic twins.

known. It clearly is not connected with reliability, or with age differences. Whatever the reason, there can be no doubt from these data that heredity plays a strong part in individual differences in ability to perform on the pursuit rotor. The correlation between phenotype measurement and genotype approximates .95!

The only other study relevant to this issue is one published by Vandenberg (1962), in which 32 pairs of dizygotic and 43 pairs of monozygotic twins were administered the pursuit rotor, as well as a number of other motor skills, personality, and cognitive tests. Three trials for each hand were given in alternating order; the total time required for each hand is stated to have been 5 min, so that it seems likely that each trial was in fact of 1-min duration. The Holzinger heritability values are .52 for the right hand and .32 for the left hand; they are thus much lower than those reported by McNemar. However, the performance estimates of the earlier study are much more reliable, being based on 7 sets of trials, each set consisting of ten 20-sec trials, making a total of over 23 min of well-spaced practice. (Ss were performing the various other tasks shown in Table 2-1 during the intervals between one set of pursuit-rotor trials and another.) In the case of Vandenberg, only 3 min (i.e., about 13% of the period used by McNemar) was spent on right-hand rotor learning, and the interpolated practice with the left hand must be assumed to have added retroactive and proactive interference factors. Vandenberg's estimate, uncorrected as it is for attenuation, must therefore be regarded as very much an underestimate of the true value; we would probably be justified in regarding McNemar's value as more closely representing the true position as far as pursuit-rotor ability is concerned.

Vandenberg also reports other motor skills as presenting significant H values: Mirror drawing (.70), Tweezer dexterity (.71), Peg board dexterity (.58), Hand steadiness (.37—not significant), Card sorting (.61), and Beam balancing (.48). He also gives an interesting table (1962, p. 233) in which he compares the percentage of measures in various areas which *failed* to give significant heritability values; primary mental abilities give the lowest value (35%), followed by motor skills (43%) perceptual tests (50%) and cognitive and achievement tests (61%) come next, while sensory and musical (62%) and personality tests (68%) bring up the rear. While these figures obviously depend on the actual choice of tests, and their mode of application, the results leave no doubt that even in their rather curtailed form the estimates of motor skill used have a strong hereditary basis. It is interesting to note, though the interpretation of the fact is obscure, that h^2 values obtained on the motor skills tests for the right hand are nearly always higher than those obtained for the left hand; the latter are frequently nonsignificant. Could this be due to greater amount of prior learning with the right hand? McNemar has analyzed the changes in intraclass correlations with increasing practice; he finds that correlations remain steady for monozygotic twins, but increase for dizygotic twins. (Comparing first with last set of 10 trials, the values are .44 and .60 for the latter, .88 and .87 for the former. h^2 drops from .78 to .67.) Vandenberg does not give intraclass correlations for his sample, so we cannot tell whether this hypothesis has any merit.

The fact that pursuit-rotor learning is strongly influenced by genetic factors does not necessarily imply that reminiscence on the pursuit rotor is similarly influenced, although the probability of such a contingent association is high. The only study to investigate this question directly is an unpublished experiment (A. R. Jensen, personal communication) in which the pursuit rotor was administered to 35 pairs of monozygotic and 34 pairs of dizygotic twins; thirty 10-sec massed trials were followed by a 10-min rest period, which in turn was followed by twenty more 10-sec trials. The reminiscence score (mean of the first two post-rest trials minus the mean of the last two pre-rest trials) showed strong evidence of heritability (h^2 = .86.) Thus the heritability of reminiscence on the pursuit rotor would seem to be almost as high as the heritability of ability on the pursuit rotor; in fact, when corrected for attenuation, the figure for reminiscence might even be the higher one. Variance due to unreliability (V_e) is often grouped with variance due to environmental factors (V_E), which is hardly logical; what is at issue is the proportion of the reliable variance attributable to G and E respectively, and to the various interaction terms (V_{GE} and Cov_{GE}). No proper biometrical genetical analysis has in fact been carried out in this field, and it is doubtful if the classical Holzinger h^2

statistic can properly be interpreted in terms of what geneticists understand by "heritability" (Mather & Jinks, 1971). The most that we can really say is that genetic factors play an extremely important part in causing differences in performance and reminiscence on the pursuit rotor; the figures should not be interpreted as estimates of heritability in the genetic sense. Corrections for unreliability would seem an unnecessary refinement.

Both McNemar and Vandenberg have failed to analyze their results fully. The early work of Seashore (1930) had already shown that motor-skill tests correlate together, although not very highly; nevertheless, there are clearly one or more general factors underlying performance on such tests, and it would be interesting to know something of the heritability of such factor scores—particularly as these are known not to be much influenced by intelligence. McNemar does in fact give the intercorrelations between his tests; these are somewhat higher than those reported previously by the authors already cited. Roughly speaking, correlations range from .2 to .5; the lowest is between card sorting and steadiness, the highest between speed drill and pursuit rotor. (These correlations have been corrected for age differences.) Correlations with mental age are all below .2, except for the speed drill which is .37. A rough factor analysis discloses a general factor running through all the motor tests, with steadiness and card sorting having the lowest loadings, and speed drill and pursuit rotor the highest. Spool packing is only slightly less highly loaded on this factor. Vandenberg does not give the figures needed to calculate similar scores. It does seem that future studies should concentrate on the task of providing heritability values for factor scores, rather than concentrate so much on individual tests; these are of interest, but as Eysenck and Prell (1951) have argued, factor scores can add considerably to the information provided by single tests.

Intercorrelations between motor tests can also solve another problem which is of some importance in considering the ability to perform on the pursuit rotor, which, as we shall see later, is inextricably mixed up with reminiscence, PRU, and other aspects of the post-rest performance of Ss on the rotor. In fact, there are two not unconnected problems. To what extent is this ability specific to the test, and to what extent is it general? To what extent does the test require identical ability patterns during various stages of practice? No very thorough discussion of the literature will be attempted, as this would take us too far afield, but the main articles relevant to the problem will be surveyed.

The first proper factor analytic study of motor tests to supercede the simple correlational presentations of earlier writers already noted was

the large-scale work of the Army Air Forces Aviation Psychology
Research Group (Melton, 1947), which will be discussed in some detail
in the next chapter. In the first study to concern us almost 5000 aviation
cadets were tested on a large battery of tests, correlations calculated and
a factor analysis with blind rotation to simple structure was performed.
Several factors are of no interest here, such as the familiar verbal,
perceptual, numerical, spatial, visualization, and mechanical experience factors. However, a factor also appeared which was labeled "coordination"; this has loadings on rotary pursuit (.58), two-hand coordination (.51), aiming stress (.35), finger dexterity (.35), complex
coordination (.45), and pilot criterion (.34)—the last named, of course,
is not a test in the usual sense, but the criterion which the tests were
used to predict. (Rotary pursuit also had a loading on another factor
which predicted the bombardier criterion.)

Another, later study used 1900 trainees and extracted 6 factors; one
of these was labeled "psychomotor," having loadings on the following
tests: complex coordination (.65), two-hand coordination (.56), rotary
pursuit (.55), finger dexterity (.45), rudder control (.43), discrimination
reaction time (.28), and mechanical principles (.27). These analyses
used the 1942 classification battery; another one was carried out with
the 1943 classification battery, again giving a coordination factor with
loadings on rotary pursuit with divided attention (.56), complex coordination (.46), aiming stress (.39), finger dexterity (.33), and two-hand
coordination (.27). Two criterion scores had loadings on this factor:
Pilot stanine (.73) and Bombardier stanine (.26). In other words, pilot
training as a whole was a better measure of the candidates' coordination ability than was any single test—not an unexpected result, perhaps, when it is realized that pilot training work involves all the
abilities measured by the specific tests, while each test largely measures
relatively specific variance. The evidence is certainly strong that pursuit-rotor performance predicts pilot training success; approximately
10% of the variance on the criterion is accounted for by this test
(Melton, 1947, p. 371.) Miles' original theory and findings have been
verified beyond doubt.

Our second problem, i.e., the change of factor loading pattern with
change in amount of practice on a test, was also first investigated,
although not very successfully, by the A.A.F. group. Melton (1947, p.
1019) points out that in one of the A.A.F. studies, "evidence was found
which indicates that during the short time period of the administration
of a psychomotor test to individuals, the ability or abilities sampled
may shift materially in importance." A special experiment was therefore set up in which part scores on various tests were ascertained and

intercorrelated. It was indeed found in the factor analysis of these scores that the character of a given test, as revealed by its factor loadings, may change materially during practice; thus on the discrimination reaction time test used two factors increased systematically in time, while two others "show precipitously declining importance of tests. This test impresses an observer who watches testees from beginning to end as changing most in character in the short span of some ten minutes' testing time." (Melton, 1947, p. 1031.) Little of interest emerged as far as the pursuit rotor was concerned, but these rather casual observations laid the foundations of the much more systematic work later reported by Fleishman. However, Melton and his colleagues were certainly justified in concluding that "there is ample evidence of function fluctuations in the results set forth. . . . The findings show systematic variations that call for explanation." (Melton, 1947, p. 1033.)

There are certain interesting regularities in the patterns of intercorrelations between successive trials on a motor skills learning task; these have been observed in many different studies (Adams, 1953; Edgerton & Valentine, 1935; Fleishman, 1953; Fleishman & Parker, 1959; Greene, 1943; Melton, 1947; Perl, 1934; Reynolds, 1952a, 1952b; Viteles, 1933). The pattern usually observed, as Jones (1966) has pointed out, is of the *superdiagonal* form, i.e., neighboring trials correlate higher than trials separated in time; "it is named after the $(n - 1)$ correlations between neighboring trials, $r, i, i + 1$, which make up the superdiagonal," i.e., the sequence of figures in a rectangular matrix immediately above the leading diagonal. "The superdiagonal form is an ordinal pattern. It requires only that the correlations decrease or remain the same across the rows and up the columns." (Jones, 1966, p. 113). Matrices so formed, however, show (Jones, 1966; p. 114) "more than ordinal pattern. These matrices are ruled by an exact regularity. All known matrices of intertrial correlations obey the *law of single tetrad differences*. This law states that every sequence of four trials satisfies the equality

$$r_{ik}r_{jl} - r_{il}r_{jk} \approx 0 \quad (i < j < k < 1)"$$

[This rule should not be confused with Spearman's (1927) law of tetrad differences, which requires that another equality be satisfied, i.e.,

$$r_{ij}r_{kl} - r_{il}r_{jk} \approx 0 \quad (i < j < k < 1)$$

and which may more conveniently be stated in matrix terms as reducing the matrix to rank one.] Jones has suggested one possible explanation of this general observation of the superdiagonal form, based on the well-established fact that "the abilities at work in successive trials become progressively fewer with practice" (1966, p. 120). Jones's simplicial theory states that where there are x trials, there are $x - 1$ common factors; one of these drops out after the first two trials, the next after three trials, the next after four, and so forth, until only one factor is left at the xth trial. The superdiagonal form of the matrix can be directly derived from this hypothesis, as can Guttman's (1954) "law of oscillations," which states the sequence of factors to be derived from a simple factor analysis of the set of learning trials; the loadings on the first component are all positive and bigger in the middle than at either end, while the loadings on the second factor undergo a change of sign from first to last trial, and those on the third factor undergo two changes of sign. Jones' hypothesis is excessively formal, and his "factors" are quite unlike those usually posited by factor analysts. "These factors should not be understood as unitary; they are composites of all differential elements which act in the first two trials, the first three, all eight, or whatever the span that the factor covers may be." (Jones, 1966, p. 120.) Such factors do not serve any useful psychological function, and thus do not represent sufficient empirical content to be acceptable. As Fleishman (1966, p. 159) has pointed out, "stopping with a simplicial analysis doesn't seem to lead us far enough along in the development of new concepts which will organize existing data more meaningfully, stimulate new experiments, or lead to improved predictions or control in new learning situations."

Among other authors who have calculated correlations between successive trials or blocks of trials, and who have observed the superdiagonal form, are Zeaman and Kaufman (1955), and Noble (1970). The substantive and theoretical problems raised by these authors will be discussed in later chapters, together with their results. Lersten (1970) is another author whose results seem to support a "simplicial" theory. Jones (1969) has actually modified his hypothesis and now prefers a dual or two-factor position, regarding practice as a process of both simplification and complication. Only the former occurs in learning a simple task, and so the superdiagonal form is weak or transitory as correlation patterns become disorganized; in complex tasks, simplification characterizes the early phases, with strong superdiagonal patterning resulting from extinction of errors. Then, as the skill is assembled and organized, complication predominates in the later stages of practice. This two-factor theory, while still purely formal, is in good accord with the work of Fleischman to be discussed presently, and also fits in well with our own theory, to be developed in a later chapter.

Fleishman's approach has been along the lines of isolating a set of motor abilities in the form of factors which could then be correlated with the different trials constituting a particular learning task; in this

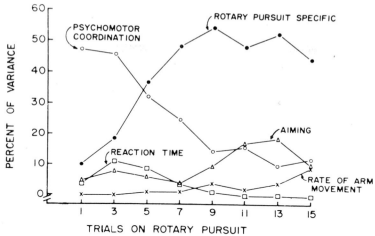

Figure 2-2. Changes in proportion of variance contributed by several factors at successive stages of practice on the pursuit rotor. Taken with permission from Fleishman (1956).

way the factor loadings on these abilities could be established for the different learning trials. A list of the main factors so discovered, with detailed references, is given in Fleishman (1966); here only a simple listing must suffice: control precision, multilimb coordination, response orientation, reaction time, speed of arm movement, rate control, manual dexterity, finger dexterity, arm–hand steadiness, wrist/finger speed, and aiming. (This list is the latest available; earlier attempts resulted in smaller and occasionally different factors. In relating psychomotor factors to pursuit-rotor performance at various times, the factors used were of course those isolated and identified at the time; hence different attempts may not give identical results, depending on the "state of the art" at the time.)

The changes in proportion of variance contributed by each of several factors at successive stages of practice on rotary pursuit are clearly demonstrated in Figure 2-2, which is taken from an early publication (Fleishman, 1956); it already demonstrates the increasing importance of specific elements in later stages of practice, the increasing importance of aiming and arm movement, and the decreasing importance of psychomotor coordination and reaction time. A more recent study (Fleishman, 1960) gives a somewhat different picture (Figure 2-3). Here we have two specific factors, one (RP Specific II) decrementing in importance, the other (RP Specific I) incrementing. There are also two nonspecific factors, control precision and rate control. Control precision is one of two factors into which the previous factor of "psychomotor

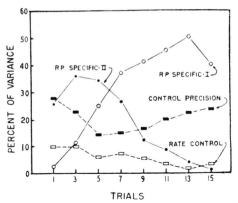

Figure 2-3. Changes in proportion of variance contributed by several factors at successive stages of practice on the pursuit rotor. Taken with permission from Fleishman (1960).

control" was found to split (also sometimes called Fine Control Sensitivity; the other psychomotor control factor became "multilimb coordination"). Rate control "appears to represent the ability to make continual anticipations and adjustments relative to changes in speed and direction of a continuously moving object. . . . This factor extends beyond pursuit tasks to other types of response involving rate." (Fleishman, 1960; p. 168.) Both analyses, although different in detail, confirm the importance of *specific* factors in rotary pursuit; six experiments previous to the latest (Fleishman, 1960) had demonstrated that communality estimates from factor analytic studies in which only single scores of rotary pursuit had been included were all between .45 and .50 (Fleishman, 1954, 1957, 1958; Fleishman & Hempel, 1954, 1955, 1956); in the study under discussion the largest amount of RP variance in common with all the other tasks at any stage of practice was approximately 48% (the sum of squared loadings of all factors excepting the two "within-task" factors). Thus it seems fairly well established that pursuit-rotor ability is specific to the extent of approximately 50%; this specificity is greater than that of most other psychomotor tasks which have been studied at all extensively (complex coordination task, 30%; discrimination reaction time, 40%; plane control devices, 42%; unidimensional matching, 34%). "The relative specificity of RP performance at least raises questions about the extent to which we can generalize from RP experiments to experiments with other tasks." (Fleishman, 1960, p. 170.) Such questions are important, but it is doubtful if the specificity of a task is particularly relevant to its usefulness as a device for studying general principles of learning. The *abilities* involved in the mastery of a task to be learned are one thing; the *course* which learning takes is another. In any case, the finding that there is an increase in a task-specific factor with increase in practice on the task is quite universal (Fleishman, 1966, p. 159); pursuit-rotor learning may perhaps be particularly typical in that respect! "Skill in later performances is more a function of specific habits acquired during practice on the task itself, relative to transfer from previous abilities, skills, and habits." (Fleishman, 1960, p. 169.)

What is relatively unique, however, is the presence of a specific factor which declines in importance. "While factors of *decreasing* importance have been found in other tasks, this is the first study in which a factor was not defined by external ability measures." (Fleishman, 1960, p. 169.) On the other hand, the interpretation of the two nonspecific factors seems fairly clear. The Control Precision factor, which contributes at all stages to pursuit-rotor performance, has been found general to performance on a variety of different psychomotor devices; it is "the ability to make highly controlled (but not overcontrolled), precise, large muscle adjustments" (Fleishman, 1960, p. 169) This factor is uniformly important throughout the stages of learning, whereas the Rate Control factor is consistently decreasing. "This is consistent with what is observed in performing on RP, where the task seems intially to be more of a pursuit task; one has difficulty in leading the target properly and even in predicting where to move in relation to it. This difficulty seems to disappear after brief practice, where the task becomes one of minimizing erratic movements while making a smooth, continuous, circular arm movement." This early acquisition of ballistic movements had already been commented on by Renshaw, Wallace, and Schwarzbeck (1930); it has found additional support in the work of Ammons, Ammons, and Morgan (1958) and Archer (1958.) The Ammons group used motion picture recordings of performance, a rational classification of "types of movements," and a "scoring stencil" employed over the film frames at different stages of practice. Scores included the number and duration of circular, tapping, looping, reverse, and crisscross movements, as well as movements ahead of the target (leading) and behind the target (following). From this analysis they concluded that "the S who can make the basic movement but whose timing is 'off' is well on the way to a higher performance level, as compared with the S who cannot make the basic movement" (Ammons *et al.*, 1958). Fleishman argues that "this conclusion fits well with the present findings that (a) an individual difference in Rate Control ability may facilitate early learning to a small extent, but this does not predict later learning; and (b) the main common factor contributing to advanced as well as early proficiency is Control Precision" (1960, p. 169).

Archer (1958) inserted a sensing device in the stylus used by his Ss and was thus able to measure the number and duration of "noncircular" movements made, and compare them with "time-on-target" scores at different stages of practice. The number and duration of these "noncircular" movements decrease as practice continues; thus his work also seems to support the notion that the ability to make the proper controlled circular movement (even though S is off in his timing, and therefore off target, during early stages of learning) facilitates later high proficiency.

These findings suggest certain disturbing thoughts regarding the measurement of pursuit learning, and the quantification of reminiscence. If learning can take place in the early stages without any improvement in the actual score, e.g., when S is improving his ability to execute the proper circular movement, but is still off target because of poor timing, then clearly the score (time-on-target) is not a perfect, and may be a poor, measure of learning. We customarily make a differentiation between learning and performance owing to the existence of certain factors which may affect learning and performance differentially; e.g., reactive inhibition may keep performance down and prevent it from being a good index of learning. However, it is usually assumed that when no such factors are present then learning will find a linear or at least a monotonic representation in performance. These analyses of Fleishman, Ammons, and Archer suggest that this may not be so, and that it is even possible that quite different results might be obtained by the use of targets of different size. Thus in the case discussed above, it is conceivable that improvement in the ability to make the circular movement might be registered when the target is very large but not when it is small, leading to different learning curves under otherwise identical conditions. (It is considerations of this kind which have prompted the construction of multiple-target pursuit rotors, of the kind described previously.)

Bahrick, Fitts, and Briggs (1957) have given a sophisticated psychometric discussion of the problems involved. Drawing attention to the arbitrary nature of many of the choices made in selecting behavior measures for use as learning indices, they set out to show "that the arbitrary choice of a cutoff point in the dichotomizing of continuous response distributions can impose significant constraints upon the shape of resulting learning curves. . . . We have chosen for illustration of this point the use of time-on-target scores as indicants of the level of skill attained in tracking tasks." (Bahrick *et al.*, 1957, p. 256.) The tracking task chosen was perceived by S as a target line that remained stationary in the center of the cathode-ray display, and a cursor which moved to the right or left depending on the direction of the error from moment to moment, incorporating an exponential time lag between the output of S's arm control and its effect on tracking error. Two types of performance measures were taken on even-numbered 90-sec trials: rms error scores and time-on-target scores. "An electronic circuit provided a means of continuously obtaining the magnitude of the error (in the form of an electric voltage), squaring this voltage, and integrating it over the period of a trial. The output of this circuit appeared on a voltmeter and the square root of this meter reading provided an index of the root mean square error (rms). . . . Time-on-target measures give the total time that the absolute magnitude of the error voltage was smaller than a given magnitude. Three such scores were taken for target zones of 5%, 15%, and 30% of the maximum possible voltage. These zones correspond to errors of .1, .3, and .6 in. of displacement of the cursor to either side of the target line, respectively." (Bahrick et al., 1957, p. 257.) These 3 zones, from smallest to largest, are referred to as A, B, and C; correspondingly, scores on these zones are referred to as scores A, B, and C. 50 male and 50 female Ss were used in all. This task was relatively difficult; an easy task was also used, in which no lag was introduced between the control output and the cursor movement.

When the males and females were compared for performance on the more difficult task, it was found that respective rates of learning were entirely dependent on the actual scores used; the males improved by 33.2%, 31.9%, and 18.7% for scores in zones A, B, and C, respectively, while the corresponding improvements for the females were only 2.5%, 17.6%, and 11.8%, respectively. The rms curves, however, indicated a greater improvement for the females, with a 22.3% reduction of error as contrasted with a 20.4% error reduction for the males. "And all these scores, it should be remembered, are derived from a single error voltage!" (Bahrick et al., 1954, p. 259.) In the easy task experiment 25 male Ss were used; quite different types of learning curves were found depending on the type of target measure used. The authors then go on to point out that "if we assume that the amplitude of tracking errors form a normal distribution during a trial, it is apparent that the percentage of this distribution which would fall within a given target zone can be determined, provided the standard deviation of the distribution of tracking errors is known." (Bahrick et al., 1957, p. 260.) Figure 2-4 illustrates the differential sensitivity of various scoring zones; the predicted are plotted time-on-target scores for five target zones of differing size as a function of the magnitude of the rms values

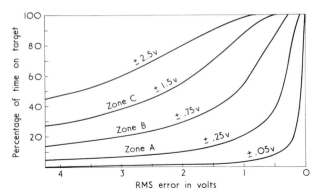

Figure 2-4. Differential sensitivity of various scoring zones: predicted time-on-target scores for five target zones of differing size as a function of the magnitude of the rms values of the error distribution. Taken with permission from Bahrick, Fitts, and Briggs (1957).

of the error distribution. "It can be seen that each of the curves . . . shows a maximal slope at a different range of variation of the rms value, and becomes insensitive to variations outside that range. The ranges of maximal sensitivity shift toward smaller rms values as we move from larger to smaller target zones. The sensitivity of a time-on-target score is maximal when the zone is of a size that includes ± 1 *SD* of the error distribution, so that S is on target about 68% of the time. For smaller or larger target zones the score becomes progressively less sensitive to changes in the rms value of the error distribution." (Bahrick *et al.*, 1957, p. 261.)

Bahrick, Fitts, and Briggs do not suggest throwing out time-on-target scores altogether; "the nonlinear relation between rms and time-on-target scores does not invalidate all use of the latter scores. For certain gross comparisons, intended only to determine the presence or absence of a significant effect, either type of score may be adequate. . . . Artifacts in the interpretation of results occur primarily when attempts are made to test for interaction effects or to interpret functional relations over an extended range of task difficulty or over an extended period of learning. Thus it would appear that a single target zone can provide a score of only limited value on an indicant of tracking performance. This is particularly true if performance on different tasks or at different stages of learning varies over a wide range, so that the percentage of time on target is either very low, or very high for some of the conditions to be evaluated." (Bahrick *et al.*, 1957, p. 266.) The authors recommend either multiple target recording, or else use of the rms error score. It is

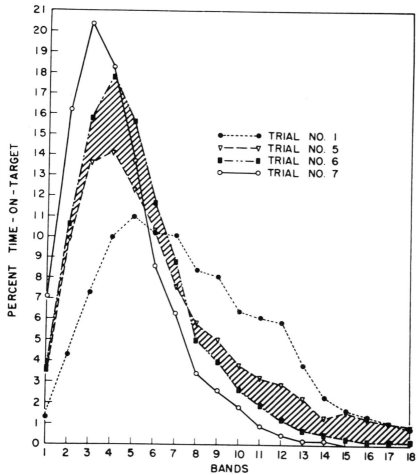

Figure 2-5. Mean percent time-on-target scores for each band during the 1, 5, 6, and 7 min of practice. Taken with permission from Humphries (1961).

fortunate that for most of the studies to be discussed in this book time-on-target scores are vitiated only to a limited extent by the errors which they have pointed out so cogently, but these criticisms of some very fundamental aspects of measurement in tracking should always be borne in mind when interpreting results. Attention will be drawn to problems of measurement whenever these appear to have caused errors in interpretation. It should of course be realized that size of target is not the only problem to arise in the measurement of pursuit-rotor perfor-

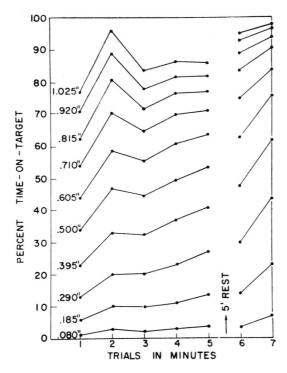

Figure 2-6. Mean percent time-on-target as a function of trials for the 10 inner rings, with the radius of each target given in inches. Taken with permission from Humphries (1961).

mance; other problems, such as the suggested transormation of scores into some form of logarithmic function to make them more truly comparable, will be taken up in the next chapter.

A direct application of the principles enunciated above to pursuit-rotor learning has been made by Humphries (1961), who constructed a multiple-target rotor with 18 concentric targets of increasing size; simultaneous scores were recorded from all of these targets. Testing sessions included 5 min of massed practice, a 5-min rest and a final 5 min of practice; initial data were summed over 10-sec periods, although these were again combined for some of the later calculations. Figure 2-5 shows the mean percentage time-on-target scores for each band during 1, 5, 6, and 7 min of practice. "The general effect of practice can be seen as a shift in the distribution toward the left, i.e., toward the inner targets, and in the pealing effect around Bands 3, 4, and 5. The usual reminiscence effect is indicated by the cross-hatched area between Trials 5 and 6 and takes the form of an increment in time-on-target scores for target Bands 2 to 7, a decrement for Bands 8 to 18, and little or no change for the inner band." (Humphries, 1961, p. 215.)

Figure 2-6 shows the mean percent time-on-target as a function of trials for the 10 inner rings; the radius of each target is given in inches. Note in this figure two features which we shall return to again in our discussion of the effects of individual differences in ability on reminiscence and on the shape of the learning curve: (1) Larger targets show a marked upswing at the beginning, followed by a marked downswing—there is no trace of these rapid changes with the smallest targets. (2) Larger targets show considerable reminiscence effects; these are completely missing with the smallest targets. Thus the occurrence of reminiscence effects can be enhanced or abolished by suitable choice of target size, and so can "upswing" phenomena and "downswing" phenomena usually observed after rest pauses. (Remember that all these curves describe *identical* test performance; it is only the measurement which is varied by different target size choice.)

Humphries also suggests a useful method for transforming the information gained into rms scores; Figure 2-7 shows the mean estimated rms error scores as a function of trials. The general pattern of scores is reassuringly similar to that with which investigators of pursuit-rotor performance are familiar. There is first a linear improvement in performance, relatively slow and unhurried, followed post-rest by a marked reminiscence jump in performance, which in turn is followed

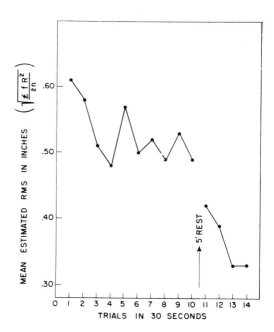

Figure 2-7. Estimated mean rms scores as a function of trials. Taken with permission from Humphries (1961).

by PRU or "warm-up", shown here of course by a decrement in rms error. There is no PRD because the final 3 min of practice post-rest have not been plotted; it is not clear why they were omitted. Had they been included it is likely that in this particular the similarity would also have been complete. It does seem, therefore, as if choice of target size is only important for the demonstration and investigation of the phenomena in which we are interested when the target is very small or very large; intermediate size targets, of the size usually used, give results very much like rms error scores. This comforting conclusion should not lead to a lack of vigilance, however, in scrutinizing experimental results for possible artifacts owing to wrong choice of target size, or overinterpretation; nor should it lead to a neglect of the rich field of experimental investigation opened up by these new methods of recording and analyzing results. Vigorous research is required in order to make us better understand, than is possible now, just what goes on when a subject "learns" pursuit-rotor performance.

CHAPTER 3

The Beginning of Investigations on a Grand Scale

Apart from Thorndike (1913), few American experimentalists paid much attention to the interesting phenomena unearthed by Kraepelin and his students, and indeed little work was done on nonverbal reminiscence until the early years following the second World War linked up pursuit-rotor reminiscence with the theoretical system of Hull, which was then very much in the ascendant. Nevertheless, a small number of empirical studies carried out during the years between the two World Wars demonstrated that phenomena similar to those observed by Kraepelin could be obtained on the pursuit rotor, and a small number of writers developed an interest in this field. In addition, there was one notable attempt to develop a theoretical account incorporating these phenomena into a general system, that of Snoddy (1926, 1935); his work gave rise to several empirical studies which attempted to test deductions from his theory (Bell, 1942; Doré & Hilgard, 1937, 1938; Hilgard & Smith, 1942). During the war, much work was done on motor tests ("apparatus tests") in an effort to improve selection batteries for prospective pilots, navigators, and other air crews (Melton, 1947). Apart from the intrinsic interest of the data collected, this major research effort, although it had severely practical objectives, succeeded in convincing a number of brilliant young experimentalists that much of scientific importance could be discovered in the field of motor skills and

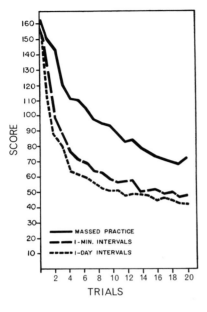

Figure 3-1. Mirror drawing under massed and spaced conditions of practice. Taken with permission from Lorge (1930).

their development, and the flowering of research in this field during the immediate post-war years owes much to their influence. These post-war developments will form the basis of our next few chapters; here we will simply outline the developmental story of research up to and including the Army Air Forces Aviation Psychology Program, to give it its full title, and its Research Report No. 4, "Apparatus Tests."

In tracing these developments we will begin with the various independent writers who made important contributions to pursuit-rotor reminiscence during the years between wars, go on to a considera-tion of the Melton A.A.F. report, and close with a discussion of the Snoddy hypothesis and the experiments to which it gave rise. Before discussing the tracking experiments, however, it may be useful to note briefly two experiments which had some influence on later writers. In the first of these, Lorge (1930) used 3 types of activity (mirror drawing, mirror reading, and code substitution) and compared the effects of 20 massed trials, 20 trials separated by 1 min and 20 trials separated by 24 hr. On all tasks the massed practice condition proved inferior; differ-ences between different legths of rest pauses were unstable and not very impressive. Lorge's results for mirror drawing (the task later favored by Snoddy) are shown in Figure 3-1. Gentry (1940) used code substitution under various conditions of distribution which ranged from (1) 20 1-min trials separated by 1-min rest pauses, to (5) 20 massed 1-min trials without rest; the intermediate conditions had 5 distributed trials and 15 massed trials in various combinations. Condition 1 was superior throughout; the other conditions showed improvement to the same extent as condition 5 when trials were massed, and similar to condition 1 when trials were not massed. Even earlier than these two writers, Carr (1919) had studied early as compared to late massing, using a pencil maze; he too found that massed or distributed conditions of work at any given moment determined performance to a greater extent than previous massing or distribution.

Outstanding as the first pursuit-rotor study to deal with the problem is a contribution by Travis (1936, 1937) who used a Koerth-type pursuit rotor. In his first paper, "Practice and Rest Periods in Motor Learning," he took up Jost's findings (1897), to the effect that two readings per day for 12 days was from 3 to 8 times more effective in memorizing than 8 readings a day for 3 days, a finding which Taylor (1915) supported to some extent in his work on the influence of rest and work periods on output and fatigue of pig-iron handlers. Travis used 4 Ss, working for 6-min periods separated by several days; results are shown in Figure 3-2. (Each point plotted represents the accumulated score for 1 min.) As Travis (1936) points out, "in the first half of the learning curve it will be noted that a significantly high jump in efficiency took place after each rest period. . . . The long rest period seemed to be more essential to improvement than the latter two-thirds of the practice period." Travis does not use the term "reminiscence" for this phenomenon, although the word had been current for almost 20 years following Ballard's (1917) original paper; possibly he was not prepared to regard the motor phenomenon as identical with that

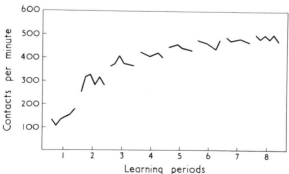

Figure 3-2. Pursuit-rotor learning: 6-min work periods separated by several days of rest each time. Taken with permission from Travis (1936).

observed in verbal learning, although he does refer to Jost and Pieron, who also worked with verbal learning. Travis also reports on the comparison of continuous and discontinuous work periods at the asymptote of learning; his results show continuous work (12 min without pause) inferior to discontinuous work (1 min work, 1 min rest.)

In his second experiment Travis (1937) pursued this question of the effect of the length of the rest period on motor learning. Six 5-min learning trials were given on his "pursuit-oscillator," with rest periods of 5 min, 20 min, 48 hr, 72 hr, and 120 hr interpolated for different groups of college students. Travis again found evidence of reminiscence, although mention of the term is eschewed; he found the 20-min rest pause most conducive to learning, followed by the 5-min rest pause. The longer rest pauses were fairly uniformly less useful than the short ones. In a later chapter we shall see to what degree these results can be generalized to other tasks and conditions, and to what degree they are dependent on Travis's setup. It would seem that Travis rediscovered motor reminiscence, 40 years after Oehrn's first demonstration, even though the similarity of this phenomenon to other types of reminiscence does not appear to have been clear at the time; Bunch (1938) in an early review quotes verbal learning experiments and animal experiments on reminiscence, but does not mention Travis.

The work of Renshaw and his colleagues at Ohio State University, some of which had been published by the data his summary was being prepared, is also not mentioned by Bunch (1938). These studies made use of a special pursuitmeter of the "prod" type, i.e., loss of contact between stylus and target stops the target, which begins to move again when contact is resumed (Renshaw & Weiss, 1926). Typically, Ss would follow the target's "complex pattern of changing directions and rates," with number of errors constituting the score. An error is defined as loss of contact with the target. Each cycle consisted of 63 revolutions; these cycles were identical, "but no portions of any one cycle were duplications." Renshaw (1928), Troyer (1930), Webb (1933), and Renshaw and Schwarzbek (1938a, b) demonstrated, with this apparatus, some of the fundamental features of pursuit learning as a function of interpractice rests.

In the main experiment of this series, Renshaw and Schwarzbek (1938a) studied 4 groups of Ss who pursued different courses of training, in the sense that the rest pauses introduced between cycles were either decreasing in length (group D), increasing in length (group I), decreasing and then increasing in length (group D–I), or increasing and then decreasing in length (group I–D). The results make it clear that, as Troyer (1938) had also found, "longer rest periods favored more rapid improvements." Each cycle was 3.57 min in length; under these conditions the authors conclude that "in all probability five minutes rest between cycles is the most advantageous condition for rapid improvement in this particular manipulative skill." At the other end, "the institution of practice cycles followed by no rest, results at any stage in the series except at the beginning, in a decrease in the proficiency of performance." Furthermore, "if no rest is given earlier in the series the decrease in proficiency is greater than if no rest is given later."

Renshaw, Wallace, and Schwarzbek (1938) complemented their statistical analyses by taking motion pictures of the performance of one subject during the course of learning, and analyzing this in detail. This analysis makes interesting reading.

The subject, stripped to the waist, was set to learn the operation of the instrument in the usual fashion. Motion pictures of the movements made by the wrist, arm, shoulder, and trunk were taken for a period of 15 seconds in various parts of the cycles. "Shots" were taken in this manner on 16 mm. film in every third cycle of a complete series of 36. The subject had one minute between cycles.

Pictures of the first cycle show that the arm moved more like a rigid rod than a coordinated compound lever. The elbow was held immobile and close to the trunk. The arm movements were of a massive sort which involved not only the elbow and shoulder but also the pectorals, latissimus dorsi, and the muscles of the lower trunk region. As soon as errorless periods of appreciable length began to occur certain of the muscle groups began to relax. At first the larger muscle groups and those near enough the surface to be readily observed, showed sustained contraction. Relaxation was indicated in two ways. First the sustained bulging of the muscles disappeared, and instead there were sudden brief thickenings, of less intensity than the sustained contractions, followed by a quick return to the immediately preceding relaxed status. Second, the pivot joints became "loose," and all of them were involved more in the pursuit act.

As the practices became more errorless the degree of relaxation, as observed in the picture, became greater and it extended to all the muscles involved. The order of relaxation was centrifugal, first the pectorals and other trunk muscles, then the deltoid, biceps and triceps groups, and finally the extensor and flexor groups of the forearms. It is noteworthy that this order is in agreement with the order of individuation of the movements in the amblystoma larvae as shown by Coghill (1929, p. 18 ff., and p. 88), and also with the findings of Minkowski and others, relative to individuation of movement in human foetus.

In the motion picture there are a number of clear-cut instances which show the effect of lost contacts on the muscular tonus. Pictures taken after the middle portion of the learning series, when the subject had become quite skilful show that errors, in which the stylus and target were thrown completely out of apposition, resulted in a tensing of the muscles. This was especially evident in the forearm, less so in the pectoral and the deltoid groups. When errors occurred the arm became rigid, and the muscle thickenings showed a sustained contraction, as at the beginning of the learning series.

In the early cycles the elbow was held close to the body. With increased skill the angle made by the upper arm and the vertical axis of the body became greater. The arm became a coordinated compound lever. Its posture then gave it the maximum mechanical advantage for subsequent adjustory movements. At the beginning the movements were jerky, whereas the skilful pursuit movements were smooth, possibly ballistic. The undue tension of the various muscle groups immobilized each pivot joint and, in the event of a specific pursuit movement, the untrained subject generally flexed only one joint at a time or if more than one the function of each was relatively disjoined from the other. With increased skill more and more pivot joints came into activity, and the action of each became more definitely related to that of the others. This interrelation has as its most apparent characteristic (and perhaps its chief characteristic) the timing of movements at the several pivot joints; head, cervical girdle, shoulder, elbow, wrist, and phalanges.

The movements of the skilful person are anticipatory in the sense that the latency has been reduced to an approximate zero. With such a wide variety of possible movements it is evident that no specific rate and direction is anticipated. It seems that learning is characterized by a more effective adjustment for an increased number and a greater variety of rates and directions. That is, the habit has become generalized. It is apparent that the requisite tactual and kinaesthetic cues have been reduced to a minimum, and visual cues which at first were helpful in the grosser adjustment not only tend to become unnecessary but also to interfere with best performance in the later stages. Subjects assume an attitude commensurate with the generalized nature of the habit. Successful learners report that the best method involves "a following attitude." It is impossible to dominate the machine. The attempt to predict, or anticipate actively the next specific movement results fatally. Subjects who fail to discard this method seldom learn successfully. Further evidence that pursuitmeter skill is a generalized habit derives from the fact that all subjects who made the attempt were able to run the pursuitmeter with the non-preferential hand as successfully as with the hand used originally in the learning. The interpretation of the above analysis of the nature and acquisition of pursuit act is quite readily made in terms of the two fundamental types of movement, the tension movement and the ballistic movement.

This classification is that of Beaunis and Richer and is followed by Stetson and Bouman (1935).

In the early stages of pursuit learning the posture of the trunk and fixation of the arm is a typical tension movement. Opposed muscle groups are contracted, and whenever pursuit occurs it is jerky and tight. It is incorrectly timed and the pursuit movement is not successful. All these characteristics might well be expected in the early stages before the ballistic type of movement has put in an appearance and while the slow tension movements remain.

The tension movement is unable to account for the smooth continuous character of pursuit movements, the velocity of which changes too rapidly to fall within the limits of maximum tremor rate. A single ballistic movement is smooth, but, being constant in velocity and being a momentum movement for the latter part of its duration, it, likewise, cannot account for a pursuit act that is both smooth and variable in speed and direction. It is possible, however, that a number of coordinated ballistic impulses may not only retain the characteristic smoothness of the single stroke but also may enable us to account for the rapidly changing velocity of the pursuit movement.

The evidence cited above, e.g., distalward relaxation, and the timing or coordination of movements of the several pivot joints, is interpreted as follows: Several ballistic impulses, involving various groups of driving muscle, determine the path of the pursuing extremity. Greater control of both the rate and direction results from the fact that several, rather than only a few, pivot joints and their corresponding muscle groups are involved. We may picture the path and the velocity of the limb as a resultant of a number of ballistic impulses. With several muscle groups capable of moving each pivot joint and with several such pivots involved, the frequency and the precision of the change in velocity (rate and direction) become quite large. Such control is the tactus eruditus of which we speak in other related skills, such as typing or piano playing and the "form" in golfing, surgery, forward passing, speaking, singing, etc. It obviously derives from the force and the timing of the ballistic impulses. These impulses, unlike those of the tension movement, are capable of being controlled by smaller increments than the .045-.050 sec. of the motor unit. The control of the "loose" ballistic movement may take place by increments of .005-.020 sec." (Renshaw and Schwartzbek 1958b, pp. 21-26.)

Renshaw and his colleagues did not measure reminiscence as such, but the relationship between reminiscence and the influence of rest pauses on the rate of improvement in pursuit learning is so close that their work is very relevant to our topic. Their main conclusions have been amply justified by later work: "the length and distribution of intercylic rest periods have great effect on the shape of the practice curve. . . . The rest conditions favoring the most rapid learning are those in which long intercyclic interims are given early in the practice series, followed by rests which are progressively decreased in length. . . . Practice without rest usually retards or reverses the practice gains. The detrimental effect is the more marked early in the learning series." Learning is seen to be "primarily a reconstruction of the form of the response. Theories of conditioned chain reflexes are not supported." (Renshaw and Schwartzbek, 1958b, p. 28.)

Renshaw contributed two further articles to the pursuit-rotor literature. Renshaw and Postle (1928) investigated the effect of explicit and detailed instructions as to how to work the prod pursuit rotor for best effects, contrasting a group of Ss so instructed with two control groups who had received no instructions. The control groups did very much better, suggesting that "conceptualization" or the making conscious of the problems involved in pursuit-rotor work actually interfered with learning and performance. "The general case in which language inhibits is one in which substitutive or surrogatory verbal habits cannot be made effective substitutes for the direct sensory stimuli afforded by the task itself." (Renshaw & Postle, 1928, p. 367.) It is of course known that overt verbalization may interfere with a highly developed skill, i.e., after the final or autonomous phase of learning has been reached; the above results suggest that such interference may occur right at the beginning of learning. Renshaw's (1928) other experiment consisted of training his Ss on the complex circuit made by the target, and then reversing this course on 2 occasions; he found that the Ss made a gain rather than a loss as a consequence of this reversal. Renshaw interprets this finding as contradicting the hypothesis that pursuit-rotor learning consists of the development of a *serial* habit; he prefers "a successive discrimination hypothesis as an alternative mode of selection in the formation of habits of this type" (1928, p. 520). One of Renshaw's students, W. W. Webb (1933) made a beginning in the field of massed versus distributed learning, but his results are of little value as his "massed" group in fact had 3-min rests between trials; furthermore, his groups were very poorly matched on ability (performance during the first trial). This may have been due in part to the very small number of Ss in his experiment.

Next in order of time comes a study by Melton (1941) which is rather closer to modern research designs; scoring is by integrating performance over quite short periods (20-sec trials) instead of over periods of almost 4 min, as in the case of Renshaw, and the design is simpler. Four groups of students were tested on the pursuit rotor with different rest intervals (10 sec, 20 min, 2 days, and 2 weeks), following 10 trials of 20-sec practice and 10-sec rest. Thus there is no properly "massed" group; the reference group is one which continues the pre-rest practice of 20 sec on–10 sec off. Differential effects of increased rest pauses will thus be less than they would have been had the reference group been completely massed, i.e., had performed without any rest pauses at all. (In the remainder of this book we shall reserve the term "massed" for the condition of work without any imposed rest; in the literature the term "massed" is often used to refer to the least distributed condition of several, although in this condition there may be rest pauses of rather short duration. As we shall see, even quite short rest pauses of 10 or 20 sec make a tremendous difference in the rate of learning, and produce quite large reminiscence effects; hence the usefulness of referring to such designs as "massed" is doubtful.)

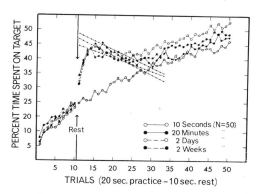

Figure 3-3. Performance on the pursuit rotor after different lengths of rest period. "Massed" practice of 20-sec practice, 10-sec rest preceded the programmed rest pause. Data by Melton (1941), redrawn by Ammons (1947) and reproduced by permission.

The actual performance curves of 4 groups of 50 students each are given in Figure 3-3; it will be seen that the 3 groups with interpolated rest show reminiscence, PRU and PRD, very much as shown in Denny's results (Figure 1-1). The length of rest, although varying from 10 sec to 2 weeks, does not seem to matter very much, although there is some suggestion in the data that terminal performance is best for the groups with 2 days' rest. All 3 groups with interpolated rest are superior at the end to the group without interpolated rest. Pomeroy (1941) using a similar schedule to Melton's but with only one group of Ss who had a 1 week's rest period, found very similar results.

Shortly after Melton's paper appeared, Buxton (1942), surveying the literature on reminiscence (Buxton, 1943a), "found reason to believe that the phenomenon should be exhibited unambiguously in the acquisition of skills." He carefully reexamined several studies on the spacing of practice, such as those of Renshaw and Travis already mentioned and those of Snoddy (1935), Gentry (1940), and Lorge (1930), and came to the conclusion that "although the experimental conditions under which data were obtained were rarely entirely favourable for the appearance of reminiscence, additional computations showed rather clearly that it was present." This paper marks the realization that the various phenomena noted by these writers in their work could theoretically be combined with the large body of work on verbal reminiscence that had been accumulated, and from then on most workers began to use the term "reminiscence" for studies using motor performance and involving improvement in performance after imposed rest pauses.

Buxton (1943b) also performed an interesting experiment whose design differs somewhat from that more usually adopted. He had 3 groups of Ss practice on the pursuit rotor to different levels of mastery

(5%, 20%, and 35% of possible score); trials were 15 sec in duration, followed by 30-sec rest periods, i.e., practice was not properly massed. After the S had reached his appropriate level of mastery, a 10½-min rest period was interposed during which he read magazines; he then returned to practice until he met his criterion a second time. A fourth group served as control; this group had no interposed rest period, but worked straight on in the 15 sec on–30 sec off rhythm. Buxton found that the experimental groups were significantly superior to the control group in every instance; relative reminiscence decreases from 47% in the group with the lowest criterion to 24% for the middle level of mastery, and to 11% for the highest level of mastery before rest. Buxton makes two interesting remarks. He finds that "the Ss who progressed by leaps and bounds and who reached the criterion early in the practice session tended to be the ones who showed the greatest gains during the rest interval." (In other words, reminiscence is a positive function of learning ability on the pursuit rotor.[1]) He further points out that in contrast to verbal learning, where optimal rest pauses are 2 min or so in duration, pursuit learning shows reminiscence for much longer rest intervals; "no study of verbal learning has produced reliable and indisputable evidence of reminiscence at an interval longer than about 5 min, if that long." He accordingly suggests "that retention curves for short intervals do not have the same form in motor learning that they do in verbal learning."

In another series of experiments, Buxton originated a further line of research which has turned out rather fruitful (Buxton & Henry, 1939; Buxton & Grant, 1939). Pointing out that "scant attention has been directed to the problem of whether or not motor learning shows the same general phenomena of retroaction as do verbal and perceptual learning," he undertook to study the occurrence (or not) of retroactive inhibition in pursuit-rotor learning, by interpolating some other task between practice sessions on a pursuit rotor; indeed, he used several different tasks in order to be able to "determine the influence of interpolated tasks of varying similarities to the original one upon the retention of the original task." His experimental design took into account the complications presented by the occurrence of reminiscence, which might wholly or partly obscure the occurrence of retroaction.

The main activity involved was of course pursuit-rotor learning; 17-sec trials were used, with 15 such trials preceding the rest pause, and 5 following it. A control group spent the rest period reading; 3 experi-

---

[1]This may of course be an artifact of measurement, along the lines of the Bahrick, Fitts, and Briggs demonstration discussed in Chapter 2.

mental groups performed different tasks during this 12-min period. These tasks were mostly taken from the Seashore (1928) motor skills battery; high reliabilities had been found for the tasks in question (Buxton & Humphreys, 1935). The tasks were: (1) a simple linear pursuit meter in which the target moved irregularly to and fro in one dimension; the design was similar to that described by Wishart (1923); (2) spool packing; and (3) stylus maze learning by mirror control. Ninety men and the same number of women, all students, took part in the experiment. Buxton and Henry (1939) discuss the results in detail, and come to the following conclusions which are also based on the observed intercorrelations, and are affected by certain failures to match the groups properly on initial trials. "1. Pursuit learning does not, like verbal learning, show a drop in performance level after interpolated practice on varying types of motor tasks. Rather, no matter what the interpolated activity, . . . a definite gain occurs. 2. Women show a relative retroaction, in that certain types of interpolated activity prevent the appearance of as large a gain as that shown by the control group. . . . The pursuit meter had the strongest effect of this type, and the maze next. Spool packing, however, produced a greater gain than that shown by the control group. Only the meter produced relative retroaction for men. The maze and spool packing performances seemed to produce a greater amount of gain for the men than simply reading in the interpolated period." We shall return to this topic in a later chapter, in view of its crucial theoretical importance, and will not discuss this experiment here in any detail.

In some additional experiments, Buxton and Grant (1939) showed that women were inferior to men on all the tasks in question; they also showed greater "fatiguability" when quite prolonged activity on the pursuit rotor was required. The authors also compared high- and low-ability Ss, defining these in terms of performance during the last 5 trials preceding the rest pause; low-ability Ss showed greater reminiscence than high-ability Ss. This conclusion must remain doubtful, however, as regression to the mean would affect the statistics, decreasing the (true) reminiscence scores of the high-ability Ss and increasing those of the low-ability Ss. Determination of ability level for such comparisons should be made on the basis of intial performance, rather than terminal performance.

Buxton and Grant (1939) make an attempt in this paper to define reminiscence more closely; they point out that "as it now is generally used, it is a rather operational sort of term, signifying any kind of gain in performance, made without rehearsal. The implicit assumptions nevertheless seem to be that recovery from fatigue is not what is meant, that changed conditions at the time of recall so as to improve performance are not what is meant . . . but that there is some sort of spontaneous change going on in the central nervous system of the organism which results in improved performance. We would propose that the use of the term be limited to the last named phenomenon. . . . We propose that reminiscence be used to describe the possible spontaneous changes in the traces which occur by the very nature of the nervous tissue in which they are laid down." This is as near as anyone has come until recently in suggesting some form of consolidation theory to account for motor reminiscence, but it will be seen that the language is very indirect and cautious. However, Buxton and Grant do recognize that several factors may be active jointly or severally in determining reminiscence; "the laws governing gains in a rest period thus should be of several kinds, dealing with, for example, amount and kind of change in traces with recovery from fatigue, amount and kind of change in traces with improved conditions of recall, such as relaxation, confidence, feelings of familiarity, etc., and amount and kind of change in traces themselves with the passage of time when the above or other factors are not significant or are cooperative." This suggestion is appealing, but difficult to follow; it requires not only an observable fact (gain in performance after rest), but also a subjective judgment based on theoretical considerations which might not be shared by other observers (absence of fatigue, of improved conditions of recall, etc.). Certainly later writers have preferred to use the term reminiscence for the observable fact.

Buxton's material had been collected at Iowa State University, which was becoming the main center for work in the field of motor reminiscence; in an unpublished Master's thesis from there Reyna (1944) contributed to our knowledge by comparing reminiscence scores of female students following a course of continuous or distributed practice (10 sec on–20 sec off), and having a rest of either 6 or 24 h. Results have been redrawn by Ammons (1947), who obtained his Ph.D. at Iowa and was later to lay the foundations for the first proper theoretical system of reminiscence; his diagram is reproduced here as Figure 3-4. It will be seen that the spaced group learns much more quickly than the massed group, and that reminiscence is much stronger for the massed group than for the spaced group. Length of rest pause does not seem to matter at this level (i.e., when the shorter of the two rest pauses is 6-hr long.) It is noteworthy that the massed group does not reach the post-rest level of the spaced group however long the rest pause; there appears to exist a permanent as well as a temporary work decrement.

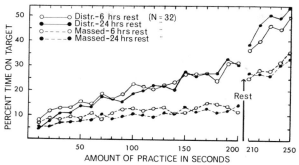

Figure 3-4. The effects of 6- and 24-hr rest pauses on massed vs spaced practice groups. Data by Reyna, redrawn by Ammons (1947) and reproduced by permission.

Reyna's study was soon followed by an unpublished report to the Civil Aeronautics Administration by Spence, Buxton, and Melton (1945), again carried out at Iowa. This work is of course linked with the air crew selection procedures later summarized by Melton in his large report, to be discussed presently, but it contains several interesting features which make separate discussion desirable. The apparatus used was an adaptation of the Koerth rotor, improved by means of the addition of automatic recording of performance and the provision for simultaneous testing of Ss in small groups. Three different samples of Ss were used: A. 240 women students; B. 120 civilian male students; C. 200 Army students. "In each of the 3 samples 4 different conditions of practice and rest were employed. In condition A the subject worked continuously for 8 minutes (recorded as 24 trials of 20 seconds each), in condition B the subject was tested for 25 seconds with rest intervals of 5 seconds between trials (16 trials), in condition C the subject worked for 20 seconds with rest intervals of 10 seconds between trials (16 trials), and in condition D the subject was tested for 10 seconds with rest intervals of 20 seconds interpolated between trials (16 trials)." (Spence *et al.* 1945.) When detailed results were tabled, "comparisons of the values in these tables indicate that under comparable working conditions the women subjects perform more poorly than men at all stages of practice." Condition D (the most spaced condition of all) gives highly superior performance for both men and women; condition A (massed) does not differ much from conditions B and C (5 and 10 sec rests between trials), suggesting that these conditions approximate complete massing. Why there should be such a complete break between condition D and conditions B and C, rather than a gradual transition, is not clear. The graph for civilian males shows much greater diversity in

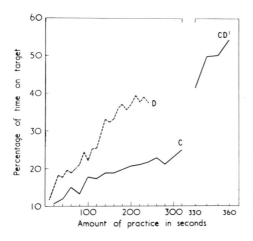

Figure 3-5. Shift in performance when group working under condition C (20-sec work, 10-sec rest) is changed to condition D (10-sec work, 20-sec rest). After Spence, Buxton, and Melton (1945).

performance between groups A, B, and C, with D still undoubtedly the best; yet here B performs considerably worse than A, which makes no sense at all. Possibly in all this we should pay attention not to the absolute values of the rest period but to the ratios of off–on periods, which are .2, .5, and 2.0 for groups B, C, and D; these ratios show greater differences than do the absolute times. Even so, the data would suggest that there is no reminiscence with rests of 5 or 10 sec, but very strong reminiscence with 20-sec rests; such a sudden rise of reminiscence when rest exceeds 10 sec seems unlikely. Later work (e.g., Adams, 1954) has shown these doubts to be justified.

An interesting graph is presented by Spence *et al.* (1945) in connection with their discussion of the hypothesis of *work inhibition,* which presumably would be present in considerable amount in condition C, as compared with D. Figure 3-5 shows the performance of the military male C and D groups, "and further results 24 hours later for the original group C when run under condition D." Two points in this figure are of interest. In the first place, there is a strong reminiscence effect; performance improves by almost 40%. In the second place, there is a change in the rate of improvement; after being changed to condition D, the rate of growth of performance now resembles that of the group originally trained under condition D, not that under which the group in question had been originally trained, i.e., condition C. This second finding has been amply confirmed, and presents many theoretical problems; we will return to it in a subsequent chapter.

Reliabilities are reported to be very high for all conditions, ranging from .91 to .98 for odd–even correlations. The product–moment correlation between total cumulative score for the first day (condition C) in the experiment described in the last paragraph, and the first four trials of day 2 (condition D) was only .68, suggesting that the relief from work inhibition variably affected different individuals. Intercorrelations were also run between 4-trial segments; "in general, adjoining segments correlate most highly with each other and, with increasing distance between segments, the coefficients decrease. Correlations between adjoining segments . . . range from .84 to .96 while those between the most distant segments, i.e., between initial and final segments vary from .69 to .82." (Spence *et al.*, 1945.) Total scores correlate most highly with the middle segments than with initial or terminal segments, and gains correlate zero with initial status, but increase their correlations consistently with later segments up to values of .60 and .70. These results are in good agreement with the "superdiagonal" hypothesis quoted in Chapter 2.

In spite of the obvious and often-mentioned similarity of verbal and motor reminiscence, no experiment to compare the two was in fact reported until the end of the period under discussion, when Leavitt and Schlosberg (1944) reported on the retention of verbal and motor skills. In a well-controlled experiment they had 48 students learn nonsense syllables for 10 trials, and practice for 10 30-sec trials on the pursuit rotor; the actual tasks and times had been carefully chosen so as to give learning to a similar degree. Subjects were divided into four groups, and retested after 1, 7, 28, or 70 days. It was found that pursuit-rotor learning showed considerable reminiscence, nonsense syllable learning none, and that pursuit-rotor performance stays up much better than verbal performance. The authors look for an explanation of reminiscence in terms of the dissipation of decremental factors which had depressed performance below the level of learning; they found that even when reminiscence was partialled out, the pursuit-rotor performance was still much better remembered than the nonsense syllables.

Leavitt (1945) submitted the same data to another form of analysis to throw some light on the problem of the relation of the speed of learning to amount retained and to reminiscence. For both verbal and motor learning correlations between score on last learning trial and score on first relearning trial were positive for the one-day rest group, and negative for the 28- and 70-day rest groups; for the 7-day rest group verbal learning showed a positive correlation, motor learning zero correlation. Considering only pursuit-rotor learning, "there is a high positive relation between amount learned and amount reminisced after 1 day (.54), up to moderate levels of mastery. After seven days there is essentially no correlation (−.06)." (Leavitt, 1945.) The figures "indicate an increase in percent reminiscence with an increase in level of learning." The term "level of learning" is somewhat ambiguous in this context; it is well known that there are quite high correlations between initial and terminal trials, so that score on last learning trial, which is Leavitt's measure of learning, is more realistically seen as a measure of total ability, i.e., of an ability already shown on the initial trial, and before any programmed learning had taken place. A proper measure of "learning" would have to be related to the slope of the acquisition curve, not to its terminal point. If we may translate Leavitt's statement, then, we might say that there is some evidence in his work that individuals of high ability show greater reminiscence effects than individuals of low ability, when rest periods of a day or so are involved; for periods of a month or longer the relationship seems to be reversed, with low ability Ss showing greater reminiscence. This reversal suggests that the Bahrick, Fitts, and Briggs paradox might not be involved. This study will be discussed again in a later chapter.

The Melton (1947) report on Apparatus Tests is a rather forbidding document of 1056 pages; it contains much information of interest to students of motor skills, but this information is largely incidental to the main purpose of the series of studies reported, namely the design and validation of selection batteries for air crews. The report is important, not only in its own right, but for two additional reasons. In the first place, the needs of military testing of thousands of recruits under conditions which combined simplicity of operation with absolute reliability of results and comparability of apparatus led to the design of pursuit rotors and other pieces of machinery which were far superior to those previously used, and set a standard of design (and maintenance) which was to become obligatory in more academic research in post-war years. In the second place, the program on which these pages report had the effect of bringing together a large number of promising young psychologists whose imagination was fired with the promise held out for theoretical and academic psychological advance by a closer study of the phenomena with which they were dealing in the restricting military environment; when at the end of the war they dispersed, they carried away with them a desire to go on working in this field and solve some of the problems which had inevitably been sidestepped during the war. The report may thus be seen either as the end of the "between wars" period, or as the beginning of the "after war" renaissance; we prefer the former interpretation in view of the failure of the A.A.F. program to produce any theoretical advances. In this chapter we will only look at results directly relevant to reminiscence; in the previous chapter we already considered the correlational results reported by Melton.

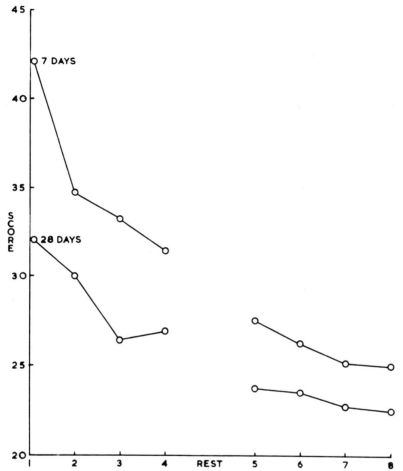

Figure 3-6. Reminiscence on Discrimination Reaction Time test. Drawn from figures by Melton (1947).

Apart from the Pursuit Rotor test, reminiscence scores are given for 5 tests which will not be described in detail. The first of these tests is the Discrimination Reaction Time. Performance is shown in Figure 3-6 of one group of Ss who performed 4 successive sets of 20 reactions during the original test, and during retest after 7 days; another group of Ss was retested after 20 days. There is clear evidence of reminiscence for both groups, amounting to 10% of their original scores, or 30% of the total amount of improvement from first to last trial. The difference in remi-

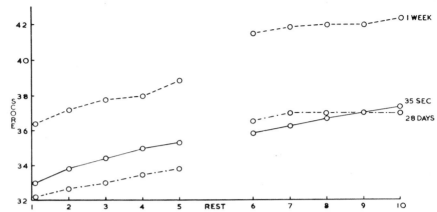

Figure 3-7. Reminiscence on Finger Dexterity test. Drawn from figures by Melton (1947).

niscence as a function of length of rest cannot be evaluated in view of the different level of pre-rest performance of the two·groups.

The second test is the Finger Dexterity test, results from which are shown in Figure 3-7. Three groups were tested with rest intervals of 35 sec, 1 week, and 28 days (approx.); reminiscence was found for the two longer rest periods, but not for the 35-sec period. Again it is not possible to compare the effectiveness of the longer periods compared to each other in view of the different levels of performance of the groups.

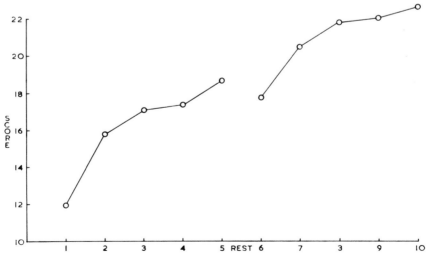

Figure 3-8. Reminiscence on Rudder Control test. Drawn from figures by Melton (1947).

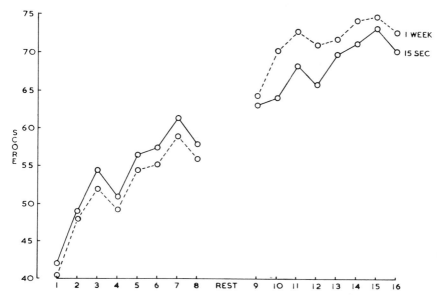

Figure 3-9. Reminiscence on Two-hand Coordination test. Drawn from figures by Melton (1947).

All one can conclude is that here, as with all motor tasks, forgetting is slow even over quite long periods, and reminiscence occurs almost irrespective of the time interval as long as this varies from a day to a month or so.

Third is the Rudder Control test, results from which are shown in Figure 3-8. Only one group was used, with a rest period of 28 days (approx.), and there appears to be forgetting rather than reminiscence. Possibly this test requires more "warm-up" than the others; there is some evidence of PRU which may indicate that "warm-up decrement" has hidden the true effects of reminiscence. Such an interpretation is of course highly speculative, and cannot be adequately defended on empirical grounds.

Fourth is the Two-Hand Coordination test, results from which are shown in Figure 3-9. Three groups were tested, having intervals of 15 sec, 1 week, and 28 days. Data from the 28-day group are not given in sufficient detail to make it possible to diagram them, although it is clear that reminiscence is present to a slightly higher extent than the 1-week group. Reminiscence for the 15-sec group is doubtful, but there may be a true effect; that for the longer period is quite strong. Another experiment supports the hypothesis that reminiscence accompanies the interpolation of rest pauses. Four groups of 50 Ss each were given massed

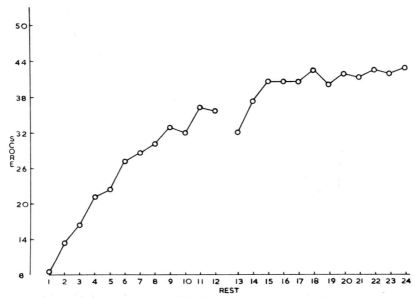

Figure 3-10. Reminiscence on Complex Coordination test. Drawn from figures by Melton (1947).

practice, for 8 min; spaced practice, with sixteen 30-sec trials with 30-sec rest intervals between trials; and two intermediate conditions using eight one-min trials with 15-sec rest pauses between trials. The terminal score for the massed group was 53.1, for the spaced group 69.8, and for the two intermediate groups 58.8 and 58.4, thus demonstrating the superiority of spaced over massed practice in this task.

Fifth is the Complex Coordination test, results from which are shown in Figure 3-10. Twenty-eight days elapsed between test and retest. Results here are similar to those on the Rudder Control test, and may be so for the same reasons hypothethized above; here too there is apparent forgetting, followed by a marked PRU suggesting "warm-up decrement" masking true reminiscence. Again this suggestion must remain highly speculative in the absence of appropriate experiments to demonstrate its correctness.

The data suggest marked reminiscence effects on motor tests, even over quite long periods, except when the test is rather complex and appears to require the operation of higher cognitive processes. Under these conditions the possibility has been suggested that "warm-up decrement" may occur and mask the existence of true reminiscence.

We may now summarize the work done during the between-war years. The phenomenon of motor reminiscence was rediscovered, and most of the detailed findings of Kraepelin and his students were replicated, although usually without acknowledgment. The apparatus used in these investigations was improved and perfected until it was almost adequate to meet the minimum requirements one might legitimately make of a simple piece of physical instrumentation. There was little theoretical sophistication, most discussions centering on such concepts as fatigue and work inhibition were usually too ill defined to be of much use. Some knowledge had been gained of the place of pursuit learning and ability in the taxonomy of motor skills, and it was known (although this knowledge was carefully disguised) that heredity played an important part in the determination of individual differences in performance. Interest in motor reminiscence and the differences between massed and spaced practice was beginning to grow exponentially, and this growth of interest was perhaps the most promising sign for future developments.

There was one exception to our generalization that theory played little part in the development of reminiscence research, and as this exception was instrumental in causing a good deal of experimental work during the between-war years, and completely ceased to affect later work, it can with advantage be discussed in this chapter. The theory referred to is that of Snoddy (1920, 1935, 1938), and although his monograph is difficult to follow, partly because of the impenetrable thicket of qualifying clauses, wrongly chosen adjectives and irrelevant adverbs, and partly because of a certain mythical assumption of global applicability of physical notions to psychological processes, it nevertheless did give rise to experimental research which advanced the study of motor learning. In view of the difficulties experienced in following his argument, direct quotation of his views would seem to be the fairest way of presenting his theory. Snoddy posits "two wholly different growth processes. . . . Let us call the early, stable form of growth, *primary,* and the later, unstable form, *secondary* growth. . . . If one is early, the other is late; if one is stable, the other is unstable; if in one individual differences are increasing, in the other individual differences are just as certainly decreasing; if one growth is increased or enhanced by the effect of passing time, the other is certainly decreased or completely lost by the effect of interpolated time, and is enhanced by the withdrawal of time. We may pass from one to the other by simple change of algebraic sign." (Snoddy, 1938, p. 15.) And again: "Primary growth comes early and is enhanced by interpolated time; it approaches its maximum as the length of interpolated time is increased. Secondary growth comes later and is enhanced by reducing the interpolated time; it is maximum when the interpolated time is zero, or when the practice may be said to be continuous." (1938, p. 15.) In other words, "primary growth is a positive function of the length of the interpolated time-interval" (p. 20); it is "always followed by secondary growth" (1938, p. 22). "The ratio of the increment for the long time-interval to the continuous-practice increment, steadily decreases. . . . The explanation that comes to mind is that continuous practice conditions are encouraging a growth process which must be *later* in terms of repetition, that is, it is not lifted up quickly by a few repetitions as is the case of the practice with long intervals." (1938, p. 22.)

On later pages Snoddy identifies primary growth with increase of entropy (1938, p. 71), speculates on the nature of time and relativity, considers the organismic basis of growth to be associated with the degradation of energy, and concludes that primary growth implies "a movement from an initial dynamic state, produced largely in the perceptual apparatus by the shock effect of early stimulation, toward an adynamic state." (1938, p. 100). Leaving out of account these far-reaching speculations, let us consider the evidence presented by Snoddy.

The task used by Snoddy is mirror drawing. A six-pointed star-shaped nicked path, 500 mm in length and 7 mm in width has to be traced with a copper stylus, and the number of contacts made are counted. "The subject is paced so that the number of errors and the number of seconds required for a circuit of the instrument are statistically equal." Pacing is achieved by instructions to go faster or slower. "A few subjects of psychopathic type could not be paced and their results are excluded from the study." (1938, p. 9.) Little information is given on the method of diagnosis used for "psychopathy", but Snoddy defines another measure used by him: Mean velocity = $(100/T + E)$. Five experiments in all are described by him:

1. 72 Ss; one circuit per day for 30 days.
2. 70 Ss; 60 continuous circuits—24-hr rest—30 continuous circuits—24-hr rest—30 continuous circuits.
3. 80 Ss; 20 circuits for 6 days, with 30-sec rest between circuits.
4. 70 Ss; 20 circuits, with 2-min rest periods, each day for 8 days. (Fourteen days elapsed between the 7th and 8th practice days.)
5. 20 Ss; 100 circuits, one-min rest between circuits.

Figure 3-11 which has been drawn from data given in Snoddy's tables 3 and 4, illustrates his contention that "primary growth is a

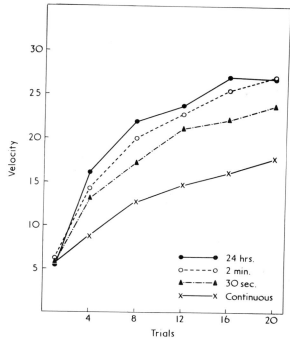

Figure 3-11. Performance on Mirror Drawing task. Redrawn from figures given by Snoddy (1936).

positive function of the length of the interpolated interval," which is little different from the old and at that time not unfamiliar rule that performance on a motor-learning task is a direct function of the degree of distribution of practice. Snoddy also publishes, as in figure 5, data in which two consecutive circuits are followed by a 2-min rest pause, then another two consecutive circuits, etc.; there are also two 24-hr rests (see Figure 3-12). He finds that the second of the two consecutive circuits is always worse (slower) than the first, i.e., all improvement in performance occurs during the rests. This, he argues, illustrates the interference between primary and secondary effect. "The conditions would . . . seem to be ideal for determining an interference effect, that is, a loss in the second member of each pair." Temporal conditions were ordered so as to accelerate primary growth, and then involve some secondary growth by continuity, in the hope of detecting interference effects. In other words, the first circuit was expected to produce primary growth and the second circuit secondary growth "since continuity is a determiner of secondary growth." (1938, p. 32.) The experimental

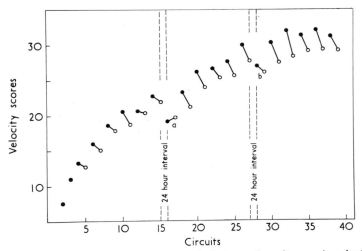

Figure 3-12. Performance on Mirror Drawing task. Redrawn from figures given by Snoddy (1936).

design is interesting and novel, but the results can hardly be cited as strong support of the hypothesis because they simply illustrate the familiar facts of reminscence and post-rest downswing; a new theory to explain the phenomenon must do more than demonstrate again the occurrence of the phenomenon to be explained. Even worse, Bell (1942) has pointed out that in actual fact the results contradict Snoddy's own assumptions. "It is clear that an interfering or inhibiting effect is present in the trials which were not preceded by a rest interval, as the velocity scores represented by boxed stations are, with the exception of one, below that of the rest interval stations. However, this denies Snoddy's tenet that secondary growth is facilitated by the reduction of time, as the losses are not smaller late in learning for the continuous practice trials. In fact, his data show an advantage for spaced practice throughout the series of trials. It is apparent also that the interference effect was present in the early as well as in the late stages of learning, which contradicts Snoddy's statement that primary growth is prominent in the early stages and secondary growth in the late stages of learning." (1942, p. 30.)

Humphrey (1936), a student of Snoddy, attempted to use the pursuit rotor in a study designed to test Snoddy's hypothesis; the data analyzed were taken from an experiment by Buxton and Humphrey (1935). Five consecutive 20-sec trials were separated by 5 min of work on other motor tasks; furthermore, there were two 48-hr rest intervals after the 30th and 60th trials. "The striking thing about the learning curve is seen at the end of every five trials, when there was an interven-ing time interval. Statistically, in the early stages of learning gains are made between practice periods, while in the later stages gains are made during the practice periods, in conformity with Snoddy's findings." (1935, p. 432.) Humphrey's study, like Snoddy's, makes the assumption that differences in scores are equal regardless of whether they occur near the beginning or near the ceiling; such an assumption is obviously incorrect particularly when, as in the present study, terminal scores are very near the ceiling. We shall return to this point again.

Doré and Hilgard (1937) studied the effects of differential spacing of rest periods in pursuit-rotor learning. Four groups of Ss practiced on the rotor for various amounts of time within one 43-min period. Three of the groups A, B, and C, practiced for one-min periods and rested 11, 3, and 1 min, respectively, between trials; within an equal number of trials, group A made the largest gains, group B next, and group C least. Group D practiced for 3 min and rested 1 min, having the same number of practice trials as the other 3 groups; its performance was the poorest. Figure 3-13 shows an interesting comparison between groups B and D; as Doré and Hilgard (1937, p. 255) put it, "the ill-effects of excessive practice are well illustrated in the performance of Group D. . . . The practice periods of Group B begin at the same time as those

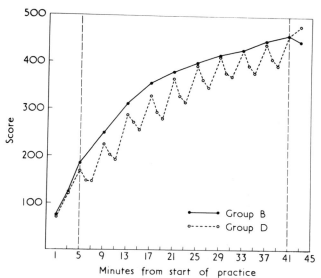

Figure 3-13. The effect of differential practice on pursuit-rotor learning. Taken with permission from Doré and Hilgard (1937).

of Group D, but Group B ceased after one minute and rested while Group D continued for three minutes. The subjects of Group D as evidenced by this curve, made poor use of the 2nd and 3rd minutes of practice. Group B remains equal to or better than Group D, in spite of one-third as much time in practice." When all the groups were prac-ticed in a final trial with fatigue effects approximately equal, the scores tended to fall in order of the amount of practice; this made the authors conclude that growth in pursuit learning may take place during rather than between trials, which is contrary to Snoddy's view.

In another study, the same authors (Doré & Hilgard, 1938, p. 360) formally deduced the following theorem from Snoddy's account: "If two equated groups of subjects are given the same number of practice trials distributed over the same total time, but the practice is differently distributed, that group which is given initial spaced practice and final massed practice should show higher scores at the end of the period than the group which is given initial massed practice and later spaced practice." This time the number of trials and the amount of time were equal for two groups of Ss, but for one group the trials were first massed and later spaced, while for the other group the trials were first spaced and later massed. Fourteen 1-min trials were given to the two groups, labeled E and F, during the 43 min of the experiment; the first 3 trials were alike for both groups, there being 1-min rest pauses between

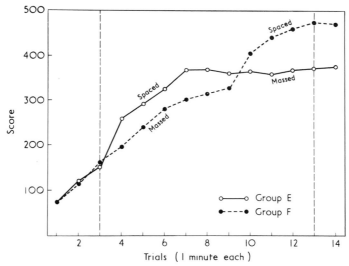

Figure 3-14. The effect of differential spacing of rest periods on pursuit-rotor learning. Taken with permission from Doré and Hilgard (1937).

trials. Group F continued with six 1-min rest pauses (called "massing" by the authors), then had gradually increasing rest pauses; group E started with an 11-min rest pause, then gradually shortened rest pauses and ended up with massed trials. There was a final trial for both groups following the last but one trial with 1-min rest (the results are shown in Figure 3-14). "The scores of the first three trials indicate that the two groups were satisfactorily matched. . . . The final scores test the theorem which predicted that the scores of Group E would exceed those of Group F. On the contrary, *the final scores of Group F exceed those of Group E by a statistically significant amount.* . . . A condition of increasing rests is more efficient than a condition of decreasing rests. This contradicts the theorem based on Snoddy." (Doré & Hilgard, 1938, p. 362.)

This study gave rise to a reply by Snoddy (1938), and two further experiments by Hilgard and Smith (1942) and by Bell (1942); however, essentially Snoddy's hypothesis never recovered from the Doré and Hilgard demonstration.[2] One reason for this failure was that Snoddy's reply was not as clear as might have been wished; he argued that the method used by Doré and Hilgard was "artificial" (what experimental design is not?), and that an "interference" factor was present, due to adaptation of group E to the time-interval conditions prevailing at the beginning of the experiment. Hilgard and Smith, in their experiment, had 3 groups of Ss each practicing for 4 daily 25-min sessions, differentiated by the number of 1-min trials within each session. The results, and the experimental details, are shown in Figure 3-15. "Scores following changes in single rest intervals between trials early and late in each day showed a 20 sec interval to be unfavourable to a 1 min rest in all comparisons. Early in learning a 3 min rest was always more favourable than a 1 min rest, but later in learning a change from a 3 min rest to a single 1 min rest occasionally brought a relative increase in score. . . . While 55 percent of the 78 subjects gained overnight between the first and second day, overnight losses were found for 85 percent of the subjects between consecutive days thereafter. These overnight changes

---

[2]The "stimulus-induced maturation" hypothesis was effectively killed when Wright and Taylor (1949) tested the theory in relation to verbal learning (serial anticipation). The task consisted of learning a list of 18 nonsense syllables presented at the rate of one every 3 sec. All Ss received a total practice period of 52 min, and all trials were 1 min in length. The length of the interpolated rest periods was systematically varied. One group of Ss practiced continuously. The other four groups received rest periods of 8, 3½, 2, and 1½ min, respectively. The attainment per trial of all four groups with spaced practice was superior to that of the groups with continuous practice but, contrary to the demands of the theory, the groups with spaced practice were not differentiated from each other.

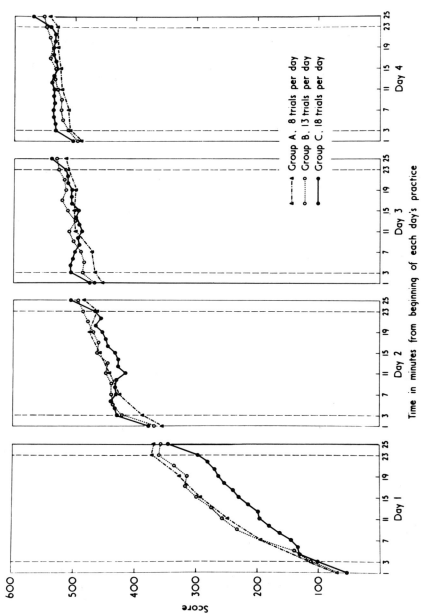

Figure 3-15. The effect of differential lengths of rest pauses on pursuit-rotor learning. Taken with permission from Hilgard and Smith (1942).

bore little relationship to the distribution of trials within each period." (Hilgard & Smith, 1942, p. 145.)

Bell (1942) gives an excellent historical discussion of the work relevant to the Snoddy hypothesis, and reports a large-scale experiment involving 457 Ss in all. "All subjects completed twenty 1-minute trials on the rotor, with the trials separated by 1-minute rest periods except for a single longer rest." A control group did not receive this single longer rest, which was either 10 min, 1, 6, 24, or 30 hr, and occurred either after the 5th or 15th trial. Thus rests might be shorter or longer, and occur early or late in practice. "The . . . data support Snoddy's contention that primary growth occurs early in learning and that it is stable when measured by the cumulative mean, but they do not agree with his claim that it is a continuous, ever-growing function. . . . The present findings support Snoddy's contention that something (similar to what he calls secondary growth) occurs late in learning and that it is unstable and hence lost over long intervals of time. They are at variance with his theory that the loss over long intervals is proportional to the amount of interpolated time, and they further question his use of the cumulative mean as a measure of primary growth." (1942, p. 28.) Bell suggests additional concepts and an alternative theoretical view as superior to Snoddy's, and Hilgard also adumbrates later theories. Before turning to these adumbrations, it may be useful to evaluate Snoddy's theory in retrospect.

It might be harsh, but would probably be true, to say that Snoddy's theory combines many features which are characteristic of bad theorizing; as such, it may with advantage be studied as a set piece by all those interested in the elaboration of psychological theories with some pretence to scientific status. What are these faults?

1. In the first place, the theory is based on a confusion between maturation and learning; Snoddy followed other writers like Coghill (1929), Wheeler (1929), and Wheeler and Perkins (1932) in "extending the concept of growth to include the changes which underlie ordinary learning. Maturation, instead of remaining a term correlative with learning and to be distinguished from it, becomes in their writings an explanation of learning" (Doré & Hilgard, 1937, p. 245). In Snoddy's hands the somewhat mythical properties of maturation as an explanatory concept for learning become so unclear that they cease to be properly definable (leave alone the desirability of *operational* definition), and cannot be integrated at all readily with the other concepts and theories arising in the field of learning. This makes Snoddy's theory very much ad hoc, rather than allowing him to derive his theorems from widely based concepts and laws.

2. The logical and mathematical analysis used by Snoddy on his own data is often faulty and unsatisfactory. To take but one example, Doré and Hilgard (1938) have challenged Snoddy's use of the cumulative mean as a measure of primary growth, by showing that he failed to note that the cumulative mean of a logarithmic curve bears a definite relation to that curve (i.e., the cumulative mean of the points on a logarithmic curve, when plotted as a straight line, is another curve of half the slope.) If primary growth is expressed as the cumulative mean and secondary growth found by subtracting primary growth from total growth, secondary growth then becomes equal to primary growth minus a constant representing initial score. This would mean that the primary and secondary growth differentials are equal after the first score, which would deny Snoddy's statement that early and late massing of practice have different effects because of early predominance of primary growth and late predominance of secondary growth.

3. Snoddy's interpretation of his own data is often erroneous and contradictory. We have already discussed the data presented in his figure 5 as one illustration of this; another example is given by Doré and Hilgard on page 368 of their account. They conclude from their examination of Snoddy's own data that "spaced practice is advantageous throughout, and continuous practice correspondingly disadvantageous, contrary to the interpretation given his data by Snoddy" (p. 369).

4. The theory is internally inconsistent. Primary and secondary growth are said to be opposite processes, but Snoddy himself finds primary growth to be correlated with the secondary growth above it to the extent of $+0.77$. Furthermore, it is evident that their measurement by subtraction from total growth supposes them to be of like sign. Addition of secondary growth to primary growth increases scores; subtraction of secondary growth decreases total scores. "An incoherence is introduced into the conception of the two processes in a section which deals with their interference." (Snoddy, 1935, pp. 29–34.) "It appears in this section that secondary growth may actually cause a subtraction of primary growth, which contradicts both the ordinary additive principle, and also the insistence upon the stability and irreversibility of the primary growth base." (Doré & Hilgard, 1938, p. 369.)

5. Problems of measurement are not faced. In almost all of the studies cited in connection with Snoddy's hypothesis, scores in later practice come very near to the ceiling of performance; group performance means are often within 10% of the maximum attainable score. Under these circumstances it becomes quite impermissible to use raw scores, or differences in raw scores, as equivalent early and late in

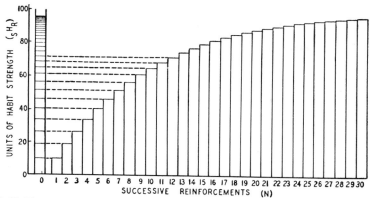

Figure 3-16. The growth of habit as a function of successive trials. Taken with permission from Hull (1943).

practice; an improvement from 10% to 20% of time-on-target is not equivalent to an improvement from 85% to 95% of time-on-target. Hull (1943) has given a very clear discussion of the problem in his note on "How to Compute Habit Strength" (p. 119); Figure 3-16 is taken from his account to illustrate his principle "that the amount of growth resulting from each unit of growth opportunity will increase the amount of whatever is growing by a constant fraction of the growth potentiality as yet unrealized." In this purely hypothetical example 1 trial would raise performance from 10% to 20% of time-on-target level, whereas 10 trials would be required to raise it from 85% to 90%; in other words, 1 trial early in practice is equal to 10 trials late in practice. These disproportions do not matter very much when we are concerned with relatively low-level performances below 50% or so of time-on-target; they become all-important when we go as close to the asymptote as was customary in the work reviewed.

Snoddy's analysis, then is clearly defective in many ways; nevertheless it had the salutary effect of (a) encouraging a number of experiments which produced genuinely new knowledge, and (b) leading a number of people to consider more seriously than before the theoretical aspects of massed and spaced learning, and of reminiscence. Doré and Hilgard (1938, p. 370), having criticized Snoddy's approach, argue that "a more conventional classification of the significant aspects of scores in skilled performances attributes improvement to learning, but recognizes that learning scores may be reduced or masked by factors producing a work-decrement. The interferences of fatigue, refractory phase, and the like, are distinguished from a more permanent disruption which is usually called forgetting. Such a conventional analysis may be outlined as follows:

1. Learning factors.
   a. Improvement with practice (Acquisition).
   b. Loss with non-practice (Forgetting).

2. Work factors.
   a. Loss within practice (Work-decrement).
   b. Improvement with non-practice (Recovery with rest)."

Similarly, Bell (1942) prefers a more orthodox interpretation of the experimental data. "The large gains over early rest intervals . . . are explained . . . as being the result of the elimination of interference during the rest interval. The advantage of spaced practice according to the theory is . . . that it tends to eliminate ineffectual responses which were interfering with the development of effective responses." Losses over rest periods late in learning are explained "by assuming that interference has been reduced to the point where warming-up is greater than interference. The losses revealed in the first trial after rest were quickly recovered in the second trial, indicating clearly that prior learning was not really lost, but could be quickly restored after brief warming-up. . . . All the factors in learning, according to our theory, are present throughout the entire course of learning, differing only in the degree to which each is effecting learning at any given stage." (1942, p. 34.) Bell also declares that his theory is entirely in line with current theories of reminiscence, which "have emphasized the removal of inhibiting or interfering factors during rest as the primary determinant in the gains which followed" (p. 35). We thus end the inter-war period with a theoretical view which, while not worked out in any detail, encompassed most of the concepts which were to form the foundation of the Hullian theories which flourished after the war, and which will engage our attention in the next chapter.

CHAPTER 4

The All-Purpose Apparatus
Meets the All-Purpose Theory

Towards the end of the war, somewhat similar theoretical attempts were made by Ammons (1947a) and Kimble (1949a, 1950, 1952) to provide a quantitative model for reminiscence in motor learning using the pursuit rotor as the preferred experimental tool, although they also used other techniques. We shall begin with Ammons, both because his attempt preceded Kimble's, and also because it is more specific and less generalized. Ammons has often spoken out in favor of "miniature models" and "small-scale theories"; Kimble has made more determined attempts to align his theories with the more ambitious ones of Hull. In spite of these differences, it will be seen that the two attempts bear quite close relation to each other.

Ammons begins his discussion (after a short dismissal of previous theories, none of which "appears adequate as originally stated to account for all particular phenomena noted") by presenting a figure (Figure 4-1) which is extremely useful in illustrating in detail the phenomena which must be explained in any workable theory of reminiscence. Curve A represents the curve of performance we would obtain under conditions of massed practice if no special rest periods were introduced; this can be obtained by the use of a control group, or by extrapolation. Normally this "curve" is a straight line, usually less steep than shown in Figure 4-1. If a rest is introduced, performance does not resume at level G (predicted level of performance on first post-rest trial if there had been no rest), but at level F; the difference between G and F is often used as a measure of reminiscence, but as we shall see Ammons

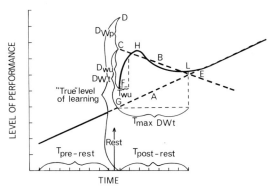

Figure 4-1. Representation of certain rotary pursuit variables. A = extrapolation of pre-rest performance curve; B = straight line fitted to the relatively decremental segment of the post-rest performance curve; C = level of line B at first post-rest trial—estimated performance level if there were no D_{wu}; D = "true" level of learning—performance level if there were no D_{Wp}, D_{Wt}, or D_{wu}; E = intersection of B and A—point at which maximum post-rest D_{Wt} is reached; F = actual performance level on first post-rest trial; G = predicted level of performance on first post-rest trial if there had been no rest; H = relative high point reached early in post-rest performance; L = relative low point in post-rest performance at the end of the "decremental" segment; $T_{pre-rest}$ = time spent practicing before rest; $T_{post-rest}$ = time spent practicing after rest; D_{Wp} = permanent work decrement on first post-rest trial (D − C where all temporary work decrement has dissipated over rest); D_{Wt} = amount of temporary work decrement dissipated over rest; $T_{max\ DWt}$ = time to reach a maximum level of work decrement after rest; D_{wu} = initial decrement in post-rest performance curve due to necessity for subject to "warm-up" after rest; and T_{wu} = time to overcome "warm-up" decrement after rest. Taken with permission from Ammons (1947a).

prefers another measure. From F to H there is a rapid rise in the curve of performance; this is often referred to as "warm-up" but the more neutral term "post-rest upswing" seems preferable, as already explained in an earlier chapter. After H the curve of performance declines again (post-rest downswing) till it reaches point L; this declining section is fitted by the straight line B, which is extrapolated backwards to point C; this point is located at the first post-rest trial. After reaching L, performance picks up again and proceeds as if rest period, reminiscence, PRD, and PRU had been nothing but a bad dream. A point D is also defined in the figure; this might be visualized as the level of performance reached after the same amount of practice (in sec.) as G, but with perfectly spaced practice. These are the main features and points introduced by Ammons; others are described in detail in the figure caption itself.

We come now to the definition of certain theoretical variables. The first of these is "warm-up decrement," defined as the "decrement on

any trial due to the necessity for the subject to 'warm-up' after rest."
This is measured as the difference between points C and F; Ammons
used the symbol D_{wu} for this concept. It should of course be noted that
this is essentially the inverse of warm-up, being the decrement in
performance due to failure of warm-up to have taken place. "At any
trial D_{wu} will be the vertical difference between line B and the post-rest
performance curve where line B is higher." The second decremental
variable to be defined is D_{Wt}—"the amount of temporary work decrement *dissipated* over rest. This is the difference between points C and G
in Fig. 1. . . . Decrement is present at all points in practice but can be
measured only by the introduction of a rest period sufficiently long to
insure its relatively complete dissipation. Then by eliminating D_{wu} (by
extrapolating line B backward) it is possible to estimate the total temporary work decrement present at the end of the last pre-rest trial. *Reminiscence* or gain over rest is due to this dissipation of temporary work
decrement. No implication is intended that temporary work decrement
is due to fatigue as commonly defined. D_{Wt} can be seen to be similar to
Hull's I_R." (Ammons, 1947a.) In this definition of D_{Wt} Ammons thus
includes the major part of his general theory; reminiscence is due to
recovery from some form of inhibition which keeps pre-rest practice
under massed conditions from reaching its proper level (i.e., the level it
would have reached under optimally spaced conditions).

A third variable is needed to complete Ammons' system; this is
D_{Wp}, or permanent work decrement. "On the first post-rest trial this
will be the difference between points C and D in Fig. 4-1, providing there
is no temporary work decrement remaining after rest. . . . There will be
an amount of D_{Wp} at every point in performance, which can be measured only by introducing a rest to eliminate the decremental effects of
temporary work decrement completely and comparing initial post-rest
performance corrected for D_{wu} with that of a control group with short
trials and long rests. The difference, by definition, would be due to
D_{Wp}. D_{Wp} is thus similar to Hull's $_sI_R$." This, Ammons tells us, "completes the isolation and definition of variables"; but as already noted, it
does more than that. We are already committed to an *inhibition* type of
theory; Ammons' nomenclature and choice of variables have predetermined the direction in which the theory to be proposed must proceed.
Note that Ammons does not present any argument in favor of this
inhibition theory; it is taken for granted that this type of theory is the
only type of theory applicable to data of this kind. Twenty-five years
after the event it is easier to see how Ammons drew a mathematically
straight line from an unwarranted assumption to a possibly erroneous
conclusion.

Ammons goes on to present a series of what he calls "assumptions"; these are essentially parametric laws indicating how a given variable will behave over time, or as another variable is changing. These assumptions are partly based on empirical evidence, partly intuitive; they clearly owe much to the grander design of Hull's system. Deductions are made from these assumptions, and these deductions have led to a good deal of empirical work.

Ammons begins with several "assumptions" about warm-up, the first of which reads:[1] "Initial post-rest D_{wu} increases as a negatively accelerated increasing function of total duration of previous practice." (A1) In other words, the more practice there has been prior to rest, the more "set" (consisting principally of various advantageous postural adjustments) has been acquired, and the more there will be to lose. "The course of acquisition of advantageous postural adjustments should follow a typical negatively accelerated learning curve." Thus PRU will be more marked with longer pre-rest practice, the increases follow a negatively accelerated learning curve. This postulate is complemented by another which says that "D_{wu} will be a positively accelerated decreasing function of the duration of practice since intersession rest." (A2) Ammons justified this by saying that "it would seem that warming-up or 'set' recovery would be more rapid at first after rest, then taper off." In actual performance, this would mean that the successive ordinate differences between line B and the actual performance curve in Figure 4-1 will constitute a negatively accelerated decreasing function. A third postulate says the "initial post-rest D_{wu} decreases as a positively accelerated function of the number of previous practice sessions"; in other words, "the more times practice is resumed, the easier it will be to warm-up." (A4) This presupposes that methods of "warming-up" will themselves be learned. A fourth assumption maintains that "initial post-rest D_{wu} is a negatively accelerated increasing function of the duration of intersession rests." This is based on the assumption that "at the start of rest there are many 'set' factors to drop out, so loss of 'set' will be more rapid then than later on in rest." And a fifth assumption reads: "Time to eliminate D_{wu} upon resumption of practice after rest is a negatively accelerated increasing function of the duration of rest." (A5) This follows from the preceding assumption; if more "set" is lost the longer the rest, the longer it should take to reacquire the lost "set." All this is of course dependent on another assumption, namely that "the shape of the curve of D_{wu} within a practice session will always be the

---

[1] The assumptions are numbered A1 through A5, following Ammons, although they are not presented in the same sequence.

'same' whatever the initial amount of D_{wu}." (A3) These "assumptions" complete Ammon's account of "warm-up decrement."

Ammons makes a number of deductions, of which the following is perhaps typical: "D_{wu} at any given time after start of a practice session will be less, the greater the number of preceding practice sessions." This follows naturally from combining A3 and A4. Another deduction reads: "The time for D_{wu} to reach a certain minimum value on resumption of practice after rest will be a positively accelerated decreasing function of the number of preceding practice sessions." This too can be deduced by taking A3 and A4 together. A third prediction, perhaps a little less obvious than the other two, is that "as the total amount of practice per session decreases, the point of maximum initial D_{wu} should come at earlier practice sessions." As Ammons points out, "it will take more sessions to build up the same amount of 'set', since 'set' is a function of amount of actual practice (A1), whereas the rate of acquisition of methods of reinstating sets will remain the same (A4)." Ammons quotes some evidence (usually reanalyses of published figures) which in a general sort of way supports his deductions; on the whole later evidence has borne out both assumptions and deductions. This does not necessarily mean that the theory of "warm-up" is true or relevant; Ammons does not in fact argue in its favor, or adduce evidence to support it. Like many others since, he simply assumes it to be true, largely by analogy from verbal learning where, as we shall see, there is some good evidence for it. Such transfer is not acceptable without good evidence, and we shall encounter several alternative theories which may fit the facts equally well.

Ammons goes on to present 3 assumptions regarding temporary work decrement. The first reads: "The increment of temporary work decrement per unit of practice time at any point in practice is a positively accelerated decreasing function of the total amount of previous practice." The argument presented in defense of this assumption is that "as a person becomes more proficient there should be less decrement from the same amount of work." Ammons recognizes the difficulty of providing evidence in favor of this assumption; he refers to the possibility that the decrease sometimes observed "is due to a flattening of the curve as it nears 100 percent performance." The second assumption reads: "Increments of temporary work decrement per unit of practice time cumulate arithmetically during practice." And the third reads: "Temporary work decrement dissipates continuously as a fixed proportion of the total temporary work decrement present at the instant." This assumption is not very clear, but presumably it applies to time spent on massed practice as well as to time spent in resting; indeed this is especially stated in Ammons's first deduction from these three assumptions: "the net level of temporary work decrement present at the end of a trial cycle will be a positive linear function of the size of the increment per unit of time, and an inverse linear function of the proportion of temporary work decrement dissipated." His second deduction states: "The net level of temporary work decrement developed serially during a practice session will be a negatively accelerated increasing function of the amount of practice since the start of that session." This, as he points out, is not contradictory to Hull's assumption of linear increase in I_R. "One actually can obtain the present deduction within Hull's system by combining his formula for I_R as a function of work and number of trials with his principle of dissipation of I_R as a simple decay function."

Ammons presents several further deductions, and then proceeds to the statement of an assumption regarding permanent work decrement. "Permanent work decrement is a multiplicative function of the amount of temporary work decrement and a negatively accelerated increasing function of the time this decrement has been present." His justification is admittedly speculative. "We can think of temporary work decrement as temporary inadequate practice methods. These will become stronger habits the longer they are practiced. This learning of inadequate practice methods can be assumed to be a negatively accelerated function since this is probably the course of 'true' learning (see Hull's $_sH_R$)." This "true level of learning" gives rise to another assumption, making clear its identity with Hull's $_sH_R$: "'True level of learning' will be a simple growth function of the amount of time spent in practice." On the other hand: "Actual performance level at any point in practice will be 'true level of learning' minus permanent work decrement, and temporary work decrement present at that point." This completes Ammons's presentation, except for one further deduction: "The proportionately shorter the rest per trial cycle, the lower the level of the actual performance curve during the practice session."

Ammons followed up his theoretical work with a large-scale study using over 500 subjects, 14 in each of 34 groups, and 34 in one group (1947b). The 35 conditions used were all possible combinations of pre-rest continuous work periods of $\frac{1}{3}$, 1, 3, 8, and 17 min and rest periods of $\frac{1}{3}$, 2, 5, 10, 20, 60, 360 min. All Ss worked continuously for 8 min after rest. Detailed results are given for each group separately, but only averaged results will be reported here. Figure 4-2 shows reminiscence as a function of duration of pre-rest practice, and reminiscence as a function of duration of interpolated rest. Note in the former that reminiscence increases as a negatively accelerated increasing function of the duration of practice up to 8 min, but falls thereafter; this fall is not easy

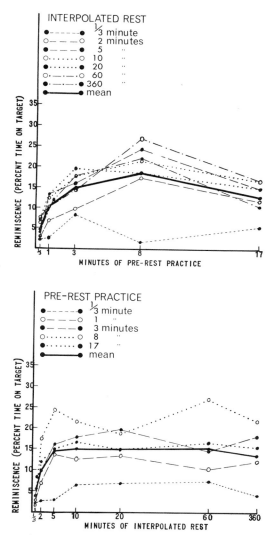

Figure 4-2. Amount of reminiscence as a function of duration of pre-rest practice and of duration of interpolated rest. Taken with permission from Ammons (1947*a*).

to account for on Ammons's principles, while the rise is of course as expected. Reminiscence also increases as a negatively accelerated increasing function of rest, but reaches a maximum at around 5 min; there is little change from a 5-min rest to a 7-hr rest. Reminiscence is here calculated in the traditional manner, i.e., as the "gain on the first post-

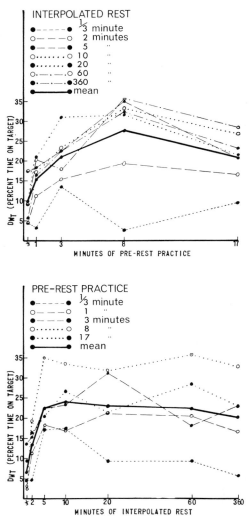

Figure 4-3. Amount of temporary work decrement dissipated as a function of duration of pre-rest practice and duration of interpolated rest. Taken with permission from Ammons (1947a).

rest trial over the level on this trial if no rest period had been introduced." Figure 4-3 shows D_{Wt} as a function of duration of pre-rest practice and interpolated rest, i.e., reminiscence calculated in the manner shown in Figure 4-1; it is reassuring to note that in their essentials Figures 4-2 and 4-3 show substantial agreement, with the latter bringing out the main points perhaps a little more strongly. Clearly, tradi-

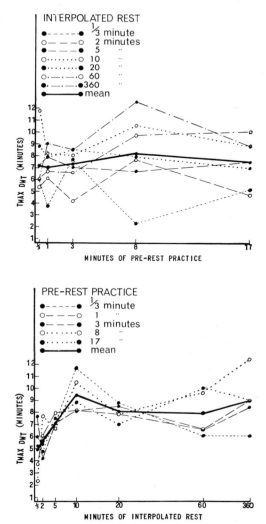

Figure 4-4. Post-rest time to maximum temporary work decrement as a function of the duration of pre-rest practice and the duration of interpolated rest. Taken with permission from Ammons (1947a).

tional reports and reports using Ammons's technique are not too disparate for transfer of information to be effected. This is important as few succeeding investigators have used his method of scoring.

As Figure 4-4 shows, time to reach maximum D_{Wt}, i.e., the bottom of the post-rest downswing, is independent of the duration of pre-rest practice; it does, however, depend on the duration of interpolated rest,

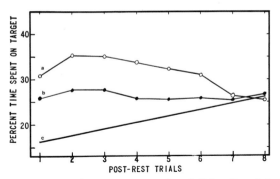

Figure 4-5. Mean post-rest performance curves for all "short" and for all "long" test groups; (a) is the mean post-rest performance curve for all rest groups of 20, 60, and 360 min; (b) is the mean post-rest performance curve for all rest groups of $\frac{1}{3}$, 2, and 5 min; and (c) is the mean for all "baselines" involved. Taken with permission from Ammons (1947a).

increasing up to 10 min. The shorter the rest, the shorter $T_{max}D_{Wt}$. Both effects are predicted from Ammons's "assumptions," but he here (1947b, p. 405) adds what is in effect another assumption not previously stated explicitly; "it may be assumed that a temporary decrement due to continuous work has reached its maximum at the point of inversion." Presumably dissipation from that point onwards is greater than accumulation of D_{Wt}, so that the curve resumes its upward path. What is not clear (and this point is crucial to Ammons's whole system of scoring) is why there is PRD at all. If his PRD is due to inhibition–D_{Wt}, then why is there no performance decrement of a similar kind during uninterrupted practice? After 5 min of rest practically all of D_{Wt} has dissipated, according to Ammons's own figures. Why then, after the very short "warm-up" period (usually not more than 30–60 sec), does the curve of performance decline, when at a similar point, after uninterrupted practice for 10 minutes or more, it is still rising without any indication of a drop? Ammons nowhere deals with this crucial problem for his system. We shall see later that there is no PRD at all when rest pauses are sufficiently prolonged; in other words, when rest periods extend to a week or so, there is no $T_{max}D_{Wt}$ because there is not D_{Wt} post-rest; this fact could not be accommodated by any form of simple inhibition theory.

Ammons presents a figure (Figure 4-5 here) which shows mean post-rest performance curves for all "short" and all "long" rest groups; "it is apparent that D_{Wt} is less for the shorter rest group." There is in fact very little deviation from a straight line for the "short" rest group; what differentiates it from the "baseline" group (extrapolation from pre-rest practice) is the slope. In fact, there is no evidence in this figure of any reversal of the PRD; the up-swing shown in Figure 4-1 after point

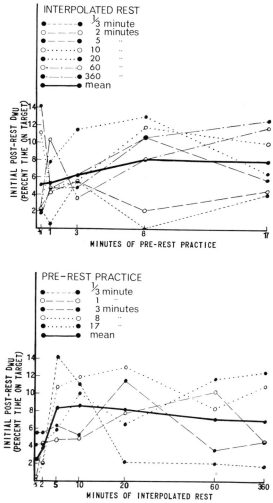

Figure 4-6. Amount of initial warm-up decrement as a function of duration of pre-rest practice and of duration of interpolated rest. Taken with permission from Ammons (1947*a*).

L is reached is conspicuously lacking. Figure 4-6 shows the dependence of D_{wu} on duration of pre-rest practice and duration of interpolated rest. Ammons interprets his findings as showing "that D_{wu} is probably an increasing negatively accelerated function of $T_{pre-rest}$, although the individual curves are quite variable and the mean curve irregular. It would seem that the potential amount of D_{wu} reaches its maximum after about 8 min practice—most of the 'set' factors which can be lost during rest have been acquired. It is also possible that D_{wu} is appreciable even before practice since the curve appears to start at a point above zero. This would represent positive transfer of 'set' to this new situation." The same Figure (Figure 4-6B) shows that D_{wu} is a negatively accelerated function of duration of rest, very much as predicted; this is because "there will be at first a rapid dropping out of advantageous postural and body adjustments; then the process should slow down—there will be fewer to drop out." A maximum is reached after about 10 min; longer rests seem to produce if anything less D_{wu}. This is unexpected and unexplained, although of course the decline may be quite nonsignificant.

Ammons (1950a) proceeded to test his assumptions in a third study, in which 7 groups of 24 female students each were tested over three periods. Periods 2 and 3 were separated by 24-hr rest; period 2 followed period 1 after 20 min. During period 1 36 22-sec trials were given (with the first 2-sec period disregarded for the purpose of scoring); these were separated by variable rest periods, i.e., 0, 20, 50 sec, 2, 5, 12 min, or approximately 24 hr. (The 24-hr group was disregarded because of various irregularities.) Periods 2 and 3 contained massed practice for 36 20-sec trials each. Performance curves are shown in Figure 4-7; the method of analysis was "to plot group mean clock scores by 20-sec trials, and fit these curves visually with smoothed curves corrected for warm-up decrement (D_{wu}). These smoothed curves are then used to obtain estimates of initial and final performance levels within periods, temporary work decrement (D_{Wt}), and warm-up decrement (D_{wu})." All curves rise during period 1, and fall during periods 2 and 3. Performance at the start and finish of period 3 is higher than at corresponding points in period 2, but not much; most of the learning clearly takes place in period 1. "There is less loss during Period 3 than Period 2 . . . presumably because less D_{Wt} is accumulated as Ss become more proficient." Performance at the end of period 1 is best for groups with 50-sec and 2-min rests; shorter and longer rests than these gave worse performance. It was expected that shorter rests would give poorer performance; less D_{Wt} is being dissipated. The fact that longer rests also lead to poorer performance is important; it cannot be accomodated within Ammons's inhibition theory. "Although D_{Wt} and performance level are correlated up to 50 sec of intertrial rest, some factor other than D_{Wt} seems to have depressed the final performance levels of the 2-min, 5-min, and 12-min groups. The amount of depression is progressively greater, the longer the intertrial rest. Inspection of curves showing D_{wu} and D_{Wp} as a function of distribution . . . indicates that changes in

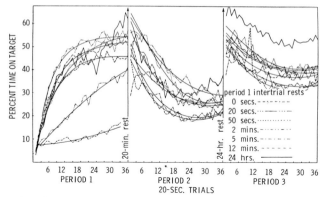

Figure 4-7. The effect of different intertrial rest periods on pursuit-rotor performance. Taken with permission from Ammons (1950).

them are not directly related to this depression." When D_{Wt} was plotted against distribution, it was found that the longer rest groups performed unexpectedly poorly. "The poorer performance of the longer rest groups indicates that a depressing factor may be operating, perhaps the same as that influencing performance levels at the end of Period 1. Whatever is depressing performance in Period 3 has an effect about as great as that produced by allowing no rests at all. The 5-min and 12-min groups do not perform much better than the continuous practice group."

D_{wu} also does not behave quite as predicted. As far as period 2 is concerned, all is well; "initially in Period 2, there is progressively less D_{wu}, the longer the Period 1 intertrial rests." For the beginning of the third period, Figure 4-8 shows the departure from expectation; D_{wu} is a curvilinear function of distribution, rather than a linear one. "The changes in D_{wu} from Period 2 to Period 3 do not parallel levels at the end of Period 1, losses during Period 2 and 3, or levels at the start of finish of Periods 2 and 3. The changes in D_{wu} therefore are not associated directly with whatever is depressing the performance of the 5 and 12-min groups." (Ammons, 1950a, p. 184.)

Ammons sums up by saying that "it would seem that two factors may be operating, one leading to better performance with greater distribution up to 50 sec or 2 min between trials, and the other leading to poorer performance with greater distribution, especially beyond two min between trials. The two factors would then work to produce the present curves showing performance levels corrected for D_{Wt} and D_{wu} as best with 50 sec or two min between trials, i.e. with best performance (or least D_{Wp}) at intermediate levels of distribution." Ammons suggests one possibility, namely that the poorer showing of the groups having

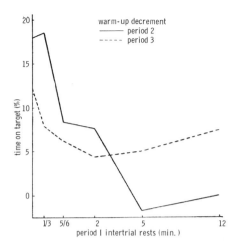

Figure 4-8. Warm-up decrement as a function of distribution of practice. Taken with permission from Ammons (1950).

longer rests might be due to the testing of performance level by introducing continuous practice periods; from what is known about stimulus generalization gradients, it could be predicted that the longer the period 1 rests, the more different would the continuous practice appear to Ss. Another hypothesis is given for the unexpected results of period 1 performance; "Perhaps the failure of distributions greater than 50 sec to lead to better performance in Period 1 is due to generalization or to interference." Longer rests permit of more activities, and hence more interference. All these are possibilities, but they do not of course form part of the original system of hypotheses and "assumptions."

In yet another experiment, Ammons and Willig (1956) investigated the effects of switching performance from massed to distributed practice and vice versa. Four groups of 26 girls were tested according to a design in which two groups, continuous and distributed, were subdivided so that half continued in their previous mode, while the other half was switched. All Ss practiced for 90 min in a training period, then practiced for 20 min in a test period. Continuous practice consisted of massed practice for 10-min periods, followed by 20-min rests; distributed practice consisted of 1-min practice periods separated by 2-min rest periods. Figure 4-9 shows the results, as far as performance is concerned, and Figure 4-10 shows some derived measures. D_{wu} does not, as expected, decrease with increasing proficiency or duration of practice. There is little D_{Wp} at the end of the first 10-min session (minute 1 in Figure 4-10), and what little there is declines to nothing by the end of period 1 (minute 11 in Figure 4-10). This is contrary to expectation, as an increase in D_{Wp} rather than a decrement would have been predicted.

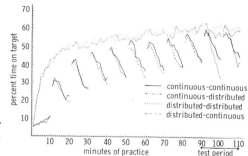

Figure 4-9. Mean performance of four practice groups. Taken with permission from Ammons and Willig (1956).

Furthermore, there is no demonstrable carry-over effect on any D_{Wp} from continuous to distributed practice. "Thus the two methods agree in showing little or no permanent work decrement." D_{Wt} is the only variable which behaves much as predicted; "D_{Wt} is large and may decrease slightly in amount as practice continues and proficiency increases." Ammons notes an interesting phenomenon; when Ss are switched from distributed to continuous practice, they show a marked "sensitivity," i.e., they develop much greater D_{Wt} than did either of the massed groups during the first 90 min. This may be a motivational effect, the unexpectedly long practice session reducing drive, or else it is possible that "the stimulus becomes increasingly different from that present during acquisition of the most adequate responses, and conse-

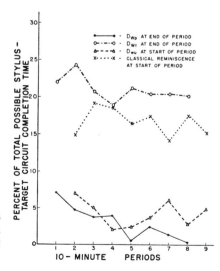

Figure 4-10. Derived performance measures as a function of duration of practice. Taken with permission from Ammons and Willig (1956).

quently fewer and fewer of these are elicited." [This latter theory has been developed by Reynolds (1945) to account for certain effects of massing and distribution in conditioning of eyelid responses.]

Ammons has made many further experimental contributions to pursuit-rotor reminiscence, but these will be discussed in later chapters under the appropriate headings; here we have only attempted to outline briefly his general theory and approach, largely because these have been so influential over the past 20 years or so (Ammons & Ammons, 1969). We must now turn to the work of Kimble, which was carried on during much the same period of time as Ammon's, but which relied in its theoretical formulations much more directly on Hull's principles of learning. Ammons's work had been carried on, first at Iowa, then at Louisville, and finally at Montana; Kimble's work was done at Brown University and his cycle of studies was apparently initiated quite independently from Ammons's. His first report was published in 1948, and deals with reminiscence as a function of length of interpolated rest (Kimble & Horenstein, 1948). Ninety-three male students were allocated to 6 experimental groups; each S received 10 learning trials (50 sec of work, 10 sec of rest), following which the groups received varying amounts of rest (10, 30, 150, 300, 600, or 1200 sec). After another 10-sec rest interval, all groups were given trials 11 and 12, two 50-sec test trials separated by a 10-sec rest. The 10-sec rest periods interspersed among the learning trials are unfortunate; they allow inhibition to dissipate to an unknown extent, and prevent the "massed" practice from being truly "massed" or continuous. The same criticism applies to the 10-sec rest between trials 11 and 12; Kimble uses the mean of these two trials as the upper point of his reminiscence measure, but the inclusion of a short rest pause ensures that learning enters into this determination. It seems likely (although this is nowhere stated) that the rests were introduced to enable the experimenter to read and reset the clock used for timing; possibly the amount of dissipation of inhibition which could take place during 10 sec was not considered important.

The lower point of Kimble's reminiscence measure was the score on the tenth trial; as the groups differed somewhat in performance he computed this in two ways, either as a mean of all groups, or as a mean of the particular group being studied. Post-rest scores were of course always calculated for a given group. Results are shown in Figure 4-11; reminiscence is as expected a negatively accelerated increasing function of length of rest, reaching an asymptote at between 300 and 600 sec, and then declining slightly (but not significantly). The similarity to Ammons's results is reassuring (Figure 4-2). Kimble explicitly invokes Hull's concept of I_R to explain the findings, and fits a formula to the

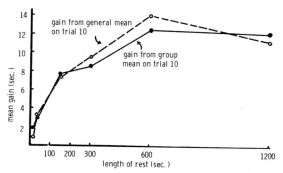

Figure 4-11. Reminiscence as a function of length of interpolated rest. Taken with permission from Kimble and Horenstein (1948).

curve by using Hull's formulation:

$$t'''I_R = I_R(10^{-qt'''})$$

where $t'''I_R$ is the amount of I_R present at any time, t''', I_R is the total amount of I_R developed during learning, 10 the base of the common logarithm, q is an empirically determined slope constant, and t''' the time allowed for rest. Figure 4-12 shows the results of fitting such a curve to the data; the fit is acceptable except for the two longest rest periods. If we consider that asymptote has been reached effectively by 600 sec, and average the two last points, then the fit is quite good. It is difficult to know if this means anything more than that the regression is regular enough to be fitted by an exponential formula; when constants in the formula (i.e., q) are based on the data to be fitted, then it would

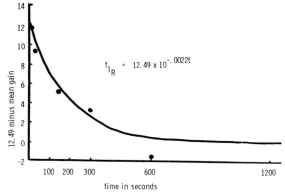

Figure 4-12. Decay of reactive inhibition as a function of time. Taken with permission from Kimble and Horenstein (1948).

require gross irregularities to prevent a reasonable fit. Nevertheless, descriptively the formula is obviously useful; what is in doubt is its relevance to the theory in question.

In his second paper, Kimble (1949a) has given the classic statement of the application of Hullian inhibition theory (Kimble calls it the two-factor theory of inhibition) as well as furnishing an experimental demonstration of its applicability. The theory distinguishes between reaction inhibition (I_R) and conditioned inhibition $(_sI_R)$; the former is essentially a negative drive state, resembling fatigue in that it results from all effortful behavior and dissipates during rest, while the latter is essentially a habit of resting, reinforced by the dissipation of I_R, which serves the purpose of drive reduction. "Since pauses, however slight, serve as reinforcements, it follows that the response of resting will become conditioned to whatever stimuli are present in the learning situation." We thus have two inhibitory factors, a drive and a habit, in which the drive component provides the motivational basis for the development of the habit. Since the general characteristics of drives and habits are known, we can predict that $_sI_R$ "must be a positive growth function of the number of reinforcements," leading to D_{Wp}. (This statement, and the term "permanent work decrement" used by Ammons to characterize this concept, must not be allowed to mislead us. Habits are permanent only if nothing is done to extinguish them; when an appropriate process of extinction, through lack of reinforcement or in some other way, is applied then of course the situation changes completely, and "permanence" disappears. Ammons made this error in arguing from his "switching" experiment that the results disproved the existence of D_{Wp}; this is true only if the changes introduced through the switching of the conditions of distribution did not lead to extinction of $_sI_R$.)

The negative drive, I_R, would be expected to accumulate at some increasing function of the amount of effort previously expended, but there is a clear ceiling to this increase. When negative drive (I_R) reaches the level of positive drive (D), the total effective drive is zero, and consequently performance would be expected to stop, in conformity with Hull's generalized equation: $_sE_R = D \times {_sH_R}.$[2] Thus a short involuntary rest pause (IRP in our terminology) will occur; during this pause I_R will dissipate, and presumably, once I_R is reduced to below the critical level, the organism driven by motivation to perform the task at

---

[2]The Hullian formulation is of course much more complete, but this does not appear to be the place for a fuller discussion. Relevant changes in this formulation are discussed by Gwynne Jones (1958) and Jensen (1961).

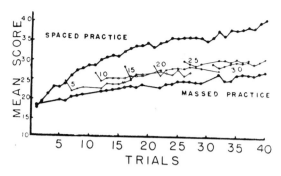

Figure 4-13. Spaced and massed practice on the inverted alphabet printing task. Taken with permission from Kimble (1949*a*).

hand will resume work and continue working until the critical level of I_R is reached again. Then it will rest, reducing I_R; start work again, increasing I_R and so on. What will eventually happen is that a state of equilibrium will be reached in which the organism rests long enough to keep I_R at or slightly below some constant specific level. Clearly, since I_R is a negative drive, acting antagonistically to the other drives in the learning situation, then the greater the motivation driving the subject to learn the task at hand, the greater the amount of inhibition which must be accumulated to produce the resting response. Kimble uses this general argument to account for the fact, observed by Ammons and himself, that there is a *decrease* in the amount of reminiscence later in the course of learning; he argues that as the S approaches the motivational goal set him by E (becoming proficient at the task), so his drive is reduced. This reduced D^+ counterbalances a weaker inhibition (D^-), and this weaker inhibition is then indexed as a low reminiscence score.

Kimble's experiment used the Kientzle (1946) inverted alphabet printing task; there were 8 groups, of which one worked under conditions of massed practice, and one under conditions of spaced practice (30-sec practice, 30-sec rest), while the other 6 groups worked under conditions of massed practice, but with one 10-min rest interpolated after trial 5, 10, 15, 20, 25, or 30. Results are shown in Figure 4-13. (Only the first 10 points after rest are plotted for the 6 experimental groups in order to keep the graph readable, and a few trials are omitted for technical reasons.) Obvious phenomena are the superiority of the spaced practice group, the inferiority of the massed practice group, and the occurrence of strong reminiscence. There is no evidence of D_{wu}, but there is clear PRD for all 6 experimental groups. Discussing this PRD, Kimble says that "what this drop probably indicates is that reactive inhibition develops more rapidly than habit." What he fails to suggest, like Ammons, is why inhibition should develop so quickly, and why, just after a rest, performance should show a downward trend when the

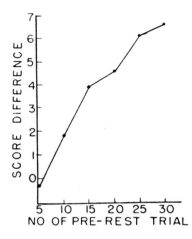

Figure 4-14. Growth of $_sI_R$ as a function of practice. Taken with permission from Kimble (1949*a*).

comparable massed practice groups, not having had a rest, show an upward trend. The reminiscence data do not show much difference between the experimental groups; Kimble argues that after 2½ min the reminiscence scores are near asymptote level, and that there is likely to have been a rapid increase at times prior to his first rest pause.

Clearly, there is a considerable amount of $_sI_R$ in the data, and these have been plotted, as a function of number of preceding massed trials, in Figure 4-14. "The result is an increasing function which shows some tendency toward negative acceleration," or just what would be expected from the growth of a habit. One may wonder why $_sI_R$ is so clearly marked here, whereas in Ammons's data it was almost completely missing. The answer may lie in the absence of D_{wu} in these data; correcting for this factor may have introduced considerable artifacts into Ammons's results, through overcorrection; where PRD is very steep corrections are very large, and if, as will be argued, PRD is quite irrelevant to reminiscence such correction vitiates the observed data. This point will be taken up again later.

Kimble and Bilodeau (1949) next took up the important question of the possible interaction between work and rest in determining performance, in an experiment employing the Minnesota Rate of Manipulation Test. 48 male and 48 female students were tested in 4 groups, giving all possible combinations of 10- and 30-sec work periods and 10- and 30-sec rest periods. The learning curves are shown in Figure 4-15; the initial difference between the two work conditions is presumably the result of a 20-sec difference in length of work period. The difference between the two 30-sec work conditions only becomes marked after 120 sec of working time, after which the longer rest condition is again superior; much the same conclusion applies to the two 10-sec work conditions. Detailed analysis of the results leads the authors to conclude that there is no interaction between the two conditions, and that their effects are additive; in a later paper Kimble (1949b), reanalyzing some published data on inverted alphabet printing, verifies this conclusion. "Given a knowledge of the separate effects of a particular variation in the length of the work and rest periods, we can predict the joint effect producible by a simultaneous variation of both factors by like amounts. It will be the sum of the two separate effects." This conclusion, of course, may not hold when work and rest periods much shorter or longer than those investigated in these studies are chosen; only a very small segment of all possible values was investigated in these studies. Within these limits, however, the conclusion seems justified.

Returning to the general outlines of his theoretical system, Kimble (1949c) reports another experiment which was designed to deal with certain critical problems. Having restated the general propositions of his theory, Kimble makes the point that I_R has a dual function; it is regarded as a drive which produces resting, and it also depresses performance, "probably by interfering with efficient muscular coordination." Kimble explains that "this dichotomizing of the function of I_R is necessary to handle a postulated instance . . . in which performance is decreased by I_R alone without the development of $_sI_R$." (An experiment reported later proves that this may in fact happen.) What precisely

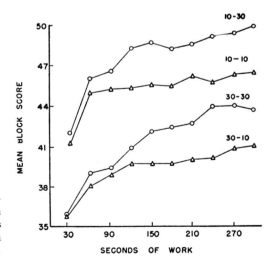

4-15. Performance on the Minnesota Rate of Manipulation test as a function of the number of seconds of practice. Taken with permission from Kimble and Bilodeau (1949).

is the difficulty? If I_R decreased performance only by producing IRPs, then it would follow that decrease in performance due to I_R would inevitably produce $_sI_R$. "It is to avoid this contradiction that we have assigned one of our major constructs two different functions." It is not entirely clear why Kimble feels it necessary to state explicitly that I_R can lead to performance decrement without producing IRPs; this would seem to follow naturally from Hull's theory. If we take a rudimentary form of his general law, then $_sE_R = {_sH_R} \times (D - I_R)$; any growth of I_R must lead to reduction in $_sE_R$, whether I_R reaches the point of equality with D (when IRPs occur) or not. Kimble's hypothesis that the growth of I_R might interfere with efficient muscular coordination does not seem in line with Hullian theory at all. However that may be, Kimble hypothesizes explicitly that "the development of $_sI_R$ is contingent upon the prior development of a certain, threshold amount of I_R." He derives 3 predictions from this hypothesis, and proposes to test them in an experiment in which Ss practice a motor task under conditions involving trials of constant length, but with different groups having different distribution of practice. After a specified number of trials, each group is given a long rest and then a final trial. Three deductions are presented.

1. Performance prior to rest will be a negatively accelerated function of the length of time between trials.

2. After rest, reminiscence will be an inverse function of length of time between trials. There are two limiting factors to this prediction: (a) if rest pauses are long enough to permit dissipation of all I_R accumulated, there will be no reminscence, and (b) the postulation of a critical, threshold amount of I_R which sets a limit to the development of this variable leads to the prediction "that groups learning under high degrees of massing may show large and identical amounts of reminiscence, if two different degrees of massing produce this limiting value of reactive inhibition. Such groups would, however, differ in the amount of conditioned inhibition acquired."

3. After the rest, at least some of the groups will show a level of performance equal to that of the most highly spaced group, i.e., will fail to show evidence of $_sI_R$. This prediction is predicated upon the notion that no conditioned inhibition may ever develop in some groups because the net amount of I_R will remain below the level required for the development of $_sI_R$ to begin. "In this case, during learning performance is depressed only by the amount of temporary I_R generated."

In addition to these predictions, Kimble raises an interesting problem, namely that of the relationship between rate of learning and distribution of practice. This, he suggests, is complicated by the rather

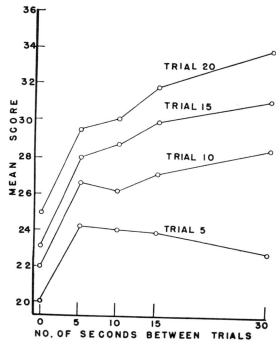

Figure 4-16. Performance on the inverted alphabet printing task as a function of the number of seconds between trials. Points plotted are mean scores of each group on the trial indicated on the individual curves. Taken with permission from Kimble (1949c).

complex relationship between performance and distribution early in practice; extreme degrees of spacing may, during early practice trials, be less beneficial than more moderate degrees of distribution. Later on in learning, however, it seems likely that rate of learning is a direct function of degree of distribution. This and the preceding hypotheses were tested by subjecting 5 experimental groups to the inverted alphabet printing task; all were given 21 30-sec trials, with rest pauses between trials 0, 5, 10, 15, or 30 sec. All groups except the 30-sec group were given a 10-min rest between the 20th and 21st trials; the 30-sec (control) group received the last trial 30 sec after trial 20. Results are shown in Figure 4-16, which shows mean scores for different trials for the 5 conditions of distribution; it will be clear that for early trials (trial 5) 5-sec rests are most advantageous, but for later trials mean scores rise pari passu with number of seconds between trials. Rate of learning is plotted in Figure 4-17, but only for trials 12 through 20; this is to eliminate the confusion predicted and found in earlier trials. Straight

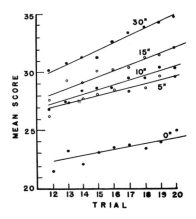

Figure 4-17. Learning curves from trial 12 to the end of the learning session. The lines through the empirical points are best fitting straight lines obtained by the method of averages. Taken with permission from Kimble (1949c).

lines fit the points well, and it is clear that slopes are progressively steeper as intertrial rest length increases.

Reminiscence data were analyzed and showed that the two groups with the shortest rest pauses (0- and 5-sec rests) showed essentially the same amount of reminscence, while groups with longer rests showed progressively less reminiscence; that of the 15-sec group is not significantly different from zero. Most important, there is no evidence for $_sI_R$ in any of the groups except the continuous practice group; "no permanent decrement in performance results from the massing of learning trials unless this massing is complete." Kimble draws two main conclustions from his data. The failure of the 0- and 5-sec rest groups to show differences in reminscence is taken as evidence that there is a critical amount of reactive inhibition that an individual will tolerate; the 5-sec rest group had the chance to dissipate I_R several times, while the 0-sec group had no such chance, yet, as shown by equal reminiscence scores, they must have developed identical amounts of I_R by the end of the 20th trial. The second conclusion is that in the case of the 0-sec rest group $_sI_R$ developed, but not in the case of the 5-sec group, although in both groups the presence of equal amounts of reminscence demonstrated the presence of D_{Wt}; this supports the points raised by Kimble in his long theoretical introduction, namely that I_R can have decremental effects on performance without generating IRPs and through them $_sI_R$.

Kimble and Shatel (1952) took up the question of the development of I_R and $_sI_R$ again, but using a pursuit rotor instead of the inverted alphabet printing task, in a particularly interesting paper. A massed and a spaced group of 10 Ss each practiced on the rotor for 15 trials a day, 5 days a week, for two successive weeks, and a total of 150 trials.

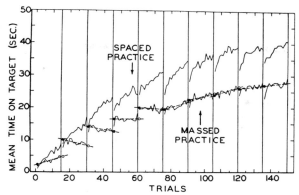

Figure 4-18. Learning curves for spaced and massed practice groups on the pursuit rotor. Taken with permission from Kimble and Shatel (1952).

For the "massed" group, each day's practice session consisted of 15 50-sec trials separated by 10-sec pauses during which the timer was read and reset. In the case of the spaced group, each practice session involved 15 50-sec trials separated by 70-sec pauses. Results are shown in Figure 4-18; the dashed lines drawn through the relatively decremental portions of the massed trials represent Ammons's correction for D_{wu}. The closed and open circles are, respectively, estimates of what performance might have been on the first trial had there been no rest, and had there been no warm up. Using this correction Kimble and Shatel obtain a graph showing the development of I_R as a function of the number of previous practice trials (Figure 4-19); also shown is the development of reminiscence uncorrected for D_{wu}. I_R is clearly greatest at the beginning

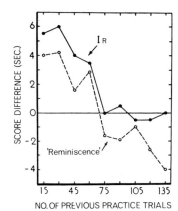

Figure 4-19. Amount of I_R and amount of reminiscence as a function of the number of previous practice trials. Taken with permission from Kimble and Shatel (1952).

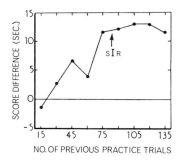

Figure 4-20. Amount of $_sI_R$ as a function of the number of previous practice trials. Taken with permission from Kimble and Shatel (1952).

of practice, and declines to zero by the 75th trial; reminiscence actually becomes negative, largely because of warm-up decrement which depresses performance during the first one or two trials. $_sI_R$ development is shown in Figure 4-20; as predicted it is negatively accelerated and asymptotic. Note that in this study, as in Kimble's earlier ones, the "massed" practice is not truly massed, containing as it does short rest pauses introduced for practical reasons; the observed rates for the development of I_R and $_sI_R$ might have been somewhat different had massing been truly continuous. It is not likely, of course, that corrections so introduced would have been very large.

Kimble pioneered another important aspect of work on the application of Hullian theories to pursuit-rotor work when he investigated the transfer of work inhibition in motor learning (Kimble, 1952). The question raised is: Is the inhibition produced by a given task general or specific, i.e., is it due to some form of localized muscle fatigue, or is it of central origin, and thus likely to generalize to similar performance carried out by different muscle groups? Skill acquired through the mechanism of bilateral transfer seemed to provide an answer to this question, in that a motor response learned without overt participation of the muscles used to perform it can be tested for reminiscence, and compared with the same response learned and tested immediately, without rest pause. Two groups of Ss were tested; both were given 60 10-sec trials on the pursuit rotor, the 60 trials being divided into two blocks of 30 massed trials each. Both groups performed the first 30 trials with the nonpreferred hand, and the second 30 trials with the preferred hand; however, group 1 received 5-min rest between sets of trials, group 2 received none. Results are shown in Figure 4-21; group 1 shows clear evidence of reminiscence, while group 2 does not. Thus the evidence indicates that the typical decremental effect of massed practice is general in that it transfers to muscle groups not actually exercised in the build up of decrement.

In a last paper related to the topics here discussed, Kimble (1950) again used the pursuit rotor. He put forward two hypotheses.

1. I_R can only grow to a value determined by the positive drive under which the S is working; this restricts the amount of reminiscence which can be obtained. If drive/motivation is increased, then more I_R can be tolerated, and greater|reminiscence should be found. An effort was made to produce greater drive by testing Ss together, two at a time, and announce their respective scores; in this way Kimble thought that the S with lower scores would become more highly motivated than the S who was "winning." The person with the lower score would conse-quently be expected to show greater reminiscence scores.

2. Taking up the theme of his 1949 article, Kimble argued that $_sI_R$ would not develop except under conditions of extreme massing contin-ued for several minutes; it should thus be possible to find a work–rest sequence which generated I_R but did not result in $_sI_R$.

Kimble used a total of 36 Ss, divided into two groups differing in the length of the practice trials and the length of the intertrial rest period, but receiving the same amount of practice and the same amount of rest. The first group practiced for 5 min and rested between practice sessions for 6 min; each of the 5-min sessions consisted of 5 50-sec trials separated by 10-sec rest pauses. The second group of Ss practiced for 50 sec and rested for 60 sec during trials. Figure 4-22 shows the results; the dashed lines and the solid circles show the Ammons' correction for D_{wu}.

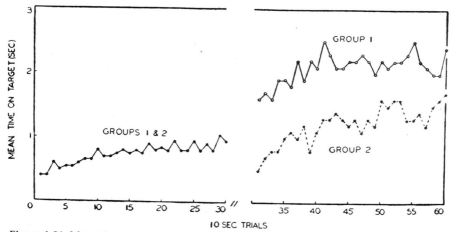

Figure 4-21. Mean time on target (a) during learning with the left hand (both groups), and (b) during test of group 1 after a rest and group 2 after no rest when practice is with the right hand. Taken with permission from Kimble (1952).

There is no evidence for $_sI_R$ under these conditions, and Kimble argues that longer periods of massed practice would be required to show such effects. Kimble and Shatel (1952) found evidence that something like 30 min of massed practice were in fact needed to produce evidence of $_sI_R$; none was found after 15 min of massed practice. Kimble argues that conditioned inhibition is not easily demonstraed, and that it is unlikely that it plays an important part in most laboratory investigations.

It is doubtful that this conclusion can be accepted. There are several features of Kimble's work which would, on his own showing, invalidate his conclusion.

1. He argues that "extreme massing" is necessary for $_sI_R$ to occur, yet massing is not "extreme" at all as 50-sec practice trials are followed by 10-sec rests; this makes it doubtful that his experiment is really relevant to the problem in hand. One would require to know what would have happened to $_sI_R$ if these rest pauses had been omitted.

2. Conditions of spaced practice used in this experiment were almost certainly less than optimal, and probably involved some growth of I_R and possibly of $_sI_R$ as well. Spacing more extreme than 50-sec trials, with 60-sec rests, might have produced a higher "ceiling" than that shown in Figure 4-22.

3. Conditions of high motivation, on Kimble's own showing, are likely to delay the appearance of $_sI_R$, by delaying the occurrence of the equality $D = I_R$. Thus the conditions of high motivation prevailing in this experiment would work against the early appearance of $_sI_R$.

These are theoretical objections, but they receive much support from Eysenck's (1956) experiment in which massed trials were truly massed, i.e., practice continued for 3 5-min periods without breaks other than the 10-min rests introduced between periods, while spaced practice consisted of 10-sec trials separated by 30-sec rest pauses. The results presented in Figure 1-8 have already shown that $_sI_R$ is clearly present after 5 min of massed practice, whether we correct by the use of Ammons's backward extrapolation or not. These subjects worked under conditions of low drive, thus making the appearance of $_sI_R$ early on in practice more likely. In view of these arguments and experimental demonstrations it may be safer to consider Kimble's conclusions as applying only to rather special conditions, and not being universally true. We shall return to the question of the "conditioned inhibition" hypothesis in a later chapter.

As regards the effect of motivation, it was found that as expected the "losers" had throughout higher reminiscence scores than the "winners"; this is interpreted in line with the hypothesis that high motiva-

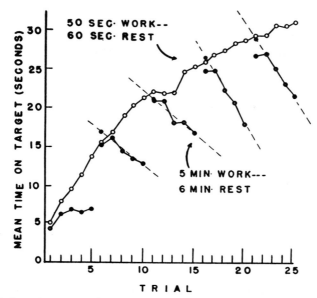

Figure 4-22. Learning curves for the pursuit rotor, using groups differing in length of practice trials and length of intertrial rest periods. Taken with permission from Kimble (1950).

tion permits Ss to store up more I_R. Kimble refutes the alternative hypothesis that poor learners might tend to have greater reminiscence; correlations between reminscence and level of performance are positive rather than negative. It is also interesting to note that the "losers" tend to improve more than the "winners"; their performance increases until they catch up. This might be interpreted in terms of Hull's system as another effect of their hypotheticated greater drive. We shall return to a discussion of this experiment in a later chapter dealing with the effects of motivation.

While this chapter is devoted to the work of Ammons and Kimble, both of whom pursued large-scale programs of investigation into pursuit-rotor reminiscence, and who jointly built up an impressive theoretical framework widely used by their successors, space must nevertheless be found for a study by Irion (1949) which appeared around the same time, and which attacked the same problem that Ammons and Kimble had set themselves. Irion was concerned with reminiscence as a function of length of rest, and length of pre-rest practice; he used 25-sec trials separated by 5-sec rest pauses, and carried out two separate studies. In the first, he varied the number of pre-rest trials (10, 20, 30, or 40), keeping the length of the rest period constant at 5 min (except for

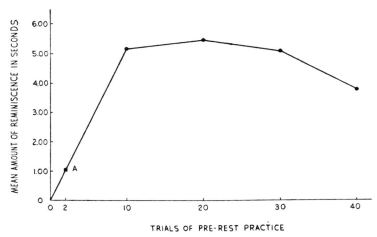

Figure 4-23. Reminiscence on the pursuit rotor as a function of number of pre-rest trials. Taken with permission from Irion (1949).

one 40-trial group which received no rest at all). Figure 4-23 shows the results. (Point A in the figure was obtained from an additional small group of Ss who had two pre-rest trials.) In the second experiment, Irion gave 20 pre-rest trials, followed by no rest, 30-sec, 60-sec, 3-min, or 5-min rest; reults are shown in Figure 4-24. In so far as they are comparable with Ammons's and Kimble's data, they are obviously very similar; replication of results is very welcome in a science as insecure as psychology, and is seldom as clear-cut as in this field.

Irion appears to have been the first writer to have noticed the fact that some Ss do not appear capable of learning to perform on the pursuit rotor. "In order to avoid the inclusion of such Ss in the experiments, a criterion was established for the selection of Ss. Any S was discarded from the experiment if, after 10 trials, he had failed to attain a score of 1.00 sec on any single trial and provided that he was not, by the end of the 10th trial, making the orthodox circular following motions." Some 3%–4% of the Ss were excluded on these grounds; unfortunately it is not quite clear from the wording what happened to Ss who failed to reach the score of 1.00 sec on target, but who made the correct type of movement. Eysenck (1964) appears to have been the only other worker in this field to have excluded Ss on the basis of absence of learning, his criterion of learning being "a score of at least one second on target during at least one of the 30 ten-second periods which constituted the pre-rest practice period." It would seem advisable for all workers in this field to adopt some such criterion as that suggested by Irion, or by

Eysenck. It would also seem important to investigate the nature of the disability affecting such incapable Ss.

Is it possible to summarize the contribution made by Ammons and Kimble to the investigation of reminiscence? They brought together the facts and rather vague notions of Kraepelin and the earlier investigators whose studies we have summarized in previous chapters, and related them, more or less explicitly, to the theoretical system of Hull; in this way they succeeded in producing a model of motor learning and reminiscence which had a considerable amount of consistency, and which in turn made possible the quantification of several of the constructs used, such as I_R, $_sI_R$, and D_{wu}. In doing this, Ammons and Kimble isolated many of the important variables which determine the appearance of these phenomena—length of pre/rest work, length of rest, distribution, motivation, and so forth. This miniature model attracted a great deal of attention, and many experimenters decided to take a hand and investigate various aspects of the model. These are important contributions, but there are also certain criticisms to be made. The most important of these is perhaps the neglect by these writers of alternative theories and possibilities; there is little indication in their papers that other explanations were feasible, and had indeed been put forward, and that an experimental decision between these possibilities would be desirable. Fortunately the particular form which the Hull–Ammons–Kimble theory has taken makes it easy to "substitute other theoretical

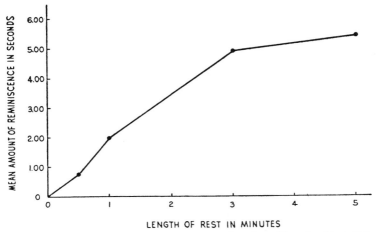

Figure 4-24. Reminiscence on the pursuit rotor as a function of length of test. Taken with permission from Irion (1949).

concepts with a minimum of fuss, and allows these alternative concepts to benefit from the quantification that has taken place. Thus if we prefer a "consolidation" theory (Eysenck, 1965) to an "inhibition" one, we can use the data on the growth of I_R to make an estimate of the growth of consolidation. Details of this proposal will be worked out later, but it seemed important to mention this point here; many readers no doubt know that Hullian inhibition theory has fallen on lean times, and may consider that a detailed recapitulation of its intricacies and applications to these particular phenomena is of little current interest. This is not so. Quantitative details and laws remain even after the demise of the theory which gave rise to the measurements in question; the substitution of Einstein's theory for Newton's does not invalidate the general measurements and laws accumulated during the preceding three centuries. If we find the inhibition theory unacceptable nowadays, we can nevertheless retain the facts on which it was built, using them as building stones for a hopefully better theory.

PART II

The Failure of the Grand Design

CHAPTER 5

Reminiscence and Motivation

The experiments described in this chapter are of particular interest, for two reasons. In the first place, reminiscence seems to be a particularly stable and sensitive index of motivation; the well-known difficulty of finding many such indicators suggests that we should cherish those we have found with particular care. In the second place, the use of motivation as the independent variable in our experimental design enables us to perform what seem crucial experiments to decide between the inhibition and the consolidation theories.

Kimble's (1950) paper, already discussed, is the first to link the problem of the effects of motivation on reminiscence with Hull's theory, and predicts that motivation-produced differences in tolerance for I_R are responsible for differences in reminiscence. His demonstration may be criticized for subjectivity; it will be remembered that he used competition between two Ss as his experimental method for producing motivation, assuming that the "loser" would be more highly motivated than the "winner." This assumption remains unproven; one might just as easily argue that the loser would lose heart and that it would be the winner whose motivation would increase. Both phenomena are (anecdotally) well known in sport; possibly there are complex interaction effects with personality, ability, and the actual size of the gap between winner and loser. Thus a narrow gap may act as an incentive for the loser, a wide gap may serve to discourage him. Thompson and Hunnicutt (1944) have shown that while praise (success) motivates introverted children, blame (failure) motivates extraverted children; it is not impossible that "winning" and "losing" in pursuit-rotor competition may similarly motivate introverts and extraverts differently. Kimble may of

131

course be right in his assumption, but it remains an assumption; there is no empirical support to back it up. It might have been better had there been an unmotivated control group, i.e., a group performing in isolation, and without the motivating condition of competition.[1] Kimble's theoretical development, although historically very important, is at points less clear in the predictions which can be derived from it than one might wish; we will return to this point when discussing alternative theories to the inhibition hypothesis.

Of particular interest in this connection is a paper by Wasserman (1951) in which he took up Kimble's theory, and reported an experiment specially designed to test the role of motivation. (A year later, Wasserman, 1952, followed this empirical study up with a theoretical paper which, however, adds little to Kimble's development and slurs over many of the difficulties which the inhibition theory encounters.) Wasserman used two motivating conditions, produced by task-oriented and ego-oriented instructions, and employed the inverted alphabet printing task. For both the high-drive and the low-drive condition, Wasserman utilized 11 groups, of which one worked under massed conditions, one under optimal spaced conditions, while 9 groups worked under conditions of massed practice except for the introduction of a 10-min rest after varying amounts of practice (2, 5, 10, 15, 20, 25, 30, 35, and 40 30-sec trials, respectively). The following predications were made.

1. A rest interval late in learning should be more beneficial (in terms of dissipation of I_R) for highly motivated groups than for poorly motivated groups. This is predicated upon the belief that high motivation allows greater development of I_R, i.e., the critical level of $I_R = D$ is reached later because D is higher.

2. Early in learning, before the threshold value of I_R has been reached, no $_sI_R$ should be present in either of the motivating conditions.

---

[1] Competition apparently has to be explicit to produce any effects, and there has to be knowledge of results; Nobel, Fuchs, Robel, and Chambers (1958) did not find positive effects on pursuit-rotor learning from having Ss tested in groups of 4 rather than in isolation. Verbal methods of increasing motivation may be more effective, but apparently interact with ability level; Fleishman (1958) found positive effects only in high ability Ss. Nobel (1959) found no positive results at all. These studies dealt with performance, rather than reminiscence, but they illustrate the complexity of the situation. Ellis and Distefano (1959), showed the effectiveness of urging and verbal praise on performance on the pursuit rotor in mental defectives; they failed to find differences in reminiscence, but their trials were too spaced to give very meaningful results. A general review of motivation studies of performance is given by Feldman (1969).

3. Late in learning the rate of development of $_sI_R$ should be less in the highly motivated group than in the poorly motivated group, i.e., the asymptote should be reached sooner with high motivation than with low motivation. This is predicated upon the belief that with the highly motivated group there will be less resting late in learning, and hence less frequent reinforcement.

4. The amount of $_sI_R$ late in learning should be less in the highly motivated group than in the poorly motivated group, due to the greater number of reinforcements produced by more frequent resting of the latter.

Results are shown in Figure 5-1. It will be seen that the performance of the highly motivated group was throughout superior to that of the poorly motivated group, whether we are dealing with spaced practice, massed practice, or massed practice with 10-min rests. There is no evidence of PRU for any of the groups, and hence reminiscence can be measured directly without using Ammons's correction. The existence of both I_R and $_sI_R$ can be directly derived from the figure, assuming the correctness of Kimble's theory. I_R was found to build up extremely rapidly. With low motivation, the maximum amount of I_R was reached after 5 min of work, with 93.4% of the maximum being present after only 1 min of work. With high motivation the maximum was reached after only 1 min of work! This would seem to be contrary to expectation; highly motivated Ss should reach the critical level of I_R later than poorly motivated Ss, and hence their maximum reminiscence scores should appear later in practice. Wasserman does not comment on this point.

Wasserman predicted that late in learning there should be less I_R with low motivation than with high motivation; this is indeed so. Only after 15 min of practice does the rest pause produce higher reminiscence scores for the highly motivated group; prior to this, in the 2½ min and particularly in the 5-min practice group, the direction of the difference is inverted, significantly so for the latter group. This is important, although Wasserman does not comment on this reversal. And while the results otherwise seem to bear out his prediction, we may now ask whether this prediction in fact follows from the theory. Until the critical level is reached for the low-motivated group, I_R should be identical for the two groups; after this point is reached, I_R should increase in amount for the highly motivated group, and remain relatively constant for the poorly motivated group. Figure 5-2 (Eysenck & Maxwell, 1961) shows in diagrammatic form the expected course of events. $I_{R(H)}$ shows the growth of reactive inhibition for the high-drive group; after 5½ min of practice the critical level is reached, and a series of involuntary rest

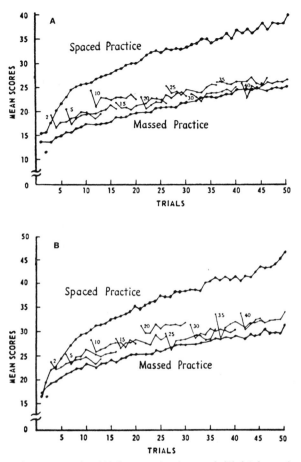

Figure 5-1. Learning curves for (A) low-motivation and (B) high-motivation groups. Taken with permission from Wasserman (1951).

pauses follow, during which inhibition dissipates until performance commences again. $I_{R(L)}$ shows identical growth of reactive inhibition, but reaches its critical level much earlier, and produces IRPs from then on; it is arbitrarily assumed that this takes place after 2 min of practice. If we now compare reminiscence scores of the two groups after 3 and 8 min, respectively, we would expect to find that after the longer practice period the high-drive group would be superior to a much more marked extent than the low-drive group. However, this model requires maximum I_R to be reached earlier for the low-drive group than for the high-drive group, and for the difference to remain constant after the high-drive group has reached the critical level; clearly neither of these conditions is fulfilled in Wasserman's experiment. Thus while he regards the results as confirming his prediction, they are in fact quite incompatible with it.

In discussing his results with respect to $_sI_R$, Wasserman makes the relevant point that part of the superiority of the spaced group may be owed to the fact that they have encountered a larger number of positively reinforced learning trials, and that their superiority may be due in part to this factor; he suggests a modification which he calls the "cumulative mean method"; in this the experimental and spaced groups are compared on trials following similar numbers of responses (letters printed) rather than on trials of the same ordinal number. In actual fact, results are similar whichever method is used. No $_sI_R$ is present very early in learning; the initial appearance of $_sI_R$ occurs later in learning with the highly motivated group; increase in $_sI_R$ levels off earlier for high-drive Ss; and amount of $_sI_R$ late in learning is less with high motivation than with low motivation. These results are of interest more in connection with our discussion of conditioned inhibition, and will therefore not be discussed further here.

The work of Kimble and Wasserman, and the theories proposed by them regarding the effects of motivation on reminiscence, were thus taken up by Eysenck and his colleagues in a series of studies which began by supporting the inhibition hypothesis, and ended up by

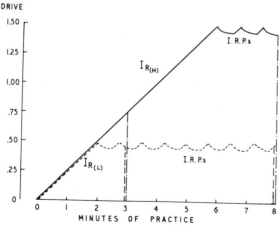

Figure 5-2. Theoretical representation of Hullian drive theory applied to pursuit-rotor reminiscence. Ordinate shows drive indexed in terms of reminiscence. Taken with permission from Eysenck and Maxwell (1961).

throwing much doubt upon its adequacy and validity. In these studies Eysenck made use of a different type of motivator to produce high-drive and low-drive groups. Previous workers had used ego- vs task-oriented instructions; competitive feelings of "Losers" as opposed to "Winners"; verbal encouragement and instructions; social vs isolated conditions. Eysenck used real-life motivation, as opposed to these laboratory-type artificial motivators; a detailed description of the method is given in "Experiments in Motivation" (Eysenck, 1964). Briefly, the low-motivation group consists of industrial apprentices at a large motor company; these adolescent boys are tested under task-oriented conditions, in that they know that the results are of interest only to the experimenter, not to the company, that the company will in fact not be furnished with the results, and that whether they do well or not will not in any way affect their future standing in the company. The high-motivation group consists of candidates who have applied to the same company to be taken on to their apprentice course, and who are being extensively tested and interviewed; they are highly motivated to do well in the experimental tests (which are included among the selection tests proper, but which are not being used for selection purposes) because the training course has a high reputation, guarantees a highly paid job at the end, and because for many young school dropouts it presents a unique opportunity of gaining access to the highly skilled working class.

Predictions concerning the superior performance of highly motivated groups as opposed to poorly motivated groups thus contrast applicants for a training course with youngsters who a year or so ago were actually accepted for the course; this comparison inevitably reduces the chances of finding such effects of motivation because (a) whatever abilities are involved in the test are possibly also involved in the tests which constitute the selection procedure, so that the low-motivation group would be slightly superior in ability, and (b) the high-motivation group is somewhat younger, and during adolescence there is probably a slight gain on most perceptual and visuomotor tests with age. Neither difference is likely to be large; age differences are known to be quite small after the age of 15 or so, and of course all the candidates would have left school and be 16 years of age or older. Also it is well known that perceptual and motor tasks of different kinds do not correlate at all highly together; neither do they show much correlation with intelligence. Thus selection on IQ tests and pegboard and other motor tests would not make much if any difference to performance on the pursuit rotor. We would thus expect there to be only slight differences, if any, due to the selection process, and those that did exist would go counter to the hypothesis that high motivation would lead to better performance. A large body of evidence has in fact been collected under these experimental conditions, ranging from eye-blink conditioning to paired-associate learning, and from mirror drawing to multiple-choice reaction (Eysenck, 1964); the results unambiguously demonstrate large and predictable differences between high- and low-drive groups on these and many other types of test. It seems quite clear that the experimental conditions are such as to produce differences in motivation which justify us in calling the groups thus contrasted high- and low-drive groups.

The experimental design of the first in this series of studies (Eysenck & Maxwell, 1961) used a total of 120 Ss, equally divided into high-drive and low-drive groups; these were in turn subdivided into a long-practice group (48 10-sec trials, equal to 8 min of practice) and a short-practice group (18 10-sec trials, equal to 3 min of practice). Massed practice for both groups was followed by a 6-min rest period, and this in turn by 4 min of massed practice (24 10-sec trials). The reminiscence score used was: first post-rest trial–last pre-rest trial. (The data were also analyzed using reminiscence maximum (rem. max.) scores, but as this analysis gave very similar results only the orthodox scores will be used here. Rem. max. scores, as explained in detail in a later chapter, use the highest post-rest score to subtract the pre-rest score from, instead of the first post-rest score.) Figures 5-3 and 5-4 show the results.

Reminiscence scores for the groups were as follows: short practice–high drive, 0.80; short practice–low drive, 0.54; long practice–high drive, 1.51; long practice–low drive, 0.51. These are the data plotted in Figure 5-2; the diagram was of course drawn to fit the data, i.e., the numbers on the abscissa and the ordinate were put in after the data had been collected. The general shape of the curves which make up the body of the diagram was of course predicted from the theory. Main effects and interaction were all significant, as expected.

Differences in pre-rest performance between high-drive and low-drive Ss are poor or nonexistent; they are nonsignificant for the short practice group, and only barely significant (at the 5% level) for the terminal portion of the curves for the long-practice groups. This is hardly in accord with Hullian theory, according to which D should multiply with $_sH_R$, giving the high-drive group much better performance. It might be argued that the high-drive group suffers from greater I_R, once the critical level had been reached, but this argument would simply suggest that differences should be apparent near the beginning of the learning curves, and then decline as both groups reach

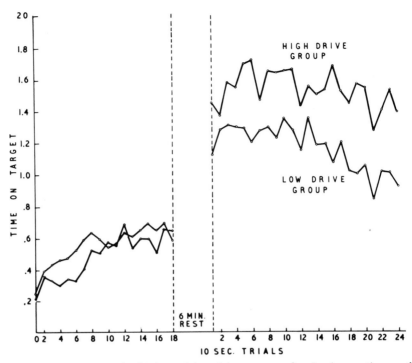

Figure 5-3. Reminiscence for high- and low-drive groups after 3-min practice on the pursuit rotor. Taken with permission from Eysenck and Maxwell (1961).

the critical level of I_R. Further comment on this point will be postponed until further evidence has been considered.

The Eysenck and Maxwell experiment was replicated by Eysenck and Willett (1961), but with two changes. As Figure 5-2 suggests, there should be no difference in reminiscence between the high-drive and low-drive groups after 2 min of practice, and maximum reminiscence should have been reached after 6 min of practice (assuming zero values for I_R at the beginning of practice). Consequently, the 6-min rest pause was introduced in this experiment either after 2 min or after 6 min of practice, and the results are shown in Figure 5-5 which also incorporates, for the sake of comparison, the reminiscence data from the previous experiment. It will be seen that for low drive the prediction is supported, in that length of pre-rest practice makes no difference between the limits of 2 and 8 min; allowing for random variations, the data fit a straight line reasonably well. For the high-drive group the 2-min practice group is also found where it should be, i.e., coinciding

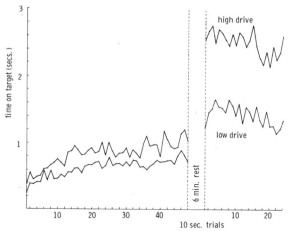

Figure 5-4. Reminiscence for high- and low-drive groups after 8-min practice on the pursuit rotor. Taken with permission from Eysenck and Maxwell (1961).

with the low-drive group. The 6-min practice group, however, shows less reminiscence than the 8-min practice group. The difference is of doubtful statistical significance, but the fact that the four points lie on a straight line must make us wary of dismissing the finding as unimportant and a statistical artifact. Clearly more evidence is required. If this straight line relationship is correct, then it must become curvilinear at values of less than 2-min pre-rest practice, as otherwise the line would cut the ordinate at a point other than zero, which is absurd.

If we accept the probability of a curvilinear instead of a linear

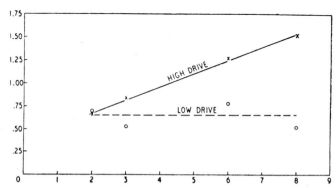

Figure 5-5. Reminiscence for high- and low-drive groups after different periods of practice (abscissa). Taken with permission from Eysenck and Willett (1961).

TABLE 5-1. Reminiscence Scores of High-Drive and Low-Drive Groups after Varying Durations of Pre-Rest Practice

Pre-rest practice period, sec	N^a	Reminiscence scores	
		High drive	Low drive
2	37	0.681	0.724
3	30	0.793	0.537
6	38	1.263	0.813
8	30	1.510	0.507
12	20	1.800	0.985
15	20	1.872	0.235

[a] Total number of subjects is 350 equally divided between drive groups.

relationship between length of pre-rest practice and reminiscence for the high-drive group, then clearly there is no reason to assume that this group has reached an asymptote at 8 min of practice, and longer periods may give even larger reminiscence scores. Willett and Eysenck (1962) replicated the Eysenck and Maxwell study again, this time using practice periods of 12 and 15-min. A summary of the results is given in Table 5-1; Figure 5-6 shows the results in graphic form. All three experiments are combined in both table and figure, and it will be seen that a very regular negatively accelerated curve results for the high-drive group. When we plot reminiscence against the log of pre-rest practice, a straight line results which shows no evidence of an asymptote having been reached (Willett & Eysenck, 1962, Fig. 2). The data for the low-drive groups do not deviate significantly from a straight line. As regards pre-rest performance, the low-drive groups are superior, but not significantly so; taking all our data together we find only random variations, with the high-drive groups sometimes superior, sometimes inferior, sometimes quite indistinguishable from the low-drive groups. We clearly cannot reject the null hypothesis with respect to the influence of drive on performance, as far as the pursuit rotor is concerned.

One important comparison was made by Willett and Eysenck (1962), in answer to the objection that the low-drive group might have appeared superior because they had been selected on the basis of motor skills, and hence not comparable in ability with the high-drive group. Comparing Ss in the high-drive group who had been accepted and rejected, these authors found no difference in pre-rest performance; clearly the criteria of selection were irrelevant to ability on this test.

Willett and Eysenck make one further point which appears to be novel. The plotted data for the high-drive groups are more clearly lawful than those for the low-drive groups, and it might seem that this could be due to the lower reliability of single trial scores for the latter groups. Accordingly, product–moment correlations were calculated for the last and last but one pre-rest trials, and the first and second post-rest trials. These were 0.62 and 0.76 for the low- and high-drive groups, respectively, pre-rest, and 0.62 and 0.74 post-rest. High drive clearly produces more reliable (less variable) performance.

The results of these experiments, as shown in Figure 5-6, are clearly lawful, but perhaps too much so; it is rare in psychology that predictions are borne out in such precise fashion. Consequently a replication of the whole research seemed advisable, particularly as the high- and low-drive groups in the Eysenck and Willett studies had been less clearly separated in overall post-rest performance than had the Eysenck and Maxwell ones; reminiscence data, depending on just one 10-sec period for their calculation, may not give an adequate picture of what is happening. Consequently a large-scale replication of these studies was undertaken by Feldman (1964b), using high- and low-drive Ss selected along similar lines to those in the studies already reviewed. A total of 600 Ss were tested, half in each condition; Ss were randomly assigned to one of 10 pre-rest practice periods, ½, 1, 2, 3½, 5, 7, 9, 11, 13, and 15 min, followed by 15 min of rest and 4 min of post-rest practice. Additional groups were tested later on, to clarify various points of interest; the results of the experiment, shown in Figure 5-7, include one such pair of additional groups which worked for a pre-rest period of 20 min. In the main, the results of the Eysenck, Maxwell, and Willett studies are replicated. The low-drive group shows an increase in reminiscence up to 2 min, followed by a roughly straight plateau up to 15 min of pre-rest practice. The high-drive group shows an increase in remi-

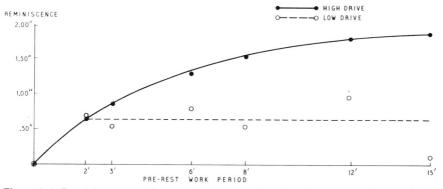

Figure 5-6. Reminiscence on the pursuit rotor as a function of pre-rest work period, for high- and low-drive groups. Taken with permission from Willett and Eysenck (1962).

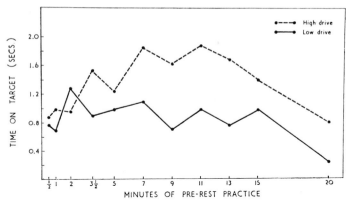

Figure 5-7. Reminiscence on the pursuit rotor as a function of pre-rest work period, for high- and low-drive groups. Taken with permission from Feldman (1964).

niscence up to 11 min of pre-rest practice, followed by a decline. This decline is statistically somewhat doubtful if we do not include the 20-min pre-rest practice period; it was added to the original experiment precisely in order to clarify this point. The data are highly significant, and as evidence for a decline in reminiscence late in learning is also apparent in the work of Adams (1952), Kimble and Shatel (1952), and Ammons (1947b), we cannot doubt that there is an inversion of the regular pattern which governs reminiscence up to about 12 min of pre-rest practice. To make assurance doubly sure, Feldman tested two further sets of high-drive Ss for 20-min practice periods. One was compared with a set of high-drive Ss tested for 11 min, using a 15-min rest pause; there was a definite decline in reminiscence with increasing length of pre-rest practice. The other group was given a 6-min rest pause, and compared with the various high-drive groups tested by Eysenck and his colleagues; again, there was a decline in reminiscence with such very long pre-rest practice periods. It is doubtful that inhibition theory can furnish us with a theoretical explanation of this phenomenon; Feldman discusses two possibilities, but neither can be said to emerge with much credit.

Having considered reminiscence, as ordinarily defined in terms of the first post-rest trial–last pre-rest trial, we may with advantage consider total post-rest performance. Pre-rest performance was found by Feldman, as by Eysenck, to be almost entirely independent of drive; statistical analysis of summated performance curves failed to produce a statistically significant difference for main effects or interactions. Hence it seems permissible to consider post-rest performance differences as a simple function of rest, and Figure 5-8 shows plots of the post-rest

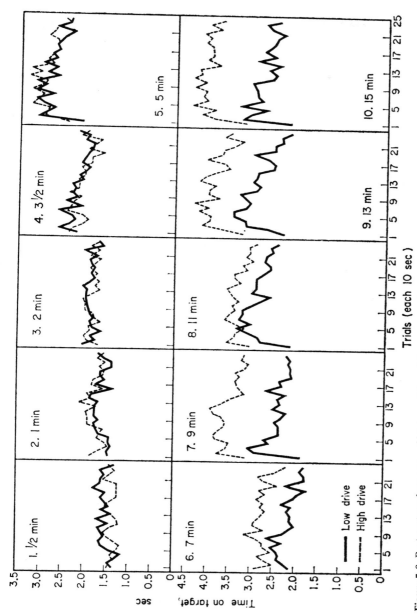

Figure 5-8. Post-rest performance of high- and low-drive groups after different amounts of pre-rest practice. Taken with permission from Feldman (1964).

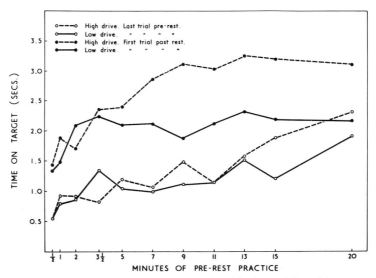

Figure 5-9. Last pre-rest and first post-rest trials of high- and low-drive groups as a function of duration of pre-rest work. Taken with permission from Feldman (1964).

performance of the high- and low-drive groups. Differentiation does not begin to be clear-cut until the 7-min practice period is reached. This suggests that total post-rest performance is possibly a less sensitive index of reminiscence than the measure plotted in Figure 5-7; however, such a hypothesis would be difficult to substantiate. In any case, these data also show that differences in post-rest performance become apparent only after some critical period of pre-rest practice has been reached. (The superior reminiscence of the high-drive groups following 3½ and 5 min of pre-rest practice is nullified by the greater PRU shown by the low-drive group.) Yet another way of looking at the data is by graphing for the high- and low-drive groups the last pre-rest and the first post-rest trials; this is shown in Figure 5-9. For both groups the last pre-rest trial show regular small increases over time, with no clear differentiation. The first post-rest trial, however, shows the flat plateau we have been led to expect from the low-drive group, from the 2-min practice to the 20-min practice period; for the high-drive group, there is a negatively accelerated growth curve ending in a plateau after 13 min of practice. The reduction in reminiscence is clearly owed to the continued improvement in performance, as indexed by the last pre-rest trial score.

One clear prediction which emerges from the general theory, and from these results, is that high-drive groups should not show any superiority when spaced practice is involved. This hypothesis was tested by Feldman (1964) in an experiment involving two groups of 30 Ss each (high vs low drive), who practiced for 15 20-sec work periods, separated by 40-sec rest periods. Results are shown in Figure 5-10; they clearly bear out the prediction. At no point are there any differences even approaching statistical significance between the high- and low-drive groups. Note the very strong reminiscence effects (comparing last pre-rest trial with first post-rest trial), and the equally marked PRD; there is no evidence of PRU. This finding is difficult to reconcile with an inhibition hypothesis; if PRD is due to inhibition, then inhibition must grow with miraculous speed (i.e., over a 10-sec period). This hardly seems reasonable, particularly when after 20 min of practice the trend of performance is still upward, not downward!

The set of experiments begun with the Eysenck and Maxwell study continues with a report by Jitendra Mohan (1966), which differs in several important respects from those discussed thus far. In the first place, his Ss were Indian students, drawn from the Punjab University in Chandigarh; this is the first cross-cultural study in this field. In the second place, Mohan used task-orienting and ego-orienting instructions to manipulate the motivational variable. In the third place, Mohan subdivided his population into 4 personality groups according to their scores on the MPI, thus reporting results for groups combining high

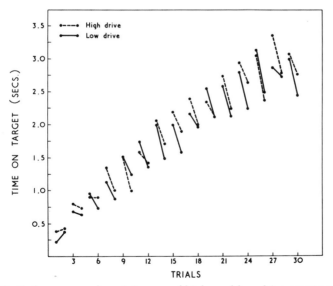

Figure 5-10. Performance and reminiscence of high- and low-drive groups after spaced performance. Taken with permission from Feldman (1964).

and low scores in extraversion and neuroticism (E+N+, E+N−, E−N−, E−N+). These groups of Ss worked for 11 periods of either 60, 80, 100, or 120 sec, and had rests of either 10, 20, 120, or 300 sec. There are thus $2 \times 4 \times 4 \times 4$ groups, or a total of 128, each containing 5 male and 5 female Ss, making a total of 1280 Ss. Apparatus and instructions were very much like those used in the Maudsley experiments, except for the specifically motivational (ego-orienting) part.

Reminiscence was scored by subtracting the last pre-rest trial from the first post-rest trial. The two extraverted groups give the highest reminiscence scores, the two introverted ones the lowest; in the order given in the last paragraph, the four groups give mean scores over all conditions of 0.28, 0.30, 0.27, and 0.26, roughly amounting to a 10% difference between extraverts and introverts in favor of the former. Motivation differences over all conditions are quite large; mean reminiscence scores at 0.35 and 0.20, respectively, for high- and low-motivating conditions. Rest periods show increasing reminiscence with increasing length: 0.23, 0.27, 0.30, and 0.30. Work periods show low reminiscence for the 60-sec trials, but little difference thereafter; this difference is entirely due to the high-drive group. Personality and motivation are both highly significant; work and rest periods only at the .05 and .01 levels, respectively. There are significant interactions for motivation × work, and personality × motivation × rest, at the $P < .01$ level. Of particular interest in this chapter is Figure 5-11, which shows the reminiscence scores of high- and low-drive groups for the 10 rest intervals, averaged over different work and rest periods. The high-drive group, as expected, is superior throughout, but this superiority is most marked in the middle, i.e., for intervals 3, 4, 5, 6, and 7; both before (intervals 1 and 2) and after (intervals 8, 9, and 10) the differences are relatively small. Both curves are curvilinear, i.e., total reminiscence (regardless of motivation) is largest for the middle intervals and smallest at the beginning and the end. With the work period being 90 sec on the average, the third interval occurs after about 4½ min of practice, the eighth after about 12 min; these figures are similar to those in the Eysenck and Feldman studies, and would seem to suggest that the interpolation of several rest pauses has not altered the general appearance of the curves for high- and low-drive subjects, and their dependence on the amount of time practiced. The actual amount of reminiscence is of course very much less, partly because of the shorter length of the work periods, and partly because of the shorter length of the rest periods.

The significant personality × motivation × rest interaction arises because high-drive extraverts are superior in reminiscence to high-

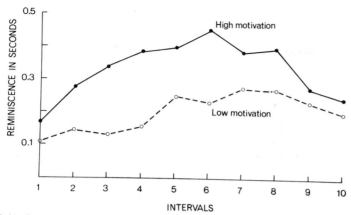

Figure 5-11. Reminiscence of high- and low-drive groups after different rest intervals. Taken with permission from Mohan (1966).

drive introverts during the 300-sec rest trials; low-drive extraverts are superior in reminiscence to low-drive introverts during the 30- and 120-sec rest trials. The 10-sec rest trials do not show any difference between extraverts and introverts in either motivating condition, although high-drive groups are clearly differentiated from low-drive groups. Altogether drive is a much more potent factor than personality, being roughly four times as influential in producing differences in reminiscence (i.e., reminiscence score differences are four times as large when comparing high- and low-drive groups as when comparing introverts and extraverts). The interaction effects are not too easy to explain on theoretical grounds, and although they are statistically significant it might be wise not to take them too seriously until replication had shown them to be a relatively permanent effect.

Mohan and Neelam (1969) reported another study incorporating both motivation and personality in their design, this time using the inverted alphabet printing task. Ss were allocated to the four quadrants of the extraversion and neuroticism personality circle; motivation was again by ego-orienting vs task-orienting instructions. Both personality and motivation were found to be highly significant. High-drive Ss had a reminiscence score of 5.0, low-drive Ss 2.9. Personality differences will be discussed in a later chapter.

In this survey we have taken together the Eysenck and Maxwell, Eysenck and Willett, Feldman, and Mohan studies because they were conceived and carried out with direct reference to each other; in doing so, however, we have omitted a few studies which appeared during the same time, and to these we must now turn. In the first of these studies,

Eysenck and Willett (1962) used a symbol substitution task with high-drive and low-drive groups, recruited as in the studies already discussed; half the Ss practiced for 3 min, the other half for 8 min, before a 5-min rest pause was introduced. After the rest pause another 5 min of practice was given. The results were clear cut: there were no drive-related differences of any kind pre-rest, the 8-min group showed greater reminiscence than the 3-min group, and the low-drive group showed greater reminiscence than the high-drive group. This last finding is of course counter to prediction and experience with other tasks, such as the pursuit rotor and the inverted alphabet printing task; no hypothesis can be suggested to explain this curious departure from orthodoxy.

In searching for possible explanations, the possibility was considered that some form of the Yerkes–Dodson Law (inverted-U relation between performance and drive) might be applicable when tasks more complex than the simple pursuit rotor were involved. As Easterbrook (1959) has shown, "the number of cues utilized in any situation tends to become smaller with increase in emotion," and in some tasks "proficiency demands the use of a wide range of cues, and drive is disorganizing or emotional." If we used a complex task requiring utilization of a wide range of cues, then (1) drive should be inversely related to performance, (2) drive should be inversely related to learning, and (3) reminiscence should be inversely related to drive. Evidence for the first two propositions has been given elsewhere (Eysenck, 1964); a test of the third proposition was attempted in another experiment by Eysenck and Willett (1966.) The task chosen was the Pathways Test (C. H. Ammons, 1955, 1960), in which the numbers from 1 to 30 are printed in random arrangements on sheets of paper, with one always in the center of the page; Ss have to trace a line from 1 to 2, 2 to 3, and so on in sequential order for 60 sec. The score is the highest number reached. There are 20 sheets, no two of which are alike. High- and low-drive Ss were tested under 3 different conditions, with no S of course undergoing more than one condition. In condition A, there were 15 min of massed practice, followed by a 10-min rest pause and 5 min of post-rest massed practice. In condition B, 5 min of pre-rest practice were followed by the 10-min rest pause and 15 min of post-rest practice. Condition C was made up of spaced practice, each 1-min trial being followed by 1 min of rest, this arrangement having been shown by Ammons (1960) not to be inferior to one containing longer rest pauses. Figure 5-12 shows the results for condition C (spaced trials); performance is better for the low-drive group, and so is learning (interaction between drive and trials.) This is in line with prediction.

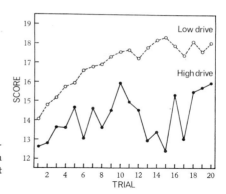

Figure 5-12. Performance of high- and low-drive groups on the pathways test. Taken with permission from Eysenck and Willett (1966).

Figures 5-13 and 5-14 show the results for the two massed groups. There is no significant difference between trials in either experiment, hence no evidence of pre-rest learning; differences between drive groups are significant, favoring the low-drive groups. As regards reminiscence, low-drive conditions resulted in significantly higher scores than high-drive conditions. Post-rest scores are significantly higher for the low-drive groups, and show a significant decline (PRD) for group A, but not for group B; in other words, long pre-rest practice is requisite for this downswing to appear. This is as predicted from Eysenck's (1965) consolidation theory, according to which the on-going and interfering effects of consolidation produce this decrement; the small amount of learning produced by 5 trials would be completely consolidated during the 10-min rest pause, while the 15 trials on condition A would not be so accommodated. Whether this experiment

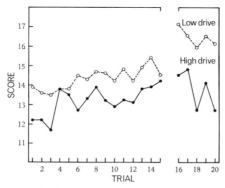

Figure 5-13. Reminiscence of high- and low-drive groups on the pathways test. Taken with permission from Eysenck and Willett (1966).

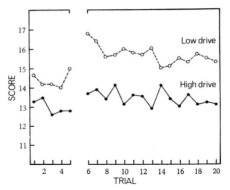

Figure 5-14. Reminiscence of high- and low-drive groups on the pathways test. Taken with permission from Eysenck and Willett (1966).

throws much light on the preceding one must remain doubtful; symbol substitution is no doubt a complex task requiring multiple cues, but there were no pre-rest differences in performance on this task between high- and low-drive groups.

Another experiment relevant to the topic of this chapter is one by Ammons (1952), in which an attempt was made to relate performance to self-reported level of motivation. Subjects followed a complex but long-continued set of pursuit-rotor tasks, containing different degrees of massing and spacing, with a 25-min rest pause intervening; work periods were quite lengthy. Ratings were required of their motivation, both before and after practice. It was found that "length of practice period had little effect on motivational levels. . . . Motivational levels remained good for long complicated conditions, and apparently were little related to level of performance in any case. No consistent relationship was found between degree of distribution of practice and motivation, so that theories attempting to account for distribution of practice phenomena in terms of changes in motivation are given no support." (Ammons, 1952.) This is an interesting and unique study; introspection is so frowned upon by modern behaviorists that it has all but disappeared from experimental reports. This is curious and probably not in the best interests of scientific study; verbal reports are "objective" in at least one sense of the word, particularly when carefully collected and quantified, as in this case. Certainly reports of high motivation, or boredom, or fed-upness, may throw light on performance data, although in this case little of interest emerged.

Ammons and Ammons (1969) review their various efforts to study the effect of motivation on rotary pursuit, including one or two unpublished studies, as well as work done by students (Ammons, Adams, &

Ammons, 1966; Ammons, Adams, Leuthold, & Ammons, 1965; Leut-hold, 1965). They used several ingenious methods for producing moti-vation, e.g., allowing Ss induced to take part in experiments lasting several hours to leave early with full credit, while others were retained and had to watch their colleagues leave; initially the performance of the groups was almost identical, but by the 4th 8-min practice period the high-motivation, early leaving group was drawing ahead, and their superiority became clear during the last 12 of the 15 8-min continuous performance periods. However, differences only extended to overall performance; there were no consistent differences in warm-up or reminiscence between high- and low-drive groups. Another method of separating high- and low-drive Ss involved taking into account their athletic achievement, higher achievers possibly having a character structure more closely geared to high motivation. No performance differences were found related to this criterion.

It may be said that the majority of experimental methods which have been used to produce "motivation" have very doubtful validity, and one should not be surprised when differing and nonsignificant results are obtained. We believe that some such "real-life" method as that used in connection with a large variety of experimental tests by Eysenck (1964) and his colleagues is indispensable for valid work in this field; the large number of positive results achieved with this method suggests that it possesses more than just face validity. Obviously it is more difficult to arrange than are within-college methods, just as the use of nonacademic Ss is more difficult to arrange than the use of sophomores. Nevertheless, if psychology is to escape from the nonre-presentative nature of the populations studied in its experiments, and the unnatural nature of the motivational conditions used, the effort will have to be made (Feldman, 1964a).

The last study to be mentioned in this chapter brings us back again to the series of Maudsley experiments which make up the bulk of material reviewed here; it was carried out by Farley (1966), again using the "selection" method for the production of high drive. His Ss were similar to those previously employed, and as his methods of testing, apparatus, etc. were also identical with those of earlier workers his results are directly comparable; indeed, he interpolated comparable results from previous research with his own to arrive at his final conclusion. This possibility underlines the great advantages in scien-tific work of standardization of all those aspects of the experimental procedure which are not relevant to the manipulation of the indepen-dent variable; if all the experimenters whose work is being summarized in this book had used identical apparatus, instructions, methods of measuring reminiscence, etc., how much easier would it be to compare

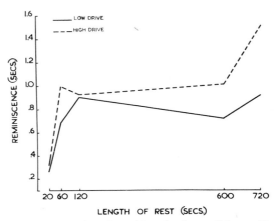

Figure 5-15. Reminiscence as a function of length of rest. Taken with permission from Farley (1966).

their results with each other, and to add results from one study to those of another!

Farley used 585 Ss in all; each S was given 8 min of massed practice, followed by a variable rest period (0, 20, 60, 120, 600, or 720 sec; one low-drive group was given a 24-hr rest period). After the rest period, Ss practiced for 15 min of massed practice. Each group contained 45 Ss, and the measure of reminiscence was the difference in score between the last 10-sec pre-rest trial and the first 10-sec post-rest trial. Analysis of variance showed that drive level was significant at the $p < .01$ level, rest interval at the $p < .001$ level. Figure 5-15 shows the main results for reminiscence scores; there is apparently no difference between groups when rest pauses are short (20, 60, or 120 sec); thereafter the low-drive group does not change in amount of reminiscence with longer rest pauses, while the high-drive group shows greater reminiscence with longer rest pauses. Even when the 24-hr rest period condition was added to the low-drive group results, no significant increase with growth of rest-pause length was found after the 60-sec rest interval; for the high-drive group, there is a significant increase ($p < .05$).

Farley extended his results by incorporating suitable data from the Eysenck and Maxwell (1961) and Feldman (1964) studies; the combined results are shown in Figure 5-16. Analysis of variance indicated significance both for the main effects (reminiscence score difference between high- and low-drive groups; rest interval) at the $p < .001$ level, and also for the drive $\times$ rest interaction at the $p < .05$ level. Second-order polynomials were fitted to the data plotted in Figure 5-16, and the results are shown in Figure 5-17. "It would appear that an asymptote

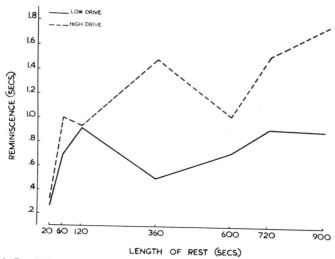

Figure 5-16. Reminiscence as a function of length of rest. Taken with permission from Farley (1966).

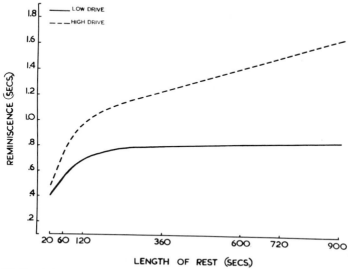

Figure 5-17. Reminiscence as a function of length of rest; consolidated results. Taken with permission from Farley (1966).

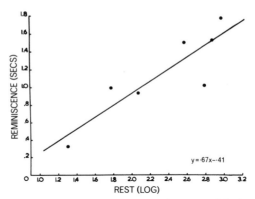

Figure 5-18. Reminiscence in high-drive groups as a function of the logarithm of duration of rest. Taken with permission from Farley (1966).

has not been reached in the high drive condition, and as a check, these reminiscence scores were plotted against the logarithms of the length of rest, with results appearing in Figure 5-18." (Farley, 1966, p. 120.) It is quite clear from this figure that an asymptote has not been reached, and that even longer rest intervals will have to be employed before the position of the asymptote in the high-drive group can be known. "The best-fitting straight line was described by the equation $y = .67x - .41$, where y is the reminiscence value and x the log of the duration of rest. The predicted reminiscence at, for instance, a one-hour rest interval would be 1.973, whereas that for a 4-hr rest would be 2.367, and for a 24-hr rest 2.898." (Farley, 1966 p. 120.)

Performance curves for the high- and low-drive conditions are reported in Figures 5-19 and 5-20. "It can be seen quite dramatically from Figure 5-19 that downswing occurs and that the downswing sections of the various curves terminate and appear to reverse, following thereupon the trend of performance of the no-rest group. Other notable features of the curves are the systematic elevation of the first approximately 5 minute post-rest period with increasing duration of rest, and the lack of pre-rest performance differentiation, which attests to the successful random assignment of subjects to groups." Statistical analysis bore out visual inspection in showing that the late practice segments of the curves all appeared to be characterized by the same stable positive slope, although in comparing pairs of curves by means of orthogonal polynomials the quadratic element was found to be significant for the longer rest periods.

A similar analysis of the low-drive group results produced essentially identical conclusions. It should perhaps be noted that as the

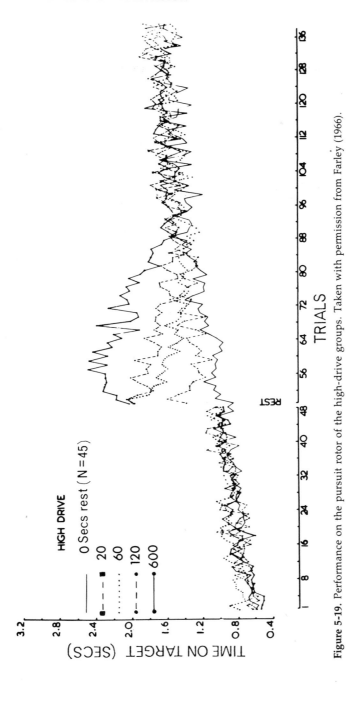

Figure 5-19. Performance on the pursuit rotor of the high-drive groups. Taken with permission from Farley (1966).

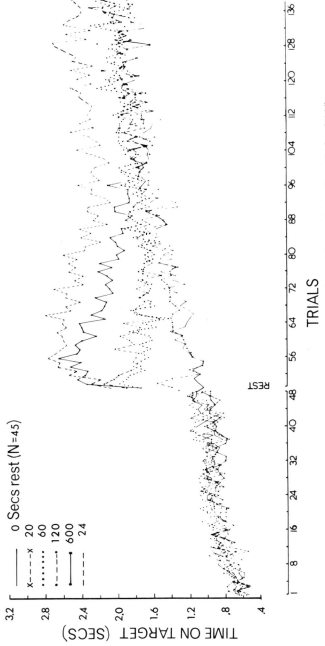

Figure 5-20. Performance on the pursuit rotor of the low-drive groups. Taken with permission from Farley (1966).

pursuit-rotor trials are not actually independent of one another, it is improper to assign the large number of degrees of freedom to the sources of variance. Geisser and Greenhouse (1958) have derived a "conservative" F test for such cases of correlated observations which effectively reduces the degrees of freedom, thus providing a more rigorous test of significance; this conservative test was used in all of Farley's analyses, as well as in the various Maudsley studies mentioned earlier.

The absence of any effects of drive on performance in Farley's, as well as in the earlier Maudsley studies, appears very clear-cut. In Farley's experiment, the 0-sec rest group (and the 20-sec rest group, which did not differ from the 0-sec group at any time) had 23 min of massed practice, probably the longest period in the literature, yet there were no even suggestive differences in performance between high- and low-drive Ss. The only study which would appear to go counter to this fairly unanimous conclusion is a report by Strickland and Jenkins (1964), in which they tested 40 male college students. Half of these were high on need-for-approval, the others low; half were tested in positive approval conditions, the others in negative approval conditions. High need-for-approval Ss, regardless of conditions, showed significantly higher rates of performance on the pursuit rotor. This might be interpreted in terms of drive, the high need-for-approval Ss being more motivated to do well on the test. Farley attempted to test the replicability of this study by administering the approval–motivation test to the high- and low-drive Ss having the 720-sec rest pause. From each group, the 15 Ss having the highest inventory scores, and the 15 having the lowest scores were chosen for analysis. There were no significant differences between high- and low-scoring Ss, nor was the interaction term significant; the only source of significance was that between high- and low-drive conditions, as might be expected. It does not appear, therefore, that the Strickland and Jenkins results are replicable, and in view of the small number of Ss involved and the doubtful status of the questionnaire used, they cannot throw serious doubt on Farley's conclusion. Having now reviewed all the studies *directly* relating to the effects of motivation on performance and reminiscence in pursuit-rotor learning, we must look at one study which has attempted to put some flesh on the theory making arousal–consolidation responsible for reminiscence, by directly measuring arousal differences following differentially induced motivation. Costello, Brown, and Low (1969) actually intended their study to provide evidence for or against their "frustration" theory of reminiscence (Costello & Discipio, 1967), but as this theory is of doubtful relevance we will here look at their results from a more general point of view; certainly the findings cannot be regarded as in any sense crucial support for a "frustration" theory.

Twenty-four female city park recreation trainees constituted the high-drive group, being motivated through a "life situation" stratagem similar to that used by Eysenck; 24 students, participating as part of their course requirement constituted the low-drive group. (It would clearly have been preferable had the two groups been selected from a more homogeneous, larger group, but it is doubtful that this small defect, which is recognized by the authors, invalidates the main results of the study.) One half of the Ss of each drive level group were given 6 min of massed practice, followed by a 10-min rest period, after which Ss were given 6 min of massed practice. The others constituted a spaced practice group, which received 36 10-sec work intervals, separated by 1-min rest periods, followed by a 10-min rest period, after which Ss were given 6 additional 10-sec work periods separated by 1-min rest periods. Also recorded were electromyograms, taken both from the active and the inactive arm, galvanic skin responses, and cardiotachograms; these measures constitute the data relevant to arousal. The following findings replicated previous work: (1) drive groups did not differ with respect to pre-rest performance level; (2) the high-drive group showed a significantly greater reminiscence effect (1.9 sec) than the low-drive group (1.1 sec); (3) the massed practice group showed a significantly greater reminiscence effect (2.3 sec) than the spaced practice group (0.6 sec).

The results from the electrophysiological measures, however, do provide important new material. Figure 5-21 shows the results for the high- and low-drive groups on the EMG measures for the active arm; Figure 5-22 shows results for the passive arm. The high-drive group is superior to the low-drive group during all three sessions, and the shift from rest to post-rest is not significantly unequal between the two groups. For the passive arm, the same facts were observed, but the post-rest differences failed to be statistically significant. For GSR measures, the high-drive group showed a lower level of resistance than the low-drive group for all three sessions, but these differences were significant only for the post-rest period. Results are shown in Figure 5-23. Logarithmic transformation of scores did not alter conclusions. Pulse rate showed high-drive Ss superior to low-drive Ss at all times, but these differences failed to demonstrate statistical significance. In view of the small number of Ss involved (12 vs 12 in the massed conditions under discussion) it is perhaps surprising that any results showed statistical significance; it would seem that the differences are very reliable to emerge so strongly with such small groups. All are in the direction of greater arousal in the high-drive group, and thus far

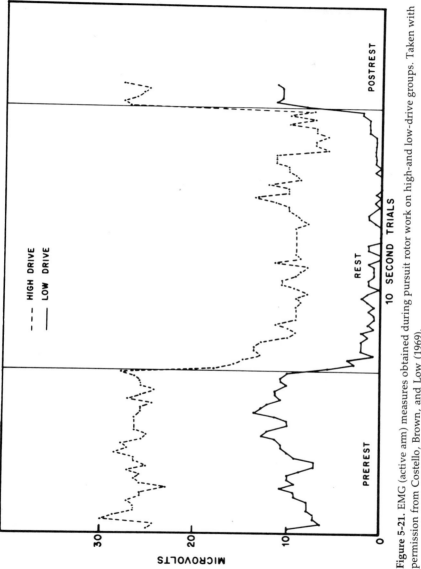

Figure 5-21. EMG (active arm) measures obtained during pursuit rotor work on high-and low-drive groups. Taken with permission from Costello, Brown, and Low (1969).

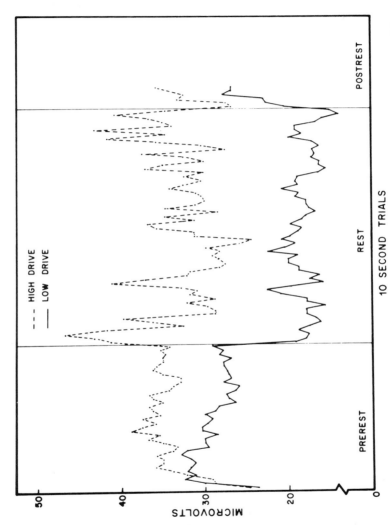

Figure 5-22. EMG (passive arm) measures obtained during pursuit rotor work on high- and low-drive groups. Taken with permission from Costello, Brown, and Low (1969).

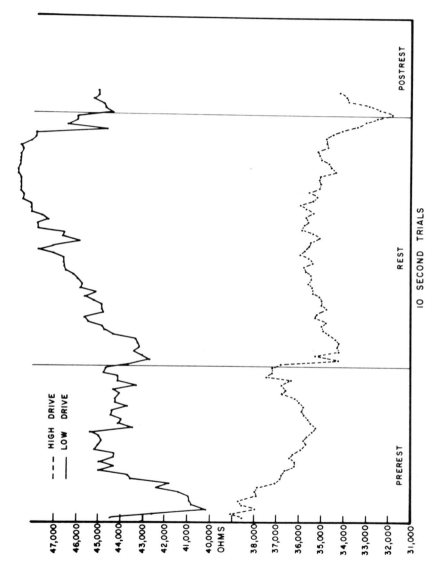

Figure 5-23. GSR measures obtained during pursuit-rotor work on high- and low-drive groups. Taken with permission from Costello, Brown, and Low (1969).

provide direct support for the arousal–consolidation hypothesis. The results would appear to be neutral with respect to the inhibition hypothesis; this hypothesis would not have predicted them, but neither would it have predicted any different results. It would require some ad hoc hypothesis to link inhibition theory with arousal differences.

We must now turn to a consideration of the deductions which can be made from the information gathered in relation to the influence of motivation on performance and reminiscence on the pursuit rotor. In particular, we shall be interested in seeing to what extent the work done supports the inhibition or the consolidation theory. Some of the results clearly can be interpreted in terms of either theory. Thus both would predict that high motivation would lead to greater reminiscence. Equally, both would lead us to expect that differences would be small or nonexistent with short pre-rest practice periods, and increase with longer practice. It is when we come to very long pre-rest practice periods that inhibition theory seems to break down, and consolidation theory might offer an explanation of the curious fact that now the differences in reminiscence between the groups decline and cease to exist. The explanation tentatively offered by Eysenck (1965) runs along these lines. The curve of learning is of the usual negatively accelerated type; thus most learning is accomplished during the first few minutes. Consolidation cannot take place until learning ceases and a rest pause supervenes; until then the learned material has to be held "in suspension" in the form of reverberating electrical circuits, or whatever may serve this particular function. There is a limit to the duration of time during which material learned can be held in suspension; consequently when the pre-rest practice period is too extended, some of the material learned drops out early in practice and is lost for the purpose of consolidation. But as the material learned early comprises a large proportion of the material learned (because of the negatively accelerated curve of learning), the total amount consolidated, will be less once the optimum length of pre-rest practice has been passed, and consequently there will be a decline in total reminiscence, and a failure for the difference between high- and low-drive groups to increase. The optimum length of pre-rest practice, on this argument, would be around 12 min, the suggestion being that learned material of the pursuit-rotor learning type (it is quite possible that the length of time in question may differ according to the particular task involved) cannot be held in suspension for longer than this. It is not clear from Figure 5-7 whether this limit is independent of motivation; it might look from that figure as if high-drive groups show a decline earlier than low-drive groups (11 min as opposed to 15 min). Clearly these figures are very approximate, and a special experiment using very large numbers of Ss would be required to settle this question. What is important here is that while inhibition theory does not seem able to furnish us with an acceptable hypothesis to explain this curious but well-established phenomenon, consolidation theory does suggest such a hypothesis. Whether this hypothesis is correct is of course another matter; there is no independent evidence on this point.

On the other hand, the detailed findings shown in Figure 5-6 can probably be handled better by some form of inhibition theory; the form such a theory would take has already been discussed. How would consolidation theory handle the data? It might be suggested that according to an individual's level of cortical arousal he can consolidate so much relevant learned material; high arousal enables him to consolidate a large amount, low arousal enables him to consolidate much less. (We are assuming a constant rest period here, possibly an optimal one.) The total amount capable of being consolidated is reached after period x for the low-drive group (x in Figure 5-6 is 2 min, but would seem to be more like 5 min according to Figure 5-8); once this critical level is reached, nothing further is in fact learned. For the high-drive group the critical period is reached much later ($x + y$ min); depending on the measure of reminiscence chosen, this might be between 12 and 15 min. High-drive groups are distinguished from low-drive groups during the pre-rest practice durations ranging from x to ($x + y$); prior to x there would not be any difference, and after ($x + y$) there would be a decline in reminiscence, leading to a lessening of the differential. Perhaps the data plotted in Figure 5-9 are the most relevant; first trial scores postrest show x for the low-drive group to be roughly 2 min, as in the Eysenck studies, and ($x + y$) for 13 min. None of the data, although derived from quite large groups, are accurate enough to narrow the range of possible values down sufficiently to be more precise.

As far as pre-rest practice is concerned, the data are not compatible with the inhibition hypothesis. According to any form such a hypothesis might take, there should be differences in performance between high and low drive groups; both the main effects and the interaction term involving trials should be significant. As we have seen, that is not so; overall there are no differences, with either the low-drive or high-drive group being slightly superior upon occasion. Never have interaction effects been observed, such as would be expected if the "critical level" of I_R had been reached at different times by the two groups. Consolidation theory does not make any differential predictions as far as pre-rest practice is concerned; this may save it from disconfirmation.

On any grounds the failure of high- and low-drive groups to be differentiated on performance is curious; not only Hull's general formulation but almost any other attempt to relate drive and performance is here put in question.

Taken all in all, the facts here reviewed tend to favor the consolidation theory, but they do not do so decisively. It is only by considering the conclusions reached in other chapters, and in particular when looking at experiments specially performed to test crucial predictions related to these two theories, that our data fall into place. An attempt to reformulate consolidation theory so as to incorporate the facts here discussed will be made in a later chapter.

CHAPTER 6

Post-Rest Upswing and Downswing

The history of the attempts to describe and explain the phenomenon of "warm-up" or "initial upswing" closely parallels that of reminiscence and indeed reveals in microcosm the history of experimental psychology. There is the rise and fall of complex theories accompanied by a shift from generality to specificity. Although warm-up has frequently been studied for its own sake, its importance in the study of reminiscence has been largely the result of the theory of Ammons (1947a) which stated that reminiscence measures as indices of reactive inhibition were distorted by the occurrence of warm-up. However warm-up had been observed long before this and so this theory will be considered later on in this chapter.

Warm-up may be defined as a temporary facilitation of performance in a task produced by previous performance of that task. Since the facilitation owing to warm-up is temporary it can be distinguished from a practice effect which is permanent. Warm-up has manifested itself in performance in two very different ways between which few authors have distinguished. Wells (1908) used the term "interserial warming up" to refer to a situation where subjects worked for five ½-min sessions separated by 2½-min rests. The later sessions were superior to the early ones. These facilitating effects were only temporary and therefore Wells referred to them as warming-up effects. However they appeared only from series to series and Wells found it necessary to distinguish this from warming-up processes occurring within a single series. It is this later phenomenon that is usually meant by warm-up.

Indeed, in his review of studies of warm-up Adams (1961) states that Wells "observed the rapid increase in initial post rest performance on a tapping task . . . identified as warm up." As we have seen Wells was very careful to point out that this was not what he observed. Thorndike (1914) is generally credited with giving the earliest clear definition of warm-up confined to a single series. He defined warm-up as "that part of an increase of efficiency during the first 20 minutes (or some other assigned early portion) of a work period, which is abolished by a moderate rest, say of 60 minutes." We shall see that these two time periods, that during which warm-up occurs and that required for the effect of warm-up to dissipate, have played crucial roles in the arguments about the underlying nature of warm-up. Eysenck (1965) has objected to the use of the term warm-up on the grounds that it implies that a particular theory (i.e., gaining of appropriate set) underlies the phenomenon. He suggests the use of the term "post-rest upswing" as being a neutral description. Such a term excludes Wells' interserial warm-up. In addition it is not really neutral. Eysenck had in mind the typical pursuit-rotor experiment in which two practice periods are separated by a programmed rest. Usually "post-rest upswing" appears to occur only at the beginning of the second practice period, hence the use of the term "post-rest." However the denial that warm-up occurs in the very first practice session contradicts the set theory, but is crucial for Eysenck's inhibition theory. Thus his term "post-rest upswing" also presupposes a theory, though in a rather more subtle way. A suitably neutral term might be "initial upswing." In this chapter we shall use the same term as the author whose work we are discussing.

EARLY STUDIES OF WARM-UP

As has already been mentioned in Chapter 1, warm-up seems first to have been described by Kraepelin's students (Amberg, 1895). Hoch (1901), writing in English, specifically uses the term warming up to describe a temporary facilitation of performance on the ergograph. "Each person was made to write three successive curves with a rest interval of fifteen minutes between. In other words the person experimented upon had to rhythmically raise the weight to the utmost, until it could no longer be stirred (the rhythm being one second, indicated by the bell signal of the metronome); then fifteen minutes rest, etc. This was repeated every day for a varied period of time. . . . In regard to warming up, . . . frequently the second curve showed a striking increase over the first, an increase which owing to its more transient character was thought to be different from the influence of practice and

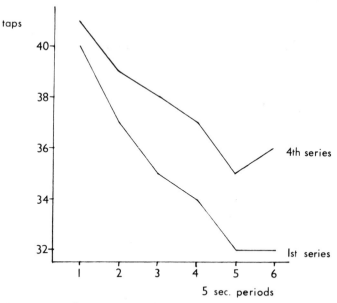

Figure 6-1. Comparison of tapping output for early and late series. Drawn after data given by Wells (1908).

which was regarded as due to 'warming up.'" This warming up is clearly identical to the interserial warm-up described by Wells (1908). Hoch reports a previous experiment in which various rest intervals were used from five minutes to an hour. The second series was consistently found to be higher after an interval of fifteen minutes than any other interval. Hoch therefore concludes that while fatigue has considerably dissipated before fifteen minutes the facilitating effects of warm-up do not begin to dissipate until after fifteen minutes. In interpretation of the warm-up phenomenon he makes the cryptic statement that "certain resistances have first to be over come before the mechanism works at its best."

Wells' (1908) experiment was very similar to Hoch's except that the subjects were required to tap a morse key rather than pull an ergograph. The subjects tapped at their maximum rate for five 30-sec series separated by rests of 2½ min. This sequence was repeated many times with intervals of at least 24 hr. Both the right and the left hand were used. The number of taps in each 5 sec of the 30-sec series were recorded. Within each series there was a steady decline in output from beginning to end, but there was a marked tendency for later series to be faster than earlier, particularly for the right hand (Figure 6-1). This was the phenomenon which Wells called "interserial warming up." A comparison of the successive 5-sec periods showed that warming up was largely due to differences at the end of the 30-sec series. Thus warm-up in this task appeared to increase immunity to fatigue. Wells also found that warm-up became more marked as the experiment was repeated. In a second experiment in which the five 30-sec series were extended to 10 he found a continued improvement (i.e., warm-up) up to the eighth series.

Matsui and Kobayashi (1935) studied warm-up in a number of tasks which they characterized as involving muscular work. In particular they studied the effects of different rest intervals. Subjects were required to grip a dynamometer with their maximum strength 5 times and to repeat these 5 pulls after various rest intervals. It was found that the longer the rest interval the earlier the maximum performance occurred. Thus with a 5-min rest warm-up was fully manifested in the second series of five pulls. It was also found that warm-up still had not dissipated after a rest of 1 hr. Maximum warm-up was found when subjects were allowed to choose their own rest interval, which varied from 6–8 min. Essentially the same results were found for tapping and the standing broad jump. In addition it was found that with practice warm-up manifested itself earlier.

The results of all these studies of very simple motor tasks seem highly consistent. A feature of all these tasks is that very little learning or practice effect is involved. The more marked appearance of warm-up in the later stages of practice is probably due to the cessation of any learning effects which would be confounded with warm-up effects. The principal process competing with warm up is fatigue. It is probably the rapid growth in the fatigue characteristic of these tasks which prevents the appearance of warm-up within the series in the form of upswing. Fatigue seems to have fully dissipated after a rest of 5–10 min. Warm-up effects, however, are still present after a rest of up to an hour. No investigations seem to have been made into how much work is required to produce warm-up in these tasks. None of these early investigators of warm-up put forward a satisfactory explanation of the phenomenon. However, there is now evidence that warm-up and fatigue in these kinds of task is basically muscular in origin. We shall present the evidence for this hypothesis later in this chapter.

Kraepelin and his students considered that mental and physical work would follow essentially the same principles, and even Hull's (1943) concept of reactive inhibition is related to the amount of physical work done. It soon became apparent that these analogies could not be supported.

Bilodeau and Bilodeau (1954) investigated the growth of inhibition when subjects had to turn a manual crank while a variable breaking

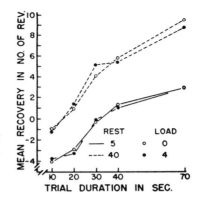

Figure 6-2. Mean difference in number of revolutions between the first 10 sec of trial 2 and the last 10 sec of trial 1 as a function of trial duration, with intertrial rest and work loading as parameters. Taken with permission from Bilodeau and Bilodeau (1954).

force was applied to the crank shaft. They investigated the effects of rest length, length of pre-rest practice, and size of load on performance and recovery after rest. Clearly, if the amount of reactive inhibition built up depends on the amount of physical work done then more inhibition should be built up when the crank is turned against a large force, and more of that inhibition should be dissipated after a constant rest. However, as Figure 6-2 clearly shows there was no difference in recovery after different amounts of physical work.

Bilodeau and Bilodeau examined the relationship between inhibition and work in other ways as well, such as instantaneously shifting the subjects from one load to another. In these experiments they also found no evidence that build up of inhibition depended on amount of physical work.

As a result of findings like these (Bilodeau, 1952; Ellis, Montgomery, & Underwood, 1952) little further work was done by psychologists on tasks in which the amount of physical work was a major variable. Thereafter, the warm-up phenomenon was studied principally in complex motor skills and in verbal learning. Although attempts were made to account for the phenomenon on these two kinds of task with the same theory, the kind of experiments carried out and the results found are, by the very nature of the tasks, rather different. It therefore seems more convenient to deal with verbal learning and motor skills separately.

WARM-UP IN VERBAL LEARNING

Experiments on warm-up in verbal learning have, by and large, been carried out within a framework of an explanation of the phenomenon in terms of set. Irion (1948) defined the warming up effect in retention in

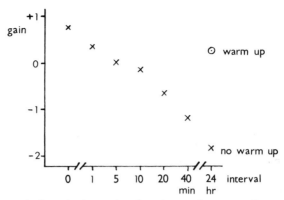

Figure 6-3. Mean gain in paired associate learning performance after varying intervals and the effect of "warming up" with a color naming task after a 24-hr interval. Drawn after data given by Irion (1948).

terms of "the greater slope of the relearning curve compared with the slope of the original learning curve at a corresponding level of proficiency." This definition requires that slopes only be compared when they are at the same level of proficiency. We shall see later that this caution is particularly necessary in the study of the warm-up phenomenon in motor learning. Irion hypothesized that warm-up was necessary because of loss of set during a rest interval. He first demonstrated that with an increasing rest interval between two sessions of ten trials on a paired associate learning list there was an increasing amount of warm-up. This warm-up was clearly due to a depression of performance on the early post-rest trials. Second, Irion demonstrated that after 24 hr of rest color naming just prior to the post-rest performance eliminated the warm-up effect (Figure 6-3) as successfully as if there had been no rest. The color naming task was similar to the learning task in that the colors to be named appeared in the slots of the memory drum where the words for the paired-associate learning task were to later appear. Thus Irion concluded that the color naming task reintroduced the set necessary for the learning task and thereby eliminated the warm-up effect during the learning task.

Other studies have further specified the warming up effects of neutral tasks on verbal learning. Irion and Wham (1951) showed that warm-up was a decreasing function of the amount of set reinstating activity.

The criterion task in this experiment was the serial learning of nonsense syllables, and the amount of warm-up needed after a rest was indicated by the rate of increase of the initial segment of the relearning curve. During the rest interval subjects had to recite three-digit numbers. As can be seen in Figure 6-4 the rate of increase of the initial segment of the relearning curve was inversely related to the amount of "warming up" activity that took place.

Hartley (1948) and Hunter (1955), in support of the set hypothesis, demonstrated that the warming up activity only produced an effect when it was given just before post-rest practice and not when it was given just after pre-rest practice. The rest in these cases was 24 hr.

Warm-up effects have been found for original learning as well as for recall. The design of these experiments is rather similar to that of Wells (1908) and the phenomenon resembles his interserial warm-up. Heron (1928) had subjects learn 2 different lists of nonsense syllables every day for three days. The temporary warm-up effect was manifested in the more rapid learning of the second list of each day. Thune (1951) performed essentially the same experiment with three lists per day for five days and confirmed Heron's findings. The within-session gains largely disappeared during the rest interval between sessions. Thune (1950) also found that color naming produced a warming up effect on the original learning of a paired associate list of nouns. He also confirmed that the warming up activity must occur immediately before the criterion task to be effective. Warming up activity 24 hr previously had no effect.

A crucial matter that does not seem to have been investigated is the

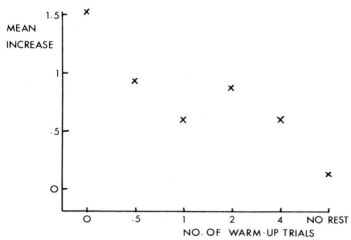

Figure 6-4. Mean increase in correct anticipations between the first and second relearning trials after a varying number of "warm-up" trials. Drawn after data given by Irion and Wham (1951).

precise nature of tasks that will produce warming up effects. If the set theory is to be made at all precise it would be necessary to know in what ways the warming up task and the criterion task must be similar and in what ways they may differ. It may be that this lack of precision accounts for the various negative findings quoted by Adams (1961). Studies by Rockway and Duncan (1952), Withey *et al.* (1949), and Hovland and Kurtz (1951) failed to show warm-up effects from color naming or number naming on nonsense syllable learning. It could well be that subtle unreported differences in the warming up tasks used by experimenters are of crucial importance.

Nevertheless, although the nature of the set reinstating activities is not clear most studies are remarkably consistent in showing a warm-up effect in verbal learning. This warming up effect, although it begins to dissipate after a mere 5-min rest is still present after 40 min [that is by comparison with a 24-hr rest, Irion (1948)]. It is not very clear how quickly the warm-up occurs. This is partly due to the nature of verbal learning experiments. One trial (e.g., a single presentation of 15 pairs of nonsense syllables) will necessarily take some time to administer. In Irion's (1948) experiment each trial took 68 sec. A comparison of curves for subjects who had either no rest, 24-hr rest, or present warm-up suggests that people with 24-hr rest reached the level of the other two groups after 5–10 trials, thus in this task warming up seemed to take at least 5 min.

The most interesting aspect of the verbal learning experiments is that some experimenters seem to have found "neutral" tasks that produce warming up effects. Neutral in this case seems to imply that no learning, or at least no transferable learning, is involved. As with the muscular tasks discussed previously the verbal learning tasks are relatively simple since, although a large amount of learning is manifested, there are no obvious effects of fatigue. The complex motor skills, and in particular pursuit-rotor learning with which the bulk of this chapter is concerned, involve both learning and fatigue, both of which are hard to separate in practice from warm-up.

WARM-UP IN MOTOR SKILLS

Bell (1942) seems to have been among the first to discuss at length warm-up in pursuit-rotor learning. He gave his subjects 1-min trials separated by 1-min rests with interpolated rests of various lengths from 10 min to 30 hr either early or late in practice. Warm-up appeared after the longer rests (1 hr or more) being particularly marked when the rests

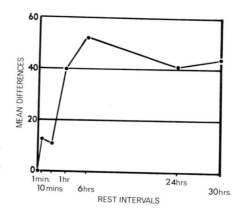

Figure 6-5. Mean differences between first and second post-rest trials after varying amounts of rest at a late stage of practice. Taken with permission from Bell (1942).

were interpolated late in practice. This warm-up manifested itself in a marked increase in performance between the first and second trial post rest (Figure 6-5). For the long rests late in practice the first trial post-rest was well below the level of the control group, having no interpolated rest. This level had been regained by the second post-rest trial. At this late stage of practice the subjects were on target about 75% of the time. There was thus much less learning to be confounded with warm-up effects.

With regard to this warm-up effect Bell (1942) reports in some detail the behavior of his subjects. "Following the longer rest intervals both early and late in learning, the subject made several preliminary adjustive movements as he resumed his task, such as changing stance, changing his grip of the stylus, and changing the position of the hand not being used. It seemed necessary, too, for him to become oriented again to the experimental situation—that is the room in which the test was given, the apparatus, and the experimenter—and to his own level of aspiration." Although he is never very explicit about the underlying mechanism of warm-up, from his observations of the subjects and his use of the term "readjustment" to describe the rapid rise in the post-rest trials it is clear that Bell favors an explanation of warm-up in terms of the reacquisition of an appropriate set lost during long rests. He allows the possibility that warm-up might be the result of the rapid relearning of short-lived habits. However it is doubtful whether such a notion would differ in practice from the theory of set. In addition the paradoxical concept of a short-lived habit is of little value.

In 1947 Ammons wrote his classic paper on the acquisition of motor skills. The importance of this paper in providing a framework for the future discussion of pursuit-rotor learning has already been demonstrated in an earlier chapter. However the paper was also very much concerned with warm-up phenomena. Ammons assumed that warm-up is manifested in the rapid initial rise in performance immediately after a rest and that this warming up is completed when the post-rest performance reaches its maximum. His speculations on the mechanisms underlying warm-up are minimal and are largely derived from Bell (1942). " . . . warm up decrement is owing to loss of 'set,' consisting principally of various advantageous postural adjustments." Nevertheless, Ammons makes a large number of "assumptions" and "deductions" about the relationship between warm-up various experimental parameters such as length of rest and amount of pre-rest practice. Support for these assumptions and deductions is derived from a large number of previous studies by Ammons and others. Indeed in many cases the assumptions and deductions are little more than descriptions of results already obtained, although they do also provide further information about what Ammons means by "set." Essentially Ammons assumed that "set" is learned and forgotten in much the same way as any other kind of material. Thus the amount of set acquired is a negatively accelerating function of the amount of practice (assumptions 1 and 2) and the amount of set lost is a negatively accelerating function of the length of rest (assumption 5). From Bell's data Ammons concluded that set is mostly lost after 1-hr rest and completely lost after 6 hours rest. Finally (assumption 4) Ammons suggested that repeated reacquisition of set will facilitate that reacquisition. The various deductions and assumptions additional to those already mentioned merely attempt to relate the basic assumptions to actual data. Ammons's assumptions about the learning and forgetting of set exactly parallel assumptions made about learning and forgetting of other kinds of material (e.g., Ebbinghaus, 1885).

One might at first wonder why set, if it is learned and forgotten in a manner so similar to other kinds of material, should be distinguished from the learning of the basic motor skill. However, it is precisely the interesting thing about motor-skill learning that it is by comparison with other kinds of material so abnormal. During continuous practice learning is extraordinarily slow and during rest there seems almost no evidence of forgetting and indeed performance is often considerably enhanced by rests. Nevertheless with regard to Ammons's account of "set" there is nothing in the various properties he assumes that are specific to the learning of "set" rather than anything else. Indeed, apart from the brief reference to advantageous postural adjustments already quoted, in justifying his various assumptions he never mentions what set might be, except something that is learned and forgotten in a standard way (e.g., at the start of practice the learning of "set" will be more rapid). It seems therefore justifiable to conclude that Ammons's theory of warm-up is largely irrelevant to the theory of set reinstatement. The theory is basically concerned with describing the form of performance curves associated with various amounts of practice and rest and to separate out the hypothetical underlying processes: warm-up, habit strength, reactive inhibition, and conditioned inhibition. It is this latter aspect of Ammons's theory that has most influenced later work, and in particular the correction he proposed for estimating the amount of reactive inhibition with the masking effects of warming up removed. Unfortunately with only one measure of performance it is impossible to separate out unequivocally the effects of four underlying processes. Ammons suggests that the warming up process has ceased when the post-rest performance curve reaches its maximum. However, there are clearly many other possible combinations of the underlying processes that could result in maximum performance. Only independant control of the underlying variables can resolve this matter.

This problem was highlighted in a paper by Adams (1952), showing that the sharp initial rise in performance known as warm-up could be obtained from just two underlying processes, increasing performance and increasing inhibition. He assumed that performance increased as a negatively accelerating function of the number of trials and that the inhibition function was ogival, i.e., inhibition first increased slowly, then rapidly and finally leveled off at an asymptote. The combination of two such processes results in the characteristic post-rest performance curve associated with massed practice on the pursuit rotor. However if warm-up is due to inhibition processes then it should not appear in conditions where inhibition does not occur, i.e., suitably distributed practice conditions. Adams therefore compared groups having massed and continuous practice. Both groups practiced for 6 min per day for five days. For the distributed practice group the 6 min were divided into 36 10-sec trials separated by 40-sec rest intervals. For both groups there were clear signs of warm-up during the first 3 or 4 post-rest trials (Figure 6-6) and Adams therefore considered that his hypothesis that warm-up was related to the growth of inhibition had been rejected. He also found no evidence for Ammons's hypothesis that with an increasing number of practice sessions the amount of warm-up decreases.

Barch (1952) also looked at warm-up under conditions of massed and distributed practice. Both groups practiced for 10 1½-min periods separated by 5-min rests. For the distributed practice group the 1½-min period consisted of 6 15-sec trials separated by 45-sec rests. Once again

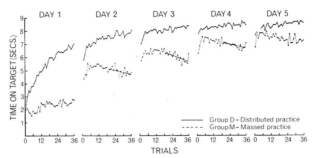

Figure 6-6. Comparison of "warm-up" for groups undergoing massed or distributed practice on the pursuit rotor. Taken with permission from Adams (1952).

both groups showed a sharp increase in performance during early post-rest practice. If anything this warm-up was greater for the distributed practice group.

Undeterred by these negative findings Eysenck (1956) also put forward an explanation of warm-up in terms of inhibition. Like Ammons Eysenck's principal interest was to use reminiscence as a measure of reactive inhibition and therefore it was necessary for him to know in what way and to what extent the warm-up phenomenon would interfere with his measure of reactive inhibition. Eysenck proposed a very detailed theory to account for warm-up, which was deliberately opposed to Ammons's "set" theory. Since, as we have seen, Ammons's was a "set" theory in name only, it was necessary for Eysenck to make suggestions about what a theory specifically concerned with set might involve so that he could contrast it with his inhibition theory.

Eysenck's theory of warm-up was based on Hullian learning theory and the extensions of it made by Kimble (1949, 1952). During massed practice, reactive inhibition, conceived of as a negative drive (I_R), is thought to build up. Eventually this negative drive is so strong that a brief involuntary rest pause is enforced (IRP). During the IRP the reactive inhibition dissipates and work can resume. However drive reduction of this kind is reinforcing and through this reinforcement the habit of not working becomes strengthened. This habit, known as conditioned inhibition $(_sI_R)$ does not dissipate during rest and results in a permanent work decrement. However, after a sufficiently long programmed rest all reactive inhibition will have dissipated. Thus at the beginning of post-rest practice the habit of not working will not be reinforced by the reduction of I_R and will therefore extinguish. Thus "warm-up" appears as the result of the extinction of conditioned inhibition, the habit of not working.

Thus a theory of the learning and extinction of a negative habit is contrasted with Ammons's theory of the extinction and learning of positive habit. Through the admirable symmetry of learning theory these two alternatives are, in practice, hard to distinguish. For example, Eysenck's hypothesis H2 "post-rest increment due to the extinction of conditioned inhibition through a failure of reinforcement will be more rapid and more extensive after the second rest pause than after the first" is effectively the same as Ammons's assumption 4, "the more times practice is resumed the easier it will be to warm-up".

There are two major differences between Eysenck's inhibition theory and Ammons's "set" theory. First, following Adams (1952) Eysenck predicts that there should be no warm-up after distributed practice. Eysenck found evidence in support of this (Figure 1-9) which seems directly to contradict that found by Adams (1952) and Barch (1952). This contradiction has yet to be resolved. The second major difference arises because Eysenck, unlike Ammons, has attempted to define a specific property of "set." Eysenck does not deny that warm-up due to set, particularly in verbal learning, occurs, but "considering the hypothesized nature of warm up, i.e., the 'shaking down' of the organism, both mentally and physically, into well practiced attitudes and muscular sets, that is quite reasonable; we would expect the organism to be 'back on the job' within ten or twenty seconds," (Eysenck, 1956). Thus upswing lasting 20 sec or less is due to the reintroduction of set while upswing lasting more than 20 sec is due to the extinction of conditioned inhibition. Once again he produces data which confirm his inhibition hypothesis since the period of warm-up is clearly a minute or more (Figure 1-9). However in this respect too data from other sources do not give such clear cut results. Both the massed and distributed groups tested by Adams (1952) show periods of warm-up lasting only 10 to 40 sec (Figure 6-6).

In his review of warm-up decrement Adams (1961) criticized Eysenck's inhibition theory on the grounds that apart from Eysenck's data there were at least six other studies in which warm-up appeared in sessions of distributed practice. He therefore concluded that Eysenck's results were anomalous and that an inhibition theory of warm-up in pursuit-rotor learning cannot be supported. He did not consider the second aspect of Eysenck's theory; the length of the period of warm-up.

Feldman (1963) attempted to refute Adams's criticisms and also presented the inhibition hypothesis in much greater detail. He pointed out that since conditioned inhibition can only appear as a result of rest pauses the length of pre-rest practice crucially determines upswing. If practice is sufficiently short not enough reactive inhibition will build up to produce rest pauses and therefore no conditioned inhibition can appear. "It follows from the above theory that there is a critical length of pre-rest practice below which warm-up will not be manifested and above which warm-up will gradually increase. The set theory would not predict this sharp break between warm up occurrence and nonoccurrence." Feldman quotes studies that support this hypothesis. Eysenck (1950c) using 1-min practice periods and Star (1957) using 1½-min practice periods found little or no warm-up, whereas Eysenck (1950) using 2-min practice periods found considerable warm-up. Unfortunately one would not expect this "sharp break between warm up occurrence and non occurrence" to appear in practice, except in individual cases which are notoriously variable for the pursuit rotor. Differential rates in the build up in reactive inhibition would lead to the appearance of rest pauses at various times after the beginning of practice. The necessity of averaging the performance of many individuals would therefore remove the sharp break between warm-up occurrence and nonoccurrence. Thus there is little to distinguish this aspect of inhibition theory from Ammons's assumption 1 which asserts that there is more warm-up after a greater amount of pre-rest practice.

Feldman then considers the influence of individual differences in drive. High-drive subjects, since they take longer to build up reactive inhibition, should show less warm-up than low-drive subjects. This prediction was confirmed by Eysenck and Willet, (1961) who found less warm-up for a high-drive group than for a low-drive group after 6 min of pre-rest practice. However it is clear from the data that this difference in warm-up appears only in the first 10 sec. Indeed Eysenck (1965) has used these very data in support of his argument for using 10-sec trials for analysis of performance since longer trials would remove the differences between the groups (Figure 6-7). It seems we must therefore abandon the notion that short warm-up is due to set and long warm-up is due to inhibition.

Finally Feldman considers the evidence that there should be no warm-up with distributed practice. He pointed out that since a small amount of warm-up was due to set, a small amount of warm-up would be expected during spaced practice, but that during massed practice would be significantly greater. He also shows that in many of the studies quoted by Adams against the inhibition hypothesis the conditions were neither sufficiently spaced nor sufficiently massed to be true tests of the theory. In spite of this Feldman's position is weak. It is much more difficult to distinguish between theories that predict more

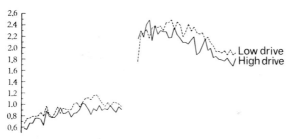

Figure 6-7. Comparison of post-rest upswing in high- and low-drive groups. Taken with permission from Eysenck and Willett, (1961).

or less upswing than between theories that predict upswing or no upswing. In particular one should bear in mind the caution of the earlier studies of warm-up (e.g., Irion, 1948) in which it was considered possible to compare warm-up slopes only when they were at the same overall level of proficiency. Since groups having massed practice are necessarily at a different level of proficiency than groups having spaced practice, comparison of the amount of upswing becomes extremely tricky.

There remains one last reason for considerable dissatisfaction with the set theory of warm-up in pursuit-rotor performance. In spite of the fact that warm-up is so slow in verbal learning (up to five minutes) both Eysenck and Adams accept an explanation for it in terms of set. This is because neutral tasks have been discovered which, if administered just before post-rest practice, eliminate warm-up. As Eysenck and Feldman point out, it is a considerable embarassment to set theory that no such tasks have been found for the pursuit rotor. Thus Adams (1963) in his reply to Feldman, having dismissed the inhibition theory on grounds similar to those we shall adopt in our chapter on consolidation, is forced to conclude "warm up decrement is considered to be without satisfactory theoretical explanation at this time."

Within the framework of the experimental methods used up to this time there was little hope of distinguishing between the two alternative theories of warm-up. Although basically different the theories had little to distinguish them in practice.

One reason for this problem may have been that the proponents of both these theories had attitudes typical of psychologists of that time. This attitude shows itself most characteristically in the dominant theory of the time; Hull's general theory of learning. This theory, because of its attempt at generality, pays little attention to the exact nature of the task being learned. Its constructs and parameters are applied with equal ease to verbal learning, alphabet printing, pursuit-rotor learning, and many other tasks. However, an analysis of task components is of course crucial in the search for neutral tasks that would reinstate set and also for discovering how a concept such as a rest pause might be recognized in practice. Hullian learning theory assumes that a large number of constructs underlie performance on the pursuit rotor. With only one measure of performance (total time-on-target) it is extremely difficult to separate out these competing processes. However because of lack of attention to the precise nature of the task no alternative measures are immediately obvious.

IS UPSWING AN ARTIFACT OF MEASUREMENT?

The important work of Bahrick, Fitts, and Briggs (1957) on methods of measuring pursuit tracking performance has already been mentioned in Chapter 3. These workers estimated tracking performance using several different hypothetical target sizes. They found that target size affected not only the level of performance, but also the shape of the learning curve. Thus, whereas performance on a small target showed a steady upward trend, the same performance considered in terms of a large target showed a bow shaped curve with both upswing and downswing present. This effect is only indirectly a result of different target sizes. It is essentially due to level of performance. Total time-on-target is a very insensitive index of performance changes when the overall level of performance is either very low or very high. Small targets naturally tend to be associated with a very low level of performance. This weakness in total time-on-target as a method of measurement is not very surprising since it is essentially a percentage score. It is well known that such scores are distorting at very low and very high levels. Indeed statisticians (e.g., Bartlett, 1947) have recommended the use of the arcsine transformation on percentage scores since this expands the metric at the extremes of the scale. The suggestion that the data should be transformed raises the problem as to what is the true metric. With one form of the data two groups at different overall levels may show different shaped learning curves. With another form the curves might be parallel. It is to some extent arbitrary which form of the data is used. Transformations are often chosen to normalize the data statistically. Alternatively it would be plausible to choose tranformations which render the curves involved parallel since this would be a "simple" structure. One is forced to conclude that it is not really possible to compare the shapes of curves when the overall performance level is different. This is precisely the cautious method adopted in the early studies of warm-up for which we now see a clear statistical justification.

Eysenck and Grey (1971) considered a number of experiments in which the shape of the learning curve was studied as a function of the overall ability of subjects on the pursuit rotor. This work is discussed in greater detail in Chapter 8. A characteristic finding was that during pre-rest practice the high-ability groups clearly showed upswing and downswing while the low-ability groups did not. This is what would be expected from the argument above since the performance of the low-ability subjects is so poor that total time-on-target scores are insensitive to subtle changes in performance. Eysenck and Grey argue that the different shaped learning curves are not the result of artifacts of measurement, but represent a true difference between ability groups. In support of this argument they present the same performance, analyzed in terms of a large "easy" target (Figures 8-17 and 8-18) claiming that the curves for the two different target sizes are essentially the same. Appearances do not seem altogether to support this contention. After an inexplicable drop in performance the low-ability group show clear evidence of upswing when their performance is analyzed in terms of the large target, although admittedly there is still no sign of downswing as in the high-ability group. In addition as has been pointed out comparison of curve shapes at different levels is a very unsatisfactory procedure. Nevertheless these results clearly show that some subjects at least show upswing at the beginning of their very first practice session on the pursuit rotor. Thus the failure of upswing to appear in the first practice session of many experiments may well be an artifact of the extremely low scores characteristic of this period.

On the basis of set theory we would expect to find upswing at the beginning of the first practice session since the various postural adjustments have to be made during the first session just as in any other. However inhibition theory cannot so easily accommodate this finding, since there has been no previous occasion in which conditioned inhibition could develop. Eysenck and Grey therefore suggest that "subjects have in the past practiced components of the task" and propose that high-ability subjects have practiced these components more assiduously than low-ability subjects. This hypothesis raises precisely the same problems as set theory when the latter posits the existence of neutral tasks that will reinstate set. What are the components of the pursuit-rotor task and what tasks practiced in the past also contain those components? We shall see in the chapter on interpolated activities that in fact there are virtually no tasks which share common components with the pursuit rotor.

MEASURES OF PERFORMANCE ALTERNATIVE TO TIME-ON-TARGET

Bahrick, Fitts, and Briggs (1957) suggest that the best measure of tracking performance would be the root mean square distance of the stylus from the target. However, this is in practice very difficult to measure and indeed impossible to measure using the standard pursuit-rotor apparatus. Thus no studies relevant to the nature of warm-up have been carried out using this measure. Alternative measures to total time-on-target are nevertheless possible using standard pursuit-rotor apparatus. These are the number of times the stylus touches the target (hits) and the mean length of unbroken contact between stylus and target (average hit length). These measures have been studied by Ammons (1951) and specifically in relation to warm-up by Frith and Tunstall (1971).

The technique for taking these measures is described in more detail in the chapter on strategies. Essentially it involves taking a continuous record of whether the subject is on or off target. From such a record it is easy, though tedious, to identify the hits and measure their length. The picture of pursuit-rotor performance given by average hit length is in at least two ways strikingly different from that given by total time on target (Figure 12-2). In terms of average hit length reminiscence tends to be zero or negative and there is much less post-rest downswing. This discrepancy between average hit length and total time-on-target implies that immediately after a rest average hit length is little changed or even lower than before the rest, but that the number of hits has considerably increased, resulting in a greater total time-on-target. Ammons (1953) also observed this large increase in hits immediately after rest and also that while both average hit length and total time-on-target showed a post-rest upswing the number of hits showed a post-rest downswing (Figure 6-8). These results imply that during the course of warm-up there is a *qualitative* change in performance. By qualitative we simply mean that the same overall level of performance is obtained in different ways. Arbitrarily choosing time-on-target as an index level of performance we can compare performance immediately after rest, and thus at the beginning of warm-up, with later performance at the same level of time-on-target after completion of warm-up and a certain amount of downswing. During this time, according to Ammons's (1953) data, the number of hits has steadily declined rather than rising and then falling. Thus during warm-up performance changes from being composed of many short hits to being composed of few long hits. Unfortunately neither set theory nor inhibition theory help us to inter-

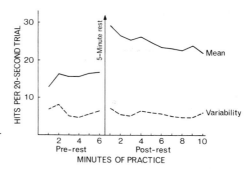

Figure 6-8. Mean number of hits per 20-sec trial before and after a five-minute rest. Taken with permission from Ammons (1951a).

pret these results. Lack of set and presence of conditioned inhibition both depress performance, but although such depression might well alter the quality of the performance there is no indication what these qualitative effects might be. For example, a naive interpretation of inhibition theory would suggest that immediately after rest conditioned inhibition results in subjects taking rest pauses which are not reinforced by the reduction of reactive inhibition. Once the conditoned inhibition has been extinguished these rest pauses no longer occur. However, for the specific case of the pursuit rotor, we have no indication of what a rest pause is or how it manifests itself in performance. Only by attempts to analyze the components of the pursuit-rotor task and thus considering the special nature of this task can further light be thrown on the phenomenon of warm-up. An attempt at such an analysis will be made in the chapter on strategies.

THE UNDERLYING COMPONENTS OF ROTARY-PURSUIT TRACKING

In his comments on the inhibition hypothesis Adams (1963) particularly criticizes the concept of the involuntary rest pause in relation to the rotary-pursuit test. He assumes that the IRP is a cessation of movement and quotes the detailed study of Ammons, Ammons and Morgan (1958).

In this study a film was made of subjects performing the pursuit-rotor task. This film was then studied frame by frame and various aspects of the stylus movement were recorded. At no time during performance was a cessation of movement ever observed. This kind of rest pause is consistent with Hull's original formulation of reactive inhibition in terms of physical work. As we have already shown there is a lot of evidence against this formulation (e.g., Bilodeau and Bilodeau, 1954), and Eysenck (1965) among others suggests a formulation in terms of mental work, "relating inhibition to the amount of continued attention required by the task." In these terms a rest pause would be a cessation of attention and not a cessation of movement. This would be impossible to detect in the performance of a subject since a subject could well be on target during a lapse of attention just as he might well be off target even when he was attending. All that can be expected is that during a lapse of attention he is less likely to be on target. These fluctuations in probability cannot be directly observed except possibly at very high levels of performance. It would thus be extremely difficult to find direct evidence for this kind of IRP.

The concept of attention rather than work immediately implies components for performance on the pursuit rotor, for attention is specifically concerned with the receiving of information and not with the production of a motor response. This suggests that pursuit-rotor performance could be divided into the following three stages: observation of the relationship between stylus and target, calculation of the necessary action to maintain or produce coincidence, and production of the appropriate motor movement. Attention is concerned specifically with the initial observation.

The observing and correcting of errors in motor skills has received much attention from psychologists working within the framework of man considered as an engineering system (Craik, 1948; Vince, 1948; Hick, 1948). Both theoretical considerations (the finiteness of reaction times) and empirical findings lead them to believe that such observations and corrections are performed intermittently and not continuously. This means that long lasting sequences of motor movements are carried out without the feedback provided by continuous visual checks. This kind of performance would seem particularly appropriate for the pursuit rotor, in which the motor movements involved are excessively repetitive. However, this model implies that the responses involved in pursuit tracking may be made at the subject's discretion so that in this sense the task is self-paced. Adams (1963) accepts that reactive inhibition and rest pauses are useful concepts in self-paced tasks. This new formulation of the task clearly has considerable implications for attempts to apply learning theory principles to pursuit-rotor performance which will be dealt with elsewhere (Chapter 12). For the moment we shall only consider their application to the phenomenon of warm-up.

Adams (1955) attempted to isolate the observing component of pursuit tracking by having a subject observe the performance of a companion and press a button whenever he was off target. Performance of this task during rest clearly depressed post-rest performance on the pursuit rotor and eliminated upswing. This observing task is clearly not neutral in relation to pursuit-rotor performance in the same way that color naming was to verbal learning (Irion, 1949), since it involves not a little of the skill also required for pursuit-rotor performance and gives rise to transferable inhibition. A truly neutral task must reinstate set without producing an increment in either skill or inhibition. Thus the elimination of warm-up found by Adams is consistent with inhibition theory and set theory since the observing task would both extinguish conditioned inhibition and reinstate set.

Frith (1969) attempted to control the rate of observing by illuminating the target of the pursuit rotor intermittently at different rates while keeping the percentage of time illuminated constant. It was argued that subjects would have to make their observing responses at the same rate as the target was illuminated. While a high rate of illumination was associated with characteristic post-rest upswing and downswing, with low rates these effects were eliminated and overall performance was slightly reduced (Figure 12-5). This would be predicted from inhibition theory on the grounds that a low rate of responding would reduce the amount of reactive inhibition and hence conditioned inhibition. On the other hand performance would be reduced because of the relatively long periods during which the subject could not check if he was tracking successfully. It is not clear whether rate of observing should interfere with the reinstatement of set, since there has thus far been no clear indication of what set might be. A slow rate of observing might well result in set taking longer to be established.

It would be desirable to specify the nature of set in more detail just as we have specified the nature of rest pauses and responses in the inhibition model. The crucial attribute of set is its neutrality. It must involve neither skill, nor habit strength nor inhibition. Since all these are assumed to have their origins in the central nervous system a peripheral source for set would be appropriate. It is therefore suprising, as Eysenck (1967) has pointed out, that no attention has been paid to the literal meaning of the term warm-up, i.e., the actual change in temperature of the body in general, and the muscles taking part in the exercise in particular. Psychologists have used the term by analogy only. It is known that only about ¼ of the extra energy derived from food is transformed into external mechanical work during muscular exercise; ¾ degenerates into heat in the body. "In muscular exercise the total energy set free may increase 20-to 25-fold as compared to energy set free at rest. Therefore, the heat production may reach values 15 to 20 times larger than in rest. Some of this heat is stored in the body, thereby causing an increase in the temperature of the exercising muscles primarily, but also in the average body temperature. This storage mainly takes place in the beginning of the work period." (Asmussen, 1965). Higher temperatures may be assumed to be beneficial to the organism; all chemical processes take place at a faster rate, internal frictional resistance in the muscles and joints decreases as the viscosity of extracellular and synovial fluids decreases, and the shape of the oxygen-dissociation curve of the blood changes so as to enhance the delivery of oxygen to the tissues. So much for theory; do higher temperatures actually accompany better performance, and is this higher performance actually due to the increase in temperature, or to some other feature of the for-exercise? The classic studies of Asmussen and Bøje (1945), the work of Högberg and Lunggren (1947), Munido (1947), and Nolite (1950, 1951) all suggest that the facts are as expected. Performance on the bicycle ergometer was consistently superior in the warm, as compared with the cold state, and this superiority was present even when the change in temperature was affected by short wave radio diathermy or by means of a hot shower. Performance times for sprint, plotted against temperature of lateral vastus muscle, is shown for one of Asmussen and Boje's subjects in Figure 6-9; the results are very clear cut, and confirm that it is the actual temperature level which is responsible for the improvement in performance. The other studies show similar results suggesting very strongly the reality of improvement in physical performance as a consequence of warm-up, strictly related to higher temperatures in the blood and the muscles, particularly those muscles involved in the work in question.

This kind of warm-up would seem almost certain to occur in the predominantly muscular tasks discussed at the beginning of this chapter, such as drawing an ergograph and tapping. Warm-up in these tasks was slow to build up and to dissipate. It did not manifest itself within one session of work, but only in overall better performance in following sessions separated by rests. The maximum warm-up appeared after a rest of 15 min and did not dissipate even an hour after the original practice session. Finally the effect of warm-up seemed to be largely one of increased immunity to fatigue. All these results are consistent with warming up of the muscles which would induce among other things an enhancement of the delivery of blood to the tissues, thus increasing immunity to fatigue.

But does this genuine warm-up apply to other tasks? It clearly does not apply to verbal learning for which, as we have seen, the set theory seems to work quite adequately. Pursuit tracking certainly involves

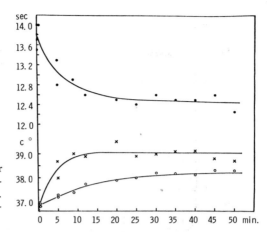

Figure 6-9. Performance times for the sprint plotted against the temperature of the lateral vastus muscle. Taken with permission from Assmussen and Bøje (1945).

muscular activity, but is the warming up of the muscles concerned sufficient to account for post-rest upswing? Upswing in pursuit tracking takes place very quickly, often being complete in 10 sec and rarely lasting longer than 2 min, at least in as far as it is manifested in the curve of performance. According to Asmussen and Bøje (1945) muscle temperature rises and becomes asymptotic only after 10 min of work.

Of course the tasks involved are different (bicycle ergometer, and sprinting), but if anything the greater energy expended in these tasks should result in a more rapid rise in temperature. Similarly "warm-up" in the pursuit rotor dissipates much more rapidly than would be expected if it was due to changes in muscle temperature. However, the hypothesis can be tested quite directly. The experiment to see if warming up the muscles passively (e.g., by short wave radio diathermy) can eliminate upswing has not been attempted, but experiments on bilateral transfer suggest that upswing can be eliminated without any warming up of the muscles.

Barch (1963) studied bilateral transfer in rotary pursuit in a carefully controlled experiment. Noting that there is some negative transfer simply as a result of changing hands he had his subjects practice with alternating hands every three trials for 18 trials before interposing a rest of one week. As can be seen in Figure 6-10 there is a considerable amount of warm-up after a week's rest as compared to a group with no rest. However, three trials with the preferred hand were sufficient to eliminate warm-up from the immediately following three trials with the nonpreferred hand, compared to a group that had received no immediately preceeding practice with the preferred hand. Since practice with the preferred hand can have little effect on the muscles of the nonpre-

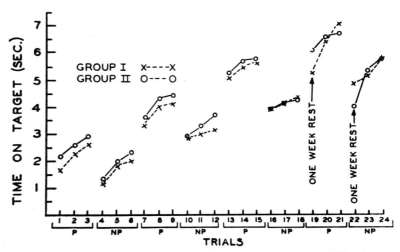

Figure 6-10. Time-on-target curves for two experimental groups. P and NP refer to trials with the preferred and nonpreferred hand. Taken with permission from Barch (1963).

ferred hand one must conclude that actual physical warming up of the muscles concerned has at the most a very minor role in so called warm-up in pursuit tracking.

The most detailed considerations of the variables that might underlie set have been provided by Schmidt and Nacson (Nacson & Schmidt, 1972; Schmidt & Wrisberg, 1971; Schmidt & Nacson, 1971). They first attempted to delineate more precisely what previous authors meant by set. They suggest that the basic assumption is that the performance decrement is caused by a decrement in either a subcomponent of the total response (e.g., the eye movement in rotary pursuit) or by incorrect postural adjustments (e.g., standing in the wrong position). However, these notions of set have failed to reveal a suitable neutral set reinstating task, at least in the case of motor learning. Schmidt and Nacson suggest this is so because this kind of set is too specific to the task/apparatus involved. They propose an "activity-set" hypothesis stating that the decrement in performance following a period of no practice is due to the loss of a generalized readiness to respond. "It is assumed that the subject has a number of supportive mechanisms which underlie the performance on any motor task and that these systems are adjusted by the subject so that they contribute maximally to the desired performance. For example, the activation (or arousal) system must operate at some optimal level, as Martens and Landers (1970) and others have shown that both too little and too much activation can lead to decrements in performance. Also, the subject must adjust his expectancies for up-coming events, with such expectancy effects easily shown in RT situations (e.g., Gottsdanker, 1970). Depending upon the objectives of the task the subject will adjust the relative importance of speed and accuracy, with such effects being shown by numerous investigators (e.g., Fitts, 1966). When the subject has practiced the task for a number of trials, the mechanisms independently attain adjustments appropriate for that activity, and this delicate adjustment defines the activity set, so termed because it is appropriate for a number of activities of a given class (i.e., with common response requirements). Thus, one might speak of an activity set for blindfold positioning, and this activity set would be appropriate for any blindfold positioning task (e.g., leg or arm positioning). Also when the response requirements change (e.g., by adding vision) a new activity set is defined for the second class of tasks and, subjectively, it seems reasonable that the activity set for threading a needle would be different from that required for attaining maximum grip force. If the subject is allowed to rest the activity set is lost, either by decay or by a process analogous to interference in which the activity set is replaced by another (possibly that for efficient resting), and the subject cannot perform well until it is reestablished. Since this reinstatement cannot occur immediately, the decrement is quickly eliminated in the next few practice trials." (Schmidt and Nacson, 1971, p. 57.)

In many ways the activity set hypothesis does not differ from either set theory or inhibition theory. "Loss of a generalized readiness to respond" sounds like a descriotion of the effect of conditioned inhibition. The great advance made by the activity set hypothesis is that it makes some very specific suggestions about the relation between the criterion task and its appropriate set reinstating tasks. The usefulness of these suggestions is proved by the considerable success of Schmidt and his colleagues in finding set reinstating tasks for a number of motor skills. So far three tasks have been studied; learning to produce a given force by squeezing or pulling, blind positioning, and production of a fast fixed movement. Figure 6-11 shows results for the blind positioning task (Schmidt & Nacson, 1971) and is typical of the results for all the tasks. The criterion task required the subject to learn to move a rod with his right hand through 50 cm from left to right while blindfolded. The set reinstating task was also blindfold positioning, but required the subject to move a block with his left hand away from his body rather than across it and through a different distance. Group REST rested for 10 min between performances of the criterion task. Group AS practiced the interpolated task during the last 3 min of the rest period. Group AS+T performed a simple tapping task for 40 sec between the interpo-

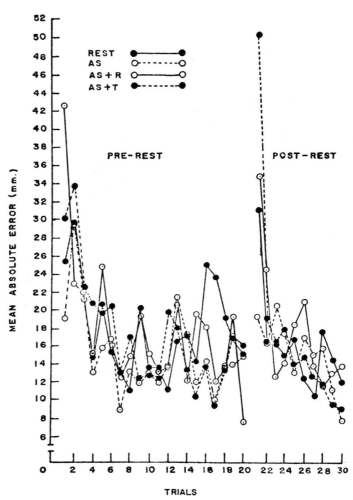

Figure 6-11. Mean absolute error for the right-hand positioning task before and after the interpolated treatments. Taken with permission from Schmidt and Nacson (1971).

lated task and the criterion task. Group AS+R rested for 40 sec between the interpolated task and the criterion task. It can be seen clearly in the figure that the interpolated activity (AS) completely eliminates the rapid post-rest improvement shown by the group that rests (REST). However, group AS+R is almost the same as group REST, suggesting the appropriate set can be lost in 40 sec. Finally, group AS + T shows an even greater post-rest decrement showing that tapping instated a set even more inappropriate than that produced by resting.

Schmidt and Nacson's results are most clear cut and elegant, but it remains to be seen whether they can be applied to the pursuit-rotor task. Although they say that their "activity-set" theory is more general than the earlier set theory, in practice the set reinstating tasks used seem to be extremely similar to the criterion tasks. Thus when the criterion task requires the subject to produce a certain force by squeezing a dynamometer using kinesthetic cues alone, the set reinstating task had to be pulling a spring with a certain force by kinesthetic cues alone. Pulling the spring with visual cues as well did not reinstate the set (Nacson & Schmidt, 1971). Thus the class of tasks that mutually reinstate set is both narrow and not very satisfactorily defined. The success of Schmidt and his colleagues in finding tasks that reinstate set is largely due to their wise choice of rather simple tasks to study. For example, the class of blindfold positioning tasks is small and well defined, while it is not at all clear what an analogous class of pursuit-rotor tasks might contain. The only safe prediction from Schmidt's results would be that pursuit-rotor performance with the opposite hand would reinstate set, which we have already seen to be the case, but few other minor changes seem to be permissable. Pursuit tracking at a different speed actually seems to enhance warm-up (Wada, 1970).

An example of how Schmidt and his colleagues derive suitable tasks for reinstating activity-set is the statement that a set for blindfold positioning will be reinstated by any blindfold positioning task (Nacson & Schmidt, 1971). However, this method only works when there previously exists a precise description of the task under investigation. Rotary-pursuit tracking is not a sufficiently precise description of the pursuit rotor for, as we have seen, set is not reinstated by any rotary-pursuit tracking task (e.g., tracking at a different speed). Thus the activity-set theory is not sufficient to account for warm up in rotary pursuit tracking. It is essential to know first what are the crucial processes underlying successful tracking.

CONCLUSIONS

We have seen how attempts to explain warm-up in various tasks have progressed from the general to the particular. Warm-up in three classes of tasks; verbal learning, muscular effort (dynamometer squeezing, sprinting), and simple motor skills (blindfold positioning), have been accounted for with a fair amount of success. However, warm-up in each class of tasks has required a different explanation. Warm-up in tasks involving considerable muscular effort is probably related to an actual increase in the temperature of the muscles involved. For both verbal learning and simple motor skills an explanation of warm-up in terms of set seems most likely, this set being reinstated by practicing an appropriate subcomponent of the task. However, while in verbal learning the practice of a very minor component of the task (e.g., watching the memory drum rotate at the right speed) seems to reinstate set, for the simple motor skills it is the major component of the task that has to be practiced (e.g., blindfold positioning for blindfold positioning tasks).

There are still no very satisfactory explanations available for the initial upswing found in pursuit-rotor performance. In later chapters we shall see that the attempts to explain aspects of pursuit-rotor performance in terms of inhibition cannot be accepted for various reasons. Since inhibition cannot explain reminiscence and downswing, then presumably it cannot explain upswing either. We must therefore tentatively conclude that the upswing found in pursuit-rotor performance does reflect a regaining of "set." This "set" is regained very rapidly (1 to 2 min) and is lost fairly rapidly (almost entirely after one hr). Some groups of subjects lose set more rapidly than others, notably schizophrenic patients, and evidence for this will be presented in Chapter 10.

The major problem for this explanation of initial upswing in pursuit-rotor performance in terms of "set" is the failure to find tasks which reinstate this "set." In the next chapter on transfer and interpolated activity we shall show that there is considerable evidence for an extreme specificity of pursuit-rotor learning. Practice on other tasks does not improve and interfere with later pursuit-rotor performance unless these tasks are extremely similar to the pursuit rotor (e.g., pursuit rotor at a different speed or in reverse). Owing to this extreme specificity it is probably impossible to discover a task that reinstates the set appropriate to pursuit-rotor performance without at the same time facilitating or interfering with the basic skill that is being learned.

After post-rest upswing is complete there follows a gradual decline in performance which, naturally enough, is referred to as post-rest downswing. Once again the typical picture is shown in Figure 2-4, which is taken from Ammons's classic study. Eysenck *et al.* (1969) investigated downswing in pursuit-rotor learning as a function of the length of practice. The practice periods varied in length from 20 to 120 sec and were separated by 1-min rests. By the second or third practice period there was marked downswing apparent whatever the length of practice (Figure 6-12). With rests of 5 min between practice periods downswing is still present, but less marked (Star, 1957) as is shown in Figure 9-4.

The use of a 24-hour rest period made it possible for Farley to test Eysenck's (1965) prediction that with greatly extended rest intervals the

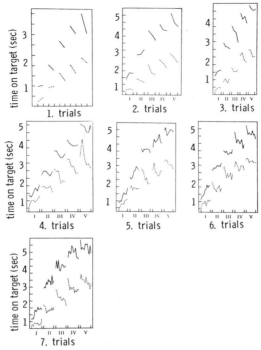

Figure 6-12. Performance of high- and low-drive groups during five practice periods of 20 sec (Fig. 1); 30 sec (Fig. 2); 40 sec (Fig. 3); 60 sec (Fig. 4); 80 sec (Fig. 5); 100 sec (Fig. 6); or 120 sec (Fig. 7) separated by 1-min rest periods. _____, low _____ , high. Taken with permission from Eysenck *et al.* (1969).

post-rest downswing would become increasingly attenuated, and overall post-rest performance elevated. The 24 hour rest group is not differentiated from the other groups pre-rest (by analysis of variance), but in the post-rest period this group is quite obviously grossly differentiated from the shorter rest groups. Of particular interest is the comparison of the 24 hour group with the 10 min one. "Both have a clear-cut upswing section, and are undifferentiated for the first approximately 8 trials or 80 sec of practice. Then the 10 minute group can be seen to fall more sharply than the 24 hour group. It is clear that some downswing occurs even in the 24 hour group, but that the duration of downswing is *shorter* than in the 10 minute condition. The reduced downswing of the 24 hour group should lead to a significant between-groups term and linear component in a comparison of the two curves, as the curves would tend to diverge, due to the reduced downswing of the 24 hour group and the extended downswing of the 10 minute group." (Eysenck, 1965, p. 146.)

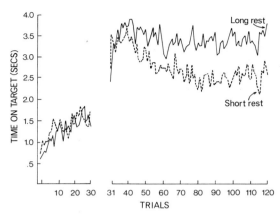

Figure 6-13. Post-rest performance of short-rest and long-rest groups on the pursuit rotor. Results from an unpublished experiment by K. Star, graphed by Farley (1966).

Both the between-groups term and the $G \times T$ linear component were in fact found to be significant, while no significance was attached to the $G \times T$ higher power terms. These results support Eysenck's prediction, but it seems that 24 hours is not sufficient to prevent some slight downswing in the post-rest curve; even longer rest periods would seem required.

Star (unpublished data) has tested this hypothesis using low-drive students who were randomly assigned to either a 10 min or a 1 week rest condition; he followed Farley's choice of post-rest massed practice period of 15 min. His results are shown in Figure 6-13; as predicted, the long-rest group has negligible post-rest downswing as compared with the short-rest group. The lack of a reminiscence difference between the groups confirms the finding of the other studies in this chapter that rest periods longer than 120 sec do not affect reminiscence. Note also that both groups are very similar in post-rest upswing; this goes counter to any hypothesis of "warm-up" as being dependent on the length of the rest period preceding it.

As we have already found with initial upswing the picture changes somewhat if we make the task easier by providing larger targets. Using such procedures Bahrick, Fitts and Briggs (1957) (see Chapter 1) and Eysenck and Grey (1971) (see Chapter 8) found that upswing and downswing tended to appear in the very first session of pursuit-rotor performance also, when the level of performance was high. However, even with these large targets subjects eventually settle down to a steadily increasing performance typical of pre-rest practice on the standard pursuit rotor.

Far fewer experiments have been undertaken to investigate downswing than upswing. There seem to be two reasons for this. First, in order to study the phenomenon fully, very long practice periods must be used which are tedious for subjects and experimenters alike. Second, until very recently there have been no theories competing for an acceptable explanation of downswing as there have with upswing.

At first sight a steady decline in performance occurring towards the end of practice must simply be a manifestation of some inhibition process. While the majority of workers accepted this explanation there was no need for further investigation of the phenomenon. However, a more careful consideration of the facts concerning downswing reveals many features that are not compatible with a simple inhibition theory. Indeed in the chapter on consolidation we shall suggest that inhibition processes play no role at all in pursuit-rotor performance. After about 10 min of post-rest practice, downswing ceases and a steady increase in performance appears. Yet inhibition should still be continuing to build up at this time. Furthermore, a group with no interpolated rest will continue to show a steady increase in performance, while another group will show a decline in performance shortly after an interpolated rest. Clearly this is contrary to our expectations since the group with no rest should have built up more inhibition.

The picture is very different with tasks where inhibition does seem to play a major role. Mackworth (1964) studied performance decrement in tasks involving vigilance, thresholds and certain perceptual-motor skills and found that the course of the decline was essentially the same in all these tasks. The decrement continued with no sign of leveling off, let alone upswing, for up to 180 min. This was true even for the tracking task that she studied. The crucial difference between this tracking task and the standard pursuit rotor seems to be that "learning appeared to be complete after about 20 minutes of testing." This is certainly not the case with the standard pursuit rotor for which learning is far from complete after 20 min of practice. Presumably the gradual increase in performance found after 10 min of post-rest practice is a manifestation of this continuing learning. Clearly if the rate of increase in performance due to learning were greater than the rate of decrease due to inhibition then a gradual increase in performance would result. However, this does not explain why post-rest downswing eventually gives way to the gradual increase in performance characteristic of subjects who have had no interpolated rest.

More serious for the explanation of downswing in terms of inhibition due to continuing practice is the failure to observe certain important consequences of this theory. Originally it was thought that reminiscence was a reflection of the dissipation of inhibition during rest. In this case the major determinant of reminiscence would be the amount of inhibition built up. However, detailed investigation of those experiments in which differences were found in amount of reminiscence showed that it was the post-rest rather than the pre-rest levels of performance that were producing the differences. For example, it had been predicted and confirmed that highly motivated subjects would show more reminiscence than less motivated subjects (Eysenck & Maxwell, 1961). This prediction was made on the grounds that high-drive subjects should be able to tolerate a higher level of inhibition before producing involuntary rest pauses. Since involuntary rest pauses should lower performance then clearly low-drive subjects should perform at a lower level at the end of pre-rest practice than high-drive subjects. However, differences between low- and high-drive subjects only appeared in post-rest performance. This, as Adams (1963) has pointed out, was a major stumbling block for proponents of inhibition theory. Since this problem concerns matters more general than the phenomenon of post-rest downswing we shall delay detailed discussion of it until the chapter on consolidation.

Precisely because of this failure of inhibition theory Eysenck (1965, 1966) attempted to account for post-rest downswing entirely in terms of a consolidation process. He assumed that while memory traces were still being consolidated this process interfered with performance to produce post-rest downswing. However, the consolidation process would eventually be complete, interference would stop, and the post-rest downswing would cease. As we shall see there are various objections to this explanation of post-rest downswing. We shall present a slightly different explanation, also purely in terms of a consolidation process. This assumes that renewed performance partially destroys consolidated learning, causing a downswing in performance. This downswing ceases when all the partially consolidated learning has been destroyed. Here again we shall leave detailed discussion of these theories for Chapter 11 which is specifically devoted to the concept of consolidation.

Another explanation of downswing which we shall only hint at here is essentially in terms of a modified inhibition theory. In Chapter 12 we shall consider the exact processes that must be involved in pursuit tracking and suggest that this is not a paced task since the major response is not moving the stylus, but detecting and correcting errors. These responses can be carried out at any rate the subject chooses. Thus it is plausible that as inhibition increases the subject reduces his response rate until a point of equilibrium is reached. At this point the inhibition produced by each response completely dissipates in between responses and so there is no further increase in inhibition. Thus downswing would cease and the gradual increase in performance that is a manifestation of learning would be revealed. Since here also there are implications for many phenomena in addition to post-rest downswing, detailed discussion of these notions will be left for Chapter 12.

We may have some success in accounting for post-rest downswing in terms of consolidation processes or modified inhibition theory, but since the reader has not yet been properly introduced to these theories a thorough assessment of them must be left for later chapters. However, it is clear that, as with initial upswing, traditional explanations of pursuit-rotor performance have little success in accounting for post-rest downswing.

CHAPTER 7

Transfer of Training and Interpolated Activity

INTRODUCTION

This chapter is concerned with two very simple experimental paradigms. In the first the experimental group learns task A and then task B and is compared with a control group that learns task B without any prior training. From this comparison we can discover whether learning task A has any effect on the learning of task B. In the second experimental paradigm task B is practiced twice, separated by an interval during which task A is practiced. Here we can discover whether the learning of task A effects the already learned task B. These both appear simple and straightforward designs. However, results from them are open to an enormous variety of interpretations. Furthermore although apparently very neutral, both experimental procedures are closely tied to learning theory and are of little use outside this framework. The most basic assumption behind these designs is that the learning of one task will indeed effect the learning of another. In the case of motor skills such related tasks have been surprisingly difficult to find. When the two tasks are related it is assumed that they have certain components in common. This notion of components is closely linked to the theory that complex activities consist of chains of stimuli and responses, and also to the theory that performance at any time will depend on a combination of underlying variables such as habit strength, reactive inhibition, conditioned inhibition, and so on. In practice it usually turns out to be very difficult to identify any of these components for a particular task. The major exceptions to this rule are tasks involving verbal learning.

We have already considered one of the components thought to determine performance, namely set, in the previous chapter. This component was investigated with precisely the experimental methods being discussed here, transfer and interpolated activity. However, a task that reinstated set was required to be "neutral" in the sense that it in no way effected the learning of the major task under investigation. This was assumed to be the case if the secondary task abolished the "warm-up" or post-rest upswing without altering the later performance. In this chapter we are concerned with interpolated tasks that are not "neutral," but affect performance of the primary task over a long term. We have already observed, in considering the set theory of warm-up, a sharp dichotomy between verbal and motor learning. This dichotomy is even greater when we consider transfer and interference effects.

As yet, no neutral set-reinstating task has been discovered for the pursuit rotor. For verbal learning, on the other hand, the situation is relatively straightforward and simple (Adams, 1961). Warm-up effects can be abolished by color naming (Irion, 1949) or learning lists of different material (Thune, 1951) just before the primary learning task of paired associate learning or list learning. These results may have arisen in part because it is so much easier to describe verbal learning tasks in terms of learning theory than it is so to describe motor skills. Adams (1961) describes a neutral task for reinstating set as one which involves "performance of S–R sequences which are neutral with respect to S–R goal sequences and which overcome warm up by restrengthening secondary responses—not the strength of goal S–R sequences." Since the goal response in verbal learning is the production of a number of specific words, we can produce a neutral task simply altering the words to be learned (Thune, 1951). Motor skills, and in particular the pursuit rotor, cannot have their content so easily changed without altering their form. Most verbal learning tasks fall naturally into an analysis in terms of stimulus and response. Paired associate learning, for example, is constructed quite explicitly in terms of S–R pairs. Few serious attempts have been made to analyze rotory-pursuit tracking into a series of stimuli and responses. We shall see in a later chapter that when such attempts are made considerable difficulties arise.

In this chapter we are concerned with tasks that directly affect "goal responses." In a paired associate learning task the "goal response" is to produce the appropriate response to a particular stimulus. Given this paradigm, it should be possible to design tasks that will strengthen, weaken, or have no effect on these stimulus response connections (S_1–R_1). In practice psychologists have had remarkable success in designing such tasks. Learning unrelated pairs (S_2–R_2) has no effect on the original

S_1–R_1 bonds. This is an example of a neutral task that will eliminate "warm-up." A task in which new responses are attached to the original stimuli (S_1–R_2) produces interference, while one on which new stimuli are attached to the original responses (S_2–R_1) gives positive transfer (Osgood, 1949). These experiments were so successful in controlling the learning and forgetting of verbal material that many authors proposed that all forgetting was the result of interference processes and, thus, that the laws of forgetting reduce to the laws of proactive and retroactive inhibition (Bugelski & Cadwallader, 1956), with experimental extinction as the process whereby responses are weakened in interference paradigms (Underwood & Postman, 1960). It was also suggested that much forgetting occurs as a result of sources of verbal interference outside the laboratory (Underwood & Postman, 1960).

A notable feature of pursuit-rotor learning (shown in Figure 8-2) is that remarkably little forgetting occurs even after long intervals (S. B. G. Eysenck, 1960; Leavitt and Schlosberg, 1945). Since everyone clearly indulges in a large amount of motor behavior outside the laboratory, why is this not interfering with learning in the same way as the external sources of verbal interference? This lack of forgetting in pursuit-rotor learning already gives us reason to suspect that studies of transfer and interpolated activity will not be very revealing. However, we shall first discuss what information has been gleaned about pursuit-rotor learning in this area before putting forward an explanation for the marked differences between verbal learning and motor learning.

Experiments involving transfer of training and interpolated activity are attempting to analyze the task being studied into components and to trace the similarities between this task and others. It is assumed that tasks producing positive or negative transfer must have elements in common with the criterion task. As we have seen the Hullian framework of learning theory, within which the pursuit-rotor task has usually been studied, is very little concerned with the exact nature of the task being learned. The theory deals with concepts such as habit and reactive inhibition and hopes that these abstract entities are the basic and essential components in the learning of all tasks. Thus decisions about whether the habit learned in one task has anything in common with that required for another depend not so much on theory as on a "common sense" analysis of what the tasks involve. Where theory does come in predictions are based on interpretations rather than explicit statements of the theory. In the early stages must of the phenomena associated with pursuit-rotor performance were explained in terms of reactive inhibition. This inhibition was supposed to build up during work and dissipate during rest. Questions immediately arise concerning the generality of this inhibition. Does the inhibition built up by one task transfer to another? Is the location of this inhibition peripheral or central?

BILATERAL REMINISCENCE

This unwieldy term simply refers to experiments in which a task is learned with one hand, but performed after a rest by the other hand. Although Hull made no explicit statements concerning the locus of reactive inhibition, his statements that it depended on the amount of physical work performed suggest that he had a peripheral origin in mind. Thus one can hypothesize that the inhibition built up during pursuit-rotor performance resides in the muscles of the hand and arm actually manipulating the stylus. The hand that was not doing the work should be entirely unaffected by this inhibition. Thus if reminiscence is assumed to be due to the dissipation of inhibition during rest, then if performance is switched to the other hand there should be no benefit gained from rest. This experiment was performed by Irion and Gustafson (1952) and the hypothesis was clearly fallacious. Two groups practiced on the pursuit rotor for ten trials with the right hand followed by ten trials with the left hand. The trials were 25-sec long with 5 sec between trials. For one group the time between switching hands (trials 10 and 11) was the normal 5 sec. For the other group there was a 5-min rest at this point. There was clearly a large gain associated with the rest (Figure 7-1). If the gain resulting from rest is due to the dissipation of inhibition then this inhibition clearly transferred to the left hand and therefore, must have a more central locus than the muscles actually involved in the work. The other notable feature of the results is that the left-hand performance is much inferior to that of the right. This could be due either to an essential inferiority of the left hand in right-handed people (as all the subjects in this experiment were) or a failure of the learning (as opposed to the inhibition) to transfer to the other hand. In terms of consolidation theory we would interpret the results of this experiment as showing that what had been learned by the right hand and consolidated during the rest was, at least in part, available to the left hand.

Grice and Reynolds (1952) and Rockway (1953) performed similar experiments on a larger scale. Rockway's subjects practiced first with their preferred hand and then with their non-preferred hands. First hand practice was for 1, 2, 3, 4, or 5 min and the intervening rest was 0,

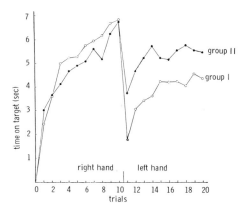

Figure 7-1. Mean time-on-target for 10 trials with the right hand followed by 10 trials with the left hand. Group 1 had a 10-sec rest between switching hands while group 2 had a 5-min rest. Taken with permission from Irion and Gustafson (1952).

2, or 5 min. Both length of rest and length of first hand practice significantly affected performance immediately after the rest. The longer the rest and the longer the practice the better was the second hand performance. This is clear evidence that either inhibition or consolidated learning is transferred from one hand to the other and cannot, therefore, be entirely peripheral in origin.

Grice and Reynolds (1952) studied transfer from right to left hand in right-handed subjects with rest lengths varying from 10 sec to 10 min. In addition, they used control groups who practiced with the left hand both before and after the rest. The gain after rest was a roughly exponential function of rest length whether subjects switched hands or not. However, the gains after switching from the right hand to the left hand were consistently smaller. Other interesting results which received little comment in the paper are shown in Figure 7-2. During pre-rest practice the performance of the left-hand groups is consistently below that of the right-hand groups. This suggests that in right-handed subjects the left hand is essentially poorer at pursuit-rotor performance. However, this lack of ability in the left hand is not sufficient to account for the relatively low gain when transferring from right hand to left hand, since performance after transfer is consistently lower than the control groups who practiced with the left hand throughout. A large amount of upswing and downswing is apparent after the 10-min rest, and after about 7 min of post-rest practice the difference between the 10-sec and the 10-min rest groups has dissappeared. Furthermore, the difference between the transfer and the control groups has also considerably decreased by the end of the post-rest practice. These results suggest that what was learned with the right hand was not completely

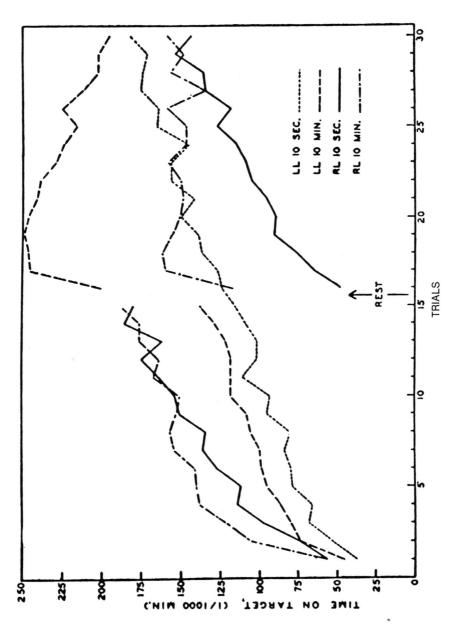

Figure 7-2. Mean time-on-target scores for 4 groups of subjects. After a 10-sec or 10-min rest the subjects either continued practicing with their left hands or switched to their right hands. Taken with permission from Grice and Reynolds (1952).

transferred to the left. However, had the trend apparent in these data continued, after about 10 or 15 min of practice the left-hand group with transfer might have reached the same level of performance as the left-hand group without transfer. This suggests that, rather than the learning in the right hand failing to transfer completely, some of the habits transferred were not appropriate for left-hand practice. These habits interfered with left-hand performance and had to be extinguished.

Kokobun and Iizuka (1969) performed a similar experiment on bilateral reminiscence, but with all the four groups required to give a complete picture of transfer effect from one hand to the other (R–R, L–L, R–L, L–R). In so far as their design replicated those described previously their results also confirmed previous findings. Reminiscence appeared for all four types of transfer when a rest condition was compared with a no rest condition. During the pre-rest period those subjects working with the left hand were consistently worse than those working with the right hand. This was also true for those subjects who continued with the same hand after rest, with the exception of the first post-rest trial at which point the left hand was at least as good as the right hand (unfortunately no significance tests are given), but thereafter failed to show such a steep upswing. Kokobun and Iizuka suggest that this effect is a result of more inhibition being accumulated during left-hand practice. The pre-rest practice performance in this experiment and in that of Grice and Reynolds (1952) show a similar effect: the difference between the left and right hand is much less marked at the very beginning of practice. However, this could well be due to an artifact of measurement at very low levels of performance. The most striking feature of this Japanese experiment is the marked asymmetry of transfer when the right–left group is compared with the left–right groups (Figure 7-3). The group that transferred from left hand to the right hand was, immediately after the rest, well below the groups that did not change hands, but after about 4-min practice had reached their level as a result of steep upswing. In contrast, the group which transferred from right to left is even more depressed below the no transfer groups immediately after rest and shows a very slight upswing. This right–left transfer effect was also observed in the Grice and Reynolds experiment (1952) and though those subjects did show some tendency to approach gradually the performance of the no transfer group they still had not reached that level after 7½ min of post-rest practice.

These four experiments have clearly shown that reminiscence transfers from one hand to the other. If reminiscence is due to the dissipation of inhibition then this result strongly suggests that the inhibition is central rather than peripheral in origin. If the reminiscence

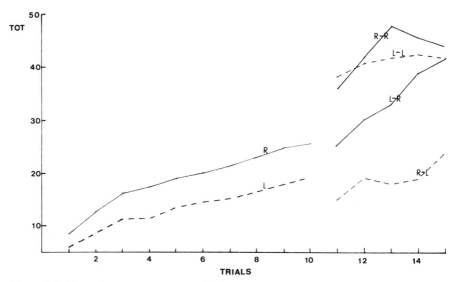

Figure 7-3. Mean time-on-target scores for four groups practicing pre-rest with either the left or the right hand and after rest either continuing with the same hand or switching to the other. Drawn from data given by Kokobun and Iizuka (1969).

is due to the consolidation of learning then something more general than the movements of a specific hand and arm must have been learned. The skill involved in pursuit-rotor performance is only partially transferred from one hand to the other since performance after transfer is consistently below performance without transfer. There are also differences between performance with the left and right hand (at least in right-handed subjects). The left hand tends to perform at a lower level than the right hand except perhaps at the very beginning of a practice period. This may reflect a greater proneness to inhibition since right-handed subjects have less experience of using their left hands. In addition there is a great asymmetry in transfer. Left to right transfer results in much better performance than right to left transfer. Left–right transfer is less depressed below no transfer performance with either hand and rapidly rises to the same level. Right–left transfer rises much more slowly, and as yet there is no evidence that it eventually reaches the same level as no transfer groups. A possible interpretation of these results is that a habit inappropriate to the other hand is also transferred, and that the right hand can overcome this negative habit more rapidly than the left. As to the exact nature of these various specific and general components we have as yet no clues.

PRACTICE AND INTERPOLATED ACTIVITY AT DIFFERENT ROTATION SPEEDS

Changing the rotation speed is probably the smallest alteration that can be made to the pursuit-rotor task and, because of the nature of the apparatus, is also the simplest. Apart from these practical considerations varying rotation speed is an ideal way of varying the degree of difference between tasks. Thus tracking at 55 rpm is more similar to tracking at 60 rpm than is tracking at 20 rpm. This dimension of the task can therefore be used to give information about how specific the learning and the inhibition produced by working on the pursuit rotor may be. Unfortunately none of the experiments involving various rotation speeds have used the simple and elegant design of the bilateral reminiscence experiments which would have enabled one to answer these sorts of questions.

Leonard *et al.* (1970) first trained subjects for 20 min at 30, 40, 45, 50, and 60 rpm and then tested them at 45 rpm after a 48-hr rest. There was no group which transferred to the 45 rpm task without rest. Thus it was not possible to test hypotheses about inhibition such as, for example, that pretraining at 60 rpm will build up more inhibition giving rise to a greater amount of reminiscence. After 48 hr all the inhibition should have dissipated (or alternatively all the consolidation should be complete). Leonard *et al.* were concerned with transfer of training and in particular the effect of task difficulty on such transfer. The results (Figure 7-4) did not throw much light on this point. At the beginning of post-rest practice the groups trained at 30 and 60 rpm performed at a significantly lower level than the others. This would

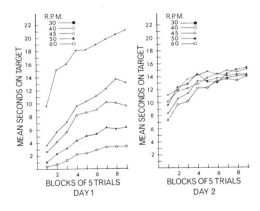

Figure 7-4. Mean time-on-target scores for 5 groups of subjects trained at various speeds on day 1, but all transferred to 45 rpm on day 2. Taken with permission from Leonard *et al.* (1970).

seem simply to imply that the greater the difference between the training task and the criterion task the less learning was transferred. However, the groups trained at 30 and 60 rpm also showed a steeper post-rest upswing and after about 8 min reached the same level as the other groups. This is the same effect as that found with transfer from one hand to the other. It suggests that these extreme rotation speeds gave rise to some inappropriate component of skill which had to be extinguished after rest, but that the basic skill was transferred completely.

Humphries (personal communication) performed an elaborate experiment in which practice for 5 min at speeds varying from 30 to 90 rpm was interpolated between two sessions at 60 rpm (5 and 3 min in length, respectively). Some groups had a 10-min rest period immediately after the interpolated learning and there were also two groups with no interpolated learning. The only measure reported is reminiscence, that is the difference between the last 20-sec trial in the original learning and the first 20-sec trial in the second learning session after rest and interpolated activity (in terms of time-on-target). The results are extremely difficult to interpret since many competing processes may be involved. Thus performance on the second session is affected by inhibition from the first session and from the interpolated activity, and by learning from the first session and from the interpolated activity. Furthermore the interpolated activity may show positive or negative transfer to the final session and may also interfere with the consolidation of the learning in the first session. The two groups with no interpolated activity had either 5 or 15 min of rest and did not differ from each other. This suggests that after 5 min all the inhibition had dissipated or all the learning had consolidated. For the groups with no rest after the interpolated activity the amount of reminiscence steadily decreased as the speed of rotation during the interpolated activity increased, being negative for speeds greater than 60 rpm. All the groups with rest after the interpolated activity showed greater reminiscence than the equivalent groups without rest. The greatest reminiscence was shown by the group having interpolated activity at 60 rpm (i.e., identical to the two learning sessions). The other groups showed about the same amount of reminiscence as the groups with no interpolated activity except the group with 90 rpm, which showed much less reminiscence. Analysis of variance revealed significant effects of rest and of type of interpolated activity. However, the interaction was not significant. Accepting that these results truly reflect the effects of the various manipulations, Humphries demonstrated that the results could be explained plausibly in terms either of inhibition theory or of consolidation theory.

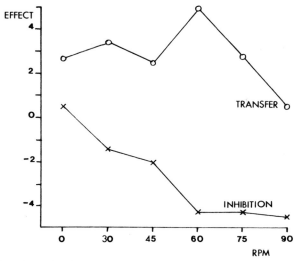

Figure 7-5. Hypothetical effects of interpolated activity at various rotation speeds. The interpolated activity may produce inhibition which dissipates during rest and transferable training which does not. Drawn from data given by Humphries (personal communication).

Since both the groups with no interpolated activity showed the same amount of reminiscence it appears that all the inhibition built up during 5 min of practice had dissipated after 5 min of rest. Thus for the groups which had 10 min rest after the interpolated activity there was no inhibition present at the beginning of the second learning session. Hence any effects of the interpolated activity must reflect transfer of skill. These groups did indeed show a typical transfer gradient with the amount of transfer decreasing as the difference between the original and the interpolated rotation speed increased. However, this gradient is asymmetric, being much steeper when the interpolated speeds are faster. The highest rotation speed (90 rpm) actually produced negative transfer. Nothing very important can be attributed to this asymmetrical transfer gradient since it depends on the scale used for describing the interpolated tasks which is arbitrarily given in rpm. The other groups which had no rest presumably show this same transfer gradient with the effects of inhibition superimposed. Thus pure inhibition effects can be derived from their results (Figure 7-5). As might be expected this shows that the faster the interpolated activity the greater was the inhibition that built up.

In terms of consolidation theory a very similar train of thought can be followed. The two groups with no interpolated activity show that consolidation is complete after 5 min. However, the interpolated activity will interfere with the consolidation of the original learning whether or not there is a rest after the interpolated learning. One might argue that in the group with no rest virtually none of the learning deriving from the interpolated activity was consolidated, so that the reminiscence of these groups reflected the amount of interference with the consolidation of the original learning. In this case it seems that the faster the rotation during the interpolated activity the greater was the interference, a very plausible result (Figure 7-6). For the groups with rest after interpolated activity reminiscence is determined by the partially consolidated original learning plus the wholly consolidated interpolated learning. Thus a transfer gradient can be estimated (Figure 7-6). Unlike the gradient derived from inhibition theory, interpolated trials at speeds greater than 60 rpm gives transfer as great as that at 60 rpm.

Both these interpretations are rather oversimplified and would have to be supported by further testing. In particular it would be interesting to study the transfer gradient unaffected by previous learning by eliminating the original learning session. Another important addition to the design, as Humphries points out, would be to introduce a rest between original and interpolated learning. This would allow the original learning to consolidate, but would not effect the build up of inhibition due to the interpolated activity. It would thus allow a critical test of the two alternative theories.

It is unfortunate that Humphries does not give any indication of what happened after the very first trial of the final relearning period. In the experiment of Leonard et al. (1970) the groups who had received pretraining at rotation speeds very different from that presented in the test session also showed depressed performance at the very beginning of that session. However, they also showed a steeper upswing and eventually caught up with the other groups. If this effect was also present in Humphries' experiment then neither of the explanations (in terms of inhibition or consolidation) would be tenable. It would be necessary to hypothesize additional underlying effects which would render the explanations even more unwieldy and difficult to test. In terms of inhibition the upswing would be explained in terms of the extinction of conditioned inhibition. Even in the absence of an interpolated rest this might occur when switching from a fast speed of rotation to a slow speed of rotation, since this switch might well be associated with a drop in the amount of reactive inhibition generated. However, it is difficult to see why conditioned inhibition should extinguish after a switch from a slow rotation speed to a fast rotation speed. An alternative explanation of this temporary supression of performance might be in terms of some sort of negative transfer which is rapidly unlearned.

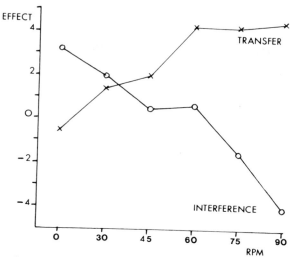

Figure 7-6. Hypothetical effects of interpolated activity at various rotation speeds. The interpolated activity may interfere with consolidation of previous learning. Only after a rest can the learning derived from the interpolated activity consolidate, giving transferable effects. Drawn from data given by Humphries (personal communication).

Since Humphries only reported reminiscence scores, all these explanations might seem rather hypothetical; however, his experiment has been partially replicated by Wada (1970), who reported the full course of a final five-minute learning session. Using a standard pursuit rotor Wada required his subjects to perform at 40 rpm for six minutes, followed by one of various interpolated activities, followed by five further minutes at 40 rpm. The various interpolated activities were rest, pursuit rotor at 20 rpm and pursuit rotor at 60 rpm. These interpolations lasted for 20, 60, or 120 sec. There was no break in performance (except in the case of interpolated rest) since the rotation speed of pursuit rotor could be changed in 0.1 seconds. This design corresponds closely to the groups in Humphries' experiment receiving no rest after their interpolated learning. Wada found that, except in the case of rest, the length of the interpolated activity had little effect on performance thereafter. Figure 7-7 shows performance after practice at 20 and 60 rpm compared with the effects of rest and continuous performance at 40 rpm. At the very beginning of the final 5-min practice session the results correspond very closely to those of Humphries. The best performance followed interpolated rest while that following practice at 20, 40, and 60 rpm was increasingly depressed. However, during the 5-min practice, there was a considerable amount of upswing for the groups that had practiced at 20 and 60 rpm though not, of course, for the group that

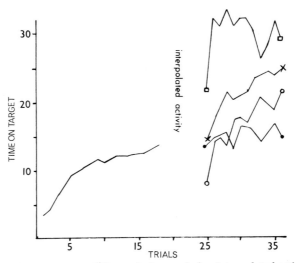

Figure 7-7. Mean time-on-target at 40 rpm before and after interpolated activity at 20 rpm (×), 40 rpm (●), 60 rpm (○) and rest (□). Drawn from data given by Wada (1970).

continued at 40 rpm without interruption. By the end of the 5-min session the 20-rpm group performed at the same level as those with interpolated rest and the 60 rpm group was well above the 40-rpm group. One rather trivial point that has never been raised by any of the authors discussed so far is that an instantaneous change in target speed is bound to produce a temporary depression of performance. The subject has first to notice that the target has changed speed and then make the necessary corrections to his hand movements. During this time his performance would be depressed even if he knew precisely what the required corrections were. The superiority of the 60-rpm group to the 40-rpm groups is particularly difficult to explain either in terms of inhibition or consolidation. The interpolated practice at 60 rpm should build up more inhibition than practice at 40 rpm. It also necessitates less experience of 40-rpm performance for consolidation. Thus even if we explain the upswing as the extinction of some negative habits learned during the practice at 60 rpm, we still cannot explain the finding that performance after practice at 60 rpm is finally better than that after continuous practice at 40 rpm.

One possibility is that any interruption of continuous performance at the same speed, whether it be by rest or by practice at some other speed, is beneficial. This might be because the interruption produced an increase in arousal, or to put it in everyday language, relieved the tedium and reduced boredom. Wada's own explanation is rather similar to this. He suggests that the change to different rotation speeds caused the subjects to try out different strategies of performance which they would not have tried had they continued to work at the same speed. This increase in flexibility made it more likely that they would discover the optimum strategy for the task.

The effects of pretraining and interpolated learning at different rotation speeds are much harder to summarize than those due to working with the other hand. This is because a number of crucial comparisons and designs have not yet been made. Thus the various processes (inhibition, consolidation, interference with consolidation, transfer) hypothesized as underlying performance have been confounded. These experiments have thrown little light on hypothetical underlying processes. The results of the experiments have, however, been fairly consistent. The greater the deviation of the speed of rotation during pretraining or interpolation from the final speed, the greater is the depression of the following performance. However, this depression is only temporary. This result suggests that, within the range of rotation speeds used, the basic skill or habit involved is the same with only minor additional components concerning the differences in speed. These minor components can be rapidly learned and extinguished. Not surprisingly there is some asymmetry in the transfer effects, with faster speeds being more detrimental than slower speeds. This is presumably because faster speeds are "harder" than slower speeds and thus may induce more inhibition or more interference with consolidation of previous learning.

PRACTICE AND INTERPOLATION OF MOTOR TASKS OTHER THAN THE STANDARD PURSUIT ROTOR

Practice on the pursuit rotor at a different speed or with a different hand still seems to involve the same basic skill. The experiments to be described in this section define the limits of this skill and show that many tasks apparently similar to the pursuit rotor show no transfer effects. Laszlo and Pritchard (1969) performed an ingenious transfer experiment in which both speed and track shape were altered. This is of course, not possible with the standard pursuit rotor. The tracks were on a plastic mask, being circular and triangular in shape and the target was a spot of light generated by a film loop and projector. The speed of the target was either constant or variable. There were therefore four closely related pursuit-rotor tasks, and transfer between all the possible combinations were studied. All subjects worked for 20 10-sec trials separated by 50-sec rests. Control subjects performed the same task for all 20 trials while the experimental groups switched to a different task after trial 10. Figure 7-8 shows the comparisons of the experimental groups with their appropriate control groups. For the most part the results are straightforward. All shifts where only one variable was changed (track shape or speed) resulted in positive transfer except with shifts to a circular track at constant speed. Thus it appears that these tasks had sufficient in common (either shape or movement) to permit learning to be transferred. In conditions where both task variables were changed there was no transfer except in one case. The shift from a constant triangle to a variable circle resulted in negative transfer, but a shift in the opposite direction gave no transfer. The reason for this subtle effect remains obscure. The condition with the circular track at constant speed was the easiest of the four and the lack of transfer when shifting to this task may be partly due to ceiling effects. Laszlo and Pritchard suggest that the constant circular task requires a different strategy from the others, depending on "receptor anticipation" rather than "perceptual anticipation." However, even though it does seem plausible to assume that different strategies are required for the various tasks, it is not clear why the lack of transfer only occured with a shift to a constant circular task and not with the shift from this task. Laszlo and Pritchard suggest that shift from constant circle required the development of perceptual anticipation in addition to the receptor anticipation already acquired, whereas transfer to constant circle required the unlearning of the perceptual anticipation strategy. If the unlearning of some strategy was involved why did it not lead to negative transfer?

It will be observed that in Figure 7-8 there is no sign of the upswing that frequently occurred after transfer from other tasks in the experiments previously discussed in this chapter. A crucial difference in Laszlo and Pritchard's experiment is that the training was spaced rather than massed and also that the time involved was rather short; 100 sec of post-transfer practice.

Apart from these minor details of interpretation the implications of Laszlo and Pritchard's experiment on transfer are clear. If either the track shape or the speed only are changed there is transfer of training. If both are changed there is no transfer. Thus the tasks they used give us some idea of the specificity of pursuit-rotor learning and it seems that it is very specific indeed. Following a target that moves round a triangular track at constant speed seems little different from following a target round a circular track at variable speed. Both tasks required the subject to follow the target with his eyes and detect whether he is in contact with it or not. Also, having detected these errors he must learn to make

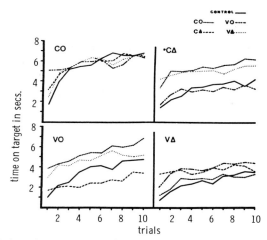

Figure 7-8. Preshift trials 1–10 or control groups and postshift trials 11–20 for experimental groups. Each quadrant shows the preshift trials of one control group compared with the postshift trials of groups shifted to the control task. Task is indicated by the symbols in the top-left corner of each quadrant. An unbroken line represents the control curves regardless of task. Symbols indicating the preshift task from which groups, other than control, were shifted, are given in the top-right corner. Taken with permission from Laszlo and Pritchard (1969).

the appropriate hand movements. It is on the basis of this kind of analysis that the pursuit-rotor task has often been referred to as a test of eye–hand coordination. Nevertheless, in spite of all that the two tasks described above have in common, learning from one does not transfer to the other. This result suggests that the precise path followed by the target is the crucial aspect of the task while more general aspects of the task, like eye–hand coordination, are not. Perhaps these general aspects of performance have been sufficiently mastered in everyday life.

The earlier studies of transfer in pursuit-rotor learning were based on an analysis which, as we have argued above, may be inappropriate. Rather than analyzing the *task* into its components as was the case in all the experiments described so far in this chapter (hand used, speed of rotation, etc.) attempts were made to isolate the components of the *psychological process*. Ammons (1957*b*) was principally concerned with reinstating set, loss of which he thought was the explanation of post-rest upswing. However, his experiment is essentially a transfer experiment. He analyzed the task into an ocular and a manual component. Ocular practice consisted of the subject following the target with her eyes for 2 min. In manual practice the subject was blindfolded and had to follow with her index finger a rivet head set in the pursuit-rotor turntable at the same distance from the center as the normal target. The subjects, who were all female college students, practiced these components for 2 min before 17 min of normal pursuit-rotor practice, some groups before the initial practice period and some at the end of an interpolated rest. The results are very straightforward, for none of the experimental groups differed in any way from a control group which did not practice any components of the task. Thus practice of these components of the task induced neither transfer of learning nor a reduction of post-rest upswing.

The only interpolated activity that did have an effect was that studied by Adams (1955) and Rosenquist (1965). This involved the subject in watching someone else practice on the pursuit rotor and holding down a button whenever the performer was on target. After an interpolated period of such active watching of between 3 and 15 min performance was impaired in relation to a control group which had rested during the same period (Figure 7-9). In addition there was less post-rest upswing for the experimental group. It was concluded that active watching reintroduced set, thus reducing post-rest upswing and also generated or prevented the dissipation of reactive inhibition thus depressing later performance. Certainly the results suggest that "active watching" is a genuine component of pursuit-rotor performance. Humphries and McIntyre (1963) used a modified form of active watching called pursuit reaction time. This consisted of pressing a button whenever a light mounted on the pursuit-rotor target came on. The light was so mounted that, in order to see it, the subject had to follow the target with a combination of eye and head movements. However, this interpolated activity in various forms clearly had no effect on later pursuit-rotor performance, suggesting that neither inhibition nor learning was transferred. Humphries and McIntyre (1963b) also used blindfold rotary arm movement as an interpolated activity (with the stylus locked to a swivel on the target), but this too had no effect on later performance.

Another method for affecting the dissipation of inhibition that can, by a small exercise of the imagination, be labeled interpolated activity, has been investigated by Rachman and Grassi (1965), Feldman (1964c), and Costello (1967). In these experiments an "alien stimulus" (a buzzer) was introduced in the last minute of pre-rest practice on the pursuit rotor. It was hypothesized that reactive inhibition was, in essence, the same as the inhibition studied by Pavlov in his conditioning experiments, and that therefore an alien stimulus would cause disinhibition. Since reminiscence was thought to be a reflection of the recovery from inhibition during rest, dissipation of the inhibition before the rest by the alien stimulus should reduce the amount of reminiscence. This

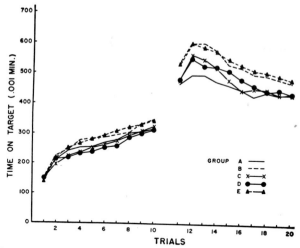

Figure 7-9. Pursuit-rotor performance before and after various kinds of interpolated activity; (A) visual responding; (B) rest; (C) button pressing; (D) rest, but standing in front of apparatus; (E) visual responding followed by 10-min rest. Taken with permission from Adams (1955).

prediction was confirmed and groups bombarded by an alien stimulus before the rest showed less reminiscence than control groups. However, detailed analysis showed that the lesser reminiscence was due, not to increased pre-rest performance, but decreased post-rest performance. This is entirely contrary to the original inhibition hypothesis. These experiments were an important reason for dropping the inhibition model of reminiscence and switching instead to a model in terms of consolidation. They will therefore be discussed in more detail in Chapter 11 in which inhibition and consolidation theories will be contrasted.

CHANGES IN THE DISTRIBUTION OF PRACTICE.

Perhaps the minimum variation that can be made in a task is to alter the distribution of practice on it. There are a number of experiments using the pursuit rotor in which the effects of changing the distribution of practice have been studied. Doré and Hilgard (1938) studied the effects of shifting from massed to spaced practice and vice versa in order to test Snoddy's theory of primary and secondary mental growth (Snoddy, 1935), which was discussed in Chapter 3. It was predicted from this theory that spaced practice followed by massed practice would result in superior performance in the last part of the session, as compared to massed practice followed by spaced practice. In fact exactly the opposite was found to be the case and spaced practice was found to be superior to massed practice whenever it occurred. Cook and Hilgard (1949) confirmed this result using a slightly different design in which the distribution of practice was changed gradually rather than suddenly. Once again spaced practice was found to be superior to massed practice whether it occurred at the beginning or the end of the experimental sessions.

This difference between massed and spaced practice became of great interest to psychologists: first, because it was so striking and secondly because it appeared to be a manifestation of various inhibition processes. Many attempts were made to explain it in terms of Hullian learning theory. The major question to be answered was, was the effect on learning or on performance? Duncan (1951) had subjects practice on the pursuit rotor for two 5-min periods separated by a 10-min rest. During the pre-rest period half the subjects were assigned to distributed practice (10-sec practice, 20-sec rest) and the other half to massed practice. At the end of the pre-rest period those whose practice had been distributed were performing significantly better than those whose practice had been massed, even though the latter had spent twice as much time actually working on the pursuit rotor. After the rest the two groups were further subdivided so that half continued with the same distribution of practice as before and the others switched.

Immediately after the rest there was no difference between the groups. At the end of the post-rest practice period those whose practice was spaced were performing better than the massed practice groups, whatever their conditions of practice before the rest. Duncan concluded from these results that the distribution of practice affected performance and not learning. However, it could be argued that those subjects who had spaced practice learned faster since they achieved the same level of performance as the massed practice group (post-rest) even though they had spent less time actually practicing.

Dey and Ammons (1956) studied this problem directly by investigating whether level of performance depended on the time spent practicing or on time since practice began (i.e., time spent practicing plus time spent resting). They tested five groups each with 1-min practice trials and with intertrial rests varying from 0 to 5 min on the Airplane Control Test (a form of pursuit tracking). They concluded that level of performance was a function of time spent practicing rather than time since practice began. However, the group with 0 min between practice sessions tended to be inferior to all the other groups. Since the distribu-

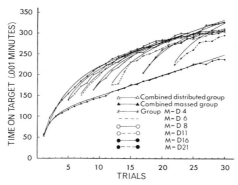

Figure 7-10. Performance curves for groups shifted from massed to spaced practice after varying numbers of trials, with hypothetical performance curves fitted. Taken with permission from Reynolds and Adams (1953).

tion of practice remained the same for all groups throughout the experiment we cannot come to any conclusions about its effect on learning.

The most thorough investigations of the effects of the distribution of practice on pursuit-rotor performance were carried out by Reynolds and Adams (1953) and Adams and Reynolds (1954). In the former experiment subjects practiced on the pursuit rotor for 30 sec at a time, separated by rests of 10 ("massed" practice) or 30 sec (spaced practice). After a varying number of trials the subjects were switched from massed to spaced practice. Figure 7-10 shows the results of switching.

It is clear from this figure that after a short upswing period of two or three trials all the groups previously experiencing massed practice reach exactly the same level as the subjects that only experienced spaced practice. Essentially the same result is obtained when subjects are switched from spaced to massed practice. After a brief period of downswing, subjects previously experiencing spaced practice reach precisely the same level of performance as those who have only experienced massed practice (Figure 7-11).

These experiments on the effects of the distribution of practice may be treated as transfer of learning experiments just like the others discussed in this chapter. In the simplest form of this design two groups are tested; one group experiences condition A twice, the other experiences condition B followed by condition A. In the examples we are currently considering A and B would be different distributions of practice. If the performance of the two groups is identical on the final session A then we would conclude that an equal amount of learning transferred from a first session of practice on task B as transferred from a

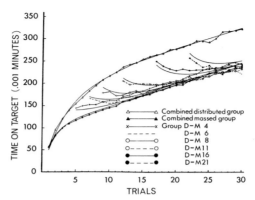

Figure 7-11. Performance curves for groups shifted from spaced to massed practice after varying numbers of trials, with hypothetical performance curves fitted. Taken with permission from Reynolds and Adams (1953).

first session of practice on task A. Thus we may conclude from the experiments discussed that the amount of learning depends on the amount of time spent practicing and is independent of how that practice was distributed. On the other hand the level of performance is dependent on the distribution of practice.

A notable feature of the work on the effects of distribution of practice is its extreme replicability and regularity. An indication of the regularity of the phenomena is given by Reynolds and Adams's (1953) successful attempt to describe pursuit-rotor performance under different practice conditions with a simple equation: $P = M (1 - e^{iT}) + bT$. In this equation P is a measure of performance, T is the number of trials, M is the limit for the exponential component and is a function of the interval between trials, i is the exponential growth parameter and is a function of the interval between trials, and b is a parameter independent of intertrial interval. With increasing trials the exponential component in this equation becomes negligible and the equation reduces to: $P = M + bT$. This defines a straight line, the level of performance on any trial being determined by M, which is a function of the distribution of practice, while the rate of increase is determined by b, which is independent of the distribution of practice. Thus the equation reflects our previous conclusions that performance is determined by the distribution of practice, while learning is determined solely by the number of practice trails. Reynolds and Adams introduced a second exponential component to describe the gradual adjustment of performance when a subject is shifted from one practice distribution to another. Figure 7-10 shows the curves fitted on the basis of this equation when subjects were shifted from massed to spaced practice, while Figure 7-11 shows the fitted curves when subjects were shifted from spaced to massed practice. The fit during the period of adjustment is not very good, but once the adjustment is complete the correspondence between the hypothetical curve and the empirical data is almost perfect.

Unfortunately Reynolds and Adams did not have a group with genuinely massed practice in their experiments. The shortest rest period they studied was 5 sec. The experiment by Dey and Ammons (1956) produced results suggesting that when practice is truly massed rather less learning accrues from a given number of practice trials than with distributed practice. Reynolds and Adams also suggest that a group in their experiment which had 21 trials of "massed" practice before being shifted to spaced practice stabilized at a lower mean level than the other groups. These observations imply that if practice is truly massed or if practice continues for a long time with only very short rests, rather less learning takes place than under conditions of spaced practice. Such observations would be expected on the basis of a consolidation theory of learning. The learned material can only be consolidated during rest. If a sufficiently long rest does not occur for a long time then some of the learned material will be lost, and thus will no longer be available for consolidation even when an appropriate rest does occur.

It is not quite clear when predictions would be made from Hull's learning theory, since paradoxically this theory is principally concerned with performance rather than learning. Denny, Frisbey, and Weaver (1955) consider that the difference in level of performance between massed and spaced practice groups is due to the build up of conditioned inhibition in the former. When subjects are switched from massed to spaced practice this conditioned inhibition extinguishes until the same level of performance is reached as a group that has experienced spaced practice all the time. Although not specifically mentioned in this model of pursuit-rotor performance the simplest assumption would be that learning depends solely on the number of practice trials. Even after a long period of massed practice, switching to spaced practice would extinguish the conditioned inhibition and performance would rise to the same level as the spaced practice group. Thus what little evidence there is from studies of shifts in the distribution of practice supports a consolidation theory of pursuit-rotor learning.

Further evidence for the regularity of distribution of practice effects was collected by Kaufman, Smith, and Zeaman (1962). These authors applied the Reynolds–Adams equations to performance on the inverted alphabet printing task. The results obtained on shifting from massed to

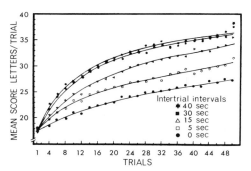

Figure 7-12. Performance curves on the inverted alphabet printing task for five constant conditions of distribution with hypothetical performance curves fitted. Taken with permission from Kaufman *et al.* (1962).

spaced practice and vice versa were remarkably similar to those obtained with the pursuit rotor, and in addition the Reynolds–Adams equations fitted the data extremely well. Figure 7-12 shows learning curves for five constant conditions of distribution. As with the pursuit rotor the equations fitted the results less well during the period of adjustment immediately after a shift in the distribution of practice. This was particularly so when conditions changed from highly spaced (30-sec practice, 30-sec rest) to completely massed practice (Figure 7-13). Nevertheless when the period of adjustment was complete the predicted performance level agreed very well with the empirical result.

However, although such similar results have been obtained for two rather different motor skills a very different picture emerges from studies of verbal learning.

Zacks (1969) concluded, from an extensive review of previous work, that in verbal learning the amount learned in a certain time is invariant, regardless of how that time is distributed. He coined the phrase "total time invariance" to describe this phenomenon. He confirmed this expectation in an experiment in which subjects learned paired associates. In the time available for learning the Ss could either study each pair for as long as they wished, or take test trials whenever they chose, or both. In spite of this freedom as to the distribution of practice, subjects learned the same amount of material as subjects for whom the distribution of practice was determined by the experimenter.

These results are precisely the opposite of those found with motor skills in which the amount of learning depended on the number of trials and not the time over which these had been distributed. However, Zacks suggests that even in the conditions in which the experimenter determined the distribution of practice, the Ss were able covertly to alter that distribution. They did this by rehearsing difficult pairs longer than easier ones and also by not necessarily switching their attention to the next pair when it was presented. Thus the difference between the distribution of practice determined by the experimenter and that chosen by the subjects was apparent rather than real. It is clear that the strategies adopted by subjects which seem responsible for the "total time invariance" effect are very specific to verbal learning (rehearsal, attention to difficult pairs) and would not apply to the learning of motor skills.

CONCLUSIONS

As we have seen many of the studies of transfer and the effects of interpolated activity in pursuit-rotor learning have been inconclusive due to the lack of certain essential experimental controls. This is due partly to weaknesses in theory. With so many hypothesized underlying processes (inhibition, consolidation, learning) confounded with one another, unduly complicated experiments are required. Nevertheless

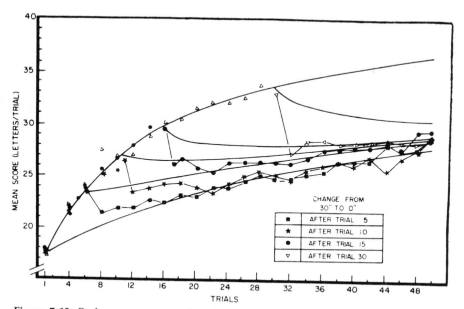

Figure 7-13. Performance curves when changing from a highly spaced to a completely massed condition with hypothetical performance curves fitted. Taken with permission from Kaufman *et al.* (1962).

the studies discussed in this chapter have provided useful information about the precise locus of these various effects and have also given some indication as to which aspects of the pursuit-rotor task are important and which are not.

The studies of bilateral transfer have shown that the inhibition built up during pursuit-rotor performance is not located in the particular limb executing the task. In addition the learning involved is largely carried over from one limb to the other and therefore cannot be concerned simply with sequences of specific muscle movements. Performance at different speeds also gives rise to transferable learning, although if the speeds differ excessively from that given finally, the final performance may be temporarily depressed. This suggests that whatever is learned about pursuit-rotor performance can readily be modified to cope with different speeds of rotation. Performance at high speeds may either build up greater inhibition or interfere more with consolidation of previous learning than performance at low speeds.

A particular pursuit tracking task is entirely defined by the variations in position and speed of the target over time. As long as two pursuit tracking tasks have one of these aspects in common then learning will transfer from one task to another. If the tasks have neither position nor speed variations in common then no learning transfers. This result might not be thought very surprising. Since the tasks have neither position nor speed in common, what learning could be transferred from one task to the other? In fact the tasks must have many other aspects in common since they are both pursuit tracking tasks. Thus the subject might have to learn how to produce effective movements of his tracking stylus, and how to take action to correct the errors that he detects. The results of the transfer experiments suggest that these more general aspects of pursuit tracking are not important components of the task, perhaps because they are already well learned in the subjects' everyday life.

Lastly, attempts have been made to analyze the performance of the pursuit-rotor task into components such as following the target with the eyes, detecting errors, and moving the stylus round the track. Moving either the eyes or the stylus round the track does not produce any inhibition that affects later pursuit-rotor performance. However, the isolated detection of errors in tracking (without correcting them) does seem to depress later pursuit-rotor performance. Practice of these various isolated components does not seem to produce any learning that is transferable to later pursuit-rotor performance.

These findings suggest the following model of pursuit-rotor performance. The subject gradually learns and consolidates an "inner representation" of the movements of the target with time (i.e., its successive positions and speeds). This "inner representation" is principally concerned with execution, but is not tied to any specific muscle groups. Only tasks for which the inner representations have something in common will show transfer and the effects of interpolated activity on learning. The subject must continuously check whether his "inner representation" is correct, i.e., whether his movements are successfully related to those of the target. This activity might generate inhibition.

These speculations are a long way from our original concerns with verbal learning and the attempt to analyze the pursuit rotor in terms of stimulus–response sequences. If nothing else the studies of transfer and interpolated activity have shown that it is not useful to analyze pursuit-rotor performance in terms of S–R sequences. Why then was this method of analysis so successful in verbal learning? One obvious solution is that the mechanisms involved in verbal learning are different from those in motor learning. This is almost certainly true. There are a few cases of brain damaged patients who show a total inability to retain verbal material for more than a few minutes while at the same time their learning of the pursuit rotor is relatively normal, showing little loss of skill after intervals of days or weeks (Corkin, 1968).

We would also suggest however that the tests of S–R theory using verbal material were bound to be successful, and tell us little about normal human learning. The theory states that learning involves the strengthening of bonds between stimulus–response pairs, and indicates circumstances in which these bonds will be strengthened and weakened. In the paired associate learning task a subject is explicitly required to build strong bonds between S–R pairs. We could in a similar fashion construct a visuomotor task in which the subject had to learn obvious S–R pairs. For example the subject might have to press a particular button when a particular light came on. With such a task we would be able to demonstrate the same effects of transfer and interpolated activity as with paired associate verbal learning. In studying these tasks the experimenter is simulating his model of behavior using a human subject instead of a computer. He may thus be able to demonstrate that his model is internally consistent and has the properties he claims. However, to demonstrate that a task which clearly involves the learning of S–R bonds is performed in a predictable way is not the same as demonstrating that it is useful to consider all tasks as consisting of S–R bonds.

It is interesting that although much of the work on pursuit-rotor learning has been carried out within the framework of Hullian learning theory, that aspect of the theory which deals with S–R bonds has been rarely evoked to account for performance of this task. Thus inhibition rather than interference has been the major variable thought to control the level of performance. The evidence presented in this chapter suggests that this was because very few other tasks interfere with later pursuit-rotor performance. In studies of verbal learning however, interference has often been demonstrated. It is doubtful that this finding represents a general distinction between "verbal" learning and "motor" learning. Had tasks other than the pursuit rotor and paired associate verbal learning been chosen the pattern might quite well have been reversed.

CHAPTER 8

Individual Differences in Ability as Determinants of Performance and Reminiscence

The study of reminiscence has concentrated mainly on general laws and has neglected the study of individual differences; the assumption has usually been that such differences would not affect the general form of the equations written to describe learning and performance parameters. In this and the following two chapters this assumption will be investigated experimentally; in this chapter we shall deal with differences in *ability* to perform the motor task in question, while in the following two chapters we shall deal with normal personality differences (mainly in extraversion and in neuroticism), and with psychotic as opposed to normal subjects. As far as the pursuit rotor is concerned, we have already seen that a person's ability to perform well on this apparatus is very much determined by genetic factors; environment only plays a very small part in causing such individual differences. What are the consequences of these innate ability differences?

Among the first to tackle this problem were Buxton and Grant (1939) who tested male and female subjects and arbitrarily divided them into high and low halves on the basis of the last five trials of the first 15 on the rotor. A 14-min rest period followed, after which another 5 trials were given. "In terms of absolute gain during the 14 minute rest period,

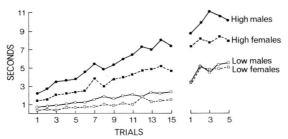

Figure 8-1. Performance and reminiscence of high- and low-ability Ss. Taken with permission from Buxton and Grant (1939).

the high and low groups in each sex are approximately equal. However, when percentages of improvement are computed, we see that proportionately more 'spontaneous' improvement is made by the poorer subjects." (Buxton and Grant, 1939.) The actual differences for high- and low-scoring men are in fact 2.85 and 2.67; those for the women 3.14 and 3.35. In percentages, the figures are 39% and 127% for the men; 65% and 256% for the women. Differences between the sexes are almost as noticeable as those between the high and low scorers. (In absolute terms the women of course score much lower than the men, as is usually found on the pursuit rotor.) Figure 8-1 shows the actual data.

Six years later, Leavitt and Schlosberg (1944) and Leavitt (1945), in a study already mentioned, reported an experiment in which 4 groups of 12 Ss each were given 10 30-sec trials to learn a list of 15 nonsense syllables, and a similar 10-trial session on a pursuit rotor, 30-sec rest pauses intervening between learning trials. The retention of material was tested after 1, 7, 28, and 70 days, one of the four groups returning after each interval. One interesting finding was that retention was greatly superior for the motor habit, as compared with the verbal one; Figure 8-2 shows the amount retained at the first relearning (11th trial). Score at the last original learning trial (10th trial) equals 100, and the ordinate is in terms of percent of the last learning trial. Note that only the motor habit shows reminiscence, after 1 and after 7 days; there is some slight evidence of reminiscence after 28 days, but none at all after 70 days. There is no evidence of reminiscence at any stage for the verbal learning.

Leavitt (1945) attacks two problems in a reanalysis of the data: "(1) the problem of the relation of speed of learning to the amount of material retained, and (2) the relation between absolute and relative amounts of reminiscence shown by individual Ss." His primary interest is in the first of these problems. He starts out with a review of previous work, showing that "the slow learner retains less of what he

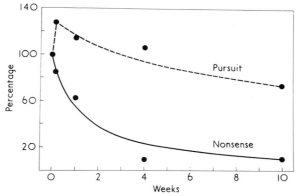

Figure 8-2. Amount retained at the first relearning trial, with last learning trial set at 100. The ordinate is in terms of percent of the last learning trial. Taken with permission from Leavitt and Schlosberg (1944).

has learned than does the fast learner." (p. 134.) The hypothesis of a positive learning–retention relationship was tested by correlating scores on last learning trial and score on first relearning trial; these are presented in Table 8-1. It will be clear that the hypothesis is borne out for the 1-day interval; for the longer intervals, however, the correlations are reversed, with the 7-day period being positive for the nonsense syllable learning and essentially zero for the pursuit rotor. "As the period between learning and relearning increases, the superiority, in terms of amount of material retained, shifts from the fast to the slow S." (p. 135.)

The same picture emerges when *relative* amount retained is considered; "relatively, too, the fast learner, after short intervals, tends to retain more than the slow learner. But again, at longer intervals, the trend is reversed and the fast learner retains a smaller proportion of what he had originally learned." (Leavitt, 1945, p. 135.) Savings scores also show the same picture. When we look simply at reminiscence, we find that "there is a high positive correlation between amount learned

TABLE 8-1. Correlations on Last Learning Trial and Score on First Learning Trial between Score [a]

	1 day	7 days	28 days	70 days
Nonsense syllables	.84 ± .05	.67 ± .10	−.26 ± .23	−.17 ± .25
Pursuit rotor	.54 ± .14	−.06 ± .29	−.68 ± .10	−.73 ± .08

[a] Taken with permission from Leavitt (1945).

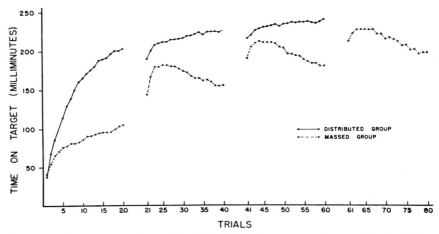

Figure 8-3. Performance of massed and distributed groups on the pursuit rotor. Taken with permission from Reynolds and Adams (1954).

and amount reminisced after one day (.54), up to moderate levels of mastery. After seven days there is essentially no correlation (−.06)." (Leavitt, 1945, p. 137.) This paper presages the important discovery that the amount learned initially, on the one hand, and amount retained, or reminisced, on the other, may be related in a complex fashion, depending on the length of the intervening rest period; the investigation of this relation has in recent years usually been concerned with Walker's theory of "action decrement" which will be discussed in a later chapter. The interesting work of Kleinsmith and Kaplan (1963, 1964), using electrophysiological measures of arousal as the crucial variable, and the work of Howarth and Eysenck (1968), using personality differences instead, have shown clearly that duration of interval between learning and relearning (or testing) is indeed vital in making any generalizations in this field. We shall return to this topic in the next chapter.

The study by Reynolds and Adams (1954) which next took up this topic is characterized by the large number of subjects employed (960 basic airmen trainees). Subgroups of 12 were assigned to either a massed or a distributed practice group, and were tested simultaneously on the pursuit rotor. The duration of each trial was 20 sec for both groups, with an intertrial rest of 5 sec for the "massed" group and 60 sec for the distributed group. The massed group was given four blocks of 20 trials each and the distributed group had three blocks of 20 trials each. There was a 30-min rest between blocks. Figure 8-3 shows the development of the habit for the two groups. There is, in the case of distributed practice, a between-session loss in proficiency, while the massed group

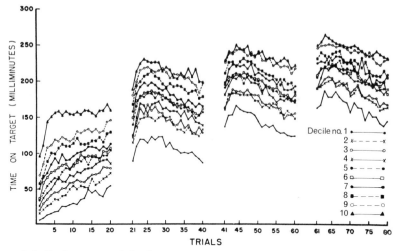

Figure 8-4. Performance of decile groups trained with massed practice. Taken with permission from Reynolds and Adams (1954).

shows reminiscence and an initial post-rest warm-up segment followed by the characteristic downward trend in the later trials of each session.

Subjects within each experimental condition were stratified into deciles on the basis of their total score for the first five trials. Acquisition curves for the 10 decile groups with massed practice are shown in Figure 8-4, and those for the distributed practice in Figure 8-5. For the

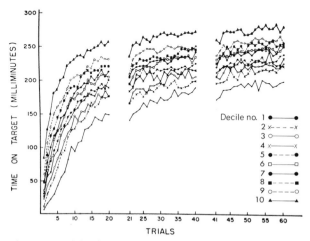

Figure 8-5. Performance of decile groups trained with distributed practice. Taken with permission from Reynolds and Adams (1954).

massed practice groups, differences are apparent between ability groups only during the first session; the curve for the poorest performers tends to be linear in shape with a slow rate of rise throughout, while with increasing level of ability linearity decreases and the initial segments show negative acceleration. The curve for the highest decile shows marked negative acceleration initially, and then essentially zero slope. "For the three later training sessions the form of the curve appears to be the same." (Reynolds & Adams, 1954, p. 271). For the groups with distributed practice, too, there are differences in slope during the first session which are related to initial level of ability, with the slopes becoming greater with increasing level of ability. The curves during the second and third sessions are essentially the same. Analysis of variance of scores on trial 60, which is the last one which is common to both groups, shows that both distribution and initial level of ability contribute significantly ($p < .01$) to variability, with interaction effects being absent.

Detailed statistical tests showed that there were no interactions between gain, warm-up, or loss within a session, and initial level of ability, as far as the massed groups were concerned. Similar results were obtained for the distributed groups. The main statistically significant finding was that low-ability groups became more variable with practice, as compared with high-ability groups; this was true even when the groups were equated for actual performance, i.e., by selecting them from different parts of the "trials" continuum. Correlations decreased with initial level as trials became more separated in time. Using total score on trials 1–5 as the X variable, and scores on trials 6–10, 56–60, and 76–80 (massed group only) as Y variables, the following correlations were found: .85 and .89 for distributed and massed practice, respectively; .57 and .61; and .57. The authors conclude that "with the exception of slope-characteristics of first-session curves no evidence has been found for the interaction of ability-level and learning variables. The data . . . support the assumption of Hull (1945) that individual differences affect the constants of a behavioural equation but not the general mathematical form. In the case of the first-session curves, the general form is apparently not affected by initial level of ability. The main characteristic which does seem to be affected is slope of the initial segment with increasing level of ability." (Reynolds & Adams, 1954, p. 275.)

The authors go on to draw attention to the fact that the curve of massed decile 10 in the pre-rest session resembled curves usually seen post-rest after massed practice, i.e., it seemed to show some form of warm-up followed by a plateau (which might have been followed, had practice gone on longer, by a decline in score.) They comment that "if the warm-up period can be regarded as a period of recruitment of previously acquired responses, then Ss in massed decile 10 would appear to be activating a pool of previously acquired relevant responses, carried over, perhaps, from psychomotor tasks encountered in everyday situations" (Reynolds & Adams, 1954, p. 276). In line with this hypothesis, they suggest a possible explanation for the increase in variability of lower-decile Ss. "One possible explanation of this phenomenon is that some Ss are initially poor performers because of lack of opportunity in the past to acquire habits which generalize to the skill being learned. When given an opportunity to practice a specific skill, they can, with sufficient training, attain the level of Ss who have had the benefit of relevant prior experience." (Reynolds & Adams, 1954, p. 276.) Also considered is the question of whether all Ss would reach a common asymptote. "Even though some Ss change status with training, . . . the mean curves are essentially parallel in the final session, with little tendency to converge. It appears that all Ss would not attain the task asymptote but rather would attain an asymptote commensurate with their own ability." (Reynolds & Adams, 1954, p. 276.) That this is correct is suggested by the work of Eysenck (1960), who trained Ss to asymptote values and found marked differences which persisted over a period of 12 months.

In the evaluation of this outstanding study, one word should be said about the term "massed." It will be recalled that in what is called the "massed" condition 20 sec of practice are followed by 5 sec of rest; thus this condition is more properly designated as "distributed" practice, the two major conditions differing in length of rest pause. Admittedly 5 sec is not much in the way of rest, but it does amount to 25% of the practice period, and it cannot be assumed that a total of $5 \times 80 = 400$ sec of rest during the total performance can be simply disregarded. Presumably the conditions of testing and the construction of the apparatus made it impossible to achieve properly massed conditions; this fact should be faced in evaluating the study.

The Reynolds and Adams finding of parallelism of practice curves for different ability groups in motor learning had been anticipated by Farmer (1927), who was concerned with psychomotor skills learned in an industrial situation, and found that Ss differentiated on the basis of initial level of ability showed parallel acquisition curves; this study would appear to be the first systematic study of the effects of ability on subsequent learning. Another study (Cieutat & Noble, 1958) attempted explicitly to test the Reynolds and Adams conclusion. The apparatus used was the U.S.A.F. two-hand coordination test. 228 Ss received 40 continuous 30-sec trials, and were stratified into 6 homogeneous ability groups, classification being on the basis of the first 5 min of practice.

Each group contained 10 Ss selected so as to insure minimum intra-group variability and equal intervals along the score continuum. There was no evidence of systematic nonparallelism among the 6 curves, and the authors concluded "that the learning rate of two-hand irregular pursuit skill, like that of one-hand regular pursuit, does not vary importantly with initial level of ability within the investigated period."

Reynolds and Adams (1953) suggested that tracking curves are best described by a two-stage equation of the type:

$$R\% = M (1 - e^{-kN}) + bN$$

where b is the empirical slope constant, m the maximum habit gain of $R\%$, and k the rate parameter; N is the number of trials or blocks of reinforced practice, and $e = 2.716$. Noble (1970) has suggested a different formula:

$$R\% = M (1 - e^{-kN}) \pm T$$

where T is the initial transfer value or origin of function when $N = 0$. [Seashore (1951) and others also prefer an equation of this type because it has an asymptote.] Adams (1954) himself provided data which invalidated the Reynolds and Adams (1953) hypothesis that after a brief curvilinear adjustive phase, tracking skill grows indefinitely in a linear fashion; Reynolds and Adams themselves recognized of course that their equation was inappropriate for asymptotic performance, but believed that it was useful for describing fairly large segments of practice (Reynolds & Adams, 1953, p. 140). Noble (1970) has provided an experiment which is relevant to this question, and which also extends our knowledge of the effects of ability on rotary pursuit.

In this study, 500 naive Ss worked on the rotor for 100 20-sec trials, separated by 10-sec rest periods, i.e., a "relatively distributed practice" scheme was used. (Noble, 1970, p. 363.) Results were analyzed in terms of 5-trial blocks, and there were (unfortunately from our point of view) no extended interblock intervals beyond the regular 10-sec rests; thus the results are not directly relevant to the theory of reminiscence. Ss were graded into pentiles (i.e., there were 5 aptitude groups for male Ss, and 5 aptitude groups for females, but in the original analysis males and females were grouped together). Noble's formula was found to fit the five groups' performance with great accuracy, goodness-of-fit percentage indices ranging from 99.64% to 99.86%, with a mean of 99.77% for all curves. Initial ability levels perfectly predicted terminal performance levels of all groups. The mathematical forms of acquisition curves are thus independent of initial level of ability. However, unlike Reynolds and Adams (1954), Noble found that the factionated groups were significantly nonparallel in their growth towards asympototic levels of proficiency; this was demonstrated by interpreting the practice ability mean square as a trend test. Pentiles 1 and 5 diverge for the first 3 or 4 blocks, then gradually converge as practice continues. It appears that "initial ability, rate of acquisition, and capacity are all positively correlated." (Noble, 1970, p. 364.)

Men and women, when grouped according to initial ability, showed good fit to the formula. "The men start above the women (T), develop skill somewhat faster (k), and are approaching a higher maximum $(M + T)$." (Noble, 1970, p. 365.) The theoretical capacity values are 68.51 for males and 63.37 for females; this sex difference is well in line with results reported by other investigators (Archer, 1958; Buxton & Grant, 1939; Noble et al., 1958). For both sexes, intratrial variances increase, then decrease over blocks, with the men reaching a maximum during block 2, and the women during block 6. From block 5 onwards, females are consistently more variable. Noble also looked at the effects of age; he found no effects between the ages of 17 to 41 years, which was the span characteristic of the sample. (At younger ages, there is a direct relationship between age and pursuit skill.)

Noble used his data, and further data from the intercorrelations between the 20 blocks, for the purpose of a discussion of four theoretical positions regarding the acquisition of pursuit-rotor skill. The "superdiagonal" matrix of intercorrelations has already been discussed in an earlier chapter; we will not go into his theoretical position here because we doubt if the data are really very relevant to such a discussion, bearing in mind the Barrick, Fitts, and Briggs (1957) criticism of the use of T.O.T. scores. Noble dismisses such doubts rather cavalierly, but they seem to us very real; in any case, we shall discuss the problems involved, in so far as they are relevant to reminiscence, in a later chapter.

The Reynolds and Adams study contains a minimum of theory; the next study to be considered, by Zeaman and Kaufman (1955), contains a maximum. Deploring the fact that traditionally the study of individual differences has been the domain of the differential psychologist and not the S–R behavior theorist, they state that "at least one S–R theory has something to say about how individual differences should behave" (Zeaman & Kaufman, 1955, p. 1). They quote Hull (1945), as had done Reynolds and Adams (1954), to the effect that individual differences may affect the various constants in the equations which represent his postulate set, but leave the form of these equations invariant, and conclude that "this would mean, for example, that in his equation for the growth of habit strength (H) as a function of number (N) of reinforcements the constants H_o, m, and i (controlling the initial strength,

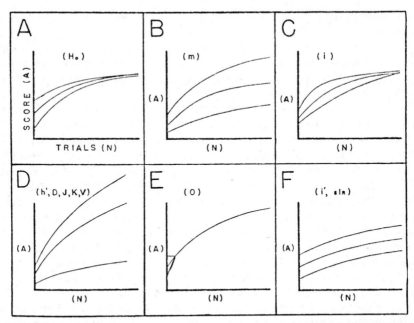

Figure 8-6. Theoretical curves showing what would happen to starting differences during practice if they represented individual differences in the theoretical parameters shown above the curves. Taken with permission from Zeaman and Kaufman (1955).

final level, and rate of rise of habit strength, respectively) would possibly vary among individuals and species. The exponential form of this equation, however, would not be expected to change: $H = (m - H_o)(1 - e^{-iN}) + H_o$." (Zeaman & Kaufman, 1955, p. 1) Zeaman and Kaufman then argue that if we take Ss with differing initial ability levels, we can deduce from Hullian principles how they should respond to training if given differences in performance were due to certain variables in the Hullian theoretical system. Figure 8-6 shows the predictions made; it will be seen that if performance differences were due to inhibition (F in the figure), then the resulting curves of Ss having different initial abilities should be parallel. The experiments reported by the authors attempt to discover which empirical result is in fact obtained, hoping that in this way the theoretical problem might be settled. This is an interesting inversion of the usual hypothesis–deduction method.

For their experiments they used the inverted printing task. In experiment 1, spaced practice was used, 30-sec trials being followed by 30-sec rest periods, this sequence being regarded as sufficient to prevent cumulation of inhibition. Forty consecutive trials were used, and the results are shown in Figure 8-7, there being 5 different ability groups of about 7 Ss each, attempts having been made to (a) maximize homogeneity within the groups, (b) heterogeneity between the groups, and (c) size of the groups (taken from an initial population of 80 Ss). It appears that "a single smooth curve gives a fair approximation to all the empirical curves," and that these curves are parallel. "The interpretation of results follows from the marked resemblance that the empirical curves bear to the theoretical curves of Fig. 8, 5 F. If a single source of theoretical individual difference is involved, the evidence points clearly to $\overset{\circ}{I}$ or i'." (Zeaman & Kaufman, 1955, p. 6.) The next experiment constitutes an attempt to make a decision between these two constructs, and the authors conclude a theoretical discussion by saying that "if during massed trials the performance curves of the various starting groups remain parallel, then we may conclude that starting differences involve negligible work differences and, more importantly, that the theoretical source of individual difference is the constant i'; if, on the other hand, the curves converge, either i' or I could be the theoretical source, and the problem would remain unsolved."

Experiment 2 was undertaken to collect data relevant to this hypothesis, the same task being used under conditions of massed practice; 40 trials were administered. Figure 8-8 shows the results. The figure indicates clearly enough that starting differences tend to be lost

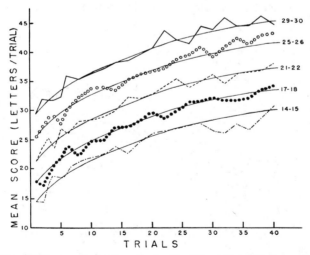

Figure 8-7. Empirical spaced-practice curves for the various starting groups. Starting scores included within each group are identified at the end of each function. Taken with permission from Zeaman and Kaufman (1955).

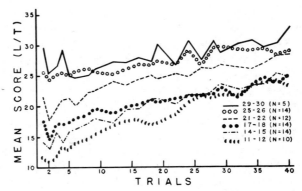

Figure 8-8. Massed-practice curves for the different starting levels. Taken with permission from Zeaman and Kaufman (1955).

during massed practice. The curves gradually converge. Furthermore, they converge in a manner described by part of the theory. "The higher starting-point curves exhibit flatter slopes than the curves lower on the graph. . . . The nonparallel form of the curves means that there are still two possible theoretical sources of the individual starting scores, either I or i'. Some further means of separating these will have to be devised." (Zeaman & Kaufman, 1955, p. 8.)

Theoretical analysis suggested that the appropriate experiment to effect such a separation would be a reminiscence paradigm, and accord-

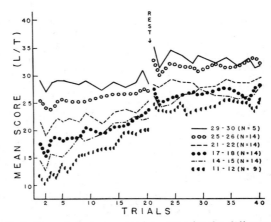

Figure 8-9. The effect of a rest during massed practice for the different starting groups. Taken with permission from Zeaman and Kaufman (1955).

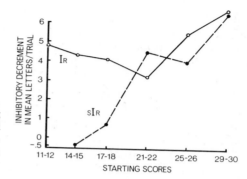

Figure 8-10. The relationship to starting level of temporary and conditioned inhibition at trial 21. Taken with permission from Zeaman and Kaufman (1955).

ingly experiment 3 provided for the interpolation of a 15-min rest period between the 20th and the 21st trial of an experiment otherwise paralleling the one just discussed. Figure 8-9 shows the results. "Before the rest a gradual tendency toward convergence of the curves can be seen. . . . On the trial following rest all the curves undergo the expected reminiscence jump, magnitudes of which are . . . our measure of I_R. With the loss of I_R there is a slight divergence of the groups, or tendency for the reappearance of starting differences, followed by reconvergence during postrest training." (Zeaman & Kaufman, 1955, p. 10.) Zeaman and Kaufman conclude that it is chiefly $_sI_R$ and not I_R that distinguishes the subgroups. "The magnitude of $_sI_R$ is directly related to starting score. A rough description of this relationship would put $_sI_R$ proportional to starting level." (1955, p. 11.) Figure 8-10 shows the nature of the argument. On the abscissa are given the 5 starting levels; on the ordinate are plotted the value of I_R and $_sI_R$, taken after the fashion of Kimble. It is clear that, to put it in simple and nontheoretical language, high starting levels correspond with large differences between spaced and massed practice, while low starting levels correspond with small differences between spaced and massed practice. The scores plotted in Figure 8-10 are those on the first post-rest trial, where reactive inhibition is assumed to be absent, leaving just $_sI_R$.

The interpretation given to their results by Zeaman and Kaufman is as follows. "The lowest starters are low because they come into the experiment with near asymptotic, generalized $_sI_R$. They, therefore, develop little or no additional $_sI_R$ in the present task, although they do develop a degree of I_R otherwise sufficient to create $_sI_R$. The intermediate starting levels show about the same amount of I_R as the lower starting groups but an intermediate degree of $_sI_R$. The highest starting levels produced the highest amount of $_sI_R$, not only because they had the lowest amount to start with (allowing the most room for new $_sI_R$—the only kind measured by our technique) but also, perhaps, because they had more I_R resulting from the higher work output."(1955, p. 12.)

To further support their hypothesis, Zeaman and Kaufman performed an additional analysis. They matched Ss from their massed, massed-with-rest, and spaced groups on ability level, and then proceeded to correlate starting score with later score. The results are shown in Figure 8-11. "For the spaced group, the first trial score starts off as a good predictor of later rank, and although it gradually diminishes in this capacity, it remains a moderately good predictor over trials. Initial rank is also well preserved over early trials for the massed and massed-with-rest groups, but the original order tends to be rapidly lost during the middle and later stages of practice. The large upward jump in the trend of correlations of the massed-with-rest group after the twentieth trial indicated a restoration of some of the starting order for this group. The fact that the correlations have been averaged in blocks of five to reduce sampling error has cut down slightly on the magnitude of this upward jump." (Zeaman & Kaufman, 1955, p. 13.) The existence of this "jump" suggests that something is occurring during rest which realigns groups in accordance with their initial ability level; this fact may throw some interesting light on the nature of reminiscence. We will take up this point again later.

This paper constitutes an extremely ingenious attempt to use Hull's theoretical system to elucidate an important problem; it is one of the high points of Hullian analysis, like the work of Kimble, but it also illustrates the weakness of this type of approach. Criticism might start with the observation that the possibility of genetic differences accounting for much of the ability variance is not even considered; we have seen that McNemar (1932) has demonstrated the great importance of such genetic factors in a variety of tasks, such as the pursuit rotor. Inverted alphabet printing has not been shown to fall into this group of tests, but it seems very unlikely that it would differ in any fundamental fashion from the other tasks used. We next have the assumption that individuals start out on the task with high levels of conditioned inhibition, while others have very low levels. It does not seem easy to see how Ss could have acquired such high levels of $_sI_R$ in the absence of any previous practice on the task. Ordinary writing, and occasionally printing, are of course undertaken quite frequently by most people, but the practice of inverting the letters of the alphabet is not so widespread as to make this a likely hypothesis.

We are less inclined than many psychologists to dismiss the possibility of conditioned inhibition appearing under appropriate circum-

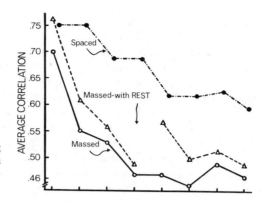

Figure 8-11. Correlations of starting scores with later scores. Taken with permission from Zeaman and Kaufman (1955).

stances [see Gleitman *et al.* (1954) for an extended criticism of the concept], but the conditions in this case do not seem propitious. A more parsimonious explanation might be that high-ability Ss, having inherited the abilities involved, or having practiced some of the skills in question, or both, write more inverted letters during massed practice and become more fatigued; they therefore do not improve to the same extent as low-ability Ss who write fewer letters and become less fatigued. During spaced practice fatigue is not allowed to build up, and hence the groups preserve their respective ability levels better. This simple hypothesis would explain the main findings, without invoking what the authors themselves call "the top-heavy theoretical superstructure of Hull's system" (Zeaman & Kaufman, 1955, p. 15). We shall return to some of these points again later. One last point should be mentioned. The curves for massed practice were shown to converge, and this, taken together with the failure to converge during spaced practice, is the main effect used to generate the hypothesis in question. But other writers, admittedly using other tasks, have not found any greater convergence for massed than for spaced practice (Reynolds & Adams, 1954; Cieutat & Noble, 1958). The effect, if there is one, may be restricted to inverted alphabet printing, and may hence be an artifact.

Rather different in conception to the experiments reviewed so far is a report by Eysenck (1964*b*). Three hundred male applicants for an apprenticeship training scheme (i.e., of high motivation) were administered the pursuit rotor. All Ss practiced for 5 min, rested for 10 min, and practiced for another 5 min. Ss who failed to learn the task were eliminated and others used to replace them, the criterion of "learning" being a score of at least 1 sec on target during at least one of the 30 10-sec periods which constituted the pre-rest practice period. Practice was massed, and Ss were divided into five equal groups according to their scores during the first 10 trials. Each of these groups, which will be denoted A, B, C, D, and E, from high to low, was in turn subdivided into two equal subgroups, according to the performance of its members during the *terminal* ten pre-rest trials; those showing the better performance will be given the subscript h for high, while the others will be given the subscript l for low. We thus have ten groups in all, divided according to initial and terminal performance. Figure 8-12 shows the performance of the A to E groups, while Figure 8-13 shows the combined performance of the h and l groups.

Before turning to the main purpose of the experiment, consider the similarities and dissimilarities of the results to those reported by Reynolds and Adams. Position of the groups is maintained pretty well, as in his study. Group A shows the "warm-up" effect, but none of the others do. Group A shows a downward trend after the 12th trial, while the Reynolds and Adams 10th decile group persevered along a plateau. After the rest pause only groups A, B, and C produce a warm-up effect; groups D and E do not: in the Reynolds and Adams experiment, all groups showed warm-up. It is difficult to say whether these differences are due to the fact that they used 20-sec trial periods, while Eysenck used 10-sec periods, or rather to the presence of intertrial rests in the so-called "massed" practice of Reynolds and Adams.

Let us now turn to the rationale of the experiment. According to the inhibition hypothesis, reminiscence is caused by depression of performance at the end of the pre-rest period; it would seem to follow that when we compare reminiscence scores of groups equated for initial ability, but differing with respect to high or low performance at the end of pre-rest practice, then those with low scores should have higher reminiscence scores than those with high scores. According to the consolidation hypothesis, differences at this point should be irrelevant to the size of reminiscence scores. We would thus appear to have a crucial test of the rival hypotheses. Table 8-2 sets out the observed mean reminiscence scores for the two groups. It will be seen that there is no difference between the h and l groups; in other words, the position at the end of the pre-rest period does *not* determine the amount of reminiscence observed. This result would appear to support the consolidation theory, and to disprove the inhibition hypothesis. An analysis of variance was performed on these data and showed this source of variance to be quite insignificant.

Differences in initial ability do not seem to give rise to differences in reminiscence; variation among scores in the last column is quite small. In the analysis of variance this source of variation also failed to disprove the null hypothesis. It might be argued that it would have

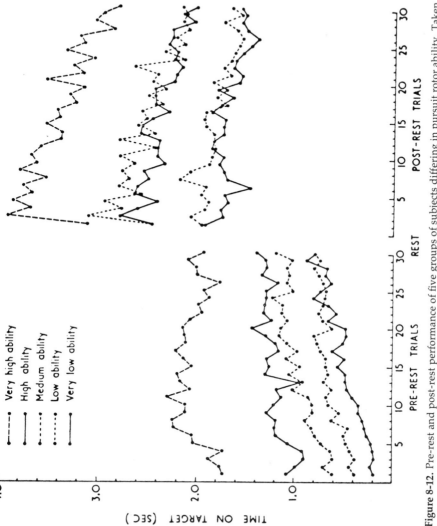

Figure 8-12. Pre-rest and post-rest performance of five groups of subjects differing in pursuit rotor ability. Taken with permission from Eysenck (1964b).

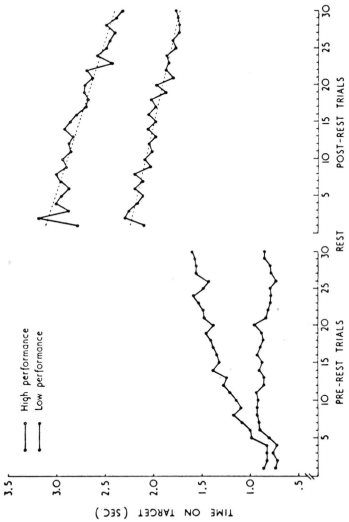

Figure 8-13. Pre-rest and post-rest performance of subjects showing depressed or elevated performance during the last ten pre-rest trials, when equated for initial ability. Taken with permission from Eysenck (1964b).

TABLE 8-2. Mean Reminiscence Scores of
High- and Low-Ability Groups [a]

	h	l	Total
Group A	.79	1.56	1.18
Group B	1.31	1.03	1.17
Group C	1.36	1.50	1.43
Group D	1.25	1.11	1.18
Group E	1.29	.98	1.14
Total	1.20	1.24	1.22

[a] Taken with permission from Eysenck (1964).

been better to have used the Ammons corrected reminiscence score, as indicated in Figure 8-13 by the broken line. The corrected reminiscence values are 1.52 and 1.38 respectively for the h and l groups; the correction thus displaces the reminiscence values in a direction contrary to the inhibition hypothesis. Even so, the differences were not significant. Initial level of performance was correlated with last pre-rest and first post-rest level of performance; the coefficients of correlation were .41 and .30, respectively. This is in contradiction to the findings of Zeaman and Kaufman (1955), who found the post-rest correlation higher than the pre-rest one. This difference may be due to task differences; it is possible that inverted alphabet printing may involve inhibition, whereas pursuit-rotor practice does not.

In making comparisons between this study and others cited, or in deriving conclusions, it should be remembered that the Ss were performing under conditions of high drive, whereas the Ss of most other experimenters were probably working under conditions of low drive. This may be important because there is some evidence of interaction between ability level and drive (French, 1957; Fleishman, 1958; Locke, 1965); effects of motivation tend to be greater on Ss of high than on Ss of low ability. In other words, there appears to be a greater difference in performance of high- and low-ability groups (where the ability level is ascertained without experimental involvement of different motivation conditions) when motivation conditions are high, than when they are low. Thus in the Eysenck experiment differences may be greater than in the Reynolds and Adams one, for instance; the trial durations and other experimental conditions do not make a proper comparison possible.

Clark (1967) repeated Eysenck's study on a low-motivation group. Using hospitalized schizophrenics, he subdivided his group into 5 ability groups of 25 Ss each, defined by rank-ordered performance level on the first 10 practice trials. (This study will be discussed in more

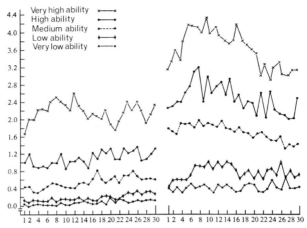

Figure 8-14. Pre-rest and post-rest performance of different ability groups on the pursuit rotor. Taken with permission from Clark (1967).

detail in a subsequent chapter.) Figure 8-14 shows the main results; they are very similar to those reported by Eysenck. Note the initial upswing of the high-ability group during pre-rest practice, and the post-rest upswing and downswing characteristically diminishing from high- to low-ability groups. Unlike the Eysenck study, however, there were very marked differences in reminiscence between the groups, which by analysis of variance exceeded a $p < .001$ level; mean reminiscence scores of the very high, high, and medium ability groups were significantly greater than the mean scores of each of the low and very low ability groups. This effect may be an artifact due to the very low level of performance of the two worst groups; with normal Ss many of these patients would have been rejected according to the rules for minimum performance laid down by Eysenck. Alternatively, the data may be interpreted as suggesting that with low-drive groups there is a tendency for high-ability Ss to show more reminiscence than low-ability Ss. The data cannot decide between these two alternatives.

Eysenck and Gray (1971) contributed several experiments relevant to the topic of this chapter. In the first of these, 8 groups of low-drive industrial apprentices were given massed practice on the pursuit rotor for either 3 or 8 min; rest periods of either 30 sec; 2 min, or 20 min followed by another 4 min of practice for all groups. Each of the 8 groups contained 30 Ss; of these the top 12 and the bottom 12 in ability were chosen for analysis, ability being defined in terms of total performance over the first 12 trials. Pre-rest performance of the 96 Ss who practiced for 3 min are shown in Figure 8-15, and that of the 96 Ss who

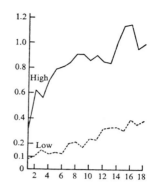

Figure 8-15. Pre-rest performance of high-ability and low-ability groups during 3-min practice period. Taken with permission from Eysenck and Gray (1971).

practiced for 8 min are shown in Figure 8-16. The comparison of the high- and low-ability groups shows much the same picture as previous reports; a gentle, linear slope for the low-ability group, and a "warm-up like" quick upswing for the high-ability groups, followed by a plateau. Analysis by orthogonal polynomials essentially bears out the visual inspection, but also demonstrates significant higher-order effects which are difficult to explain, and probably not relevant to our purpose here.

Details regarding the post-rest performances of the various groups are given in the original article; the main point of interest is that there is no warm-up effect for rest periods of less than 6 min and at all rest intervals the effect is clearly stronger for high-ability groups than for low-ability groups. However, our main interest is in reminiscence scores. Analysis of variance was carried out on reminiscence as a function of high and low ability, long and short pre-rest practice, and length of rest period. High-ability groups in each case showed greater reminiscence; longer pre-rest periods produced greater reminiscence;

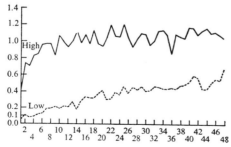

Figure 8-16. Pre-rest performance of high-ability and low-ability groups during 8-min practice period. Taken with permission from Eysenck and Gray (1971).

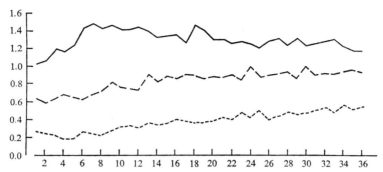

Figure 8-17. Pre-rest performance of high-, medium-, and low-ability groups, using the small target. Taken with permission from Eysenck and Gray (1971).

and longer rest pauses produced greater reminiscence. The differences due to ability level were the most significant ($p < .001$); length of rest was significant ($p < .05$); but length of pre-rest practice failed to reach an acceptable level of significance. "It is notable that ability level is a much more significant determiner of reminiscence than either of the other factors." (Eysenck & Gray, 1971, p. 205.) None of the interactions were significant. It would seem that the difference between the results of Eysenck (1964) and Clark (1967), with respect to the influence of ability level on reminiscence, may have been due to the use of high- and low-drive Ss, respectively.

In the second experiment, Ss did 6 min of massed practice, followed by a rest of 30 sec, 10 min, or one week; post-rest consisted of a further 7 min of practice. Two concentric targets were used in order to study the effects of ease or difficulty of the task. [Bahrick *et al.* (1957) have drawn attention to the fact that learning curves may contain large artifacts due to choice of target size, and it seemed important to span the gap between the largest and the smallest target that could in practice be used without either making the performer reach a perfect score too early, or else making the task impossibly difficult for a large number of Ss.] Ss were low-drive student volunteers, and there were approximately 70 in each group; these were divided into three groups again on the basis of their performance over the first 120 sec of practice, constituting a high-, medium-, and low-drive group. Figure 8-17 shows the pre-rest performance of these 3 ability groups; it will be seen that results agree well with those hitherto considered. This figure shows results with the small (difficult) target; Figure 8-18 shows the results for the large (easy) target. On both graphs the groups are seen to converge; on both graphs the high-ability group shows the typical warm-up and downswing effect noted before, while the low-ability groups start with

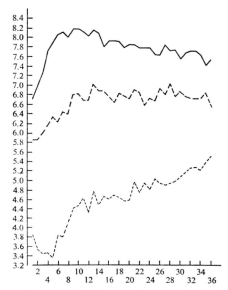

Figure 8-18. Pre-rest performance of high-, medium-, and low-ability groups, using the large target. Taken with permission from Eysenck and Gray (1971).

a downswing (a kind of inverted "warm-up" effect, and then go up in a linear fashion. There is some slight evidence of this downswing in Figure 8-14, but we have not seen this effect in any other report.

Post-rest curves for the different rest groups show the great importance of length of rest in the shape of the curve. For the 30-sec rest pause groups all the curves proceed essentially along a straight line, without significant rises or decrements in performance; these lines are parallel with each other (Figure 8-19). (The linearity of the lines was assessed by orthogonal polynomial analysis, as were all the statements made about

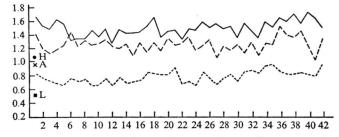

Figure 8-19. Post-rest curves for high-, medium-, and low-ability groups after 30-sec rest pause. Taken with permission from Eysenck and Gray (1971).

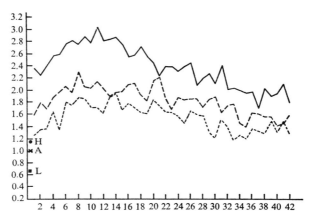

Figure 8-20. Post-rest scores for high-, medium-, and low-ability groups after 10-min rest pause. Taken with permission from Eysenck and Gray (1971).

the shape of curves in relation to this study.) The 10-min rest pause produced a very marked effect, with linear, quadratic, and cubic components all significant for all groups (Figure 8-20). For the 1-week groups, linear components are insignificant, quadratics very significant for the high-ability Ss, and insignificant for the low-ability Ss. Cubics are significant only for the high- and average-ability groups (Figure 8-21). "These data leave no doubt that groups of different ability levels show highly significant post-rest performance curves provided the rest is long enough to permit consolidation (or dissipation of inhibition) to take place to a sufficient degree." (Eysenck & Gray, 1971, p. 207.)

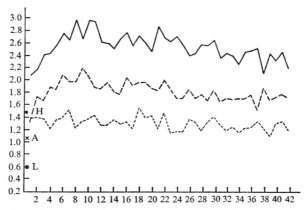

Figure 8-21. Post-rest scores for high-, medium-, and low-ability groups after a 1-week rest pause. Taken with permission from Eysenck and Gray (1971).

TABLE 8-3. Correlations between Reminiscence and "Maximum Reminiscence" Scores and Regression Coefficients a and b, Representing Pre-Rest Performance Level and Decrement

Group	Coefficients	Reminiscence	Rem. max
30-sec group	a	0.153	0.469^b
	b	-0.261^b	-0.239^a
10-min group	a	0.082	0.338^b
	b	-0.210	-0.265^a
1-week group	a	0.032	0.413^b
	b	-0.416^b	-0.245^a

[a] $p < 0.05$.
[b] $p < 0.01$.

Terminal pre-rest scores of the 3 groups are shown in Figures 8-19 through 8-21, labeled H, A, and L, for high, average and low ability, respectively; thus it is possible to demonstrate reminiscence effects directly. There is a significant interaction effect between reminiscence, ability, and rest period. The low-ability group shows a continued increment in reminiscence over the 3 rest periods; the other 2 groups show a rise from 30 sec to 10 min, followed by a fall. These results are in good agreement with what one might have expected from Leavitt's findings, that is a positive correlation between ability and reminiscence for short rest pauses, and a negative one for long rest pauses.

Eysenck and Gray performed a more detailed analysis of these data. A linear regression coefficient b was computed for the final 4½ min of the pre-rest practice period to indicate depression of performance during this time, i.e., following any initial upswing. A regression coefficient a was calculated to represent the level of ability measured 1½ min after performance started. These coefficients were correlated with reminiscence scores, determined as usual, and also with a new coefficient, called rem. max.; this calculates the difference between terminal pre-rest performance and the mean of the two highest trials occurring at any time within the first 2 min of post-rest practice. (The rationale of this measure is discussed in the next chapter.) The correlations between reminiscence and rem. max. on the one hand, and a and b on the other, are given in Table 8-3; there is a gradual decrease in the correlations between reminiscence and a with increasing length of rest, but this change is not significant. The increasing correlation with b is also not significant, and the changes in size of correlation with rem. max. are neither systematic nor significant. These data suggest that level of ability in this study is mainly correlated with rem. max., i.e., an index which combines the twin effects of the slight correlation of reminiscence with ability, with the strong PRU characteristic of high-ability subjects.

Results from this study using older brighter and possibly more highly motivated Ss than the previous one confirm in most respects the conclusions already reached. Pre-rest performance shows high-ability groups giving rise to upswing followed by downswing, while low-ability groups show the opposite pattern. Post-rest performance shows PRU and PRD to be phenomena peculiar to subjects in the higher-ability groups, and missing in the lower ability groups; length of rest pause of course also enters as an important factor. Reminiscence was not found to be determined by ability level to anything like the same extent as in the first experiment, or that of Clark (1967); it is possible that this may be due to greater motivation, making this group more comparable to Eysenck's (1964) high-drive group where no relation was also found between reminiscence and ability. The apprentice group used in the first experiment was on the whole rather poorly motivated, if one may use personal judgment based on observation, whereas the university students used in the present experiment seemed to be more ego-involved (Alper, 1948). Clearly motivation is an important variable in untangling the relationships between ability and reminiscence, and equally clearly our data do not provide the required measure of motivation without which these suggestions cannot be regarded as anything but speculation.

A final experiment reported by Eysenck and Gray is based on the hypothesis that the failure of Reynolds and Adams (1954) to obtain post-rest differences between their different ability groups was due to the fact that they used distributed rather than massed practice, even in their miscalled "massed practice" groups. If this were true, then it should be possible to compare groups of low-drive apprentices, similar to those used in the first of these 3 experiments, engaged in distributed learning on the pursuit rotor; if distribution of practice is responsible for the failure of ability differences to mark differences in the shape of the learning curve, then such an experiment should result in essentially similar curves, excepting of course the course of learning preceding the first imposed rest. 15 high- and 15 low-ability Ss were chosen from 45 Ss who had practiced on the rotor for 11 1-min periods, separated by 5-min rest pauses; Figure 8-22 shows the results. It will be seen that PRU is universally missing in both groups; PRD is observed equally in both groups. The only trial on which the groups differ significantly (by orthogonal polynomial analysis) is the first; as previously observed, the high-ability group shows a rapid upswing while the low-ability group shows no change at all. (A medium-ability group, formed from the

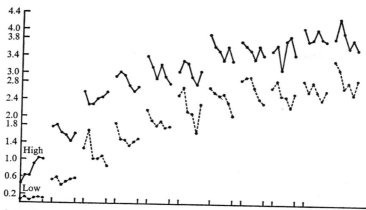

Figure 8-22. Scores of high- and low-ability groups during eleven 1-min practice periods separated by 5-min rest pauses. Taken with permission from Eysenck and Gray (1971).

remaining 15 Ss, showed intermediate upswing, followed by a plateau. This group remained intermediate between the other two throughout practice.) These results support the view that massing is responsible for the major differences between high- and low-ability groups.

Certain theoretical arguments may fittingly bring this chapter to a close. In explanation of the relation observed between ability and reminiscence, but only in low-motivation groups, one might argue that the higher-ability groups would, by and large, be more highly motivated; motivation and success are unlikely to be entirely separated. This relationship would be presumed to operate along the lines: high ability → successful performance → high motivation, in expectation of future success, whereas on the other hand we have the progression: low ability → unsuccessful performance → low motivation in expectation of future failure. The opposite possibility of high motivation leading to good performance seems ruled out by the findings (discussed in another chapter) that high- and low-motivation Ss are not distinguished in terms of pre-rest performance. If this were so, then in groups not specifically motivated for pursuit-rotor performance, reminiscence (which is known to be a function of motivation) would be greater in high-ability Ss; this differential would be wiped out when an external motivating factor is introduced, bringing the low-drive Ss up to the level of the most highly (internally) motivated ones. This additional hypothesis would explain the observed relationship between ability level and reminiscence in low-drive groups, and its failure to be observed in high-drive groups. The hypothesis appeals to characteristics in task and subject which are difficult to observe and measure, and which certainly have not so far been measured; the main point in proposing such a highly speculative theory is of course that it may lead to further investigations geared more specifically to testing the various parts of the theory in question.

One final hypothesis to be considered is concerned with the vexed problem of measurement of reminiscence and performance. The conclusions of Bahrick *et al.* (1957) regarding the problem of target size have already been mentioned; in this connection the work of Humphries (1961) is very relevant. It will be remembered that he used a rotor in which circular target areas, insulated from each other, were surrounded by a very small central disk; recording from each of these target areas was done separately, thus enabling scores to be obtained simultaneously from target areas differing in size. In Figure 2-6 are plotted his results from 5 min of massed practice, followed by a 5-min rest pause and another 2 min of practice. It is clear that the large target sizes give results similar to those obtained by our high-ability subjects, while the smaller target sizes give results similar to those obtained by our low-ability Ss. The former show pre-rest upswing, pre-rest downswing, and marked reminiscence, while the latter show neither pre-rest upswing, pre-rest downswing, or reminiscence, although the scores are derived from the same Ss on the same occasion! This similarity is striking, but it does not prove that the phenomena are artifacts when observed in high- and low-ability Ss. The second Eysenck and Gray experiment has shown that shifting from a small target to a large one does not obliterate or change the observed phenomena; they are more dramatic in the case of the larger target, but they are identical with those produced by the smaller target in most respects. Future work will undoubtedly benefit from incorporating multiple targets into the design, as in the Humphries experiment; we doubt if such innovations will alter the main conclusions drawn from the work reviewed in this chapter.

CHAPTER 9

Individual Differences:
Extraversion

As we have pointed out in the first chapter, the early German workers implicitly (and sometimes explicitly) introduced the concept of individual differences into their discussions; they found it impossible to account for the peculiarities of individual protocols without postulating (often ad hoc) personality qualities which might explain such departures from expectation. It would be easy to read too much into these early efforts; there is little there of systematic theorizing regarding the influence of personality on reminiscence. Nevertheless, what is noticeable is the marked contrast present in these early accounts as compared with the later, largely American work, where the very mention of "personality" would have been regarded as an anathema. This early interest in normal variations in personality, and the possibility that they might account for individual differences in reminiscence, was matched by an interest in the possibilities of "work curves" and reminiscence being used with psychiatrically abnormal groups as diagnostic measures, or as indicants of the severity of illness. These two strands, concern with normal personality and interest in abnormal behavior, became the focus of attention in a large-scale research program which has been pursued at the Institute of Psychiatry for a period of some twenty years. In this chapter we shall be dealing with studies using normal personality variates as the independent variable; we shall deal with abnormal and psychiatric conditions in the next chapter.[1]

[1] Peters (1973) has doubted the existence of individual differences in reminiscence in pursuit-rotor work and other similar tasks, on the grounds that crude gain measures of change are inadequate, and that reminiscence scores are not independent of perfor-

255

The first study to recognize explicitly that personality variables might play an important part in determining the size of the reminiscence effect was based on a theory of personality which owed much to Pavlov and to Hull (Eysenck, 1956). This theory, which was developed in some detail by Eysenck (1957), is now of mainly historical interest, having been superceded by a more physiologically oriented theory (Eysenck, 1967), but it will nevertheless be restated here briefly in order to make intelligible the reasons which led the author to predict that extraverts would show greater reminiscence in pursuit-rotor learning, and that under suitable conditions subjects scoring high on the N (neuroticism, anxiety, emotionality) scale might also show greater reminiscence. Basic to these predictions was the "typological postulate," which was formulated as follows:

> Individuals in whom reactive inhibition is generated quickly, in whom strong reactive inhibition is generated, and in whom reactive inhibition is dissipated slowly, are thereby predisposed to develop extraverted patterns of behaviour and to develop hysterico-psychopathic disorders in case of neurotic breakdown, conversely, individuals in whom reactive inhibition has developed slowly, in whom weak reactive inhibitions are generated, and in whom reactive inhibition is dissipated quickly, are thereby predisposed to develop introverted patterns of behaviour, and to develop dysthymic disorders in case of neurotic breakdown. (Eysenck, 1957.)

It would seem to follow from this formulation that if reminiscence were due to the dissipation of inhibition, then extraverts, prone under identical circumstances to generate more inhibition than introverts, would also have more inhibition to dissipate; this should lead to greater reminiscence in extraverts, as compared with introverts. Precise parametric predictions would of course depend on greater knowledge of the rate, asymptote, and other details of inhibition acquisition; thus if rates of acquisition were equal between extraverts and introverts, then the difference in reminiscence would only become apparent after introverts had reached their asymptote, with extraverts still continuing to acquire more inhibition. If the rate of acquisition of extraverts were quicker, but asymptotes equal, then differences should be more apparent after short practice periods, only to vanish later on. If differences were present in both rate of acquisition and asymptote, then differences would appear at all points regardless of length of pre-rest practice. No

---

mance level. In reply, Eysenck (1974) has pointed out that personality is related to reminiscence, but not to performance; that crude gain measures may have disadvantages, but that they could not produce the regular and replicable results found; and that the discovery of significant relations between reminiscence and personality features, such as extraversion, disproves Peters' point *a fortiori*.

detailed predictions were made regarding these points. Anxiety-neurot-icism-emotionality, on the other hand, was conceived, very much in the manner of Spence, as a drive variable; high N constitutes a drive under anxiety-provoking circumstances, and high-N subjects will therefore behave differently to low-N subjects under such circum-stances. We have already established in a previous chapter that under high-drive conditions reminiscence is greater than under low-drive conditions; it would seem to follow that high-N subjects, under suitable conditions, would show greater reminiscence than low-N subjects. Failure to find such differences could of course always be blamed on the conditions of the experiment; trait anxiety which is measured by the typical personality scales used may not issue in state anxiety, which has typically not been measured in the experiments to be reported. This difference between trait and state anxiety, which dates back to Cicero, is of considerable theoretical and practical importance. Cicero, as already noted, made a firm distinction between *angor* (which is transi-tory, a sudden access due to external stress of a well-defined kind) and *anxietas* (which is an abiding predisposition, a semipermanent trait). As he points out, "anxium proprie dici qui pronus est ad aegritudinem animi, neque enim omnes anxii, qui anguntur aliquando; nec qui anxii, semper anguntur." The notion of situational stress, for him, is the de-fining mark of *angor*; "angor est aegritudo premens." Spielberger *et al.* (1970) and Sarason (1966) recently put this distinction, and the empirical measurement of state anxiety, on a proper experimental footing. Lewis (1967) has given a thorough historical discussion of the growth in the use and meaning of the term "anxiety" over the centuries.

Eysenck's experiment used three 5-min work periods, separated by 2 10-min rest periods; this makes possible the calculation of two separate reminiscence scores for each subject, using the first and second rest periods, respectively. The general shape of the resulting work curves has been reported already in Chapter 1 (Figure 1-7). The pre-rest and the post-rest curves follow the traditional form. Fifty Ss were given the pur-suit-rotor test, as well as the MPI, and correlations calculated between E and N on the one hand, and the two reminiscence scores, on the other. Also calculated was the correlation between the two reminiscence scores, which gives us an approximation to a reliability estimate for pursuit-rotor reminiscence. This reliability turned out rather low ($r = .44$); this is of course not unexpected. It is well known that the reliability of difference scores is greatly inferior to the reliability of the component scores (Lord, 1956; Cronbach & Farley, 1970; Stanley, 1971), and the reliability of the component scores (i.e., in this case 10-sec time-on-target scores for the post-rest score, and the average of 3 10-sec time-on-target scores for the pre-rest score) is itself not very high, and not exceeding .6 for the typical trial-to-trial correlation. It is important to bear in mind throughout this chapter the low reliability of pursuit-rotor reminiscence scores, because this sets an obvious limit to the size of the correlations which can be obtained with personality variables, and also the size of the differences which can be obtained between groups made up on the basis of personality test scores; even if reminiscence were a perfect reflection of a person's degree of extraversion, the observed correlation between E and reminiscence would still be below .44! It is of course possible to argue that our measure is not a good estimate of the reliability of the reminiscence score; as we have pointed out in an earlier chapter, the abilities entering into pursuit-rotor performance change with amount of practice, and reminiscence scores taken at different points of the work curve may reflect different combinations of abilities. Such an objection is well taken, but it seems unlikely to us that even if full value were given to this argument, the "true" reliability of this measure could be very much higher than the value observed.

Correlations with personality were low; with E they were .29 and .10 (the former significant at the .02 level by the appropriate 1-tail test, the latter not significant) and with N they were .40 and .27, the former being significant at the .01 level. Purely as a statistical exercise, it may be instructive to correct these observed values for attenuation, using reasonable estimates for the reliability of E and N (.8) and of reminiscence (.5); this gives us corrected values for the correlation between the first reminiscence score and E of .5, and N of .6. As E and N are independent, we might say that reminiscence is determined by personality factors E and N to the extent of 60% approximately. These calculations are of course purely notional, in view of the large standard errors involved, and the assumptions which require to be made; nevertheless they may serve to give a more realistic idea of the sort of relationship that would exist between personality and an error-free measure of reminiscence. However we may regard these statistical exercises, the data do give some weak support to the hypotheses which are being tested.

Warm-up effect and practice score (improvement during the first 5-min practice period) were both uncorrelated with E or N; this finding should perhaps have served as a warning that the theory of E which served to make the prediction was not in fact correct. It follows directly from any inhibition theory of reminiscence that the crucial score differentiating between extraverts and introverts should be the last pre-rest score; this in theory is lower for extraverts due to the action of reactive inhibition. The first post-rest score should be equal for the two groups,

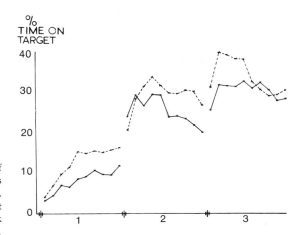

%
TIME ON
TARGET

Figure 9-1. Performance of introverts and extraverts (broken and solid lines, respectively) on the pursuit rotor. Data from Eysenck (1956), drawn by Star (1957).

as the inhibition in both should have dissipated completely. But a lower terminal pre-rest score for extraverts implies a negative correlation with practice score; although the observed score was negative $(-.10)$ it was clearly insignificant, and this failure to achieve significance cannot be blamed entirely on unreliability of data as it was based on the difference between two sets of data based on 3 successive 10-sec trials. Inspection of the mean pre-rest and post-rest scores for extraverts and introverts, respectively (carried out later, after the alternative theory of consolidation had been proposed), showed that the higher reminiscence of the extraverts was partly due to their lower pre-rest performance, partly to their higher post-rest performance (Figure 9-1). These data are therefore equivocal with respect to these two theories— the former predicting that personality types should differ on the last pre-rest trial, the latter that they should differ on the first post-rest trial, i.e., when consolidation is at work.

In 1962, Eysenck returned to review the progress that had been made, and to suggest an extension or revision of the theory. He gives a table which attempts to construct in scoreboard fashion a survey of the 20 or so results reported by various authors; this table is here reprinted (Table 9-1). It will be seen that practically all the studies report positive (although not always significant) results for E, but that for N there is little by way of replication to be found. Before turning to the revision of the theory contained in this paper, we may with advantage look at some of the papers quoted, and discuss points of interest arising.

Star (1957, 1963) worked with 100 male apprentices, and used a 60-rpm instrument, as opposed to Eysenck's use of a 72-rpm instrument;

TABLE 9-1. Summary of Studies Relating Reminiscence and Personality[a]

Author	N	Type of S	Type of test	Criterion	Result: E	Result: N	Remarks
Eysenck (1956)	50	Students	Pursuit rotor	MPI	++	+++	
Treadwell (1956)	40	Students	Stylus tracking	Minnesota T Scale	++	(not included)	Criterion questionable; Gwynne Jones (1960)
Star (1957); 1	100	Apprentices	Pursuit rotor	MPI	++	− −	Sixteen 90-sec trials; 5-min rests
Star (1957); 2	79	Students	Pursuit rotor	MPI	−	+	One 90-sec session
Das (1957)	68	Students	Pursuit rotor	MPI	++	(not included)	
Das (1957)	68	Students	Pursuit rotor	Nufferno test	++	(not included)	
Rechtschaffen (1958)	47	Students	Inverted alphabet	Guilford R Scale	+	(not included)	Extraverts have significantly lower performance scores
Ray (1959)	240	Students	Pursuit rotor	MPI	=	=	Extraverts have significantly lower performance scores
Claridge (1960)	48	Soldiers	Pursuit rotor	Factor loading	+++	=	Several reminiscence scores used, of which only one correlates significantly with E
Becker (1960)	62	Students	Pursuit rotor	MPI	+	=	
Eysenck (1960a)	240	Apprentices	Pursuit rotor	MPI	+	=	Significant rest-extraversion interaction
Eysenck (1960b)	45	Apprentices	Pursuit rotor	MPI	+	−	Eleven 1-min trials
Eysenck & Eysenck (1960)	62	Apprentices	Rotating spiral	MPI	+	=	One correlation with E significant
Lynn (1960)	40	Students	Inverted Alphabet	MPI	++	+	Extraverts have significantly lower performance scores
Lynn (1960)	40	Students	Inverted alphabet	Spiral after-effect	++		
Lynn (1961)	82	Children	Inverted alphabet	Factor loading	++	++	
Germain & Pinillos (1962)	300	Drivers	Pursuit rotor	MPI	++	+	Personality × length of rest pause interaction significant at 1% level
Bendig & Eigenbrode (1961)	160	Students	Pursuit rotor	Guilford–Zimmerman temperament survey	++	=	Factor analytic study
Meier (1961)	128	V.A. patients	Inverted alphabet	MMPI	+++	+	Hypothesis erroneously stated by author
Costello & Feldman (1962)	120	School children	Pursuit rotor	Junior MPI	++	=	Unpublished data

[a] In this table a rough indication of the significance of findings has been given by using an = sign to denote absence of any relationship between personality and reminiscence. A single + or − sign denotes results tending to confirm or infirm the hypothesis, but at levels of $p > 0.05$. A double ++ or − − sign has the same import, but at levels of $p < 0.05$, while a triple +++ or − − − denotes levels of $p > 0.01$. Occasionally, as in the case of Becker's (1960) work, several results are reported from one study; in this case a (subjective) overall estimate has been attempted.

he also added a third rest period and a fourth work period, so that a third reminiscence measure could be obtained. He found a significant correlation between reminiscence after the first rest pause and E ($r =$ .17), but as in Eysenck's experiment the later reminiscence scores failed to give significant results. The correlation between N and the first reminiscence score was significant ($r = -.24$), but opposite in sign to that found by Eysenck. No obvious explanation is available, other than that the faster rate used in Eysenck's experiment may have put a greater stress on Ss; there is evidence in the work of Jensen (1962) that time stress of this kind can significantly alter the amount of correlation between N and task performance (in his case, short-term memory). This explanation might account for the failure of Star to find a significant positive correlation between N and reminiscence; it cannot account for the discovery of a significant negative correlation. (Correlations with later reminiscence scores were all not significant). Star's subjects were specially selected to fit into the four quadrants of the $E \times N$ space, i.e., they were $E+N+$, $E+N-$, $E-N+$ or $E-N-$.

Star attempted to estimate the reliability of the first reminiscence (rem.) score, using the formula for the reliability of a difference score (Lindquist, 1951, p. 614.) The reliability of the 1st post-rest trial was taken to be its correlation with the 2nd post-rest trial. The reliability of the mean of the scores on the last 3 pre-rest trials was taken to be the average intercorrelation of scores on those 3 trials concerned, corrected by the Spearman–Brown formula. The reliability of Star's first rem. score turned out to be .54, which agrees quite well with the estimate made on the basis of the rem. 1 vs rem. 2 correlation. When Star tried out the same formula, using Eysenck's data, a much higher reliability was obtained ($r = .77$). This value does not agree at all closely with the rem. 1 vs rem. 2 correlation, but it is impossible to say which is more likely to prove "correct."

Star's results, comparing the 26 highest E scorers, are given in Figure 9-2. It will be seen that there are two features in this figure which contradict the theory of inhibition: (1) extraverts do not show poorer pre-rest performance than introverts, and (2) their superior reminiscence is due to better initial post-rest performance, rather than to poorer terminal pre-rest performance. While Star's study thus confirmed Eysenck's in the sense of also finding a significant positive correlation between E and rem. 1, the precise way in which the difference was produced was quite contradictory to Eysenck's theory. The superior rem. scores of the low-N scorers also seemed to be due to differences in post-rest performance, not to differences in pre-rest performance; this is shown clearly in Figure 9-3. Star pointed out the

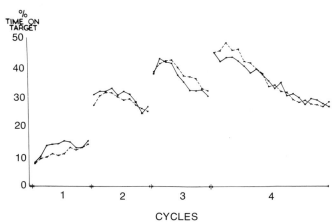

Figure 9-2. Performance of introverts and extraverts (broken and solid lines, respectively) on the pursuit rotor. Taken with permission from Star (1957).

failure of the experimental details to conform with the theory of inhibition, but did not advance an alternative theory.

Eysenck had suggested that possibly measurement of Hullian inhibition (I_R) in these experiments might be invalidated by the growth of $_sI_R$, and that a better experiment might involve shorter practice periods (e.g., 90 sec); this would enable I_R to grow but would fall short of the

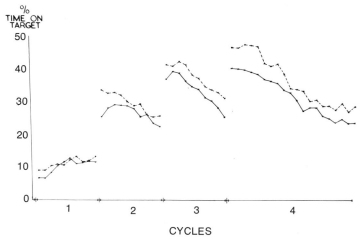

Figure 9-3. Performance of high- and low-scorers on N (solid and broken lines, respectively) on the pursuit rotor. Taken with permission from Star (1957).

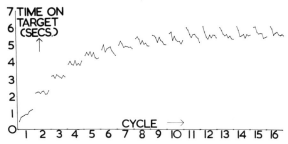

Figure 9-4. Performance on 16 90-sec performance trials, separated by 15 5-min rest periods. Taken with permission from Star (1957).

critical level where IRPs arise, and where $_sI_R$ makes its appearance. Star (1957) performed a second experiment to test this prediction, using 79 volunteer students, selected on the basis of their MPI scores as falling into one of the four quadrants: $E+N+$, $E+N-$, $E-N+$, and $E-N-$. Sixteen 90-sec work periods were interspersed with fifteen 5-min rest periods; the general shape of the resulting work curves is shown in Figure 9-4. This figure has many features of interest; it will be seen that each rest pause is followed by reminiscence, and the amount of reminiscence did not decrease over trials, but varied at random around a mean value. Reminiscence scores were correlated over all Ss; these correlations were uniformly low (none exceeding .40), and some attaining nonsignificantly negative values. By corrected split-half (odd–even) reliability, the value for the mean reminiscence score was .57. Factor analysis of the matrix of intercorrelations suggested the presence of only one general factor, with positive loadings throughout; these ranged from .12 (for the first reminiscence score) to values above .60. There is no obvious pattern to the distribution of high and low values, except that the first and last values are the lowest. There is no obvious post-rest upswing in most of the records, but a marked post-rest downswing from the sixth trial onward.

As regards personality correlates, Star found no evidence of any correlation with E or N in either the 15 individual reminiscence scores, or in the combined reminiscence score. Das (1957), using 63 volunteer Ss, administered a 90-sec work period, followed by a single 10-min rest pause, followed by a 180-sec work period; this experiment may tell us whether Star's negative results might be due to the choice of too short a rest period. Das also failed to obtain any correlation between rem. and E, although he did report that both level of performance and rem. correlated with the speed score on the Nufferno test (Furneaux, 1955);

the correlations are .42 and .26, respectively. This may be relevant as speed, as opposed to accuracy, has been found to be correlated with extraversion (Eysenck, 1947.) However, the general conclusion to be drawn from the Star and Das studies is clearly that as far as question-naire measurement of E is concerned there is no evidence at all for any correlation with reminiscence. This clarifies the situation; short practice periods do not generate reminiscence related to E, while long practice periods may. Most later workers have accordingly used longer practice periods; it may be noted that the failure of short practice periods to produce E-related reminiscence goes counter to the inhibition theory.

One might ask whether it is in fact reasonable to derive more than one reminiscence score from a given experiment; it seems possible that the experience of the sequence work-rest-work will change individual performance and reminiscence levels in unpredictable ways, so that the second and other later reminiscence values would not be comparable with the first. This does not appear to be so. Carron and Leavitt (1968) report an experiment devoted to precisely this problem. They argue that the quantitative measure of individual differences is provided by the true-score variance. Thus, the reliability coefficient, which can be dem-onstrated to be equal to the ratio of true-score variance to total variance yields an estimate of the proportion of total variance which can be accounted for by individual differences in the skill. "If the adjacent trial correlations and the variance of performance scores for each trial are available, the total variance can be readily fractioned into true-score (individual difference) variance (S_t^2) and within-individual variance ($S_{w/i}^2$). Then, if the apparatus is calibrated and an estimate is made of the errors in observation, it is possible to fractionate the within-indi-vidual variance into real error variance (S_e^2) and intra-individual vari-ance (S_i^2)." These techniques for separating the components of total variance have been used in a study of pursuit rotor performance and of performance on the stabilometer; we will be concerned only with the former measure.

Fifty high school students were given five 4-min blocks of practice with 5-min rest pauses intervening. Practice schedules called for 4 trials of 50 sec separated by 10-sec rest pauses in each of the so-called "massed practice" periods. Strong reminiscence effects were obtained. It was found that the greatest change in the sources of variation occurred during and immediately following the first 4 practice trials. "Individual differences increased 60% and intra-individual variability increased 40% during and immediately following the first 4 practice trials. Further practice from Trial 5, the trial following the first 5 min. interpolated rest, to Trial 20 did not have any additional effect upon intra-individual variability." (Carron & Leavitt, 1968, p. 502.) These results would seem to suggest that continued practice and multiple reminiscence trials do not increase individual differences or intra-individual variability to such an extent that only one reminiscence score can legitimately be derived from one study.

Rechtschaffen (1958) was the first American author to test the predictions made from Eysenck's theory; he used the inverted alphabet printing task. Ss were first given five 30-sec trials separated by 30-sec rest intervals (distributed practice). Ss were then given a one-min rest interval, followed by 5 min of massed practice. This sequence was followed by 49 Ss; the remaining 47 Ss were given a one-min rest following the last trial of massed practice, followed by two consecutive 30-sec trials (in order to obtain reminiscence scores). Personality was assessed on the basis of Guilford's R scale, probably not a very good measure for the purpose. Rechtschaffen's main concern was with the predicted inhibition effect during massed practice, i.e., the hypothetical greater falling off in the performance of extraverts; he calculated an "inhibition score" by subtracting the number of letters printed during the last five trials of massed practice from the number of letters printed during the five trials of distributed practice. This score was thought to be a direct measure of I_R; this score correlated .18 with the score on the *rhathymia* scale, which is significant on a one-tail test, but is certainly not impressive. "The extreme extraverts had a mean inhibition score of $-.10.9$ as compared to a mean inhibition score of $-.15.7$ for the extreme introverts. The difference was in the predicted direction but was not significant ($t = 1.26.$)" (Rechtschaffen, 1958, p. 286.) The correlation between inhibition and reminiscence was .35, which is significant but probably somewhat spurious as the number of letters printed on the last two trials of massed practice enters into both scores; the correlation between reminiscence and R was .08, which is quite insignificant. This study does not help us much in deciding upon the value of the inhibition hypothesis; the significance is borderline, and compatible with either the inhibition hypothesis or some alternative.

Lynn (1960), whose results were much more positive than those of Rechtschaffen, criticizes the latter on various grounds. He believes that "Rechtschaffen's failure to get large reminiscence scores for his extraverts could be due to an insufficiently long rest pause; the rest given was only 1 min., which is considerably less than most investigators have used with the inverted alphabet printing task. . . ." It is likely that the 1-min rest is insufficient for reactive inhibition to dissipate fully in extraverted subjects. Hence they would not show the full reminiscence effect obtained with a longer rest interval. He also criticizes Rechtschaffen for inappropriate choice of length of practice; he believes that $_sI_R$ may not yet have reached its asymptote for the introverts. Using parameters based on these hypotheses Lynn was in fact able, as we shall see, to obtain much more convincing results than Rechtschaffen.

A study by Ray (1959) is of more interest due to its superior design. Ss were selected on the basis of their MPI scores as extraverted or introverted, and then sub-divided into high-N and low-N groups, making 4 groups in all. All Ss were given 5 min of massed practice on the pursuit rotor, followed by variable periods of rest (0, 30, 60, 180, 600, or 900 sec) for different groups; this in turn was followed by 2 min of massed practice. Learning in the 240 Ss was analyzed over the massed practice period, and significantly steeper slopes found for the extraverts (trials $\times$ extraversion); this would be in line with expectation from the inhibition hypothesis. There were however no significant differences in reminiscence between the four groups, for any of the rest intervals. E correlated only .08 with reminiscence after the 600-sec rest interval. None of the results for N proved to be significant.

A much more complex study was undertaken by Claridge (1960), and our brief account will not be adequate to do full justice to it. He used 4 groups of male army recruits, of about 24 years of age, living in a military psychiatric hospital: hysterics, dysthymics, schizophrenics, and normals. Intelligence did not differentiate significantly between these groups. All Ss were administered the MPI, several MMPI scales, and a number of experimental laboratory tests. These tests covered, in addition to pursuit-rotor reminiscence, vigilance, time error, time judgement, suggestibility (body sway), spiral after-effect, and auditory flutter fusion. The testing schedule for reminiscence followed that used by Eysenck. Reminiscence scores for the groups were significant only for the very low values obtained by the schizophrenics; this, as well as their marked post-rest upswing, is discussed in the next chapter. Figure 9-5 shows the performance data for all groups.

A factor analysis was carried out by Claridge on the matrix of intercorrelations calculated over all 64 Ss, as well as on a matrix calculated for 48 Ss, i.e., excluding the psychotics. In view of the virtual absence of reminiscence for the latter group, the analysis excluding the 16 schizophrenics may be more apposite. Four main factors were extracted and rotated. The first factor extracted was clearly one of intelligence, having a loading of .73 on the IQ test. The second factor was identified as neuroticism, the N scale, and some of the MMPI scales, having high loadings on this factor. Few of the objective tests had loadings on this factor, having been chosen as measures of E rather than of N.

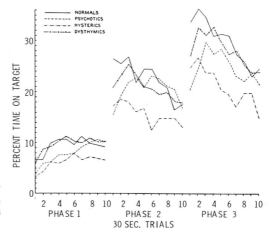

Figure 9-5. Pursuit-rotor performance curves for normal, neurotic, and psychotic groups. Taken with permission from Claridge (1960).

Interpretation of the third factor is less certain than in the case of the other three factors. It has loadings of -0.56 on Vigilance Fall-off, .52 and 0.32 on RS_1 and RS_2, respectively (i.e. the two reminiscence scores), 0.50 on the Spiral, and 0.42, 0.67, and 0.78 on the performance level measures for the three phases of the pursuit rotor experiment. In addition, the N scale of the MPI has a moderate loading of 0.31. The pattern of loadings suggests that the most likely interpretation is that this is a "drive" or "motivational" factor. Undoubtedly supporting this are the high positive loadings of pursuit-rotor performance level, of which one of the major determinants is certainly drive. Similarly, low degrees of fall-off in vigilance may be meaningfully interpreted as being closely associated with high drive levels, while . . . the latter is also likely, other things being equal, to result in increased amounts of reminiscence. Finally, the moderate loading of the N scale on this factor lends support to the interpretation, in so far as neuroticism as measured by this scale can be said to have drive properties. (Claridge, 1960, p. 147.)

This interpretation may of course be correct, but as we have pointed out in our chapter on motivation, the evidence does not by any means support the Hullian notion that drive increases performance on the pursuit rotor in any monotonic fashion. However, with the exception of the pursuit-rotor performance scores the remainder of the high loadings appear to support Claridge's hypothesis. Certainly the positive loadings of the reminiscence scores fall in line with the hypothesis, as does the positive loading of N. Here we would appear to have some slight support for the hypothesis linking reminiscence and N through the postulation of "anxiety as a drive"; possibly the results are not adequately summarized in Table 9-1 in terms of a "=" sign.

It is Factor 4 which is of most interest in the context of this chapter. "It may be interpreted with some confidence as the factor of 'extraversion' which we predicted would emerge from the analysis, the loading of the E scale being 0.48. Its identification with an underlying factor of 'inhibition' is supported by a number of loadings on the objective tests. The loadings of −0.67 and 0.46 shown by Tests 1 and 3, for example, indicate that poor overall vigilance performance and rapid fall-off on this test, both indicative of high levels of inhibition, are positively associated with extraversion. Similarly Test 5 (Vigilance change) has a loading of 0.67 on this factor and confirms our hypothesis that disinhibitory effects will be greater among extraverts. . . . Turning to the other tests, RS₁ RS₂ have loadings of, respectively, 0.58 and 0.36, reminiscence, as predicted, being higher in extraverts. . . . Auditory flutter fusion has a loading of −.39 on the factor. . . ." (Claridge, 1960, p. 146.) The discussion of the test loadings on this factor is continued by Claridge, but there seems to be little doubt that the identification is correct, and that reminiscence has reasonably high loadings on this factor of extraversion. Note that again RS₁ has a higher loading than RS₂, just as in the original Eysenck study the correlation between E and reminiscence was higher for the first than for the second rem. score. On the whole, Claridge's study provides support for the general hypothesis that E is positively correlated with rem., but says nothing about the explanation of this correlation in terms of the inhibition hypothesis: it is clearly possible to explain all the observed phenomena in terms of differences in arousal, rather than of inhibition (Eysenck, 1967).

Becker (1960) reported a study which in design had many similarities to that of Claridge. He too attempted to measure inhibition–satiation by means of laboratory tests, and to correlate the results with extraversion in a factor-analytic design. "Of the eight experimental tests used, two clearly measured reactive inhibition effects (pursuit-rotor reminiscence) and response alteration (sic!), three fitted the definition of a satiation effect (kinesthetic after effect, Archimedes spiral, and the Necker cube difference score), while three approximated basal type measures (GSR conditioning, aniseikonic lenses, and CFF)." (Becker, 1960, p. 54.) We shall of course here be concerned mainly with the reminiscence measures on the pursuit rotor. Personality was assessed by reference to the Guilford Temperament Schedules, Cattell's Revised 16 PF, and the MPI extraversion scale. Sixty-two college students constituted the population tested.

The procedure used by Becker for the reminiscence trials was somewhat unusual. "Each S was given up to 20 practice trials of 30 sec duration, separated by 10 sec rest. When a male reached a criterion of 14 sec on target, or a female a criterion of 12 sec, for two consecutive trials, the practice period was ended. The average number of trials to criterion was 13.2 ($\sigma = 4.6$). Three males and five females were eliminated for failure to reach criterion. After a 5 min rest, two 7-min continuous performance trials were given separated by 5-min rest periods. The final rest was followed by a 2-min trial. During retesting, an additional reminiscence score was obtained using a 7-min performance trial, 5-min rest, and 2-min performance. Reminiscence scores were based on the difference between the minute's performance preceding each 5-min rest and the minute's performance following each 5-min rest." Becker claims that this departure from Eysenck's practice, involving as it does confounding between reminiscence and post-rest upswing, was undertaken in order to improve reliability; this aim does not seem to have been achieved. Becker gives correlations between his three reminiscence measures (two during the first testing, one during the retest session) as .52, .41, and .37; the average score for the former two values correlates with the latter .44. These values are very similar to those obtained by Eysenck and Star. It should be noted that the mean values of the reminiscence scores vary greatly, decreasing from the first (14.8) through 12.1 for the second to 8.0 for the third.

Becker's general findings were rather negative; he claimed that "the concept of basal cortical inhibition . . . appeared as a unitary factor, but was not found to be related to extraversion–introversion. No empirical evidence was found to support Eysenck's assumption that satiation and reactive inhibition form a unitary trait. Satiation and reactive inhibition measures were found to have some common variance with the basal inhibition measures, but they did not covary with each other. There was no evidence to support Eysenck's hypotheses that satiation measures covary with extraversion measures." (Becker, 1960, p. 65.) Becker did, however, find significant correlations between his retest reminiscence score and extroversion (his 3 main measures of extraversion correlated .21, .22, and .19 with rem.) Also, the reminiscence measure loaded .24 on his extraversion factor. He acknowledges that the accumulation of "such correlations of borderline significance suggests that Eysenck's results may be replicable," although he does not really seem to think so (Becker, 1960, p. 64). How can we explain Becker's failure to discover the kinds of relations found by Claridge in a rather similar experiment? Failure to replicate is of course endemic in psychology and is often dismissed without attempting to find valid reasons for it; proponents and antagonists of a theory select the positive or negative findings to prop up their views, without attempting to discover the possible causes for the apparent disagreement. As the literature on reminiscence is especially rich in "failures to replicate," it may be useful to look a little more closely at Becker's work.

Note, in the first place, that his experimental paradigm of the reminiscence phenomenon does not constitute a replication of the original studies which found positive correlations with E. There are two important differences. In the first place, Becker's Ss worked at a much higher level of achievement, due to the pre-test practice which brought them up to a level of almost 50% of time-on-target for the men (somewhat less for the women). This level was at no time achieved by Eysenck's (or Star's) Ss; in Eysenck's experiment the level at which reminiscence was occurring was about 12% of time-on-target for the first measure, and 22% for the second. Clearly, Becker was working at quite a different part of the learning curve, well after the major portion of a response acquisition had taken place; this is an important difference, particularly as Becker himself found "that less reminiscence occurs with a higher level of skill" (p. 62). In the second place, Becker used as his measure of reminiscence the difference between 1-min periods; in other words, the post-rest period used for the comparison was 6 times as long as that used by Eysenck and Star. This extended measure confounds reminiscence and post-rest upswing; as will be seen in the figures contrasting extraverts' and introverts' post-rest performance from the work of Eysenck and Star, the differences are most marked in the first trial or two, and then decrease and vanish. Rescoring Eysenck's and Star's work according to Becker's method showed that all correlations with E became insignificant; thus there is no question of "failure to replicate"—Eysenck, Star, and Becker all get identical results when the same method of scoring is used! It is not clear why Becker failed to use the original method, which had been found to be successful, thus properly replicating the original studies; his purpose of achieving greater reliability by the use of the scoring method adopted clearly failed, and there was no apparent reason why he could not have gone back to the method of scoring which had shown promise in previous work.

The general failure of the factor analysis to support Eysenck's theory, or to replicate Claridge's results, may be due to two causes. In the first place, Becker constructed his tests and adopted parameters for his experiments which were different to those used by workers who had previously found positive results; often his choice was such that from a consideration of the theory one might have predicted a negative outcome. In the second place, Becker failed to pay attention to three important rules in factor analysis; this failure makes his results difficult to interpret. In the first instance, he used correlations between 58 variables when his total population was only 62; it is a well-known rule in factor analysis that the number of Ss should be greatly in excess of the number of variables correlated. In the second instance, many of Becker's scores were not experimentally independent; this confounds results, and makes for the extraction of "apparatus factors." Third, and most important, Becker used an orthogonal method of rotation (vari-max) which forces these "apparatus factors" into orthogonality, elimi-nating any correlations that might be present between them, and between them and "questionnaire factors." It seems doubtful if the matrix of factor loadings is capable of meaningful interpretation; the glimpses of positive outcome which do emerge suggest that a properly conducted and analyzed experiment would have given results closer to the outcome of the Claridge experiment.

In the same year in which Becker's article appeared, Eysenck (1960a,b) published two further studies. In the first, 240 engineering apprentices were tested in eight groups, subdivided according to length of pre-rest massed practice (3 vs 8 min) and duration of rest (30 sec, 2 min, 6 min, and 20 min). Ss within each group were divided into extravert, ambivert, and introvert on the basis of their scores on the short version of the MPI. In the case of overlapping scores, Ss were allocated on a random basis. Reminiscence was found to be an increas-ing function of both amount of practice and rest; mean values for the two practice periods were .69 and .98; for the four rest periods, they were .61, .72, 1.15, and .84. Extraverts, ambiverts, and introverts have decreasing reminiscence scores: .94, .88, and .69. This effect is just short of significance, but there is a significant $R \times E$ interaction, shorter rest periods producing greater differences between groups (with the excep-tion of the 20-min rest period, which produced the greatest difference). This general trend had been predicted, and this prediction had formed the basis for Star's second experiment; the results cannot be regarded as support of the theory in view of the failure of Star's experiment, and the anomalous nature of the 20-min rest pause. Possibly the short work periods in Star's experiment account for his faulure.

In his second study, Eysenck (1960b) again tried to use short work periods, this time using one-min trials, separated by 5-min rest pauses; there were 11 such trials. Ss were 45 engineering apprentices, who were also administered the MPI; unfortunately these Ss were rather homoge-neous with respect to E, which would of course lower any relationships found. The product-moment correlations of the E scale with the 10 reminiscence scores were nearly all positive; only one correlation with E was statistically significant, but 8 out of 10 were in the predicted direction. Mean reminiscence score over all trials correlated .21 with E and $-.19$ with N. A factor analysis of the reminiscence scores, E and N, did not greatly clarify the results; the first factor extracted had loadings on all except the first and the two last rem. scores, and the second had a high loading on E (.54) and the majority of the reminiscence scores; however, it also had a negative loading on N (−.60). Again, therefore, results are in the predicted direction on the whole, and on the borderline of significance.

R. Lynn (1960), working with 40 students, used as his measure of extraversion the MPI and also the Archimedes Spiral After-Effect. It had been shown that, in line with theory, the after-effect is longer for extraverts, and Lynn also found this to be so ($r = −.43$). Reminiscence was measured on the inverted alphabet printing test, massed practice being given for 14 1-min trials, followed by a 2-min rest period, and one further 30-sec trial. Extraversion correlated with reminiscence .42, which is statistically significant; the correlation with work decrement was .21, which is insignificant. The spiral after-effect also correlated significantly with reminiscence ($r = −.34$). There was a slight correlation between E and the recovery of the spiral after-effect after rest ($r = .18$); this score might be regarded as a reminiscence score, although of course it differs in many ways from the orthodox type of reminiscence measure.

Lynn selected two groups of 12 extreme extraverts and 11 extreme introverts from his group, and printed a figure demonstrating the tendency of the extraverts to slow down during the massed practice, and to show greater reminiscence (our Figure 9-6). It will be noticed that in this study both groups converge on an identical post-rest performance score, having started out on an identical pre-rest first trial score. This test, therefore, agrees perfectly with the inhibition theory, and gives no support to any form of consolidation theory. Lynn failed to find any significant correlations between any of his measures and N.

Lynn followed up this work in an unpublished study, in which 82 children were exposed to the same test of inverted alphabet printing. He again found a significant correlation between reminiscence and E, but this time the correlation with N also proved to be significant. It seems clear that the inverted alphabet printing task can with advantage be used for the purpose of analyzing relationships between personality and reminiscence. We shall argue in a later chapter that in a proper taxonomy of tasks, pursuit-rotor learning shows only consolidation as being responsible for reminiscence, while at the other extreme vigilance tasks show only inhibition in the same role. Inverted alphabet printing lies in an intermediate position, with both consolidations and inhibitions concerned in mediating reminiscence. Spiral after-effects are in the same class as vigilance tasks.

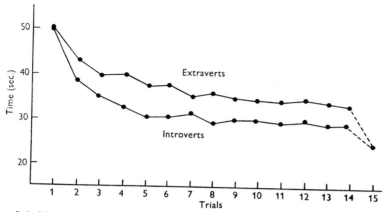

Figure 9-6. Mean times and reminiscence of introverts and extraverts on the inverted alphabet printing task. Taken with permission from Lynn (1960).

We next encounter an exceptionally well designed study by Germain and Pinillos (1962), using an occupationally homogeneous sample (professional drivers), aged between 20 and 35, medically fit, and with IQs neither in the top nor the bottom decile. Ss with high lie scale scores were excluded, and so were subjects falling into the middle 50% of the distribution on E and N, leaving only extremes in the four quadrants. A 10-min rest followed one of five periods of massed practice on the pursuit rotor: 60, 180, 360, 600, and 900 sec. Sixty Ss were assigned at random to each of these conditions, except that the Ss were equally taken from each of the four quadrants of the personality circle. The groups showed no correlation between reminiscence and age, IQ, spatial ability, humidity, and temperature at time of testing. There were no differences between high-N and low-N Ss, but extraverts scored 23% above introverts on reminiscence: 1.27 vs 1.01 sec. Unfortunately one of the two recording clocks did not function properly during the experiment, and consequently reminiscence was scored as the third 10-sec post-rest trial minus the last pre-rest trial; this is probably not an optimal score for use in this connection. The main outcome of the analysis of variance was a significant interaction ($p < .01$) between E and conditions; it appeared that the difference between extraverts and introverts on reminiscence was maximum after 3 and 6 min of massed practice, slight and negative after one min, or after 10-and 15-min periods. To some extent this agrees with our own findings; we obtained positive data with 5-min practice periods, and insignificant data with short practice periods. The possible reason for obtaining insignificant data with long practice periods has already been discussed in relation to the effects of motivation on reminiscence.

It may be useful to restate at this point the exact position reached. The studies summarized have shown (1) that the reminiscence phenomenon can only be measured with a moderate degree of reliability, probably not exceeding .5, and not infrequently below that value. It follows directly that (2) correlations with personality variables cannot be very marked, and are likely to be low to middling; this is what has in fact been found. (3) Under favorable conditions, E has usually been found to correlate positively with reminiscence, correlations not usually exceeding .3 or thereabouts, and sometimes failing to reach acceptable levels of significance. (In this context, the term "favorable" is used to denote test parameters which can be deduced from theory, i.e., reasonably lengthy pre-rest practice, reasonably long rest period, avoidance of compounding "warm-up" and reminiscence effects, etc.) (4) There has been little consistent correlation of N and reminiscence, although both positive and negative correlations have been found; there is some evidence of a negative correlation between N and performance of motor tasks, particularly when these are complex. (5) Doubt has been thrown on the inhibition hypothesis because of the failure in many studies to find pre-rest decrement in the performance of extraverts, and because there was some evidence that post-rest performance of extraverts was superior.

These doubts led Eysenck (1964) to consider the possibility that reminiscence might be a more complex phenomenon than had been hypothesized. It will be recalled that Hovland (1951) had defined reminiscence in terms of increments in *learning* which occurred during a rest period, while Osgood (1953, p. 509) had defined it as "a temporary improvement in *performance*, without practice." These two definitions may contain a clue to the fact that there are two different phenomena, either of which may give rise to reminiscence, but which require entirely different explanations. The first kind of phenomenon we may be dealing with is properly considered an inhibition effect; massed practice sets up cortical inhibition effects which depress performance below what it would be under conditions of spaced practice, and this performance decrement is reinstated after rest. This phenomenon follows Osgood's definition, can be subsumed under Hull's and Kimble's theories, and is perhaps most clearly shown in vigilance phenomena (Eysenck, 1967). The fact that vigilance tests show introverts superior in maintaining a state of high arousal supports the general theory linking inhibition with personality. The second kind of phenomenon we may be dealing with is properly considered a consolidation effect; massed practice sets up reverberating memory circuits which require a rest pause in order to permit transfer into permanent memory storage. This phenomenon follows Hovland's definition, cannot be subsumed under Hull's and Kimble's theories, and is pehaps most clearly shown in pursuit-rotor learning, as we shall argue in a later chapter. We have already discussed some of the evidence indicating that in general the consolidation theory is more appropriate for the usual paradigm of pursuit-rotor learning; the argument is presented at some length by Eysenck (1965). Here we shall be concerned more with the relevance of this argument to the findings as far as personality is concerned.

When first contrasting these two hypotheses, Eysenck (1964) was unwilling to accept the consolidation theory as being able to account for the personality correlates (particularly E); given that introverts are characterized by a higher level of arousal, and given also that high arousal level is a precondition for effective consolidation, it seemed that the natural prediction would have to be that introverts would succeed better than extraverts in achieving high post-rest performance, i.e., in showing greater reminiscence. This, as we have seen, is counter to fact; it is extraverts who show greater reminiscence. Consequently, Eysenck tried to develop a theory depending on inhibition, but not implying greater pre-rest performance decrement in extraverts. Two theories were in fact developed; they are here presented only very briefly because both were abandoned in favor of the consolidation theory (taken in conjunction with Walker's "performance decrement" hypothesis) shortly afterwards.

The first of these theories posits that conditioned inhibition ($_sI_R$) arises because of the reinforcing effect of the "blocks" or involuntary rest pauses (IRPs) which are the results, in Hullian theory, of reactive inhibition building up to the level of drive (D) under which the individual S is working. Now if introverts condition better than extraverts (Eysenck, 1967), then it might be predicted that they would also accumulate more conditioned inhibition; this should depress their performance post-rest, but might not affect it pre-rest. The theory is outlined in some detail in Eysenck (1964b); it demands (as does the consolidation theory) that the difference between introverts and extraverts in reminiscence should be determined by the post-rest trials, not by the pre-rest trials, as demanded by the reactive inhibition hypothesis. As this is clearly an important empirical question, which had only received a rather ambiguous answer in previous work, a special experiment was set up to test the hypothesis. From a larger number of apprentices, 28 extraverts and 23 introverts were selected as extremes; these were then tested on the pursuit rotor on a 5-10-5 schedule. Results are shown in

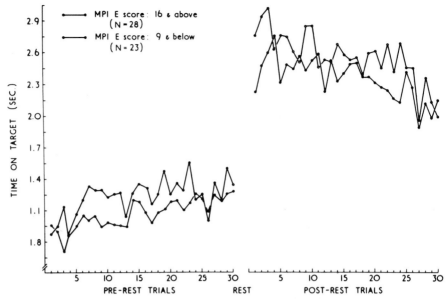

Figure 9-7. Pre-rest and post-rest performance of extraverted and introverted subjects on the pursuit rotor. Taken with permission from Eysenck (1964b).

Figure 9-7; extraverts had a significantly higher reminiscence score than introverts (1.67 vs 1.09.) More important, it is clear that the difference arises exclusively from the post-rest difference in performance; pre-rest performance shows no even suggestive difference. This result goes counter to the reactive inhibition theory.

The other alternative theory (Eysenck, 1962) also depends on the concept of IRPs, and asserts that because of greater inhibition in the extravert, there should be more and longer IRPs, and consequently the extravert would more frequently be in a state of not working; this would lower his score on the average for any given period of time. However, this hypothesis would lead to the postulation of lower performance pre-rest in the extravert, and it can therefore not be supported in view of the results just mentioned.

It will be clear that the existence, and hypothetical differential occurrence in extraverts and introverts, of IRPs has become an important theoretical issue. Eysenck (1957) has reviewed the evidence on the existence of these "blocks" (e.g., Bills, 1931, 1935; Bjerner, 1949; Geldreich, 1959; Williams *et al.*, 1959); we have already seen that they had already been encountered explicitly in the early work of the Kraepelin school towards the end of last century (Voss, 1899). Spielmann (1963) made a special study of the occurrence of IRPs, using tapping with a metal stylus on a metal plate as her task; she measures the length of each tap (contact between stylus and plate) and each gap (time between contacts). Concentrating her analysis on the gaps (which are more accurately measured, for technical reasons) she found that the average frequency of IRPs (objectively defined) was significantly higher in extraverts than in introverts, the total number of IRPs observed being 15 times as high in the former than in the latter group. The average onset of IRPs was significantly earlier in the extravert than in the introvert group. Testing was done for 5 min on each of 5 successive days; during this time the 5 most introverted Ss produced 25 IRPs of which none was longer than .5 sec while the 5 most extraverted Ss produced 370 IRPs of which 44 were longer than .5 sec. Diagrams showing the actual performance of the 9 most extraverted and the 9 most introverted Ss are given by Eysenck (1967). Eysenck (1964c) has also reported a study in which extraverts showed significantly more IRPs in a tapping task than did introverts, although the difference was much less marked than in the Spielmann study; this may have been due to the fact that only 1 test of 1-min length was given. Longer periods may be required in order to produce sufficient inhibition for IRPs to occur in any number.

A tapping task was also used by Wilson, Tunstall, and Eysenck (1971); 187 apprentices were asked to tap for 1 min on two occasions separated by 24 hr, and their performance summed for the four 15-sec periods into which each 1-min work period was split. There was a distinct tendency for extraverts to begin each session at a higher level of performance (faster rate of tapping) than did the introverts, but to become much slower in the last 15-sec period. They also showed a distinct reminiscence trend after the 24-hr rest period, beginning at a faster rate than that on which they had finished the day before. The difference from day to day was in almost equal degree due to lower performance pre-rest and higher performance post-rest. This suggests that a certain amount of learning may be involved in this test, as well as recovery from inhibition. It should be noted that special conditions of testing included feedback of speed of performance by a rate meter; Ss were instructed to keep the needle of the meter on a red mark, corresponding to a rate of 5 taps per sec. In addition, Ss tapped the morse key with the middle finger of their preferred hand while the remaining fingers and the hand were held flat by a perspex bar passing under the working finger; this clamping system was designed to prevent Ss from counteracting the build-up of inhibition by transferring the work load to different muscles, so that fatigue effects would be manifested more quickly.

These studies have been introduced to show that the postulation of inhibition-produced IRPs is not unreasonable in itself; however, their use in the theory of conditioned inhibition is still quite speculative, and although we would not dismiss Hull's theory of $_sI_R$ out of hand in view of some positive, direct evidence in its favor (e.g., Kendrick, 1958, 1960), nevertheless, for reasons given in detail in a later chapter, we would prefer to rely on the consolidation theory as being more direct and as being able to explain certain aspects of pursuit rotor and verbal learning reminiscence which could not be handled by a theory involving $_sI_R$. Before discussing the precise form such a theory would take in dealing with personality differences, it may be useful to complete out account of empirical studies.

A particularly interesting study was reported by Yates and Laszlo (1965); their experiment was concerned not with reminiscence, but with the prediction made by the inhibition hypothesis that greater I_R would accrue to extraverts than to introverts during massed practice. For this purpose they decided to build up maximum $_sH_R$ for rotor performance through a process of spaced practice not giving rise to either I_R or $_sI_R$; this was followed, after a rest of 10 min, by 7 min (42 10-sec trials) of massed practice. Pre-rest practice consisted of ten 12-sec trials (with only the last 10-sec scored), with 58-sec rest between trials. The results are shown in Figures 9-8 and 9-9. There is clear evidence that asymptote has been reached by the 10 extraverted and by the 10 introverted Ss (chosen as extremes on the basis of questionnaire and objective performance test); it can also be seen that these two groups do not differ in learning. Neither do they differ in the downward trend which eventuates after the rest pause, when massed practice is introduced. This downward trend is a clear manifestation of I_R on the inhibition theory, and the failure of extraverts to perform at a lower level than the introverts at any point during this 7-min period is fairly conclusive evidence against any explanation of personality differences in terms of inhibition (at least as far as this apparatus and experimental paradigm are concerned). It is interesting to note the complete absence of post-rest upswing; post-rest performance begins at a slightly lower level than is manifested at the end of pre-rest performance; thus there is no reminiscence either. This also speaks against the inhibition theory, and for a consolidation theory; once asymptote has been reached, no further learning takes place.

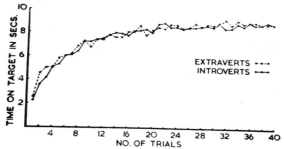

Figure 9-8. Pursuit-rotor learning (spaced practice) of extreme extraverts and introverts. Taken with permission from Yates and Laszlo (1965).

We next turn to a series of studies carried out in India by Jitendra Mohan and his students at Amritsar; these are not well known in the U.S.A. and the U.K. because many of them have been published in Indian journals, but they present interesting data which are very relevant to our discussion. In the first study, Mohan (1968a) tested 80 adult Ss who were grouped into the four quadrants of the E and N circle on the basis of their MPI scores. Each S worked on the rotor for 60 sec, rested for 10 sec, and followed this procedure until 11 work periods separated by 10 rest periods had been completed. Ten reminiscence scores were thus available for each S, scored in terms of 10-sec periods pre- and post-rest. In the analysis of variance, personality was significant at the $p < .01$ level; both E and N had a positive effect, with that for E being the stronger. In a second study, Mohan introduced an inhibiting stimulus (a bright light, lit up for 2 sec, 10 sec before the end of a 5-min period of massed pre-rest practice); this was followed by 10

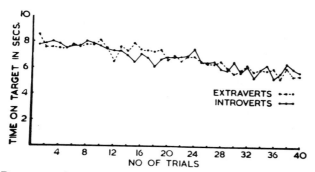

Figure 9-9. Decrement of pursuit-rotor performance from asymptomatic level in extreme extraverts and introverts. Taken with permission from Yates and Laszlo (1965).

min of rest, and 1 min of practice. Forty female students, again sorted into four quadrant groups, constituted the sample of Ss; under these conditions, extraverts showed significantly less reminiscence than introverts ($p < .05$). N played no systematic part in the results. Thus under disinhibiting experimental conditions (Mohan, 1968b) the direction of the extraversion–reminiscence connection may be reversed; this conclusion is of course subject to replication, as this one study is not sufficient in itself to establish such a far-reaching conclusion.

A third study by Mohan and Neelam (1969) used eighty students, half male, half female, selected on the basis of their MPI scores as belonging into one of the four quadrants (stable introverts, stable extraverts, unstable introverts, unstable extraverts). Half the Ss were tested under ego-orienting conditions, half under task-orienting conditions; the test used was the inverted alphabet printing test. Nine 30-sec trials of massed practice were given, followed by a 10-min rest, and one further 30-sec trial. Analysis of variance demonstrated significance for the personality variables ($p < .01$), motivation ($p < .01$), and the $P \times M$ interaction ($p < 0.1$.) Extraverts had greater reminiscence than introverts, low-N Ss greater than high-N Ss, and high-motivation greater than low-motivation Ss. Unfortunately the data given in the paper do not make it possible to explicate the precise nature of the $P \times M$ interaction.

In a further experiment, Mohan and Shashi (1972) again studied 40 male and 40 female students, divided into four personality groups, on the basis of the EPI. inverted alphabet printing and symbol substitution were the two tasks employed; for both, 5 min of pre-rest practice was followed by 2-min rest and a final 1-min practice period. Reminiscence scores for both tests disclosed a personality difference at the $p < .01$ level, with motivation also being significant ($p < .01$ and .05, respectively); extraversion and high motivation are the variables linked with high reminiscence. There were also peformance differences on the alphabet printing task, with personality having a significant influence ($p < .01$); high-E and high-N Ss performed better. Motivation failed to show significant influence on scores.

We come next to a study by Farley (1966, 1971) which is much more directly relevant. Farley argued that the uncertainty and the numerous marginally significant data of previous research were due largely to the relatively small numbers of subjects employed, or, when larger numbers had been used, the failure to preselect high-E and low-E Ss. Clearly, with the reliabilities of the reminiscence measure being as low as we have found it to be, no large effect can be expected, and only the use of large preselected samples is likely to give us unequivocal results.

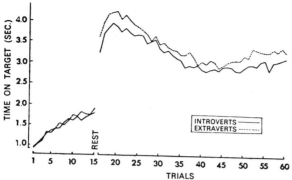

Figure 9-10. Performance curves of 90 extraverts and 110 introverts on the pursuit rotor. Taken with permission from Farley (1971).

Accordingly Farley selected a total of 110 introverted and 90 extraverted Ss from a much larger group of 623 male students; extreme dissimulators (i.e., with high scores on the lie scale of the EPI) had been excluded from either group. These Ss were given a pursuit-rotor test using the 5-10-15-min paradigm; reminiscence was measured by using the last two pre-rest and the first two post-rest 10-sec trials. Results are given in Figure 9-10, scored in terms of 20-sec periods. The reminiscence score of the extraverts was 16% higher than that of the introverts (3.50 vs 2.92), a difference significant at the $p < .03$ level using the appropriate one-tailed test.

The groups were not differentiated on the terminal pre-rest test, but were significantly differentiated on the initial post-rest test ($p < .025$). This result supports the consolidation hypothesis, and goes counter to the inhibition hypothesis. Separate analyses were carried out on the three 5-min periods which make up the post-rest performance; although the figure shows clearly that introverts are inferior throughout the 15-min period, this difference is only significant during the first 5-min period ($p < .05$ by analysis of variance).

Farley also constituted two samples of high and low N; several additional Ss were included in this study in order to obtain more extreme Ss. The final sample contained 51 high-N and 37 low-N Ss. These groups failed to show any differences whatsoever, either in performance or in reminiscence. Farley concludes that N played no great part in producing individual differences in reminiscence, possibly because of the nonthreatening nature of the situation; he also draws attention to the fact that in the Maudsley studies of the effects of drive this failed to show any effect when 5-min practice periods were employed, but became obvious with longer periods. As far as extraversion is concerned, Farley concludes that his results support either the "conditioned inhibition" hypothesis, or else the consolidation hypothesis. This is by far the most careful and well-designed study in the field, and the results agree well with the general tenor of our survey.

We must now turn again to a discussion of the value of the inhibition and consolidation theories in accounting for the observed higher reminiscence of extraverts. The main argument against the consolidation hypothesis, in relation to personality differences, is of course the direction of the difference; we would expect introverts, who according to the theory have high cortical arousal, to show greater consolidation and reminiscence than extraverts, who according to the theory have low cortical arousal. Walker's "action decrement" theory resolves this difficulty; according to this theory the strong arousal of the introvert, mediating a strong consolidation process, makes the subject less able to use the acquired knowledge or skill while consolidation is still going on. Thus during the first few minutes after learning, extraverts should do better than introverts; after a long rest period, when even the most powerful consolidation process has ceased, introverts would do much better. After a long rest period, therefore, introverts would show reminiscence, extraverts forgetting; after a short rest period, extraverts would show reminiscence, introverts failure to do well. This theory will be discussed in much greater theoretical detail, and adapted to pursuit rotor learning results in a subsequent chapter; here we shall be concerned rather with the empirical results of looking for the "crossover" effect which according to the theory would be a function of differences in rest period duration. The most clear-cut evidence has come from experiments using verbal (rote) learning.

Using paired associate learning as the task, Howarth and Eysenck (1968) 5 groups of 11 introverts and 5 groups of 11 extraverts learned the associates to a set criterion, and were then tested for recall after rest intervals of 0, 1, 5, 30 min, or 24 hr. It was predicted that the introverts would recall poorly after short rest intervals and well after long rest intervals, while the extraverts would show the opposite pattern. Figure 9-11 shows the outcome of the experiment; it will be seen that the prediction is borne out in detail.

A more complex study was undertaken by McLean (1968, 1969), who not only used extraverted and introverted Ss as low- and high-arousal groups, but also used white noise and control conditions to produce high- and low-arousal reactions, respectively. In his first experiment, Ss were given a single presentation of 6 paired associates.

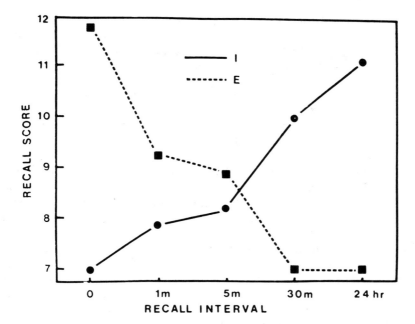

Figure 9-11. Mean recall scores of extraverts and introverts at the recall interval stated. Taken with permission from Howarth and Eysenck (1968).

Half of the Ss received white noise (85 dB) simultaneous with the pairings of the items. Half of the Ss from both noise and no-noise groups were given a recall test 2 min following paired associates presentation, while the remainder were tested 24 hr later. The learning of this experiment was incidental. Skin resistance recordings indicated that white noise presentation increased arousal during the associative phase of learning of the experimental Ss. A significant interaction between noise and recall interval condition was found in the direction predicted by consolidation theory. When noise conditions were collapsed and the recall of associates compared as a function of the within-subject arousal present during the associative phase of learning (i.e., using the Kleinsmith and Kaplan scoring procedure, based on skin resistance decrements), similar interaction was found.

McLean (1969, p. 181) also found that "Eysenck's theory that introverts function at relatively higher levels of arousal was supported in this experiment. Introverts performed relatively poorly on the immediate paired-associate retention test but reminisced to a strong advantage over extraverts, who performed optimally immediately and poorly on the delayed recall test. This interaction between personality and recall interval was statistically significant ($p < .01$). Furthermore, it was clear that personality derived arousal (introversion–extraversion) and induced arousal (white noise) were additive in their effects on paired-associate recall performance." Other measures of arousal, such as TFT and several electrodermal response measures, failed to relate to either paired associate recall performance or personality dimensions (E and N).

A second experiment, similar to the first, was performed to see if the interaction between arousal and recall interval could be demonstrated when awareness was involved. The interaction between noise and recall conditions in this case was significant and in the predicted direction. However, the interaction between within-subject arousal categories and recall interval in this experiment failed to reach statistical significance. Details regarding this experiment are given in Eysenck (1973); this source also gives a review of studies relating personality (extraversion–introversion) to short-term recall. Over a dozen such studies leave little doubt that, as demanded by our consolidation theory, extraverts show better recall after short intervals. This better performance is not always indexed in terms of reminiscence; both extraverts and introverts may show poorer performance after a short rest, but the decline would usually be greater for introverts. These findings are in good agreement with the greater reminiscence of extraverts on the pursuit rotor after short intervals of rest. On the whole, therefore, as far as verbal learning and reminiscence are concerned, the consolidation hypothesis seems to fit the data reasonably well. The results of these studies may also serve to explain the reasons for Buxton's statement about verbal reminiscence as the "now you see it, now you don't" phenomenon; the interaction of personality, arousal property of the orders and syllables used, and length of interval require more explicit control than they have received in the classical literature!

Results with the pursuit rotor have been contradictory. Farley (1969) reported several experiments, using the traditional Maudsley paradigm, in which personality was assessed both by questionnaire and by the "lemon test." In this test the increase in salivation consequent upon having 4 drops of lemon juice on the tongue is measured; the evidence supports the hypothesis that this increase would be larger for introverts than extraverts (Corcoran, 1964; Eysenck & Eysenck, 1967). In each experiment Farley observed the predicted "cross-over" effect, although the significance level was not always high enough to make the results acceptable; out of 3 experiments only 2 gave statistically significant effects. The "short" rest period was 10 min, the "long" period was 24 hr. Unfortunately this very important paper has not been published (it was delivered as a talk at the 1969 International Congress of Experimental Psychology in London), and consequently no further details are available.

In our own laboratory, Gray (1968) has also attempted to test the "cross-over" hypothesis, but with less success than Farley. Using 3 different rest intervals (30 sec, 10 min, and 1 week), he employed 72, 71, and 66 Ss, respectively; all were male volunteers, with an average of 26 ± 5 years. Two-flash thresholds were measured as an index of arousal; so were skin conductance, and the orienting response to the simultaneous presentation of 1 sec of white noise and a bright light. The pursuit-rotor target consisted of a central disk surrounded by 3 concentric rings, so that time-on-target scores for targets differing in size could be obtained; this was done to take into account the criticisms of Bahrig, Fitts, and Briggs (1957) discussed in an earlier chapter. Pre-rest practice was continued for 6 min, post-rest practice for 7 min. Two measures of performance were used; T.O.T. for the small target (0.5-in diameter), and a root-mean-square (rms) measure derived for the large target (1.71-in diameter). This latter score was calculated using the formula provided by Humphries (1961); it was used in preference to a simple T.O.T. score for the large ring because it suffered less from ceiling effects, while still correlating very highly with the T.O.T. score. Reminiscence was measured in two ways: (1) conventional reminiscence scores (rem.) were calculated as by Eysenck (1956); (2) Maximum reminiscence scores (max rem.) used as the post-rest measure the mean of the two highest trials occurring at any time within the first 2 min of post-rest practice. This score was designed to measure reminiscence to the top of each subject's post-rest upswing which, it was hypothesized, would provide a measure less influenced by conditioned inhibition than the first post-rest trial. The modal trial, i.e., the trial on which most Ss produced their highest performance, differed for the 3 rest conditions; for the 30-sec group the modal trial was the first, for the 10-min group it was the eighth, and for the 1-week group it was the twelfth. The two methods of scoring correlate .53 for the small target and .69 for the rms score. Max. rem. is about twice as large as rem. for both scores, with almost identical variances. Reminiscence scores, however measured, are approximately twice as large when the large target is used for the measurement. Reminiscence scores correlate .56 between small and large target (−.68 for small target and rms); for max. rem. the correlations are .17 and −.53. Large target correlates with rms −.97 and −.91. Clearly size of target determines reminiscence score to a marked extent.

Gray undertook to investigate directly the problem of inhibition or consolidation determining reminiscence by correlating pre-rest perfor-

TABLE 9-2. Correlations among Reminiscence Measures and
Measures of Depression of Pre-Rest Performance (b) and
Ability (a) (N = 209)

	b	a	b with a partialled out
Reminiscence			
Small target	−.29	.09	−.29
rms	−.37	−.06	−.49
Rem. max.			
Small target	−.17	.31	.02
rms	−.30	−.20	−.50

mance depression with reminiscence, his argument being that on the consolidation hypothesis this correlation should be zero. The measure of depression of pre-rest performance, calculated for each S, was the linear regression coefficient (b) for the final 4½ min of the 6 min pre-rest practice period. The initial 1½ min were excluded because very little improvement in performance was evident after that time. The regression coefficient (a) represented the level of ability measured 1½ min after performance started. Table 9-2 shows the results taken over all 3 groups, as these did not differ significantly in pre-rest performance. It is clear from the table that Ss who show the most depression of performance have the highest reminiscence scores, however calculated. As in Eysenck's (1964) study there is no significant relationship between ability level and reminiscence (rem.); there is, however, a significant relationship with Max. Rem., in the sense that high levels of ability are associated with high reminiscence scores. (The negative sign of the correlation between a and rms arises because good performance is reflected in low rms scores.) Eysenck's (1964) results show a similar pattern when his Fig. 1 is looked at from this point of view; he did not of course use rms scores. In the present study the relationship between ability (a) and the depression of pre-rest practice was highly significant (small target $r = .60$; rms $r = -.56$); Ss who show a relatively high level of performance after 1½ min show a considerable decline in performance during the remainder of the session. Partialling out this ability factor tended to increase the size of the correlation between decline in performance and reminiscence. It seems that in this study at least reminiscence is in part determined by dissipation of inhibition, and in part only by consolidation. This means that to test the "cross-over" hypothesis properly it is necessary to partial out the effects of pre-rest performance (b) on the reminiscence scores. (Detailed figures are given by Eysenck and Gray, 1971.)

The hypothesis was evaluated by analysis of covariance, using the pre-rest measures employed in the calculation of the reminiscence scores as the covariates, and the reminiscence measures as the dependent variables. To achieve proportional numbers in the cells of the $2 \times 2 \times 3$ table (2 levels of E, 2 levels of N, 3 rest conditions), small numbers of Ss had to be dropped by random exclusion. Figure 9-12 shows the results; there is little difference between extraverts and introverts after the 30-sec rest pause, a marked difference in the predicted direction after the 10-min rest pause, and a slightly reduced difference, in the same direction, after the 1-week rest pause. The predicted cross-over has failed to occur; the shorter rest pause gives results in line with prediction, but the 1-week group fails to show greater reminiscence for introverts. Using the rem. measure, extraversion ($p < .004$) and length of rest pause ($p < .015$) are both significant; for max. rem. the p values are .10 and .001. The failure of the max. rem. measures to show significance for E is due to an interaction effect with length of rest.

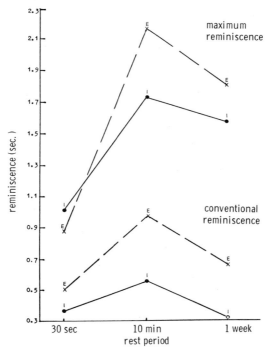

Figure 9-12. Conventional and maximum reminiscence scores of extraverts and introverts after different rest periods. Taken with permission from Gray (1968).

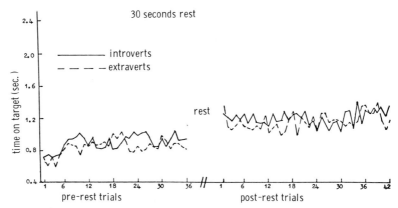

Figure 9-13. Performance of extraverts and introverts pre- and post-rest, with rest interval of 30 sec. Taken with permission from Gray (1968).

When the means of the 10-min and the 1-week groups are combined, extraverts have significantly higher max. rem. scores at the $p < .01$ level. There is not even any suggestive significance for N in the data.

The significant differences in reminiscence scores must have arisen mainly from differences between groups in the post-rest scores for calculating reminiscence, because the analysis partialled out the effects of the pre-rest measure used in calculating reminiscence. Nevertheless, Eysenck's (1964) finding that introverts and extraverts did not differ in terminal pre-rest performance was confirmed; personality did not affect

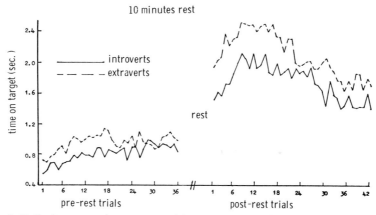

Figure 9-14. Performance of extraverts and introverts pre- and post-rest, with rest interval of 10 min. Taken with permission from Gray (1968).

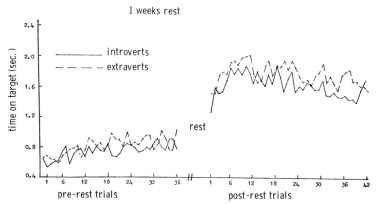

Figure 9-15. Performance of extraverts and introverts pre- and post-rest, with rest interval of 1 week. Taken with permission from Gray (1968).

terminal pre-rest level of performance, and the effects of E and length of rest on rem. were significant when pre-rest levels were not partialled out. Figures 9-13 through 9-15 show the actual performance curves of extraverts and introverts; it will be seen that only the 10-min rest period produces really decisive differences over the whole post-rest period between extraverts and introverts.

The overall differences in post-rest performance between the three rest groups are of interest; they are graphed in Figure 9-12. Rem. scores fail to show a difference between the 30-sec and the one-week groups, but max. rem. shows a very marked difference. This may be due to the need of the 1-week group for a more prolonged "warm-up." Even for max. rem., however, the 10-min group had higher scores than the 1-week group ($p < .05$). The 10-min group, however, also had a steeper slope for its post-rest downswing ($p < .001$), supporting the hypothesis that long continued dissipation of inhibition would lessen the extent of the downswing, or the alternative hypothesis that consolidation has ceased to interfere with performance after 1 week. The results suggest a "forgetting" loss when periods of 1 week of rest are involved; this agrees with findings by Koonce, Chambliss, and Irion (1964), but not with Jahnke and Duncan (1956). Clearly the amount of forgetting is not large, and may fail to reach significance. It may also be affected by differences in motivation, personality, size of target, and other conditions.

Performance curves for extraverts and introverts are shown in Figures 9-13, 9-14, and 9-15, for the three different rest intervals, respectively. Figure 9-16 shows a comparison between the overall per-

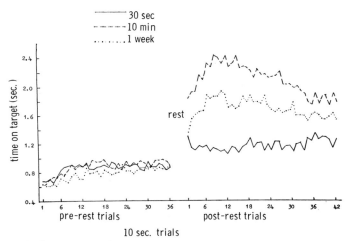

Figure 9-16. Performance on the pursuit rotor pre- and post-rest, comparing effects of three different rest intervals. Taken with permission from Gray (1968).

formance curves after the three rest intervals. The observed differences in post-rest performance are very clear, with the 10-min rest group clearly superior to both the others.

Two-flash threshold measures did not show significant relations with reminiscence, although results for max. rem. approached significance. Low arousal Ss showed higher max. rem. scores to the extent of 5% overall, there being no significant TFT × rest interval interaction; nor was there any correlation between TFT and extraversion ($r = .08$). The orienting response also failed to correlate with reminiscence; however, low arousal Ss (small ORs) had significantly higher pre-rest scores than high-arousal Ss. Range corrections did not alter the conclusions. Skin conductance was monitored throughout the practice blocks, and results are shown in Figure 9-17. During the minute prior to the start of practice, conductance rose very sharply to reach a peak within the first 20 sec of practice. Thereafter conductance declined, in a negatively accelerated manner, so that after about 5 min of practice it was dropping relatively slowly. However, when the S was told to cease working there was again a rapid rise in conductance similar to that observed when the S had been told to commence working. The same pattern occurred during the second session, and the findings are similar to those reported by Kling *et al.* (1961*a*, 1961*b*). (See also report by Costello *et al.*, 1969.) Analysis concentrated on two scores as potential measures of arousal: the highest point of log conductance during the first 30 sec of practice ("top conductance"), and the decline from this point to the lowest log conductance level occurring during the final 30 sec of pre-rest practice ("drop conductance").

Top conductance, assumed to signify high arousal, was significantly related to max. rem. ($p < .01$), in the sense that low-arousal Ss had higher scores than high-arousal Ss; this was true under all conditions, there being no significant interaction with length of rest pauses. This finding, that low-arousal Ss showed higher max. rem. scores, is consistent with the previous results where extraverts, subjects with high TFT and subjects with small range corrected ORs were found to have the slightly higher reminiscence scores. Drop-conductance failed to show significant effects of any interest. Nonspecific fluctuations did not show a significant effect on max. rem. Finally, an estimate was made of each S's "maximum arousal level," using a procedure suggested by Lacey's principle of "response stereotypy" (Lacey & Lacey, 1958). The individual's scores on each arousal measure discussed, except N, were expressed in standard form and the highest standard score for each S taken as his maximum arousal score. This method also failed to show any consistent effects.

To clarify the position with respect to arousal measures, Gray attempted to use an "inverted-U" model, but failed to obtain any significant results. Intercorrelation and factor analysis of the measures used disclosed a pattern of very low correlations, and the absence of any clear-cut "arousal" factor. The general tendency in this study of finding

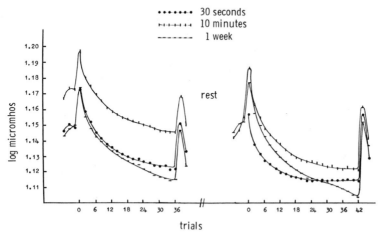

Figure 9-17. Skin conductance during performance on the pursuit rotor, comparing groups having three different lengths of rest interval. Taken with permission from Gray (1968).

high reminiscence related (weakly) to low arousal would not be acceptable as a conclusion were it not for the fact that similar results have been
reported by Corteen (1967); he too found that low levels of skin conductance were associated with high reminiscence scores. His explanation is in terms of a differential forgetting theory (McGeoch & Irion,
1952), but the evidence for a differential forgetting theory of reminiscence is not particularly strong (Osgood, 1953), and in particular seems
to apply less to motor performance than to verbal behavior. Gray
suggests an explanation in terms of Eysenck's (1964) hypothesis, i.e.,
that extraverts condition less $_sI_R$ which depresses post-rest performance. Spain (1966) has found that eyelid conditioning was significantly related to arousal, measured by skin potential in both normal and
schizophrenic Ss, a finding which would fit in well with such an
hypothesis.

Gray argues thus: "High arousal subjects would condition more $_sI_R$
which would not consolidate during pre-rest practice and would not
therefore affect their level of pre-rest performance but, following the
rest, when the $_sI_R$ had consolidated, it would impair the performance of
high-arousal subjects more than low-arousal subjects and result in
lowered reminiscence" (Gray, 1968, p. 175). It is difficult to reach any
conclusion at this point of time on the adequacy of the different theories
involved, although it seems clear that the inhibition theory is irrelevant
to the results of Gray's experiment in view of the fact that he partialled
out pre-rest decline effects. What does become apparent, however, is
that the results of the two relevant experiments (Farley & Gray) reach
opposite conclusions; the former finds a distinct "cross-over" effect,
while the latter does not. Another attempt to demonstrate this cross-
over effect was made by Seunath (1973). 120 school boys aged 15 were
divided into four groups on the basis of their extraversion and neuroticism scores. They practiced the pursuit rotor for two sessions separated
by either a 10-min or a 1-week rest. The apparatus used was a standard
pursuit rotor with the metal target disk replaced by an illuminated
panel and a photocell in the tip of the stylus. Seunath found no
differences between the personality groups with either the long or the
short rest. Reminiscence was significantly greater after 10 min than after
1 week, confirming Gray's finding that with a rest of one week some
forgetting takes place. Typically, this is not an exact replication since
different apparatus and a different type of subject were used. Nevertheless, the results are disturbing since as far as personality effects are
concerned, neither Farley's nor Gray's findings were replicated. One
might be inclined to dismiss the issue as just another "failure to
replicate," but this would not be an adequate response to the situation.

As we shall see in the next chapter there is direct evidence for a cross-over effect associated with arousal (as measured by the TFT), and there is the evidence from the experiments of Howarth and Eysenck, and of McLean, which also demonstrate this effect. Clearly, there is some evidence for the underlying theory, but unfortunately we do not yet know which of the many parameters governing performance on the pursuit rotor is responsible for the observed divergence in result. The fact that such a simple variant as size of target can produce very different sorts of results must act as a warning; major effects, such as reminiscence differences between extraverts and introverts, can be reproduced with a wide array of experimental conditions (provided that there is sufficient pre-rest practice and a sufficiently lengthy rest interval), but more complex effects, such as the "cross-over," are contingent on parameter choices which cannot as yet be specified. The discovery of the appropriate parameters to make this phenomenon replicable is the most urgent task awaiting experimentalists at the moment.

There is evidence of genetic differences in response to intertrial intervals which comes from animal work with mice. In one study (Wimer et al., 1968) both the active shock escape learning and passive shock avoidance learning of C57BL mice were better under a long (24 hr) intertrial interval condition than with brief (5–40 sec) intervals; for DBA/2 mice, the converse was true. Another mouse study on distribution of practice has yielded strain differences (Bovet et al., 1968). In shuttle box avoidance learning, 500 trials were presented either in one continuous 250-min session or in five 50-min sessions at daily intervals. The distribution of practice over 5 days resulted in a dramatic enhancement of learning compared to the continuous session performance in DBA/2 mice, but resulted in poorer performance in C3H and BALB/c mice. Similar strain differences were found in continuous sessions when the intertrial interval was either 30 or 120 sec. As McClearn (1972, p. 62) points out, "these demonstrations of strain differences have amply shown a genetic influence on memory and consolidation mechanisms." They also show our postulated "cross-over" effect.

Also of relevance in this connection are studies by McGaugh and colleagues (McGaugh et al., 1962; McGaugh & Cole, 1965) on the influence of distribution of practice on the behavioral differences between decendants of the Tryon maze-bright and maze-dull strains. As McClearn (1972, p. 62) argues convincingly, "this particular parameter of the learning situation is a central one, because it is related to the consolidation of the memory traces. . . . The results clearly imply genetically influenced differences in rates of neural consolidation." Of the greatest importance here is the fact that strain differences depended crucially on the length of rest interval; 30-sec intervals demonstrated clear-cut differences, longer intervals did not. It is always chancy to argue from animals to men, but the analogy is too close to omit from our account, again demonstrating the "cross-over" effect.

Our discussion, and our conclusions, have been formulated largely in terms of work with the pursuit rotor, although at times we have included results obtained with other tests, particularly the inverted alphabet printing test. In view of the fact that our taxonomy of tasks places inverted alphabet printing at a point where both consolidation and inhibition may be active in producing reminiscence, results from this task (and even more from other tasks, such as vigilance or spiral after effect) should be looked at as essentially dissimular from the pursuit rotor. However, for the sake of completeness, and in order to make comparisons possible, brief mention has been made of investigations using tasks other than the pursuit rotor.

A brief statement was given on a previous page, listing the conclusions which might be reached from a study of the reports referred to in Table 9-1. Do the later papers add anything to these conclusions?

1. The evidence now seems conclusive (where it was previously only suggestive) that extraversion is positively correlated with reminiscence on the pursuit rotor when pre-rest practice is continued for at least 5 min and the rest pause is of around 10 min duration.

2. The studies of Farley and Grey (Figures 9-12 and 9-16) are particularly convincing evidence in this respect; they also make it clear that it is the whole post-rest performance of the extraverts which is raised, rather than merely the first few post-rest trials. It might have been maintained on the previously available evidence [even including the Eysenck study (Figure 9-10)] that introverts show a failure to preserve set, consequently have poor post-rest performance immediately following rest, but catch up with the extraverts soon afterwards. Such a hypothesis, implying exaggerated warm-up, will be found to account for the behavior of schizophrenics; it clearly does not account for that of introverts.

3. The correlation between reminiscence and extraversion is replicable, but it is not strong; the observed value will in part depend on experimental conditions (length of pre-rest practice, length of rest, difficulty level of task, ability level of Ss, range of E in subject sample, etc.), but is unlikely to be much above or below .25. This suggests that experiments to test the hypothesis should (a) use groups of extreme Ss, as was done by Farley and Grey, and (b) should use reasonably large numbers. A correlation of .25 on an unselected sample of 100 Ss would

just fail of significance at the 1% level; thus a study finding precisely the predicted correlation would declare this finding to be insignificant! Many studies have used too small numbers of Ss to arrive at meaningful results.

4. It should not be thought that such a small correlation, even though replicable, is of no importance. What is at issue is the correlation between the two phenomena, extraversion and reminiscence, rather than the observed correlation between very imperfect and unreliable measures of these variables. Given that the reliabilities of the two variables concerned are roughly .75 and .50, the "true" correlation would not be .25, but in excess of .40; correction for attenuation gives a much more reasonable estimate of the relations involved. Assuming that the empirical correlation was more like .3, and the reliability of the reminiscence score .45, would raise the "true" correlation to .50. Such statistical games should not of course be taken too seriously, but nevertheless they suggest that the observed relation may be of some importance, and deserves explanation.

5. The data make it plain that no inhibition hypothesis can account for the findings, although the original prediction was made in terms of such a theory. It is possible that the consolidation theory, amplified and strengthened by Walker's "action decrement" hypothesis, can account for the observed facts, but the evidence is by no means clear. This may be due to the fact that few investigators have looked for the "cross-over" effect, and that the optimal conditions for its observation are not known. The proof that such an effect can be demonstrated quite clearly in the verbal learning field is of great interest, but does not imply that the same effect must be demonstrable with the pursuit rotor; if this book shows anything, it is that different tasks may involve quite different mechanisms. We shall return to the problem of explaining the observed correlations theoretically in a later chapter, where we attempt to suggest a solution in terms of differential strategies adopted by extraverts and introverts. Such an alternative explanation does not necessarily disprove the consolidation + "action decrement" hypothesis here canvassed; both might be correct. No final answer can be given without much further work on the "cross-over" effect.

6. We have noted, for the sake of completeness, correlations between personality and reminiscence involving other types of tests, particularly the inverted alphabet printing task. Even though equally small correlations have been found in these tasks between extraversion and reminiscence, it does not follow that these are produced by the same mechanisms. It has often been demonstrated that "reminiscence" in vigilance tasks correlates with extraversion (Stroh, 1971; Buckner &

McGrath, 1963); this effect is due almost entirely to inhibition, and not at all to consolidation. (In vigilance tasks, performance typically declines with time, and recovers completely after rest; there is no learning, and hence no consolidation. The term "reminiscence" is put in quotes here because the measure actually taken is the decline over time from the starting level; this effectively equals reminiscence multiplied by -1 because each S returns to his starting point after the rest, provided the rest is long enough. Hence for the sake of rapid communication we will use the term "reminiscence" in this rather unusual connotation.) Inverted alphabet printing would appear to demonstrate characteristics of both types of task; there is learning, and hence presumably consolidation, and there is inhibition, and hence presumably dissipation of inhibition. In complex tasks like this it is not possible to be certain about the mechanism responsible for the observed correlation. The advantage of tasks like vigilance and pursuit-rotor learning is precisely that they demonstrate the activity of one single mechanism, i.e., inhibition or consolidation, so that testable predictions can more easily be framed for them.

CHAPTER 10

Individual Differences: Schizophrenia

Kraepelin appears to have been the first to extend work on mental and motor performance, and on reminiscence, to abnormal groups; he reports on the performance of schizophrenics on a simple addition task (massed practice for 10 min), followed by a pause of 5 min (Kraepelin, 1913). Performance increased markedly after the rest pause, but then sank to a low level. Hoch (1901), a pupil of Kraepelin's, used the ergograph in his experiments; he found that manic-depressives showed a reversal of fatigue effects. Performance was found to increase in strength before a reduction appeared with exhaustion. These experiments were not particularly well controlled, they lacked proper comparison groups, and neither the statistical treatment nor the description of the experiment is adequate for a proper evaluation. This work did, however, set the stage for later more adequately controlled studies which have thrown some light on the performance characteristics of psychotic groups. Several pioneering studies investigated learning in insane Ss (e.g., Kent, 1911; Boring, 1913; Hull, 1917), but the first experiments relevant to the topic of this chapter were those of Huston and Shakow (1948).

This work was predicated on the view that schizophrenics had poorer learning ability than normals, a view supported by much previous work (e.g., in addition to the references given above, Gardner, 1931; Babcock, 1933; Kendig & Richmond, 1940). The schizophrenic group contained 122 male patients, of whom 46 were tested 3 times (at intervals of 3 months). The normal control group contained 60 male Ss, of whom 22 were tested a second time. In addition there was a small group of 13 manic-depressive patients, none of whom were tested twice. On each occasion the pursuit rotor was administered for ten 10-sec trials, interspersed with 20-sec rest pauses. The work was thus not massed. Manic-depressives and normals performed much better than schizophrenics, who showed little evidence of learning, although there were marked differences by subtype of illness: paranoids, unclassified, hebephrenic, indeterminate, and catatonics performed in this order. Duration of illness was not found to be important. Schizophrenics were also found to do worse on other tasks, such as tapping the reaction times. The main item of interest to our present concern is that patients showed reminiscence after the three months' interval, while normals showed forgetting; in terms of an arousal–consolidation hypothesis we would interpret this as evidence for high cortical arousal in schizophrenics. This interpretation, however, is not very compelling in view of the fact that the practice was spaced, rather than massed; furthermore, the difference is not likely to be very significant.

An experiment by Venables and Tizard (1956) is rather more illuminating. 30 male schizophrenics and 10 men suffering from endogenous depression were used as Ss. The task was a continuous self-paced reaction time measure, in which 5 choices were possible, and where the depression of the correct key corresponding to one light lit up the next stimulus light. Ss were sorted into groups on the basis of age and of short-stay vs long-stay in hospital. A run of 10-min practice was followed by a 1-min rest, and a further 10 min of practice. Figure 10-1 shows the results for the 7 subgroups. There were no significant differences among the schizophrenic groups in slope, all showing a tendency to rise during the first 10 min and to fall during the second 10 min. With respect to level, age was not a significant variable, but short-stay patients did better than long-stay patients. A significant reminiscence effect was observed for the schizophrenic groups; depressives showed only a slight improvement after rest. The authors conclude that "schizophrenics might be said to show an exaggerated tendency to develop reactive inhibition in contrast to depressives" (Venables & Tizard, 1956, p. 25). Comparing their results with those of Kraepelin and Hoch, they argue that "while the findings on these three studies are thus susceptible to a theory of differential development of reactive inhibition, other explanations are possible. Kraepelin himself dismisses the notion of fatigue as being responsible for the decrement in schizophrenic performance and favoured an explanation in terms of diminishing 'willed attention' (*Willenspannung*)." This is not necessarily a true discrepancy; if we regard I_R as a central variable (i.e., not in terms of the Mowrer–Miller "work hypothesis"), then rise in central inhibition

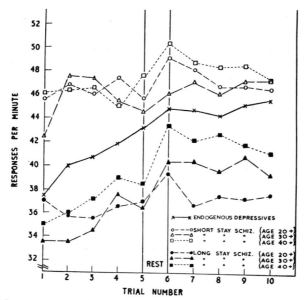

Figure 10-1. Mean scores per minute of schizophrenics and endogenous depressives on a repetitive task. Taken with permission from Venables and Tizzard (1956).

might be described as lessening in *Willenspannung*. As we have noted before, the evidence against the "work theory" is overwhelming, and it is no longer seriously upheld.

Mednick (1958) had proposed a theory of differential arousal with respect to the various stages of schizophrenic illness; early and advanced stages of the disorder are conceived of as poles of a learning process continuum. "This continuum proceeds from a state of heightened arousal (Early Stage) to a state of reduced, eventually subnormal, arousal resulting from the acquisition of anxiety avoidant associative responses (Advanced Stage.) In terms of arousal level, the normal individual might be expected to fall somewhere between the heightened arousal of the early schizophrenic and the lowered arousal of the advanced schizophrenic." (Higgins & Mednick, 1963, p. 314.) Basing themselves on the finding that greater arousal results in greater psychomotor reminiscence, these authors predicted that under identical test conditions, Early Stage schizophrenics would exhibit greater reminiscence effects than Advanced Stage schizophrenics; reminiscence of normals were expected to fall between the two psychotic groups. There were 16 patients in each of the "stage" groups, and 16 normal controls. Inverted alphabet printing was used as the test, each S being given five 1-min massed learning trials, a 2-min rest, and then

TABLE 10-1. Reminiscence Effects Displayed by Experimental and Control Groups [a]

Reminiscence	Early stage schizophrenics	Normals	Advanced stage schizophrenics
None	3	4	8
Moderate	5	7	6
High	8	5	2

[a] Higgins and Mednick, 1963.

another two 1-min practice trials. Results were reported in terms of an "all-or-none" statistic, each S being scored as showing reminiscence either moderately or strongly, or not showing it. Table 10-1 shows the main findings. It will be seen that the hypothesis is on the whole supported, although the statistical significance is only borderline; again one wonders why so few cases were tested in order to test such a clear-cut hypothesis. If groups of 50 or so Ss had been employed we would be more certain of our facts. It also seems that the method of scoring is not optimal; it would have been more sensible to have used actual scores, rather than to categorize them into three groups (no, moderate, or high reminiscence), a procedure which throws away information and has no rational basis.

The work of Claridge (1960) has already been mentioned in the preceding chapter; it will be remembered that he found very much reduced reminiscence in pursuit-rotor learning in schizophrenics; in this his results are like those of several authors summarized here (see Figure 10-2). His work, and that of several other Maudsley workers, was carried out in connection with a theory of schizophrenic disorder rather different from that of Mednick; this theory, with particular reference to inhibition and pursuit-rotor learning, has been developed by Eysenck (1961). Stated quite briefly, Eysenck postulates that schizophrenics differ from other groups (neurotics and normals) in that they dissipate inhibition more slowly; it is this that makes them work for most of the time under a lower drive (D) than other groups. (This theory was of course based on Hull's view that I_R was a negative drive state, which subtracted from D). If we identify, with Hebb, "drive" and "arousal," then our theory would coincide to a marked extent with Mednick's; both theories would attribute low arousal to schizophrenics, at least to "advanced stage" schizophrenics. It is the latter with whom most of our experiments have in fact dealt.

There is one important way in which this theory suggests novel experiments which would not follow from the Mednick type of approach. Given short rest pauses (meaning by this now rest pauses of up to 10 or 20 min) both theories would predict that schizophrenics would show little reminiscence. However, for long rest pauses (meaning by this rest pauses of several hours, perhaps 24 hr or even more) schizophrenics should dissipate all their inhibition, and have reminiscence scores as high as, and perhaps even higher, than normals. Thus this conception suggests what has proved a very interesting modification of the usual paradigm, by introducing into the experiment an important variable (short vs long rest pauses). (The older literature is of course full of comparison between different length rest pauses, but these were always "short" in our sense, and consequently irrelevant.) Looking at the literature already reviewed, we see that Claridge, Mednick, and others using short rest intervals found little if any reminiscence, while Huston and Shakow using a long rest pause (3 months) found considerable reminiscence. However, these are not experiments planned to test a theory, and consequently their support for the hypothesis in question cannot be regarded as very strong.

P. Ley, in an unpublished study (cf. Eysenck, 1961), tested 10 schizophrenics and ten normals on the pursuit rotor with a rest interval of 10 min; he also tested another 10 schizophrenics and 10 normals with a rest interval of 24 hr. He found, at a good level of statistical significance, that while after the 10-min rest pause the normals had high positive reminiscence scores, those of the psychotics were for practical purposes equal to zero (very much as in the study by Claridge). After 24 hr, he found that the reminiscence scores of the normals were somewhat lower than after the 10-min rest pause; those of the psychotics however, were now higher than those of either of the two normal groups. Eysenck (1961, p. 202) concluded that "it would appear, there-

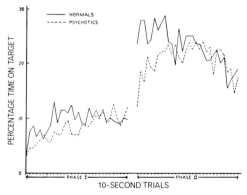

Figure 10-2. Performance curves of normals and schizophrenics on pursuit rotor. Taken with permission from Claridge (1960).

fore, that the hypothesis relating psychotic behaviour to low drive is untenable and that we must conclude that psychotic reactions are characterized by an excessive slowness of dissipation of inhibition." The possibility that the effects observed might be due to better consolidation accompanied by Walker-type "action decrement," on the part of schizophrenics was not considered; such a hypothesis would imply greater arousal among schizophrenics.

Ley's work was replicated, and taken farther in one important aspect, by Rachman (1963). Long-stay schizophrenics constituted his sample; 20 nonparanoid, male, chronic schizophrenics being assigned randomly to experimental and control groups. Both groups practiced for 5 min (i.e., 30 trials) before resting (either 10 min or 24 hr); rest was followed by a further 30 sec. of massed practice. Figure 10-3 shows the main results. There are no differences in performance pre-rest; note the failure for the usual improvement (however slight) to occur. This bears out several of the findings already quoted. Reminiscence scores are clearly as predicted; the 10-min group has a small negative score

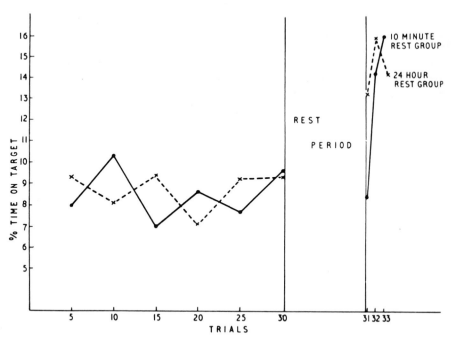

Figure 10-3. The effect of different periods of rest on reminiscence in schizophrenics. Taken with permission from Rachman (1963).

(−1.23%), while the experimental group has a mean score of +3.94%. Thus, with a pre-rest score of 9% of time-on-target, the 24-hr group jumps to 13%, while the control group falls to 8%. This difference is statistically significant ($p < .05$). A normal group of 20 Ss produced a reminiscence gain of 1.62% after a 10-min rest (Rachman, 1962) when tested under identical conditions. Rachman (1962, p. 94) concludes that "the hypothesis that schizophrenics dissipate reactive inhibition slowly is supported."

Rachman (1963) went on to consider the problem of disinhibition, very much in the manner in which he had attacked this problem in normal Ss (Rachman, 1962). Of 3 reports in the literature, 2 had failed to find evidence of disinhibition in schizophrenics. Kessell (1955) and Tizard and Venables (1957) used distraction and extraneous auditory stimulation in order to produce disinhibition in Porteous Maze and concellation tests (Kessell), and in a RT task (Tizard and Venables). Kessell's use of simple and regular distraction made failure to observe disinhibition almost certain; disinhibition is usually caused by sudden and unexpected stimuli. Tizard and Venables found differences between "withdrawn" (introverted?) and "sociable" (extraverted?) patients, with the former showing disinhibition effects, the latter not. Pascal and Swensen (1952) found disinhibition to occur among schizophrenics in a RT task, sudden noise being the disinhibiting stimulus. In view of the disparity of the tasks and conditions used, predictions on pursuit-rotor performance cannot be made with any confidence. Using an identical paradigm to his earlier work on normals, Rachman again used 20 schizophrenic patients, 10 of whom had a rest pause of 10 min, the others one of 24 hr. Both groups, however, were administered a buzzer for 2 sec at the end of the 5-min massed practice period preceding the rest (after 4 min, 35 sec) Results are shown in Figure 10-4, which gives performance scores during the 55-min pre-rest period for the "disinhibition" (experimental) group, and the groups whose performance has been graphed in Figure 10-3 (control). It will be seen that there is a very marked disinhibition effect; the buzzer is sounded during trial 28, and trials 29 and 30 show clear evidence of better performance. The difference between experimental and control groups is clearly significant ($p < .05$).

Rachman also predicted that disinhibition would produce a diminished reminiscence effect; Figure 10-5 shows the relevant findings. This comparison uses the experimental and control groups exposed to the 24-hr rest conditions; it will be remembered that the 10-min rest groups showed no evidence of reminiscence anyway. The disinhibition groups clearly fail to show any reminiscence at all; the difference is fully

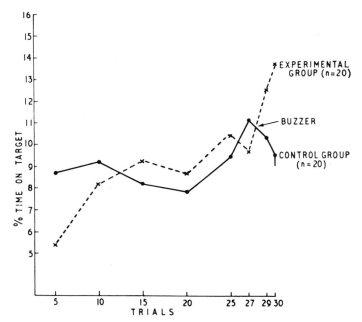

Figure 10-4. The effect of a disinhibiting stimulus on pursuit-rotor performance in schizophrenics. Taken with permission from Rachman (1963).

significant ($p < .01$). The difference is not due, as one might have thought, to the terminal improvement of the experimental group, but much more to the post-rest improvement of the control, and the slight decline in performance of the experimental group. This effect is similar to findings with normal Ss (Rachman, 1962); it raises many important questions which are dealt with elsewhere in this book. Whatever the explanation, Rachman (1962, p. 97) concludes that "the introduction of an alien or extraneous stimulus late in the practice period will produce (i) disinhibition and (ii) a decreased reminiscence period in chronic schizophrenics."

Another group of investigators from the Maudsley laboratories investigated reminiscence and the effects of massed and spaced practice in schizophrenics, replicating Eysenck's original 5-10-5-10-5 design. Forty-two chronic schizophrenics were randomly assigned to one of two groups given either massed or spaced practice on the pursuit rotor, and a group of 16 depressives were given massed practice only (Broadhurst & Broadhurst, 1964). Ss showing no evidence of learning on an objective criterion were eliminated from an original larger group; results are shown in Figure 10-6. The authors comment on several noteworthy features of the curves shown in the figure. "The first is the generally lower level of the performance of the psychotic groups. This is doubtless an example of the psychomotor slowness frequently associated with the performance of psychotics. The second striking feature is the apparent absence of reminiscence among the massed practice groups of psychotics, which is in strong contrast with the findings for the normal groups." (Broadhurst & Broadhurst, 1964, p. 324.) Neither depressives nor schizophrenics show any post-rest improvement after either the first or the second rest pause. A third striking feature of the results is that, "turning to the spaced practice groups, we find that the generally beneficial effect of spacing practice is less among psychotics than among normals" (Broadhurst & Broadhurst, 1964, p. 325). Furthermore, in the psychotic group there is an actual decrement in performance following the 10-min rest period in the spaced practice groups; the difference from the normal group is significant in respect to the first rest period. Another curious feature of the schizophrenics' spaced practice curve is the apparent warm-up (post-rest upswing) effect, which is not usually found with normal samples which have been exposed to spaced practice. We thus have several marked differences

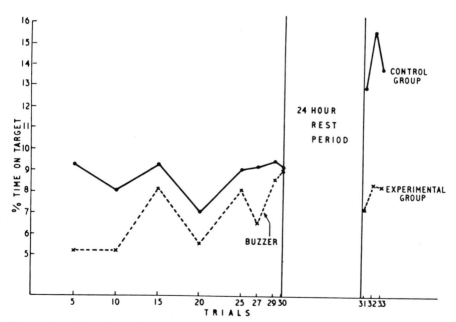

Figure 10-5. The effect of disinhibition on reminiscence in schizophrenics. Taken with permission from Rachman (1963).

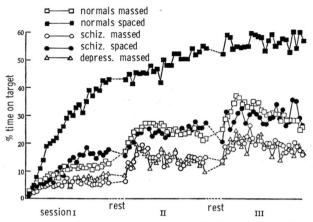

Figure 10-6. Performance curves of normal and psychotic groups on the pursuit rotor. Taken with permission from Broadhurst and Broadhurst (1964).

between normal and psychotic Ss, in addition to the previously established failure of schizophrenics to show reminiscence after massed practice, which emerges again very clearly.

Does the hypothesis of a slower rate of dissipation of I_R (Venables, 1959; Eysenck, 1961) explain all the facts? As the authors indicate, there are several difficulties which such an hypothesis encounters. "The first is the presence of the warm-up effect in the massed practice of psychotics in both Sessions II and III. If we postulate that reactive inhibition has not dissipated during the rest periods, how then can we use its absence to account for the extinction increment effect during the first few trials of the resumed practice?" (Broadhurst & Broadhurst, 1964, p. 328.) This objection depends on a particular theory of post-rest upswing; if it is regarded, for instance, as a true "warm-up" effect, then no problem arises. This objection should be seen in the light of our discussion of this effect in another chapter. A second difficulty is the fall-off in the spaced practice of the schizophrenics during the 10-min rest intervals; this is not predictable in terms of the failure of reactive inhibition to dissipate. The explanation may lie in the presence of "warm-up" effects properly so called; if schizophrenics lose set more quickly than normals (an effect for which there is evidence in the work of Shakow and others), then this would account both for their apparent performance loss in spaced practice, and for their post-rest upswing after spaced practice. On the whole we would argue that the data are not incapable of an explanation in terms of poor dissipation of inhibition in psychotics; we would merely add that an explanation in terms of high arousal leading to strong long continued consolidation and Walker-type "action decrement," can serve equally well as an explanation; the data cannot serve to decide between these alternative hypotheses.

The fact that psychotics show poor dissipation of I_R (or else strong "action decrement") does not tell us whether they also show a stronger build-up of I_R. A study by Bills (1964) was designed to measure the rate of build-up of inhibition, as indexed by "blocks" in performance. Mailloux and Newburger (1941) had found that the average block length of psychotics was over twice that of the normal population, with the severity of blocking roughly proportionate to the degree of deterioration of the individual patient; they were unable to find differences between different diagnostic categories of psychotics. Bills used a self-paced multiple choice reaction time design, differently colored lights constituting the stimuli, and each response producing the next stimulus. The behavior variables studied were average responses per minute (each S was permitted 5 min of practice and a short rest, followed by 20 min of continuous responding), blocks per minute, errors per minute, average block length, and overall variability. Blocks "were arbitrary defined as response latencies exceeding the model reaction time by at least twice" (Bills, 1964, p. 100). "The concept variability refers to the average of the deviations of each response from its antecedent, with blocks excluded," Ss of the experiment were chronic schizophrenics, brain-injured psychotics, brain-injured nonpsychotics, and nonpsychotic controls; a group of paranoid schizophrenics was also included. Figures 10-7, 10-8, and 10-9 show typical response patterns of control Ss, paranoid and undifferentiated schizophrenic Ss; each record represents a run of 120 responses extracted from the 20-min work session.

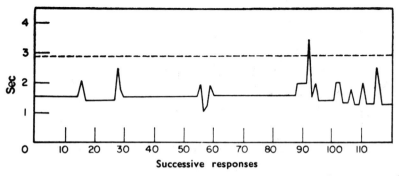

Figure 10-7. Block frequency and length in control subject. Taken with permission from Bills (1964).

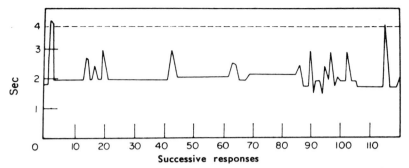

Figure 10-8. Block frequency and length in paranoid schizophrenic subjects. Taken with permission from Bills (1964).

Vertical distances on the graphs represent reaction times. The abscissa represents consecutive reactions. The broken line drawn parallel to the base represents the criterion of a block, for this S, being twice his modal RT. All RTs rising above the broken line are blocks, as well as those just reaching it. "Variability is shown by the number of jiggles in the graph line which fall short of the block criterion."

These examples were chosen to demonstrate the general findings of the study. "All experimental groups differed from the control group to a significant degree in every one of the variables, except that the paranoid schizophrenics differed only in number of responses and slightly in variability. A comparison of the two schizophrenic groups shows them in sharp contrast, for the chronic, undifferentiated type exceeds all others in frequency and average length of blocks, but had significantly fewer errors than the brain-syndrome patients; the latter were highest in errors and variability." (Bills, 1964, p. 105.) The study seems to

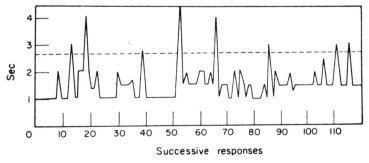

Figure 10-9. Block frequency and length in undifferentiated schizophrenic subject. Taken with permission from Bills (1964).

establish that psychotics (and brain-damaged Ss) show much more blocking than normals, although paranoids seem less affected than other types of schizophrenics.

Our next study returns again to the performance and reminiscence of schizophrenics. Broadhurst and Eysenck (1973a) tested 24 normals and 24 schizophrenics on the pursuit rotor, 5 min of practice followed by rest pauses of 2, 12, and 30 min, and 1, 6, and 24 hr (in counterbalanced order). It was thought that schizophrenics would show greater reminiscence after the longer periods of rest, normals after shorter periods of rest. The results are shown in Figure 10-10; there is some slight evidence of a cross-over effect, but this is clearly insignificant.

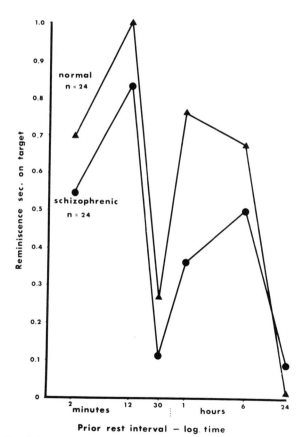

Figure 10-10. Reminiscence on pursuit rotor of normal and schizophrenic subjects after various rest pauses. Taken with permission from Broadhurst and Eysenck (1963a).

Order effects were not significant for the different rest pauses, but the fact that each S was exposed to 6 rest pauses of varying length may have caused results to differ from those reported by Ley, Rachman, Broadhurst, and others. This experiment ought clearly to be repeated, with each rest period being applied to one group of Ss only. There is a curious and remarkably consistent fluctuation in reminiscence score for normals and schizophrenics alike; it is difficult to account for this. It is noteworthy that throughout the experiment (except for the 24-hr period) schizophrenics have lower reminiscence scores than normals; departure from previous work is thus not too extreme.

The same Ss were used in a tapping task (Broadhurst & Eysenck, 1973b), the aim being to replicate Bills' findings of greater number of blocks in schizophrenics. A recording apparatus similar to that originally used by Spielman (1963) was employed, and the score was length of IRPs in sec. Seven periods of massed practice were used, each lasting

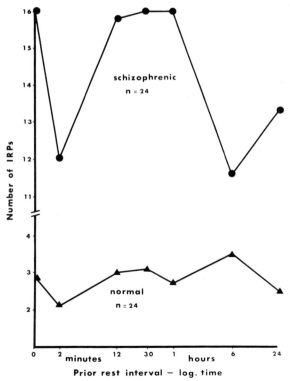

Figure 10-11. Number of IRPs in normal and schizophrenic subjects. Taken with permission from Broadhurst and Eysenck (1973b).

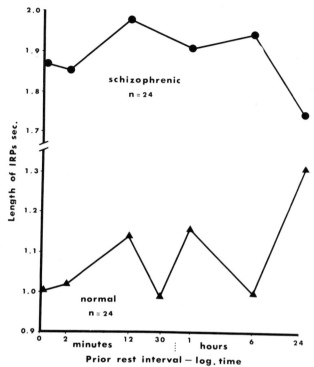

Figure 10-12. Length of IRPs in normal and schizophrenic subjects. Taken with permission from Broadhurst and Eysenck (1973*b*).

for 5 min, separated by rest intervals as described in the experiment above. As in the Spielman study, gap IRPs were identified as any gap frequencies isolated from the main distribution of gaps and from its predecessors by two or more intervening class intervals (or more than 0.10 sec duration). There were no order effects, and no effect of different rest intervals. Schizophrenics showed many more IRPs than did normals ($p < .01$) (see Figure 10-11). The average median length of IRPs in 5 min of tapping by normal and schizophrenic Ss is plotted as a function of prior rest interval in Figure 10-12; the only suggestive finding is that after the 24-hr rest interval the length of IRPs decreases for schizophrenics and increases for normals. Even so the differences are still pronounced.

It seems reasonable to expect that IRPs would increase with length of practice. Comparing first and last minute performance for normals and schizophrenics, it is seen that there is some increase, but more so for schizophrenics than for normals. This might suggest a build-up of inhibition in schizophrenics that is faster than in normals. However, the movement is not regular over the 5-min period, nor is the difference large; chance deviations would not be ruled out as an explanation of the observed differences. The data certainly support Bills' conclusion of greater numbers of IRPs in schizophrenics, but they do not go much beyond this point.

The studies summarized so far have been concerned mainly with the differential performance levels and reminiscence scores of schizophrenics and normals; Clark (1967) attempted to answer a more fundamental question, namely that relating to the causes of the observed differences. We have noted several times that findings are usually compatible with an inhibition hypothesis as well as with a consolidation hypothesis; Clark attempted to collect evidence which would make it possible to decide between these two hypotheses. He started out with a general formulation of the arousal–consolidation hypothesis (Figure 10-13) in which are given, on the left, certain sets of determinants of arousal (*conditions*, such as white noise, which are supposed to increase arousal, and *groups* which are believed to differ in arousal level.) There are also *indices* of arousal, such as GSR measures, the Funkenstein test, etc.; these serve to measure the amount of arousal present. Last, on the right, we have the effects (determinates) of high arousal, such as reduced cue utilization and slower consolidation of memory traces (action decrement). If this general picture is along the right lines, then it should be possible to constitute groups differing in degree of arousal as indexed by one of the physiological measures indicated, and to test the hypotheses expressed on the right of the diagram. For example, high-arousal Ss should show reduced reminiscence with short rest pauses, and increased reminiscence with lengthened rest pauses. If this could be done, our interpretation of the performance (reminiscence) of groups listed at the bottom right of the diagram would be strengthened correspondingly.

Clark made use of the two-flash threshold (TFT) as the measure of arousal to be used. Lindsley (1957) had reported that two brief light flashes separated by about 50 msec, presented to the eye of the cat, will produce one fused evoked potential when not accompanied by stimulation of the reticular system, whereas with stimulation identical flashed separated by the same temporal interval will produce two evoked potentials. Jung (1957), recording from individual neurons, has shown that with reticular stimulation the CFF of these neurons is increased significantly over control conditions. Eysenck and Warwick (1964) have shown that Ss under high drive conditions were able to identify two flashes with closer interflash intervals than Ss tested under low-drive conditions. Kopell, Noble, and Silverman (1965) studied the effects of

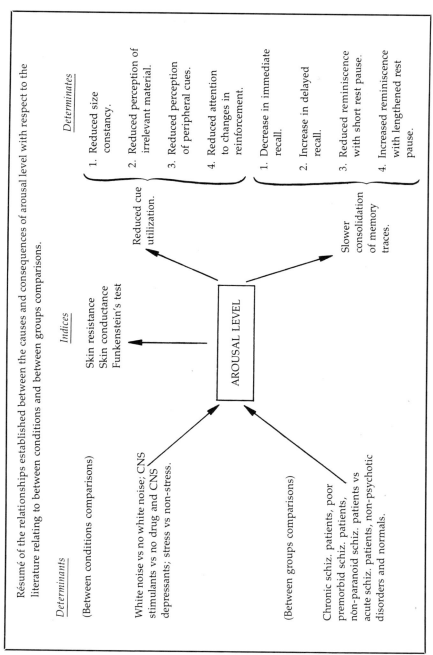

Figure 10-13. Determinants and determinates of arousal level in learning. Taken with permission from Clark (1967).

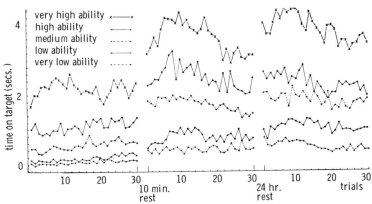

Figure 10-14. Performance of schizophrenic patients on pursuit rotor, divided into 5 different levels of ability. Taken with permission from Clark (1967).

drug administration on TFT and established that, relative to the control condition of saline injection, amphetamine administration reduced the threshold of paired flashes whereas barbiturate injection raised it. Venables (1963c) found that increasing amplitude of integrated alpha activity on the EEG was associated with higher TFT in a linear fashion, the correlation being +0.56. The evidence (which could of course be extended) suggests very strongly that TFT is a useful measure of cortical arousal, even though Venables (1963a) has found that it correlated with tonic palmar skin potential in opposite ways in normals and schizophrenics. (Lykken & Maley, 1968, found the anomaly less extreme).

The method of TFT measurement adopted was very similar to that described by Venables (1963b). Intelligence was measured but found not to be correlated with either TFT or reminiscence; neither was length of hospitalization. Clark was careful to investigate the influence of ability level in his 125 schizophrenic Ss on their reminiscence scores. Figure 10-14 shows the performance of 5 ability groups of 25 Ss each; Ss were given 5-min practice periods separated by a 10-min rest pause in the first place, and then a 24 hour rest pause. Reminiscence was found higher in the very high, high, and medium ability groups than in the low and very low ability groups; this effect was partly but not entirely due to differences in intelligence. TFT was not significantly associated with ability grouping. Paranoid Ss were not found to differ substantially in any relevant ways from nonparanoid schizophrenics.

The sample was then split into a high-TFT and a low-TFT group, using threshold scores of 56.6 msec as the dividing line. Analysis of variance showed no main effects on reminiscence either between groups or between rest pauses, but did show a very significant groups × rest pauses interaction ($p < .001$). This is in good accord with Clark's (1967, p. 166) hypothesis, which he had stated in the following form:

> Relative to patients distinguished by low two flash threshold levels, patients who are characterized by having high two flash threshold scores will demonstrate greater reminiscence after the ten minute rest pause, and less reminiscence after the twenty four hour rest pause.

Figure 10-15 shows the actual outcome; "as predicted, patients characterized by high two flash threshold scores are seen to achieve greater reminiscence after the shorter rest interval than patients distinguished by low scores on the threshold measure, with the corollary situation in evidence after the twenty-four hour rest pause. It should be noted too that this significant interaction is accompanied by a significant separation of the mean reminiscence levels of the two groups after each of the rest pauses." (Clark, 1967, p. 191.)

The post-rest performances of the high- and low-arousal groups were analyzed in some detail, the pre-rest performance of the two groups having been found not to differ significantly (see Figure 10-16). Analysis by orthogonal polynomials disclosed significant quadratic and cubic trends. Performance after the 10-min interval did not significantly differentiate the two groups (except of course for the reminiscence score), but significant differences, additional to the reminiscence score, were found for the two groups after the 24-hr interval. Results are

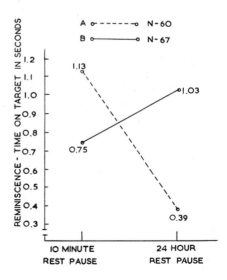

Figure 10-15. Mean reminiscence scores after 10-min and 24-hr rest for groups characterized by (A) two-flash threshold scores equal to or greater than 56.6 msec; (B) two-flash threshold scores less than 56.6 milliseconds. Taken with permission from Clark (1967).

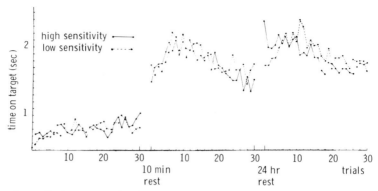

Figure 10-16. Performance of schizophrenic patients characterized by high and low arousal, as measured on the two-flash threshold test. Taken with permission from Clark (1967).

shown in Figure 10-17; this shows curves representing the best fit to trial data in relation to linear, quadratic, and cubic trends. Notable is the absence of post-rest upswing in the high arousal patients; such upswing was clearly present after the shorter rest interval.

Clark's work is important in demonstrating that phenomena similar to those discovered by Kleinsmith and Kaplan (1963, 1964), Kleinsmith, Kaplan, and Tarte (1963), Walker and Tarte (1963), and others with respect to arousal properties of stimuli can also be obtained with respect to arousal properties in different tasks.[1] This clearly shows that the theory of "action decrement" applies to the field of individual differences, as well as being a general law applying to S–R relations. We shall turn to a consideration of this aspect of the theory presently, but first we must discuss the light Clark's work throws on the problem of the arousal level of schizophrenics. Assuming that reminiscence is indeed mediated by consolidation processes which are themselves influenced by arousal level, we must conclude that schizophrenics are not a cohesive group homogeneous with respect to drive level; both high-arousal and low-arousal Ss can be found within this diagnostic group. The question originally asked, and the hypotheses put forward, are therefore not capable of a direct or meaningful answer. Verma and Eysenck, (1913), as a result of a detailed study of hospitalized psychotics, concluded that there were marked differences within the group with respect to extraversion–introversion; this suggests that the differences in arousal (high in introverts, low in extraverts) hypothesized in

[1]Other workers to find evidence for the inimical effect of high arousal on immediate recall are Grand and Segal (1966), Berlyne *et al.*, (1965, 1966): but see Berry (1962).

normals may equally be found in psychotics, and determine the direction of reminiscence scores. This conclusion fits in well with the work of Venables and Wing (1962) on level of arousal and subclassification of schizophrenia; their main grouping is in terms of "withdrawal" and "sociability." A scale developed by Venables (1957) and Venables and O'Connor (1959) was used to measure behavior on this activity–withdrawal dimension, lower arousal scores being found to go with greater withdrawal.

An experiment by Venables (1963c) may be very apposite here. He distinguished the habitual arousal level from the "arousability" of Ss in response to specific stimuli, testing schizophrenics and normals as his experimental and control groups. After dark adaptation for 4-min TFTs were determined in 63 chronic schizophrenics and 47 normals. One minute subsequent to the threshold being established, white noise of 80 dB intensity was presented and maintained for 3 min. Just prior to the termination of the noise, a second threshold level was determined. There were no differences in resting arousal level, and no differences in mean threshold change after the onset of noise. However, it was established that, while in the normal group the amount of change varied randomly about zero, among the schizophrenics the amount of change was significantly related to initial threshold level. Those patients whose original threshold levels were low tended to show an increased threshold in noise conditions, while those with a high threshold exhibited a lowered threshold in noise. There is thus a distinctive difference in arousal response between normals and schizophrenics, with the former apparently possessing some regulatory mechanism imposing limits to arousal levels which the latter group did not possess. It seems possible

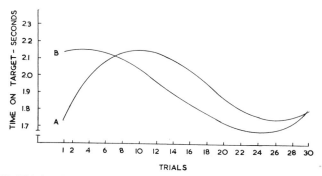

Figure 10-17. Third-order orthogonal polynomials fitted to the post 24-hr rest pause performance curves of high- and low-arousal schizophrenics. Taken with permission from Clark (1967).

that the existence of a cortical–reticular loop might be relevant here, by imposing a continuing suppressive and facilitatory cortical effect on the arousal value of stimulation; this might provide the mechanism of regulatory control suggested in relation to the maintained threshold levels prevailing among the normal Ss in this study. If this were so, then the change in threshold level manifested by the schizophrenic patients under conditions of white noise might be supposed to be due to a failure of this cortical–reticular control mechanism to mediate the arousing effects of stimulation. The fact that those patients whose initial TFT scores were indicative of high resting arousal levels showed a decrease in threshold level with noise might be due to something akin to Pavlov's "transmarginal inhibition," i.e., a mechanism postulated by Pavlov to protect cortical cells from further stimulation which might be harmful to them.

The relation between "arousal" and schizophrenia is therefore clearly not a simple one. Lynn (1963) concluded from his review of the Russian literature that there exists a majority group of schizophrenics characterized by low sympathetic tone and reactivity, and a minority group with unusually high sympathetic tone and reactivity. Gellhorn (1957), Venables (1960), Mednick (1958), and many others have come to similar conclusions, and Fenz and Vellner (1970, p. 27) summed up this agreement by saying that "reviewing the literature on arousal in schizo-phrenia, one comes to the conclusion that depending on the physiologi-cal measures used, the selection of Ss, and the experimental situation, schizophrenics fall anywhere along the continuum of arousal, although in most cases towards the high or low ends of this continuum. In addition, some schizophrenics show marked and sudden shifts in autonomic activity, now being 'overaroused' and now 'underaroused'." This difference in arousal may be related to such a distinction as that suggested by the terms "process" and "reactive" schizophrenia, and it is interesting to note that Armstrong et al. (1967) have demonstrated a high correlation between extraversion–introversion and the process vs reaction types of schizophrenia (see also Thayer & Silber, 1971). When, in addition to all these complexities, we consider that the very term "schizophrenia" denotes substantially different symptom sets to differ-ent investigators (it has been shown that the same or similar groups of patients are diagnosed "schizophrenic" 5 times more frequently by American than by English psychiatrists—Cooper et al., 1972), then it is remarkable that there is any agreement at all among investigators of reminiscence phenomena in this ill-defined group. Nevertheless, the fact remains that many different workers have discovered poor remi-niscence in schizophrenics after short rest pauses, and high reminiscence after long rest pauses, a pattern which is contrary to that usually found in normals, and which agrees with that of the "high-arousal" group in Figure 10-15. In terms of the general considerations discussed above, this may mean that most of the schizophrenics tested show a low arousal level in the resting state, but a high arousal level in response to the test situation. The available evidence does not permit us to evaluate this hypothesis, most of the studies having been carried out with some other hypothesis in mind.

The hypotheses which gave rise to the various studies here reviewed dealt with "reminiscence," regarded as an undifferentiated phenomenon which could be measured by the classical method of taking the difference between last pre-rest and first post-rest score. However, as Ammons pointed out, and as we shall conclude in a later chapter, the phenomenon of reminiscence must be sharply differentiated from that of warm-up or PRU: reminiscence proper would then be measured in terms of Ammons' formula, or else, and more simply, in terms of Grey's rem. max. For most practical purposes this differentiation is not important, because the course of post-rest practice is parallel for Ss working at different ability levels; thus measures of reminiscence along these different lines would be reasonably highly correlated, certainly over groups. However, when the detailed post-rest records of psychotic (particularly schizophrenic) Ss are studied, it will become clear that these groups present a clear exception to the rule; psychotics appear to be differentiated from normal samples mainly in their exaggerated warm-up; there is little difference in rem. max. or in Ammons' measure. In other words, psychotics compared with normals of similar pre-rest performance show very poor performance on the first few post-rest trials, a very rapid and strongly marked upswing, and a level of performance following this upswing which is indistinguishable from that of the controls. The original Claridge study (1960), reproduced in Figure 10-2, is an excellent example. The normal and the schizophrenic Ss score equally at about 10% T.O.T. at the end of the pre-rest period. At the beginning of the post-rest period the schizophrenics score at exactly the same level, while the normal controls have more than doubled their score (approximately 25% T.O.T.). Less than 2 min after the rest pause, however, both groups again score at an identical level, the schizophrenics having shown a rapid PRU.

The same extremely rapid PRU is apparent in the Rachman study (Figure 10-3) for the 10-min rest period. The Broadhurst and Broadhurst study (Figure 10-6) also shows the same effect as the Claridge study, except that the average level of performance of the groups is different throughout; when this is taken into account, schizophrenics again differ only with respect to warm-up and the first few post-rest trials. A similar phenomenon is noticeable in Figure 10-16, although this is of course a comparison between high-arousal and low-arousal schizophrenics, not between schizophrenics and normals. It is the low-arousal Ss who show the marked upswing, and the failure to produce reminiscence as traditionally measured. This was after the 24-hr rest; no such differences were observed after the 10-min rest. For short rests, therefore, it would appear that all schizophrenics act in much the same way, i.e., by requiring a particularly long warm-up period.

This finding makes good sense in terms of what is known about the functioning of schizophrenics in experimental situations. Shakow (1962, 1963, 1967) has postulated that the schizophrenic's major difficulty is his inability to maintain a major set, i.e., a state of readiness to make a response at some time in the future. Instead, he is controlled by minor sets with the result that he shows segmented patterns of behavior, and is subject to distraction far more than is a normal or neurotic person. This hypothesis fits in well with larger-scale theories such as the immediacy view favored by Salzinger (1973), according to which schizophrenic behavior is primarily controlled by stimuli that are immediate in the environment. There is good experimental support for the view that schizophrenics are poor at preserving set (King, 1954; Rodnick & Shakow, 1940; Shakow, 1946), and that they are unduly prone to disruption and distraction (Ludwig *et al.*, 1962; McGhie, Chapman, & Lawson, 1965; Rappaport, 1968; Stilson & Kopell, 1964; Stilson *et al.*, 1966), and such a theory would adequately account for the observed phenomenon of greater PRU or warm-up in schizophrenics, if we are willing to assume that PRU is indeed to be explained in terms of loss of set and reacquisition of set. To what extent this loss of set is related to arousal (if at all) remains to be seen; it is not clear that the available data enable us to answer this question.

PART III

The New Look in Reminiscence

CHAPTER 11

Consolidation: The Failure of Inhibition Theory

When the inhibition concepts proposed by Hull were first applied to reminiscence in learning (Kimble, 1949) they seemed to provide a simple and elegant solution to the problem. Ten years later however the situation was very different. Inhibition theories of reminiscence had evolved into complex and unwieldy forms as a result of the new phenomena that had been uncovered. In spite of this evolution many of the new phenomena remained unexplained.

The theories assumed that during massed practice on the pursuit rotor there was a build up of reactive inhibition (I_R) which eventually induced a rest pause (IRP) in performance. In conjunction with drive (D) a habit of nonresponding was learned in addition to a habit of correct responding. The IRPs resulting from I_R lowered performance. During a rest the I_R dissipated so that after a rest performance was improved (reminiscence). The habit of nonresponding remained however, so that performance after a rest was still inferior to that with spaced practice. During the initial post-rest period the habit of nonresponding extinguished resulting in post-rest upswing. The post-rest downswing that followed was presumed to be due to the renewed increase in I_R.

Even if this model successfully accounted for performance on the pursuit rotor it would still be too complex and unwieldly to be of any value. In itself pursuit-rotor performance is of little interest. Study of this task is only valuable if it can be used to measure quantitatively variables such as I_R, sI_R, habit, or some other set of more general

323

variables. The inhibition model is too complicated to permit us to do this. Low performance after a rest can be the result of the failure to build up the habit of correct responding, the failure of I_R to dissipate, or the acquisition of a strong habit not to respond ($_sI_R$). Furthermore the strong habit not to respond might be slowly acquired from many rest pauses or rapidly acquired from a few rest pauses. Although some of the processes can be sorted out by varying the length of work and rest, enough information is never available particularly when only one measure of performance is taken (total time-on-target) to assign values unambiguously to all the variables involved in the inhibition model.

This objection could be overcome if there were independent ways of observing or controlling some of the hypothetical entities such as $_sI_R$, I_R and rest pauses. Such methods have never been found. I_R was originally thought to be a function of the actual amount of physical work done by the organism, but this has proved not to be the case (Bilodeau & Bilodeau, 1954). It is now suggested that I_R may be related to the amount of continuous attention required for the task (i.e., a "mental work" hypothesis rather than a physical one, Walker, 1958). This type of work might also be amenable to independent quantification and control except that, as we have seen in the chapter covering transfer and interference, it seems to be entirely specific to the task being performed.

Furthermore, it has not been possible to identify or observe rest pauses in pursuit rotor performance. This identification is important "as the concept of conditioned inhibition stands or falls with the presence of I.R.P.s in massed practice" (Eysenck, 1965). Rest pauses have been identified in vigilance tasks (Broadbent, 1953) and in tapping tasks (Spielman, 1963 and Eysenck, 1964), although curiously enough there is no indication of conditioned inhibition occurring in the tapping task. It may well be impossible to identify rest pauses in pursuit-rotor performance since the index of performance used does not distinguish between no attempt and an unsuccessful attempt at performance. This problem will be dealt with more fully in the chapter on strategies where it will also be suggested that massed practice on the pursuit rotor is perhaps not really massed practice in the learning theory sense at all. This would imply that even if the task is analyzed in terms of Hullian learning theory one might not expect rest pauses to occur.

More important than these theoretical considerations in the downfall of inhibition theory were certain experimental results which even the complex version of the theory cannot account for and these results will now be discussed. Kimble (1950) suggested that subjects working under conditions of high motivation should show greater reminiscence than subjects working under conditons of low motivation. This prediction has been supported by a large number of experiments (Wasserman, 1951; Eysenck & Maxwell, 1961; Feldman, 1964). Kimble's hypothesis was based on the assumption that I_R was, as Hull had postulated, a negative drive state; Subjects working under a high drive would be able to tolerate a high degree of I_R, and would thus be able to dissipate more I_R during rest. Although it is not completely clear how exactly these processes would manifest themselves in pursuit-rotor performance, any such interpretation would require that high-drive subjects should be superior to low-drive subjects pre-rest and even more superior post-rest. In fact, as the pictures from Eysenck and Maxwell (1961) (Figures 5-3 and 5-4) clearly show, all the experiments have found no differences in pre-rest performance between high- and low-drive groups. The differences have only appeared post rest. As Adams (1963) remarks, "the authors puzzle over this and rightly so."

On grounds rather similar to Kimble, Eysenck (1956) had predicted that extraverted subjects should show greater reminiscence than introverted subjects. A number of experiments (Eysenck, 1962) gave support to this prediction although not very strongly. According to the hypothesis extraverts are more prone to the build up of inhibition. This should result in a greater pre-rest performance decrement in the extraverted group; the dissipation of this greater performance decrement during rest would then show up in the form of greater reminiscence. Thus the hypothesis clearly requires that the difference between the personality groups should occur pre-rest rather than post-rest. Eysenck (1964b) found that the opposite was the case (Figure 9-9).

A third experiment grounded in similar arguments was performed by Rachman (1962). Rachman argued that any strong "alien" stimulus, such as a loud buzzer, if applied shortly before the rest period on a massed practice pursuit-rotor task, should have the effect of disinhibiting part of the I_R accumulated up to that point. This should improve performance and lower reminiscence. If we accept this rather dubious equation of Hull's inhibition with that of Pavlov, it is clear that we would expect reminiscence to be reduced because of improved performance in the experimental group immediately pre-rest. In contrast to this prediction both Rachman (1962) and Feldman (1964) found a lowering of reminiscence due to a lowering of post-rest performance.

Another kind of experimental result that inhibition theory cannot deal with involves various manipulations during the rest interval. Rachman and Grassi (1965) gave four groups of subjects two 5-min sessions of massed practice on the pursuit rotor separated by 4-hr rest. During the first ten minutes of the rest three of the groups practiced on

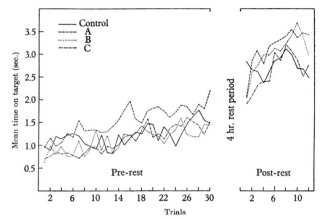

Figure 11-1. Performance curves for four groups of subjects. The control group shows normal reminiscence, group A a slight negative reminiscence. Taken with permission from Rachman and Grassi (1965).

a mirror reversed pursuit rotor for 3 min; one group (A) for minutes 1–3, the second (B) for minutes 4–6, and the third (C) for minutes 7–9 of the rest. These three minutes of reversed cue practice should have no effect on inhibition since all groups had four hours rest in which this could dissipate. Learning the reversed cue pursuit rotor might be expected to interfere with the original habit of pursuit-rotor performance, but this should be unrelated to the time during the rest at which the reversed cue practice took place. Reminiscence was indeed reduced for the groups which practiced the reversed pursuit rotor, but this reduction was significantly greater for the group which practiced during the first three minutes of the rest than for the other two experimental groups (Figure 11-1). Once again this finding is incompatible with inhibition theories of reminiscence.

THE NEED FOR A NEW APPROACH

When theories become very complex and unwieldy and yet still fail to account for all the facts the time has come for new approaches which will hopefully result in theories that are radically simpler. Inhibition theories of reminiscence essentially assume that some inhibiting factor is at a maximum at the beginning of the rest and gradually dissipates during the rest. There is a converse theory which will account equally well for many of the same facts. In this theory it is assumed that there is some potentiating factor which is at a minimum at the beginning of the rest and gradually increases during the rest. In most of the experiments discussed previously inhibition theory failed because differences between groups (e.g., low and high motivation) occurred at the end of the rest rather than at the beginning. These results are, of course, entirely consistent with the converse theory of potentiation. Such a theory of memory had indeed been suggested by Müller and Pilzecker in 1900, but had been largely ignored by psychologists until there began to appear in the literature strong physiological evidence in its favour.

THE CONSOLIDATION THEORY OF MEMORY

According to the theory of consolidation a neural fixation process is assumed to continue after the organism is no longer confronted with the set of stimuli which constitute the learning task. This fixation process plays a crucial part in efficient retention and anything that interferes with perseveration is assumed to have an adverse effect on the subject's ability to transfer material acquired to the permanent memory store.

Some of the earliest evidence for this hypothesis came from studies of retrograde amnesia. Russell and Nathan (1946) surveyed 1029 cases of head injury and found 840 patients reporting amnesia for events occurring from several minutes preceding the injury. Having ruled out the possibility of hysterical repression, the authors conclude that loss of the material is due to a blocked perseveration process:

> It seems that the mere existence of the brain as a functioning organ must strengthen the roots of distant memories. The normal activity of the brain must steadily strengthen distant memories so that with the passage of time these become less vulnerable to the effects of head injury.

More convincing than these clinical and hence poorly controlled studies are the results of experiments with electroconvulsive shock in both animals and humans. All these experiments essentially involve periods of learning separated by rest periods during which electroconvulsive shocks may be given. With an interpolated shock subsequent performance is considerably impaired. Furthermore recent learning is more affected than remote learning. This has been found with patients learning paired associate lists while undergoing shock treatment (e.g., Cronholm & Molander, 1958) and also with rats learning various tasks (reviewed by Glickman, 1961). Although the empirical results of interference with performance by postlearning electroconvulsive shocks has not been questioned, the interpretation of the results is not so clear. The most radical alternative to interpretation in terms of consolidation, proposed by Miller and Coons (1955), suggests that ECS interferes with performance because of its aversive qualities. However, those experiments in which these two interpretations of the "forgetting" have been opposed, favored interpretation of the effects in terms of consolidation (Essman & Jarvik, 1960; Pearlman, Sharpless, & Jarvik, 1961). Apart from ECS there are other treatments that give evidence of interfering with consolidation. These include anoxia (Hayes, 1953; Thompson & Pryer, 1956), anaesthesia (Leukel, 1957), and stimulation of certain midbrain structures (Glickman, 1958; Thompson, 1958).

These experiments demonstrate that recently acquired learning can be impaired by gross disturbance of the brain such as are produced by convulsions. Remote memory, however, is not impaired by such disturbances. It is concluded that immediately after learning a "consolidation" process occurs which changes the "memory traces" in such a way that they are protected from such disturbances. There is however, another class of experiments the results of which suggest that the consolidation process must have more than a protective function.

In a series of studies McGaugh and Petrinovich (1959), McGaugh, Westbrook and Thompson (1962), and Breen and McGaugh (1961) have injected stimulant drugs into rats after the completion of learning periods, and tested the rats after the drug effects had worn off. Comparison with control groups demonstrated the superiority of the drug-treated animals, and the authors concluded that the experiments could best be interpreted as showing that drug administration "improves maze performance by facilitating post-trial consolidation of the neurophysiological process underlying memory" (McGaugh *et al.* 1962, p. 172).

A slightly different design was used in a series of investigations of the consolidation process by Garg and Holland (1967*a*, *b*, *c*). Rats selected from the Maudsley reactive and nonreactive strains were given practice of one trial per day in problem 4 of the Hebb–Williams' maze. Immediately after two-minutes feeding in the goal box of the maze the animals were given various treatments followed by 24-hr rest. The maze training was given for ten consecutive days. Two groups of animals were given intraperitoneal injections with stimulant drugs (Nicotine and picrotoxin), one with a depressant drug (sodium pentobarbital) and three groups were given various control treatments (injection with distilled water, dry needle, and no injection). The results, in terms of the number of errors committed each day, are shown in Figure 11-2. It is clear from this figure that the two groups treated with stimulant

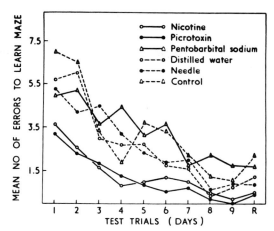

Figure 11-2. Mean number of errors made per day under several different kinds of treatment. The points marked R are retention scores. Taken with permission from Garg and Holland (1967).

drugs learned much more rapidly than any of the other groups. The group treated with the depressant drug on the other hand learned slightly, but significantly more slowly than the injected control groups. The reactive group of animals learned faster than the nonreactive group under all treatment conditions.

It is difficult to explain these treatment effects in terms of any process other than consolidation. The various drug treatments were clearly most active during the period of rest. Their effects on the animals while they were running the maze (once a day for one trial) must have been minimal, since the effects of the treatments had had 24 hr to wear off. Thus there must have been some process going on during the rest which related previous learning to later performance. This process was enhanced by stimulant drugs and impaired by depressant drugs.

Albert (1966) found that polarizing currents applied to the medial cortex altered consolidation in a similar manner. Surface positive currents enhanced consolidation while surface negative currents interfered with it. Albert, who was studying avoidance learning in rats, also found evidence that there were two information holding mechanisms present during the consolidation period, one allowing for recall during consolidation and the other involved in the actual consolidation process, perhaps serving as a template for the formation of the permanent retention system.

It is clear from these studies that consolidation has two distinct functions and perhaps Albert's two information holding systems are related to these. First, consolidation protects the memory traces from being destroyed by future events affecting the brain. This is shown by the many studies in which after a sufficient time lapse electric shocks, drugs, and so on no longer destroyed the memory traces. The second function of consolidation is to improve performance. This is shown by the studies in which administration of stimulant drugs during rest facilitated post-rest performance. This second function of consolidation is, of course, crucial in explaining pursuit-rotor reminiscence but has received relatively little attention. In particular it is necessary to explain how a process that protects memory traces also improves performance. This question will be considered in some detail in the next section.

It might also have been expected that from these large numbers of carefully controlled studies of consolidation we would know something about the time course of consolidation. However, estimates vary from minutes to hours and the results found seem to depend on the task being learned and the nature of the agent being used to manipulate the consolidation process. This confusion could be a result of a failure to recognize that the consolidation process has more than one stage.

HOW DOES CONSOLIDATION IMPROVE PERFORMANCE?

It will be remembered that in place of the factors suggested by inhibition theory we had hypothesized that the learning of motor skills involved some potentiating factor that rose from a minimum to a maximum during the course of a rest interpolated in massed practice. Does consolidation fulfill this requirement? The increased protection of a memory trace does not potentiate performance and hence, the first function of consolidation does not fulfill this role. To account for improvements in performance we must hypothesize a process whereby learning cannot fully be manifested until after consolidation is complete. This, as we have seen, is the second function of consolidation.

A hypothesis to explain this effect of consolidation has been put forward by Walker (1958). He proposed a mechanism called "action decrement" which was intended to replace the discredited processes known as reactive inhibition and conditioned inhibition. Action decrement is thought to be an additional component of the basic consolidation process. Walker and Tarte (1963) made the following proposals. "(1) The occurrence of any psychological event sets up an active, perseverative trace process which persists for a considerable period of time. (2) The perseverative trace process has two important dynamic characteristics; (a) permanent memory is laid down during this phase in a gradual fashion; (b) during this active period, there is a degree of temporary inhibition of recall, i.e., action decrement (this negative bias against repetition serves to protect the consolidating trace against disruption). (3) High arousal during the associative process will result in a more intensely active trace process. The more intense activity will result in greater ultimate memory, but greater temporary inhibition against recall." Proposal 2 clearly fulfills our requirement for a process whereby learning cannot fully be manifested until consolidation is complete. Furthermore a very plausible reason for this is given in that the consolidating trace must be protected against disruption.

THE EVIDENCE FOR ACTION DECREMENT

Unfortunately, apart from the various phenomena associated with pursuit-rotor learning, the evidence for action decrement is rather weak. What evidence there is comes from two main areas: the study of response alternation in animals (Walker, 1958) and the study of verbal learning in humans (Walker and Tarte, 1963). Although the animal experiments described by Walker clearly show an effect that can justifiably be labeled "action decrement" (ceasing to perform the original response) no evidence is provided that this relates to learning. In the first experiment (Walker, 1956) it was shown that rats tend to alternate responses separated by a short interval, but not by a long interval. In this experiment the rats were placed in a T-maze and it was observed whether the animals turned right or left. After various intervals the animal was again placed in the maze and its subsequent response was observed. After a short interval the rats tended to alternate rather than repeat their responses. Thus if they turned to the right the first time they turned to the left the second time and vice versa. With delays of up to half an hour animals repeated their first response only 20% of the time. With delays of two hours or more the animals repeated their responses about 50% of the time, i.e., at a chance level.

This phenomenon was unaffected by whether animals were reinforced for making the original response. In the second experiment it was shown that increasing motivation increases this alternation tendency, but again this effect was independent of reinforcement. In the third, and most interesting experiment, (Walker and Paradise, 1958) it was shown that response pairs that induce the most pronounced alternation were also the most easily learned. In this experiment the alternative responses that could be made by the rats consisted of three independent components: stimulus (black vs white goal box), place (position of goal box in room), and pattern of motor movements required to enter the goal box (a twist in three dimensions). In one condition the reward remained with the same stimulus, the same place, and the same movement all at the same time. In another the reward followed the stimulas, but was random with respect to place and movement. There were 8 conditions, altogether involving various such combinations of the three response components. This experiment clearly showed that response alternatives that produced the most alternation were also the most easily learned. This shows that "action decrement," the tendency to alternate, is related to learning, but this does not mean that action decrement is the result of the consolidation of learning. In order to make the alternate response the animal must in some sense remember which response it made previously. The more discriminable the two alternatives the easier this memory task will be. Similarly the more discriminable the two alternatives the more easily will the animal learn which one of them is associated with reward. This seems to be what Walker and Paradise have shown. Response alternatives that differed in all three components (by definition the most discriminable) induced the most alternation and were the most easily learned. Once again it is not shown that action decrement is a consequence of learning as would be necessary to support Walker's theory. These studies seem to show that rats have a tendency not to repeat a response they have recently made and this is not a passive inhibition type of process, but a more active choice perhaps akin to "curiosity." There is no evidence that the action decrement is caused by some learning process.

The verbal learning studies support Walker's theory rather better, but only that part which states that high arousal favors long-term retention while low arousal favors short-term retention. In these studies subjects were given one opportunity to hear a list of paired associates and then tested at various intervals for retention. Arousal was either manipulated by the type of word (e.g., rape vs pond) or measured at the time the pair was presented (GSR). Kleinsmith and Kaplan (1963) used this technique and found a clear cross-over effect such that low-arousal items were recalled best after 2 min whereas high-arousal items were recalled best after 1 week (Figure 11-3). This was partially replicated by Walker and Tarte (1963) who found that high-arousal words were much better recalled than low-arousal words after 1 week. However, the two kinds of words were not differentially recalled after 2 min. Figure 11-4 shows their results and suggests that the low-arousal words were much more rapidly forgotten than the high-arousal words. Furthermore there is no sign of reminiscence in this study (i.e., the high-arousal words were not recalled better after longer intervals) and indeed this is not a notable feature of verbal learning.

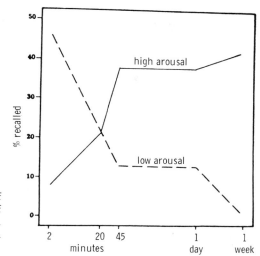

Figure 11-3. Differential recall of paired associates as a function of arousal level and rest interval. Taken with permission from Kleinsmith and Kaplan (1963).

Howarth and Eysenck (1968) also studied short- and long-term recall in verbal learning measuring arousal in their subjects in terms of the extraversion dimension of personality. They clearly showed that extraverts (low arousal) were better at short-term recall, but worse at long-term recall than introverts (Figure 9-13).

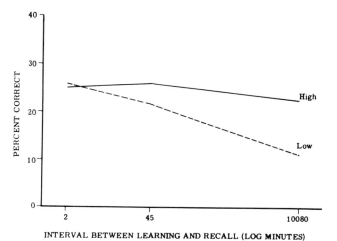

Figure 11-4. Differential recall of paired associates as a function of arousal level and rest interval. Taken with permission from Walker and Tarte (1963).

A more complex study was carried out by McLean (1968, 1969) involving three different methods of measuring or manipulating arousal. Subjects were divided into high- and low-arousal groups on the basis of their extraversion scores on a questionnaire. Also within-subject variations in arousal were measured in terms of skin resistance decrements (based on Kleinsmith and Kaplan's scoring procedure). Finally arousal was manipulated by subjecting subjects to white noise and control conditions to produce high- and low-arousal reactions, respectively. All these effects related to the recall of incidentally learned paired associate lists. Words learned in low-arousal conditions were recalled well immediately, but poorly on a delayed recall test. The reverse effect was shown for words learned under conditions of high arousal.

As has been emphasized in previous chapters a great deal is lost in an analysis if overall performance only is considered. Detailed analysis of results in this verbal learning study, as in so many areas, throws much more light on the underlying mechanisms of recall. Walker and Tarte have made a start in this direction by providing the serial position curves for short- and long-term recall (Figure 11-5). As is usually found in studies of verbal learning, words at the end of the list were better recalled after a short interval while words at the beginning of the list were better recalled after a long interval. Furthermore there does seem to be evidence for a reminiscence effect in that words at the beginning of the list are better recalled after a long interval than after a short one. This effect is not visible in the overall results since it is counterbalanced by forgetting of words at the end of the list. If we accept these detailed results then a rather different interpretation of reminiscence than Walker's seems necessary. It appears that, at least in verbal learning, two memory stores are involved: a short-term store into which go items from the end of the list (Craik, 1971) which functions better at low levels of arousal (Gale et al., 1974) and a long-term store into which go items at the beginning of the list. The concept of action decrement seems to apply to this long-term store, since items can only be retrieved from this store after a relatively long interval. This delay that is necessary before material can be retrieved from the long-term store may be used to "recode" the material and perhaps to fit it into a complex verbal "filing system." It has been suggested that material in long-term store is coded semantically while material in the short-term store is coded phonemically. The evidence for this notion is reviewed by Baddeley and Patterson (1971). This idea about two stores and their relation to reminiscence could be tested by presenting different kinds of material (codeable or uncodeable) or by studying the kind of clustering that seems to occur

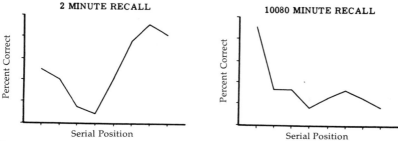

Figure 11-5. Differences in the serial position curve after different rest intervals. Taken with permission from Walker and Tarte (1963).

with the free recall of lists (Tulving, 1962). A slight amount of support for this model is derived from McLean, who provides means for the serial position curve in an experiment in which arousal was manipulated by subjecting some subjects to white noise (McLean, 1968). It appears from these data that the loss from memory shown by the low-arousal groups occurs in words at the end of the list, whereas the gain in recall shown by the high-arousal group occurs in words at the beginning of the list. Unfortunately we do not know if this effect is significant. However, these results are precisely in line with the speculations we made on the basis of Walker and Tarte's data.

These speculations have been largely confirmed by some recent and as yet unpublished work by Steven Schwartz of Northern Illinois University. Schwartz compared recall for sentences and random word strings with and without white noise during presentation. With no noise sentences are recalled better than random word strings, but the high-arousal state induced by the noise resulted in a loss of this superiority. Since the superiority is due to the subjects' use of semantic cues we may conclude that under high arousal subjects use these cues to a lesser extent. Such an interpretation is also consistent with the finding of Hormann and Osterkamp (1966) that white noise induced arousal leads to a decrease in semantic category clustering in free recall.

Schwartz used the same technique to compare the recall of semantically similar and phenemically similar word lists under different levels of arousal. Since attention was paid to phonemic aspects of the list high arousal favored the recall of semantically similar words for both immediate and delayed recall (although the delay was only two minutes). Schwartz performed similar experiments in which personality was used as an index of arousal. In accordance with the results of the experiments with white noise he found that neurotic introverts (high arousal) recalled lists of semantically similar words better than lists of phoneti-

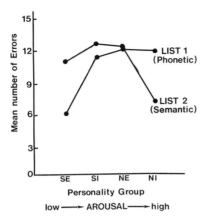

Figure 11-6. The effects of personality on recall of different kinds of verbal material. Taken with permission from Schwartz.

cally similar words. For stable extraverts (low arousal) the order of difficulty of the lists was reversed (Figure 11-6).

On a free recall task he found that low-arousal subjects (as indicated by personality measures) clustered words together on the basis of semantic category at higher rate than high-arousal subjects.

It is clearly necessary to repeat these experiments with short and long intervals between presentation and recall before we can conclude that the results found by Walker and Tarte (1963), Kleinsmith and Kaplan (1963), and Howarth and Eysenck (1968) are due to the effects of arousal on the organization of memory rather than on a simple consolidation process. However, whatever the results of such experiments, Walker's model of the consolidation of verbal learning will have to be considerably modified to take into account the different kinds of memory organizations the subject may use. It is clear that such a model will be very specific to verbal material. Even if there are different possible organizations for the memory of motor skills they will not depend on semantic and phonemic cues. Nor is there evidence that there is a distinction between short- and long-term stores in the learning of motor skills. In a later chapter we shall suggest that two independent mechanisms (feedback and motor programs) are involved in the performance of motor skills and also that a rest is necessary for control of performance to be transferred to the second mechanism. However, these two mechanisms are merely analogous to the short- and long-term stores of verbal learning and by no means identical.

The memory process may be considered to have three basic stages: registration, storage, and retrieval. Walker's action decrement theory hypothesizes that material passes from the registration to the storage stage via the process of consolidation and that this process is affected by level of arousal. However, by the nature of things, it is impossible to study the registration and storage stages without also involving the retrieval stage, for we cannot discover whether or not material is in store without first retrieving it. It is, however, possible to look at the retrieval stage of verbal memory in isolation, for example by asking the subject to name items in a particular category such as fruit. This has been done in a number of experiments by M. W. Eysenck (1974). He has shown very clearly that level of arousal and personality have very marked effects on retrieval from this "semantic" memory. High arousal improves retrieval in extraverts (more items are retrieved, each item is retrieved more rapidly, and there is a greater semantic clustering of the items). With introverts, on the other hand, high arousal has a detrimental effect on retrieval.

These results suggest that we must exercise great caution in interpreting the verbal learning experiments which purport to support Walker's action decrement theory. Conclusive experiments in this area will require the development of techniques to separate out the registration, storage, and retrieval stages of memory in addition to the different kinds of store we have already discussed.

We conclude that, although a concept such as action decrement can explain why learning cannot be fully manifested until consolidation is complete there is little direct evidence for such an effect. The animal studies which originally generated the concept do not in fact provide any evidence for it, at least in the sense that the decrement is the result of the consolidation of learning. The studies of verbal learning do suggest that some such process is operating, but the details of this process are probably rather specific to the learning of verbal material.

There are at least two mathematical models of learning based on neuroanatomical and neurophysiological concepts (Marr, 1972; Grossberg, 1969) in which reminiscence-like phenomena play an important role. Marr suggests that certain restructurings of the nervous system necessary for learning can only take place during sleep (the penultimate rest pause). Grossberg has devised mechanisms that might exist in the nervous system in which memory would spontaneously improve after moderate amounts of practice. Both these explanations are clearly closer to consolidation than to inhibition theories of reminiscence. However, both models are extremely speculative. Grossberg's version is completely general and does not distinguish between learning of different kinds of material. One of the themes of this book has been that such generality does not accord with reality. Marr's theory does provide for some specificity of learning and will be dealt with more fully in a later chapter. In the current state of knowledge about the details of the nervous system these kinds of theories need to seek support from empirical studies of learning rather than vice versa.

EVIDENCE FOR CONSOLIDATION IN PURSUIT-ROTOR LEARNING

Clearly then support for a consolidation theory of pursuit-rotor reminiscence must come largely from studies of the pursuit rotor itself. The two studies most compelling in this respect have already been discussed at the beginning of this chapter. First there was the well documented fact that the difference between high- and low-drive groups appears only after a rest pause (Eysenck & Maxwell, 1961). Second, there was the demonstration by Rachman and Grassi (1965) that reversed cue learning interfered more with later performance if given at the very beginning rather than later in a rest. Other studies which are more easily explained in terms of consolidation also concerned various manipulations of the subjects during the rest.

Catalano and his colleagues have reported a number of studies in which attempts were made to increase the arousal level of the subjects during a rest after massed practice on the pursuit rotor. Catalano (1967) suggests that continuous massed practice on the pursuit rotor causes a reduction in the arousal level of the subject below the optimum for that task. Such reductions in arousal have also been inferred from changes in the GSR during pursuit rotor performance (Gray, 1968). During the rest the subject's level of arousal increases and hence his performance after the rest is at a higher level. Catalano tested this theory by interpolating activating events during the rest. Both induced muscular tension (Catalano, 1967) and auditory stimulation enhanced reminiscence beyond that found with rest alone. Hammond (1972) enlarged these findings by showing that flashing a bright light or immersing the nontracking hand in cold water during a series of 15-sec rest pauses interpolated between sessions of massed practice on the pursuit rotor also enhanced reminiscence beyond that found with rest alone.

Frith (1968) found that small doses of nicotine administered orally at such a time as to be active at the beginning of a rest between two sessions of pursuit-rotor performance slightly improved the post-rest performance. This experiment is essentially a replication of those carried out by Garg and Holland with rats.

All these experiments demonstrate that increasing arousal during a rest produces an improvement in the post-rest performance.

Since the effect is obtained with such widely differing means of increasing arousal it seems that nonspecific arousal is concerned. The results clearly support Catalano's theory, but would equally support consolidation theory. Walker (1958) hypothesized that increased arousal would strengthen the consolidation process and there is some evidence of this from the animal studies quoted earlier. The two theories could easily be contrasted by varying the time during the rest at which the arousing event occurred. Arousal at the beginning of the rest will increase reminiscence if consolidation is involved, whereas arousal at the end of the rest will increase reminiscence if the arousal level during the following performance is the important variable. Such crucial experiments have not yet been carried out.

The issue will, of course, be confused if Walker's hypothesis about the length of rest also plays a part. This stated that high arousal favored performance after long rests whereas low arousal favored performance after short rests. Attempts to demonstrate this effect in pursuit-rotor learning have not been very successful. Eysenck and Maxwell (1961) showed that high-drive subjects were superior to low-drive subjects after all but the shortest rest lengths. Studies in which levels of arousal were measured in terms of the extraversion dimension of personality have given equivocal results. Farley (unpublished) confirmed that extraverts showed greater reminiscence after a short rest and introverts after long rest, but Grey (1968) and Seunath (1973) failed to find this effect.

Clarke (1967) found some support for the hypothesis when arousal was measured using the two-flash threshold (Venables, 1963). However, the group tested were schizophrenic patients who are considered by many authors (e.g., Venables, 1966) to be abnormal in the way their arousal relates to physiological indices. Furthermore as we have seen in the chapter on abnormalities this group of patients is abnormal with regard to pursuit-rotor learning.

CONSOLIDATION IN THE EXPLANATION OF REMINISCENCE AND OTHER PHENOMENA OF PURSUIT-ROTOR LEARNING

We began this chapter by suggesting that explanations of pursuit-rotor reminiscence in terms of inhibition were too complicated to be of any use. It was hoped that a radically new approach might be found that would also provide a simpler explanation of the phenomena. Consolidation theory has certainly provided a new approach to the problem, but has it also provided a satisfactory explanation of it?

The only major attempt to apply consolidation in the explanation of reminiscence is found in the work of Eysenck (1965, 1966). In the detailed examinations of the proposals that follow we shall show that they contain many flaws. However, as a result of this examination we are able to propose a new explanation which is hopefully more satisfactory.

There are three major objections to Eysenck's account of pursuit-rotor reminiscence. First, it is even more complex than the inhibition theories it is supposed to replace. Second, contrary to Eysenck's claim, the account cannot explain downswing. Third, the concept of "action decrement," which plays an important part in the account, turns out on close examination to be essentially indistinguishable from the discredited concept of reactive inhibition. In fairness to Eysenck it should be remembered that his model (Eysenck, 1965) was not concerned to explain reminiscence only in pursuit-rotor learning, but also in other tasks. Eysenck suggested that there were many task-specific features of reminiscence and that there were several dimensions along which tasks could be ranged. In the first place, for tasks which involve new learning such as the pursuit rotor, consolidation will be of prime importance. For tasks involving no learning such as vigilance[1] and tapping, consolidation will play no part, but reactive inhibition will be important. Other specific features mentioned by Eysenck were the effects of "blocks" or "rest pauses" on performance and the influence of motivation on performance. A major theme of this book has been that more attention must be payed to the specific nature of the task being studied

---

[1] The question of whether vigilance decrement is caused by some form of reactive inhibition or perhaps rather by a falling off of arousal (assuming that these are in fact different hypotheses leading to different consequences) is of course not finally settled. The inhibition theory would predict that vigilance decrement should be significant over trials; that it should be significant between extravert–introvert groups; and that the *interaction* should be significant (extraverts falling off more quickly than introverts, having started at pretty well the same level). Such interaction effects were found by Bakan, Belton, and Toth (1963) and by Carr (1971), but not by Claridge (1960) or by Harkins and Geen (1974). The latter attempt to explain these differences between investigators in terms of different levels of arousal generated by the different tasks used, taken in conjunction with the inverted-U hypothesis. Clearly no final judgment is possible at the present time regarding the possibility of accounting for personality differences in vigilance performance in terms of reactive inhibition, partly or wholly.

and thus Eysenck's 1965 paper was an important step in this development. Our criticisms of the paper are directed solely against the application of the theory to pursuit-rotor reminiscence.

The very title of Eysenck's paper; "A three factor theory of reminiscence," (1965) indicates the complexity of this account of pursuit-rotor learning. Rather than replacing the previous inhibition model, Eysenck added to it the concept of consolidation. Thus his account states that all learning must be consolidated before it can be manifested in performance. It is this consolidation that produces the improvement in performance after a rest. Interpolated activities at the beginning of the rest will interfere with the consolidation process producing a lowering of post-rest performance as found by Rachman and Grassi (1965). Furthermore, consolidation cannot occur without a rest and hence little or no learning will be manifested before the programmed rest pause takes place. As a result the faster learning that results from high motivation cannot be manifested until after a rest. This accounts for the failure to find differences between the performance of the high- and low-motivation groups during pre-rest practice.

Post-rest upswing is, however, still explained basically in terms of inhibition theory. Reactive inhibition builds up to produce involuntary rest pauses and this habit of not responding is learned (conditioned inhibition). However, this negative learning too must be consolidated and so can only be manifested after a rest. After such a rest the conditioned inhibition suppresses performance, but is gradually extinguished since reactive inhibition has not yet built up and so the conditioned resting is no longer rewarded. In accord with this account is the empirical observation that upswing is greater after longer rests, since the conditioned inhibition has had greater opportunity to consolidate.

Downswing is affected by length of rest in the opposite way, so that the longer the rest the less the post-rest downswing. This could be the effect of a gradually decreasing consolidation process. Eysenck has attempted to explain post-rest downswing in this manner by assuming that consolidation has two functions (Eysenck, 1966). Primary consolidation takes place during rest during which time neural traces are made available to the experimental subject for actually improved work. This is followed by secondary consolidation which protects the already laid down trace against retrograde amnesia. Secondary consolidation takes much longer than primary consolidation. Two stages of consolidation have to be posited since maximum gain in performance due to rest occurs after about ten minutes (primary consolidation) whereas post-rest downswing only begins to disappear after extremely long rests, perhaps as long as 175 days (Koonce, Chamblis, & Irion, 1964). An explanation is required as to how this ongoing process can produce a gradual decrease in performance. Eysenck (1965), following Walker (1963), suggests that consolidation and work are mutually interfering processes (action decrement). "This interference produces post-rest downswing, which in turn ceases when consolidation is complete; at this point we may then return to the gentle upward sloping course characteristic of massed practice without rest pause interference." Detailed examination of this explanation shows that it is not feasible. If consolidation interfered with work it would certainly depress performance, but such depression is by no means the same as a downswing in performance. Downswing in performance implies that the interference from the consolidation increases over time, since the depression of performance is greater at the end of the downswing than the beginning. It would, on the contrary, be expected that as the protective consolidation neared completion its interference with performance would decrease. This would result in an upswing in performance.

Finally Eysenck attempts to account for the greater reminiscence shown by extraverts than introverts. He suggests that introverts, being more highly aroused, consolidate conditioned inhibition better and therefore their post-rest performance is depressed below that of the extraverts. This too is in accord with the experimental findings. However, in terms of this argument, should not the introverted subjects also consolidate the pursuit-rotor skill itself better, resulting in a better overall performance post-rest as is found in high-drive groups? In those studies where personality differences have been found it was the extraverts that showed the better overall pursuit-rotor performance (Farley, 1966; Gray, 1968).

A flaw in this account more basic than any of those already pointed out relates to the concept of "action decrement" itself. We have already seen that an action decrement resulting from the continuing secondary consolidation cannot account for post-rest downswing. Some kind of action decrement is presumably implicated also in Eysenck's statement that while the subject is working "no permanent memory traces are laid down." This is the other aspect of action decrement; not only does consolidation interfere with performance, performance also interferes with consolidation. An extreme interpretation of Eysenck's position would suggest that during pre-rest practice performance prevented consolidation from taking place, whereas after the rest it was the consolidation that interfered with the work. This seems somewhat implausible. It would be necessary to know when and how this reversal of roles took place. It would be more plausible and still consistent with Eysenck's position to assume that both before and after the rest performance and consolidation interfered with one another mutually. Indeed one might argue that the pre-rest learning cannot be manifested in performance because of the interference from the ongoing consolidation process. Only after a rest when this interference is no longer present can the pre-rest learning appear in performance. Unfortunately this account of the effects of action decrement is essentially identical to those models in which reactive inhibition is used to explain reminiscence. During pre-rest work there is a build up in some process that interferes with performance, and this interfering process decreases during a rest. It makes little difference whether we label the process reactive inhibition or action decrement caused by consolidation. Both accounts fail to explain the experimental results we listed at the beginning of the chapter.

It is interesting that explanations in terms of reactive inhibition and action decrement attempt to deny the paradox of reminiscence. Both assume that learning is already available at the end of pre-rest practice, but cannot be manifested because of interference from other processes. It is clear that such explanations as to why learning cannot improve performance until after consolidation is complete are unsatisfactory. A more radical alternative would have the learning in a form unsuitable for improving performance. Consolidation would be necessary to change the learning into the correct form. A model of this kind will be described in the chapter on "strategies." This is not a particularly far-fetched notion. It is analogous to the process whereby a man turns his knowledge of the internal combustion engine into a car in which he can drive along the highway at 90 mph.

It is clear that Eysenck's three factor theory of reminiscence has failed to provide a model which accounts for all the phenomena associated with pursuit-rotor learning. However, it may well be that such an all embracing model is not particularly desirable. It is not a good strategy to define the set of facts to be explained by a single theory in terms of a particular task, since performance of the task may involve the combination of a relatively arbitrary collection of components that may not be intrinsically related to one another. The collection of facts that a theory is supposed to explain is better brought together on the basis of some underlying process that all may have in common (e.g., memory, learning, etc.). The difficulties encountered in constructing a general theory of pursuit-rotor performance may well indicate that there is no single process underlying behavior on this task and that the various phenomena encountered may be better explained in isolation and without reference to each other.

A ONE-FACTOR THEORY OF REMINISCENCE

In constructing this new theory of reminiscence we have tried to take account of all the problems and criticisms that have arisen in relation to previous theories. Recognizing the need for simplification we have abandoned all the inhibition concepts and tried to account for reminiscence entirely in terms of a consolidation process. Furthermore we have not tried to account for all pursuit-rotor phenomena with this one theory. Post-rest upswing we accept provisionally as a manifestation of "set" reinstatement relating it to a rather different body of evidence which has been discussed in a previous chapter. Differences between introverts and extraverts are, we suggest, related to different strategies adopted in the performance of the task. This topic will be dealt with in the chapter on strategies.

The facts left for our theory to explain are therefore those relating to reminiscence, downswing, and the effects of various rest and practice lengths. These facts can be summarized as follows: a small, but steady, amount of learning is manifested during pre-rest practice; after 15-min rest there is a considerable amount of reminiscence; however, a downswing in performance follows which eventually reaches the same level as a group having no rest; after a very long rest there is less downswing and final performance remains above that of a group with no rest. All these effects can be seen in Figure 5-20 and 6-13 from Farley (1966).

To these facts must be wedded what we know about the consolidation process. Consolidation has two functions as a result of which before the consolidation process is complete, (a) learning cannot be fully manifested in performance and (b) learning can be destroyed.

To apply such a consolidation process to pursuit-rotor learning it is necessary to specify the nature of these two functions in more detail. It is convenient to imagine the learning and consolidation process passing through three stages. In the first stage the learning is neither available for improving performance nor is it protected against destruction. In the second stage the learning is available for improving performance, but is not protected against destruction. In the third stage the learning is available for improving performance and is protected against destruction. This specific ordering of the consolidation stages is clearly open to empirical testing. However, it is of course possible that this account of the consolidation process may only apply to the learning of motor skills.

In order to explain pursuit-rotor learning in terms of consolidation, we must specify more precisely the agents that can destroy the partially consolidated learning. We have already seen that there is ample experimental evidence that this learning can be destroyed by major disturbances of the CNS such as convulsions. We propose that in addition the partially consolidated learning can be destroyed by performance of the task being learned. This would be plausible in physiological terms (not that such plausibility is necessary to our model) if the performance of the task involved precisely the same small area of the CNS as the consolidating trace. Other activities would not affect the trace since they would not involve precisely the same areas of the CNS. However major disturbances affecting the whole of the CNS would interfere with all consolidating traces.

In the chapter on interference and transfer we presented evidence that pursuit-rotor learning is extremely specific. Activities carried on between sessions of pursuit-rotor performance have very little effect on pursuit-rotor learning, unless they are tasks very similar to the pursuit rotor. Such tasks would include performance on a pursuit rotor going backwards or at a different speed. A task only slightly more different from the standard pursuit rotor than these will interfere little with pursuit-rotor learning. The interpolated task which interferes most with pursuit-rotor learning in these terms is clearly performance on the pursuit rotor itself. Indeed this is really what the phenomenon of reminiscence is all about.

Figure 11-7 shows how this hypothetical consolidation process can explain many phenomena appearing in pursuit-rotor performance. During a period of uninterrupted practice little learning can get through to the latter stages of the consolidation process since the consolidating traces are destroyed by the continuing performance. Thus only a slight and slow improvement in performance appears. During a short rest some of the learning passes into the second stage of the consolidation process where it is available for improving performance, but is also destroyed by that performance. Thus, immediately after the rest (and after the post-rest upswing), there is a marked improvement in performance due to the partially consolidated learning. However, the performance also destroys that partially consolidated learning causing a downswing in performance. Eventually all the consolidated learning is destroyed and performance returns to the level that would have been achieved if no rest had been interpolated.

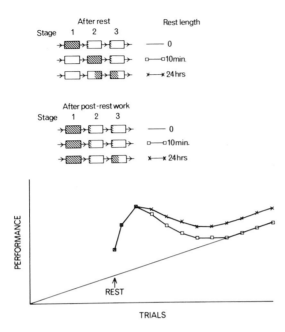

Figure 11-7. The hypothetical course of pursuit-rotor performance based on a three-stage model of consolidation. With continuous work very little learning passes beyond stage 1. After a short rest learning has passed to stage 2 improving performance; however, post-rest work destroys this learning causing downswing. Only after a long rest when learning has passed to stage 3 is learning retained permanently.

If the rest is longer more learning is partially consolidated and hence there is more reminiscence, but also more downswing since there is more learned material to be destroyed by the performance. Only after a relatively long rest does any learning become fully consolidated, i.e., it is both available for performance and immune from destruction. After such a rest what partially consolidated material still remains will be destroyed by the performance causing downswing, but the performance will remain at a higher level than would have occurred without rest, because the fully consolidated material is not destroyed. The greater the proportion of the learned material that becomes fully consolidated the less downswing there will be. If all the material is fully consolidated there should be no downswing.

The amount of material consolidated during a rest (both temporary and permanent) is indicated by the difference between the last pre-rest trials and the maximum post-rest trials (i.e., performance after post-rest upswing). This was the measure used by Grey (1968) and labeled rem. max. The amount of material permanently consolidated as a result of rest is indicated by the difference between performance after post-rest downswing is complete and performance at an equivalent time in a group which had no interpolated rest. These measures are illustrated in Figure 11-7.

Most of these effects are illustrated in Figure 5-20 from Farley (1966). This figure also gives some indication of the times necessary to pass through the various stages of consolidation. There is little further increase in reminiscence (in terms of the top point of the post-rest upswing curve) after 10-min rest. However, there is a considerable degree of downswing and the performance returns to the level shown by groups with no rest. This observation suggests that all learned material has passed into the second stage of the consolidation process after 10 min, but that none of it has at that time passed to the third stage. After a 24-hr rest there is still some post-rest downswing, but the performance stabilizes at a level above that shown by groups with shorter rests. This suggests that some, but not all material has reached the final stage of the consolidation process after a 24-hr rest.

It is interesting to note that the 24-hr rest will necessarily include the occurrence of sleep. Marr (1971) has suggested that the restructuring of the CNS that may be necessary for learning may only be able to occur during sleep. If the final stage of the consolidation process involves such restructuring then it is possible that it is sleep, rather than a long rest that is necessary for material to reach the final stage of consolidation.

If, after a sufficiently long rest, no downswing occurred we would conclude that the final stage of consolidation had been reached by all the learned material. What little evidence there is on this matter suggests that the time involved may be very long indeed. The data collected by Koonce, Chamblis, and Irion (1964) suggest it may be as long as 175 days.

The simple model proposed here will also account for the difference between spaced and massed practice and the shifts in performance that occur when subjects are switched from one condition to the other. Spaced practice will always be superior to massed practice since the partially consolidated learning is available for improving performance and is never fully destroyed because performance never continues long enough. If the subject is switched from spaced to massed practice then the partially consolidated learning will be fully destroyed and his performance will decline to a lower level. Switching from massed to spaced practice increases the amount of partially consolidated learning available for improving performance and hence produces an increase in the overall level of performance. The effects of motivation and arousal can be explained by assuming that high-motivation/high arousal increases the speed at which consolidation takes place. Post-rest performance after massed practice fails to reach the level of performance with the same amount of distributed practice. This would be expected if the first stage of the consolidation process has a limited capacity. Thus if the first stage was filled and no rest occurred enabling material to be transferred to the later stages, either new material would not be able to enter the store or old material would be lost. Evidence for the existence and extent of this limited capacity is indicated by the finding that increasing the length of pre-rest practice beyond about 15 min does not produce any further increase in reminiscence (Willett & Eysenck, 1962).

The finding that there is no post-rest upswing after short rest intervals (e.g., Feldman, 1964, who had subjects practice for 20-sec periods separated by 40-sec rest periods) is probably best explained in terms of the speed at which set is lost. Only after a five-minute rest has a sufficient degree of set been lost to produce a pronounced post-rest upswing.

The one factor model of reminiscence does not cope very well with the observation that high-ability groups show upswing and down-swing even in the pre-rest practice period. One proposal has been that such groups have a high ability because they have had previous experience with tasks similar to the pursuit rotor and hence the pre-rest practice is, for them, equivalent to post-rest practice. However, we have seen in the chapter on transfer and interpolated activity that almost no task is similar to the pursuit rotor in the sense that learning or inhibition acquired on this task will transfer to pursuit-rotor performance. Thus, this explanation of the behavior of high-ability groups is very unlikely.

Another possibility is that the performance of the high-ability group is due to an artifact of measurement. We have seen in the chapter on measurement that subjects performing with a large target get high scores and also tend to show upswing and downswing in their pre-rest performance. Briggs, Fitts, and Bahrick (1957) have also shown that the shape of the performance curve will depend to some extent on the level of performance. These difficulties are a result of the crude measure of performance normally used. Measuring the subject's mean distance from the target, rather than simply whether he is on or off, might help to resolve the problem.

We hope that by now the reader is convinced that the concept of consolidation can provide a simple model of pursuit-rotor performance that is consistent with most of the phenomena that have been observed. There is however one aspect of this model that places it very much in the neo-Hullian tradition of the inhibition theories proposed by Kimble and Eysenck. Like these models it is not concerned with what it is that the subject learns or how this learning enables him to improve his performance. Thus these models would be of no help if we wished to construct a machine that would follow a target. This problem will be discussed in the chapter on "strategies." In that chapter we shall see that there are certain systematic changes in the style of pursuit rotor performance during continuous practice which are entirely outside the scope of either the consolidation or the inhibition models.

CHAPTER 12

Strategies in Performance: What Is This Thing Called Learning?

The model of pursuit-rotor performance that we presented in the last chapter was a radical departure from previous neo-Hullian models, since all Hull's concepts such as reactive inhibition, conditioned inhibition, and involuntary rest pauses were abandoned in favor of the single factor of consolidation. However, in another, and perhaps more important, sense this new model was very much within Hull's tradition. For, as in Hull's models of behavior, there is nothing in our explanation of pursuit-rotor performance that relates specifically to the task being performed. There is nothing in the model to tell us that it applies to the tracking of targets and not to the learning of poetry. Thus we do not know *what* is learned, merely that this learning improves performance. Hull was justified in such an approach since he believed that all learning was fundamentally the same. However, as we have seen in previous chapters, much evidence has accumulated indicating that different tasks require different learning models. In this chapter we shall consider the problem of reminiscence from a very different angle that places a major emphasis on the exact nature of the pursuit-rotor task. We may contrast the two approaches as follows. The first approach, based on Hull, attempts to derive a set of hypothetical variables which would account for observed courses of learning and performance. The second approach, based on applied, engineering psychology, attempts to design a blueprint for a machine that would perform the task under study.

PROBLEMS IN THE MEASUREMENT OF PURSUIT-ROTOR
PERFORMANCE

Virtually all the experiments discussed so far have used only one measure of performance, the proportion of time-on-target. The experiment by Briggs, Fitts, and Bahrick (1957) showing that this is a very crude measure giving results dependent on the size of the target and the level of performance has already been described in Chapter 2. Many of the drawbacks of this measure are however quite obvious and do not need to be demonstrated by experiments. It would be possible for a subject to follow the target round very accurately, but a few millimeters behind it. This very good performance would have a very poor score in terms of total time-on-target. The only way to overcome this difficulty is to use a continuous measure of the distance of the subject's stylus from the target. This is extremely difficult to do using the traditional pursuit-rotor apparatus. However, we shall see that it is nevertheless possible to obtain more detailed measures of performance using the traditional on or off target measure.

Another criticism is that most studies have failed to consider the special nature of the skills required for pursuit tracking. The single measure of performance has of course helped in the persistence of this error, by minimizing the difference between the pursuit rotor and other learning tasks. Few attempts were made to define concepts like "response" or "rest pause" specifically in relation to pursuit tracking. In the experiments to be described below such attempts have been made and have led unavoidably to the conclusion that pursuit-rotor learning is very different from other kinds of learning and also that the Hullian model of stimulus and response sequences is singularly inappropriate.

HITS AND AVERAGE HIT LENGTHS

Given a standard pursuit-rotor apparatus the basic information available about performance is whether the subject was on or off target at any particular time. Such information could be displayed on a chart recorder as in Figure 12-1, but the amount of such data involved in even a few minutes practice would be too great for analysis from such a display to be feasible. The display of pursuit rotor performance shown in Figure 12-1 can be said to consist of an alternate sequence of "hits" and "misses." Each hit and miss will have an associated length. Total time-on-target is one of many possible summary scores for the

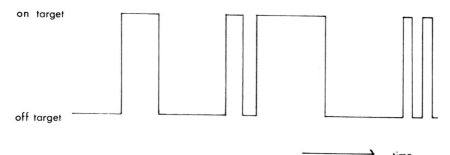

on target

off target

time

Figure 12-1. Part of a continuous record of pursuit-rotor performance based on knowledge of whether the subject was on or off target.

sequence, being the sum of the hit lengths in the usual trial length of 10 sec. Another summary score that is easy to measure, but that has been largely neglected, is the number of hits in ten seconds. A third measure, average hit length, can be derived from the first two by dividing the total time-on-target by the number of hits. The nature of the method of measurement imposes certain restrictions on these scores. For example, a small number of hits can be associated either with very bad performance where the subject very rarely makes contact with the target, or with very good performance where the subject very rarely breaks contact with the target. Thus, on its own, number of hits is not a good measure of performance. Consideration of these three scores suggests that there might be novel dimensions of pursuit-rotor performance. For example, a given total time-on-target could be built up from many short hits or a few long hits. Wherever the same level of performance (i.e., total time-on-target) is achieved by different means in this way, we have chosen to label these as differences in "strategy."

A number of studies (Ammons, 1951; Frith, 1968; Frith & Tunstall, 1971) have investigated the relationships between these three variables and found essentially the same results (Figure 12-2). Immediately after a rest there is a significant increase in total time-on-target (reminiscence), but a significant decrease in average hit length. Associated with these changes is a very pronounced increase in the number of hits immediately after a rest compared to the number immediately before a rest. During the period of post-rest downswing where there is a gentle decline in total time-on-target there is no significant change in average hit length.

Thus it seems that an alternative measure of performance, average hit length, gives a very different picture of the changes occurring during pursuit-rotor learning. This measure reveals neither reminiscence nor post-rest downswing. As we have seen, complex theories

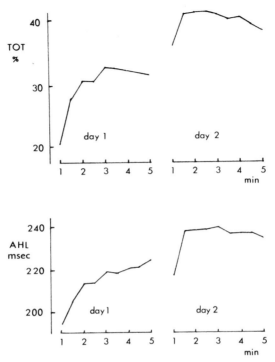

Figure 12-2. Comparison of two different measures of pursuit-rotor performance (total time-on-target and average hit length). Drawn from data provided by Frith and Tunstall (1971).

have been based upon these changes which seem largely dependent on which measures of performance happen to have been chosen for study.

Frith (1968) studied the relation between these three measures of pursuit-rotor performance, total time-on-target, hits, and average hit length, paying particular attention to individual differences and changes in the relations between the measures over time. The apparatus used was not the standard pursuit rotor, but a device displaying a moving light which could activate a photo-cell in the tip of the subject's stylus. Such a device gives a much cleaner distinction between the states on and off target. This apparatus was used rather than the standard pursuit rotor because of the poor quality of the mechanical contact involved in this latter apparatus. This depends on a metal stylus making electrical contact with a metal disk while sliding over its surface. The infinitesimally short makes and breaks which result unavoidably from the unevenness of the two surfaces will hardly affect the total time-on-target score, but may well give rise to spurious additional hits. The photoelectric system largely avoids this problem. The target in this apparatus is provided by a radial strip of light set in a revolving turntable. Above this is placed a sheet of glass the underside of which is covered with lightproof paper. Tracks of any shape can be made by cutting away the appropriate parts of this paper. The target is then seen as a path of light moving around the track. Two tracks were used in this experiment, one shaped like a triangle and the other like a six pointed star (Figure 12-3). The light rotated beneath them at a speed of 37.5 rpm. Since all points on these tracks are not equidistant from the center of revolution, the target changes speed, moving fastest along those parts of the tracks (the corners) which are furthest from the center. These tracks are both more difficult to follow than the simple circle of the standard pursuit rotor. However, the rotation speed of the target was much slower than in the standard pursuit rotor (60 rpm). The resultant level of performance was in the region of 50% time-on-target which is rather higher than that usually obtained with the standard pursuit rotor and is also optimal for time on target to be sensitive to changes in performance (Briggs, Fitts, & Bahrick, 1957).

Two groups of subjects worked on the two tracks for three 5-min sessions separated by 15-min rest periods. Performance on the star shaped track was consistently worse than performance on the triangular shaped track throughout the 15 min of practice. The shape of the learning curves was however similar for both tracks and its essentials have already been described. In terms of total time on target there was a marked reminiscence effect after rest; there was also a period of post-rest upswing lasting about 30 sec followed by post-rest downswing. The number of hits in each ten seconds had also been recorded and

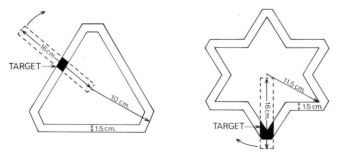

Figure 12-3. Scale diagrams of the two tracks used in the variable pattern polar tracker. Taken with permission from Frith (1968).

from this an average hit length score was calculated. In terms of this measure there was no reminiscence after rest and no post-rest down-swing. There was however, a marked post-rest upswing. The results were essentially the same therefore as those shown in Figure 12-2 for which the triangular track was used. It should also be noted that for these tracks, which give rise to somewhat better performance than the traditional pursuit rotor, there is some evidence of an upswing in the pre-rest practice session.

The differing course of change in average hit length as opposed to total time-on-target suggests that the relationship between hits and time-on-target changes during the course of each session of work. This relationship was therefore investigated in more detail. As we have already seen the relation between hits and time on target must necessarily be curvilinear since there can only be few movements on or off target (and hence few hits) when the total time on target is either very low or very high. The simplest curve with these properties is a parabola. Figure 12-4 shows the best fit parabolas for the twenty subjects given the triangular track. (The exact expression fitted was: Hits $= a + b.\text{TOT} + c.\text{TOT}^2$.) It was possible for the resulting relationship to be a straight line or even an inverted parabola, but as can be seen for the vast majority of subjects the fitted curves as expected show zero hits at about 0% and 100% time-on-target. The principal difference between the subjects in Figure 12-4 is the number of hits at 50% time-on-target. Such a difference corresponds to the strategies that have already been outlined. Some subjects are achieving 50% time on target with many short hits while others are achieving it with a few long hits. We shall refer to these as short-hit and long-hit strategies, respectively. For both the star shaped and the triangular shaped track there was a significant relationship between strategy and personality. Extraverts tended to adopt a long-hit strategy, while introverts adopted a short-hit strategy (Figure 12-4).

The change in strategy during the course of practice was investigated by comparing the actual number of hits at the beginning and end of each five minute session with that predicted from the fitted parabolas. There was a significant shift from a short-hit strategy to a long-hit strategy confirming the results obtained by comparing average hit length with total time-on-target.

During the period of post-rest downswing we have seen that the total time-on-target decreased while the average hit length remained constant. This implies that the average miss length increased. Clearly these increasingly long gaps appearing towards the end of performance

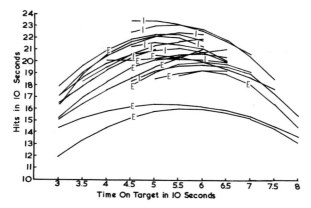

Figure 12-4. The best fit parabolas relating time-on-target and average hit length for 20 subjects performing on a triangular pursuit rotor. E = extraverts; I = introverts. Taken with permission from Frith (1968).

could be a result of subjects taking involuntary rest pauses as hypothesized by Eysenck (1957). Thus we can also hypothesize that a "long-hit strategy" is a type of performance involving rest pauses. Thus the performance of extraverts appears to involve rest pauses which also agrees with one of Eysenck's hypotheses about individual differences. However, there still remains the problem of why the performance of extraverts is not worse than that of introverts if it includes rest pauses.

REST PAUSES AND RESPONSES

Consideration of what exactly a rest might be should help us to deal with some of these problems of interpretation. The nature of the rest pause is intimately tied up with the nature of the response since a rest pause is a failure to respond. At the simplest level of interpretation a response could be a movement of the stylus. In this case during a rest pause the subject should cease to move the stylus. Ammons *et al.* (1958) carried out a painstaking frame by frame analysis of films of pursuit-rotor performance. They demonstrated that such a cessation of movement virtually never happens. We may therefore assume that movement of the stylus occurs continuously. Indeed, the task is not to move the stylus, but to equate the movement of the stylus with that of the target. Thus we might conclude that the response is the detection and correction of mismatches between stylus and target. Such a response has two components; a visual one required for detecting the discrepancy between the stylus and the target and a movement component by which this discrepancy is corrected when necessary. In terms of this model when the subject takes a rest pause he will cease to detect and correct errors. Thus the discrepancy between stylus and target will tend to be larger during a rest pause. However it is clear that just as a subject continually detecting and trying to correct errors may fail to get on target so another subject may stare out of the window and nevertheless hit the target by chance. There are thus considerable problems in detecting a rest pause of this type.

Are we justified in assuming that the detection and correction of errors occurs at discrete intervals in this way? Hick (1948) has suggested that the phenomena of refractory period, threshold and reaction time necessitate that in a tracking task the human must operate intermittently. Vince (1948) and Beggs and Howarth (1970) have shown that extinguishing the illumination of the target after an aiming movement has started makes little difference to accuracy, suggesting that no further correcting movements are made after a certain time. Beggs and Howarth (1972) have further demonstrated that such corrections are made no more frequently than at 290 msec intervals (the visual corrective reaction time for their subjects). Although these results are for simple aiming tasks they strongly support the notion that errors are corrected intermittently in all tracking tasks.

Identifying the response with the detection and correction of errors sheds some interesting light on some of the old Hullian concepts. For example, even in the so-called massed practice condition the rate at which the subject chooses to make this kind of response is not fixed. It would be possible for the subject to respond at a slow rate, and thus avoid the build-up of reactive inhibition and hence the occurrence of rest pauses. This could account for extraverts taking more rest pauses than introverts, but achieving the same level of performance. They could manage this by responding at a faster rate between the rest pauses. However, this difference between personality groups is one of performance strategy (i.e., preferred rate of responding) and need have nothing to do with differences in proneness to the build-up of reactive inhibition or the efficiency of the consolidation process.

In the following section we shall consider attempts to demonstrate the existence of these responses and rest pauses in pursuit-rotor performance. Frith (1969) attempted to control the rate of responding by intermittently illuminating the target. For obvious reasons the photoelectric pursuit rotor could not be used in this experiment and therefore

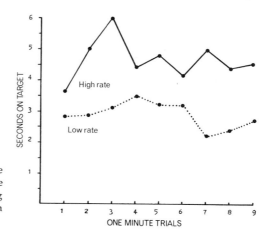

Figure 12-5. Comparison of the post-rest pursuit-rotor performance of two groups of subjects viewing the target at different rates. Taken with permission from Frith (1969).

the standard apparatus was used. Because of the drawbacks of this apparatus only the standard performance measure total time-on-target was recorded. For all subjects the target was illuminated only 25% of the time. For one group the target was visible 5 times a second for 50 msec. For the other group it was visible twice a second for 125 msec. All the subjects practiced on the standard pursuit rotor for two 9-min sessions separated by a 5-min rest. Figure 12-5 shows that there were striking differences between the groups particularly after the rest. The group which saw the target at a high rate of illumination showed both upswing and downswing whereas the other group did not.

The rate at which the target was illuminated roughly determined the maximum rate at which the subjects could detect errors in their performance. Thus the subjects for whom the target was illuminated only twice a second could only make their detection and correction responses at a slow rate. The results may readily be interpreted in terms of the Hullian framework that has been discussed in previous chapters. We could assume that inhibition causes a reduction in response rate. During the period of post-rest upswing the conditioned inhibition extinguishes and the response rate increases. During the period of post-rest downswing reactive inhibition builds up and the response rate decreases. All these effects appeared in the group with a high rate of target illumination since these subjects were able to respond at a high rate. The other group could only respond at a slow rate and therefore did not build up reactive inhibition or extinguish conditioned inhibition. They therefore performed continuously at the same rather low level.

THE SEARCH FOR THE REST PAUSE

We have redefined the rest pause as an abnormally long gap in between the successive corrections of errors. Such rest pauses will be manifested in performance as a temporary decrease in the probability of being on target. Thus there will be a different distribution of hits and misses lengths during a rest pause as compared to the distributions during normal performance. At the end of performance when rest pauses are interspersed with normal response intervals, the hit and miss distributions should differ from those at the beginning of performance. In particular distributions at the end of practice should have an increased number of long misses.

Frith (1971) analyzed performance on the photoelectric pursuit rotor with the triangular track already described using a LINC-8 computer and was thus able to measure individual hit and miss lengths and plot hit and miss distributions at different stages of practice. Figure 12-6 shows the distributions of miss lengths for the first and fifth minutes of work for 30 subjects. It is clear that the difference between these distributions is in the very short misses and not in the long misses. In the fifth minute of work there was a marked reduction in the proportions of very short misses. There was no difference in total time-on-target between the first and fifth minute since upswing and downswing were roughly equal. Thus the difference between the miss distributions cannot be attributed to differences in level of attainment. Can we conclude from this result that rest pauses did not appear towards the end of performance? Long misses were very rare throughout performance and therefore it is difficult to measure changes in their frequency. It is probably impossible to come to definite conclusions therefore about the existence of rest pauses without observing the error correction responses directly. Nevertheless the change in the distribution of miss lengths over time is more consistent with an overall decrease in response rate rather than the appearance of abnormally long gaps in sequences of responses that remain at the same rate. With an overall decrease in response rate the very rapid correction of errors will cease resulting in a drop in the frequency of very short misses. Both models of performance change predict an increase in average miss length as was found in the experiments comparing total time-on-target and average hit length.

In the experiment described previously (Frith, 1967) individual differences in performance strategy were found which were similar to the differences in performance at the beginning and end of work period. It was hypothesized that this might be due to extraverted

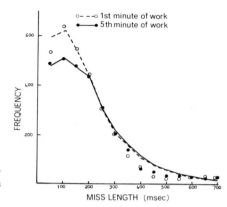

Figure 12-6. Miss distributions from different stages of pursuit-rotor practice. Taken with permission from Frith (1969).

subjects producing more rest pauses than introverted subjects. Does the comparison of hit and miss length distributions between such subjects reveal the existence of rest pauses or is the performance of extraverts characterized by a slower overall rate of responding?

Frith (1971) found a number of characteristics of performance that distinguished introverts from extraverts. The major variable defining this dimension of performance was the short-versus long-hit strategy described. At 50% time-on-target extraverts were producing fewer and therefore longer hits than introverts. It was clear however, that his long-hit strategy was not due to the occasional appearance of extralong misses, but to a greater frequency of medium length misses and hits. In particular the hit length distribution of the extraverted subjects tended to be bimodal, having peaks at 200 and 450 msec. The introverted subjects tended to have only one peak on the hit length distribution at 200 msec (Figure 12-7). Such a difference in the distributions would clearly result in the extraverts having longer average hit lengths for the same time-on-target, but can have little to do with the production of rest pauses. The position of these two peaks in the hit length distribution was constant and independent of level of performance and other factors and was thus probably related to properties of the track, which it should be remembered was triangular. Another measure of performance relating to the long-hit strategy was rhythmicity. Fourier analysis of the sequence of hits and misses in the performance of a single subject revealed a strong rhythmic component corresponding, as one would expect, to one revolution of the target around the triangle. Subjects who showed a long-hit strategy and a bimodal distribution of hits also showed a stronger rhythmic component of this kind.

An explanation of this cluster of variables which defined the low-

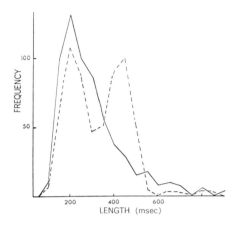

Figure 12-7. Comparison of hit length distributions for introverted and extraverted subjects (straight line = introverts; dashed line = extraverts). Taken with permission from Frith (1969).

hit strategy was discovered by direct observation of tracking performance. Two subjects were chosen whose performance was characterized in one case by extreme bimodality of the hit distribution and in the other by extreme lack of bimodality. The two subjects worked for a further two minutes on the triangular pursuit rotor and their performance during the last 2½ min was filmed. For each subject the position of the stylus in relation to the track was plotted for frames of the film (Figures 12-8, and 12-9). The gross behavior of these two subjects was revealed by this technique to be remarkably different. The subject with the bimodal hit distribution (and hence the long-hit strategy) followed a roughly circular course which therefore tended to cut the corners of the triangular track and also to swing out at the center of each side (Figure 12-8). The subject with the short-hit strategy followed a triangular course closely related to the track (Figure 12-9). Another difference between the two subjects lay in the relation between the tracking stylus and the position of the target. The subject following the circular course matched the radial velocity of the target very well. Thus he was always radially in line with the target even though he was not always on the track. The subject following the triangular course, although nearly always on the track, was often in front of or behind the target. He showed a strong tendency to be behind the target immediately after rounding a corner and then to catch up with it rapidly to the extent of overshooting, especially since in terms of linear velocity the target was slowing down at this stage.

These two types of performance relate to the cluster of measures that had been found to define the long- and short-hit strategies. The subject following a circular course and matching the radial velocity of

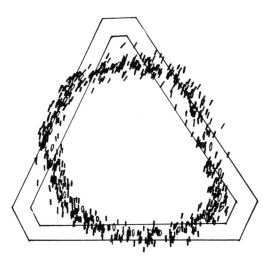

Figure 12-8. Positions of stylus in relation to track for a subject with a "long-hit" strategy. Taken with permission from Frith (1971).

the target must produce a strong rhythmic component in his performance relating to one revolution of the target. His cutting of the corners of the triangle will produce misses at regular intervals. The subject following a triangular course will not produce so rhythmic a performance. The subject following a roughly circular course will also produce a bimodal distribution of hit lengths. With such a path he will not only cut the corners of the triangle, but also will sometimes swing too far out

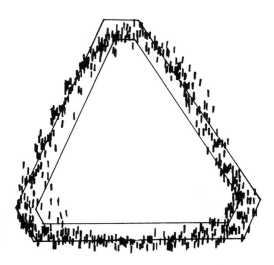

Figure 12-9. Positions of stylus in relation to track for a subject with a "short-hit" strategy. Taken with permission from Frith (1971).

from the center of the sides. When this happens he will gain two hits with length approximately under half a side. When he does not swing too far out he produces one hit of approximately double the length. Hits of intermediate length will be less frequent. This pattern of performance corresponds very well to the actual distribution of hit lengths shown in Figure 12-7.

It is clear from this analysis that the different strategies of performance (long hit and short hit) found for extraverts and introverts has nothing to do with the greater or lesser production of rest pauses. The long-hit strategy involves matching the radial velocity of the target at the expense of its exact position. The short-hit strategy involves attention to the exact position of the target. This involves trying to match the changing linear speed of the target (in the triangular track) and prevents making use of the much easier constant radial velocity. Thus it seems the major dimension of strategy in pursuit-rotor performance varies from an exclusive attention to the position of the target to an exclusive attention to the radial velocity of the target. At the same time the two strategies involve a high and a low rate, respectively, of detecting and correcting errors. In the next section we shall try to show why a low rate of detecting and correcting errors is associated with attention to the radial velocity rather than the precise position of the target.

WHAT HAPPENS IN BETWEEN RESPONSES?

We have presented reasons for believing that pursuit tracking consists of a discrete series of detections and corrections of miss-matches between stylus and target. There remains the question of what happens in between these responses. We know that the subject continues to move his tracking stylus, but what determines the course of this movement? The simplest option open to the subject is to continue moving his tracking stylus in the same direction and at the same speed until he makes the next error correction. If the target changes its direction of movement fairly slowly and infrequently and if the responses are made fairly rapidly in relation to the movements of the target then performance of this kind would be reasonably successful. For example, a circle can be well represented by a regular polygon with a sufficient number of sides. Such performance is entirely determined by the relationship between stylus and target each time the subject makes his detection and correction response. He does not need to know the shape of the track or to predict the future position of the target. In engineering terms we would describe this type of performance by saying that the relation between stylus and target produced by the system man/pursuit rotor was "fed back" into the system and used to modify the system's future behavior. Thus we can characterize this kind of performance as being controlled by feedback. This feedback is visual, being the relationship between stylus and target seen by the subject. The subject who adopted the short-hit strategy on the triangular track may well have been controlling his performance by feedback in this way. Thus he made frequent responses, followed the track of the target well, but failed to cope with the constantly changing speed of the target.

Models of tracking performance based on feedback of this kind have been widely studied (Noble *et al.*, 1955; Poulton, 1967), but almost all have been concerned with situations where the movement of the target was completely unpredictable. In this case feedback is all the subject can use to guide his performance. However, it is characteristic of rotary-tracking tasks that the future position of the target is very easily predicted. This knowledge about the movement of the target can be used to determine movements of the stylus in between responses.

Instead of moving his stylus to the current position of the target the subject can, from his knowledge of the target's future movements, move his stylus to the position the target will be in when he makes his next response. He could move by the most direct route as with feedback control, but with his knowledge of future target movements he can do even better than this. He can initiate movement sequences which will correctly track the target. In the hypothetical ideal case once he had initiated these movement sequences he would not need to look at the relation between stylus and target again. Evidence that people can make accurate movements in the absence of feedback has been noted in a number of situations (Craik, 1948; Vince, 1948; Beggs & Howarth, 1972). These sequences of movements which are controlled by previously acquired knowledge and not by immediate feedback have been called "motor programs" (Keele & Posner, 1968; Conolly, 1970). It is clear that by making use of these motor programs the subject can make detection and correction responses at a slower rate. The subject with the long-hit strategy who followed a circular course around the triangular track must have been making use of a motor program. He had learned that the target moved around the track with a constant radial velocity. He then used this knowledge to anticipate the future position of the target. It was such anticipations that enabled him to cut the corners of the triangle.

We conclude, therefore, that pursuit tracking involves two components. The first is a "response" by which the relation between stylus and target is observed and the appropriate corrective movement is made. This is control by feedback. The second involves sequences of movement which anticipate those of the target and which, having been initiated, are continued without visual feedback. This is control by motor programs. To be effective feedback control requires a high rate of responding, but does not require much knowledge about the movements of the target. Control by motor programs requires the subject to make detection and correction responses as well, but the more effective his programs become the less frequently he needs to make these responses. The development of a motor program requires the subject first to gain knowledge about (construct an internal model of) the movements of the target and then to translate this knowledge into sequences of corresponding hand movements. The major dimension of individual difference in this system relates to whether subjects depend more on control by feedback (with the associated high rate of responding) or on control by motor programs (with the associated low rate of responding).

Having proposed this new and rather specific mechanism for pursuit tracking, we must consider how it relates to the results and theories discussed in previous chapters. Immediately after a rest subjects produce a very large number of short hits and then change from this short-hit strategy to a long-hit strategy. We would now interpret this as a shift from control by feedback to control by motor programs. At the very beginning of practice the subject has no suitable motor programs available and must therefore rely on feedback control. Similarly immediately after an interpolated rest performance must depend on feedback control since it is of no value to initiate the preprogrammed sequence of movements until the stylus is already tracking the target with reasonable success. This change in the form of control probably underlies the period of post-rest upswing. During the period of post-rest downswing there is a decrease in the rate of responding, but little increase in the efficacy of the motor programs. Our main concern, however, is to relate this new model of performance to the phenomenon of reminiscence.

WHAT IS LEARNED IN A PURSUIT-TRACKING TASK?

We have stated that the production of motor programs depends on gaining knowledge about the movements of the target and translating this into appropriate motor movements. This then is the most obvious feature of a tracking task that has to be learned. However, there is another, less obvious feature. A subject may have to learn what are the appropriate movements to correct the errors that he detects in the feedback mode. This kind of learning is particularly important in mirror drawing tasks where the relation between vision and movement had been deliberately disrupted. It would be easy to discover how large a role this kind of learning played in pursuit tracking tasks by investigating how much performance with unpredictable target movements improved over time. There would probably be very little improvement. If this is the case, reminiscence must be due to an improved efficacy of the motor programs after a rest. Such improvement will depend not only on the subject constructing some kind of internal model of the movements of the target, but also on translating this model into appropriate sequences of motor movements.

Frith (1973) studied learning and reminiscence in a considerably modified pursuit-tracking task in an attempt to elucidate some of these problems. It was hypothesized that the successful use of motor programs would enable the subject to reproduce in his movements any rhythms present in the movement of the target. It was therefore important to be able to measure the subject's hand movements continuously and independently of the movement of the target. Since movement in two dimensions presents formidable problems of data analysis and storage a one-dimensional analog of the standard pursuit rotor was used. In this task a target moves backward and forward along a straight line. The target was displayed on the scope of a LINC-8 computer. The subject controlled the position of a cross on the screen by moving a stick from side to side. His task was to keep the cross inside the square defining the target. The movements of the subject could be recorded continuously and related to those of the target. To be directly analogous to the circular track of the standard pursuit rotor the movement of the target over time would be a single sinusoid. (This means that the target moves backward and forward along its straight line path regularly, but changes direction gradually and smoothly rather than abruptly.) However, in this experiment the track was more complex. This was achieved by producing target movements that were derived from three independent sine waves. By performing a frequency analysis on the successive positions taken by the subject it was possible to discover to what extent each of these sine waves (and perhaps others) was reproduced in his performance. Several tracks were constructed from various combinations of sine waves. The major variation in the tracks that concerns us here was speed. Some tracks were composed of three low-frequency sine waves (e.g., 0.5, 1.0, and 1.5 c/sec) while others were composed of three high-frequency sine waves (e.g., 0.6, 1.25, and 1.9 c/sec). In addition to the measure of the extent to which each component of the track was reproduced in the subjects' perfor-

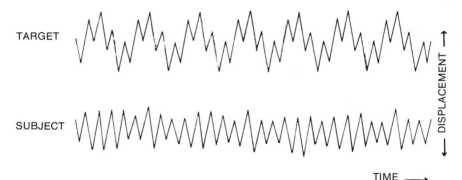

Figure 12-10. Subject tracking a target whose displacements are derived from the sum of two sinusoids. The subject is seen to reproduce only the faster of these two components.

mance the traditional measures of time-on-target and average hit length were taken. Subjects worked at the task for two 5-min periods separated by 5-min rest. Their learning of this task followed a similar course to learning of the traditional pursuit rotor. In particular there was little increase in success during the 5-min work periods, but a marked increase immediately after the 5-min rest. This was true of all the measures of performance. However, there were striking differences in the extent to which the different components of the tracks were reproduced. The faster tracks were clearly more difficult than the slow ones and, corresponding to this result, the fast component of a fast track was less well reproduced than the fast component of a slow track. Within a track however, the situation was reversed. Thus the fastest component of a track was better reproduced than the slowest component of the same track. Furthermore the greatest reminiscence effect was shown in the fastest component of each track.

This tendency to concentrate on reproducing the fastest component of each track is illustrated in Figure 12-10 (taken from a pilot study). In this case the track consisted of two sine waves, one double the frequency of the other. The subject is clearly shown to be reproducing only the faster of these two components.

We have already stated that prediction of target movement and control by motor programs is essential for tracking targets that are moving fairly rapidly. With the limitations produced by refractory periods, reaction times and so on, targets that are rapidly changing direction cannot be tracked using feedback. Thus the finding that fast components within a track were reproduced better than slow components suggests that control by motor programs was used more by the subjects than control by feedback. Furthermore the fast components showed the most reminiscence and hence the most rapid learning. This is clearly an optimum strategy since good reproduction of the fast components depends most on predicting the future position of the target. We would suggest therefore that reminiscence in pursuit-rotor learning reflects an increased efficiency of the motor programs used by the subject to control his hand movements. One is obviously tempted to suggest that rest is essential for the laying down or consolidation of these motor programs.

A SUMMARY OF THIS NEW MODEL OF PURSUIT TRACKING AND ITS IMPLICATIONS

When tracking a target a man must observe whether his stylus is in contact with the target and make the necessary corrective movements. Because of limitations to the system such as finite reaction times and refractory periods, the man will make these detections and correction responses intermittently. In between these observing responses the man controls his movements by predetermined sequences of muscle contractions (motor programs).

It follows from this analysis that there are three major determinants of level of tracking performance. The first major determinant of performance is the rate at which the man detects and corrects errors. Clearly the more frequently he makes such responses the better his performance will be. In this respect the tracking task is very similar to a vigilance task in which a man also has to detect signals and take appropriate action. The major difference is that in most vigilance tasks the signals are very infrequent, whereas in tracking tasks errors occur very frequently. Nevertheless if the responses in tracking are in any way analogous to those made in a vigilance task we would expect these responses to produce a build-up in some kind of inhibition. This would produce a gradual decrease in the rate of responding during a period of continuous practice. Presumably there would also be recovery from this type of inhibition during rest. Thus some of the changes in performance that occur during practice on the pursuit rotor might be the manifestation of an inhibition process just like that found in a task involving no learning such as tapping.

Such a process will give rise to a gradual decrease in rate of responding (post-rest downswing) during continuous practice until some equilibrium point is reached. At this equilibrium point all the inhibition built up by the response must dissipate between responses since there is no longer any reserve of energy from which to draw. After a rest the inhibition has partially dissipated, but will build-up more rapidly after a short rest giving rise to faster post-rest downswing.

If the man has to pay attention to some other signal as might be provided by a secondary, distracting task then the rate at which he makes corrective responses on the pursuit rotor will be decreased and his level of performance will decrease correspondingly. This result has been shown by Eysenck and Thompson (1966). In this experiment five groups of subjects first practiced the pursuit rotor for two minutes and then had a ten minute rest. They then practiced for 4 min 30 sec with distraction. This distraction consisted of having to press either a right or left foot pedal in response to one of two distinctive signals, a high- or low-pitched tone. The difficulty of the distracting task was determined by the rate at which the signals were presented. In the easy distraction condition the subject responded to 20 tones/min (B); the medium distraction condition required a response to 47 tones/min (C); the difficult distraction condition required a response to 72 tones/min (D). Control group A had no distraction and control group E ignored the tones, but pressed the foot pedals once a second. Figure 12-11 shows that distraction has a large effect on performance and that the depression of performance produced by the distracting tasks is a direct function of the number of signals per minute. Figure 12-11 also shows that this effect of distraction was less towards the end of the period of continuous practice. This would be expected since those subjects who made their correction responses less frequently because of a high degree of distraction would have built up inhibition more slowly.

Eysenck and Thompson also found that the distraction had no effect on the learning of the skill as shown by later, undistracted performance (experimental period II in Figure 12-11). This suggests that the learning (as opposed to the performance) of the pursuit rotor has little to do with the detection and correction of responses.

In the chapter on warm-up we discussed experiments by Rosenquist (1965) and Adams (1955) in which subjects had to watch someone else's pursuit-rotor performance and press a button while the performer was on target. In terms of the analysis of pursuit-rotor performance proposed in this chapter such a task is essentially the response component of the pursuit-rotor task performed in isolation. If repeated production of these detection responses produces a build-up in inhibition and a resulting reduction in the rate of such responding then we would expect a reduction in the level of pursuit-rotor performance carried out immediately after such a task. This is precisely what Adams and Rosenquist found as can be seen in Figure 7-9.

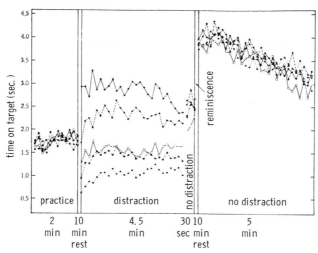

Figure 12-11. Pursuit-rotor scores for three practice periods with distraction during the second period. ●————————●, no distraction; ●——————●, easy distraction; ●—·—·—·—●, medium distraction; ● · · · · ●, difficult distraction; ○————————○, control group with distraction. Taken with permission from Eysenck and Thompson (1966).

The second major determinant of performance on the pursuit rotor is the ability the man has to make the appropriate corrective movement having detected an error in his performance. In the normal pursuit rotor the relationship between the perceived error and the appropriate corrective movement is a very direct one. It corresponds very closely to the kinds of movement we are accustomed to make all the time as, for example, when we reach out for something. With such an action also we move our hand to make contact with a target. Thus in the pursuit rotor we would expect this ability to be well learned from previous experience and thus to change little during practice on the task. However, there are closely related tasks for which this relation between errors and movements would not be so direct. The most extreme example is mirror drawing in which the relation between the visually perceived errors and the necessary corrective movements is reversed. Improved performance on this task will depend almost entirely on the learning the new relationship between the errors he sees and the movements he makes. Any task in which hand movements are not directly related to the movements of the device tracking the target will also involve learning of this type. For example the man may control the position of a pointer by rotating a wheel. In such circumstances the man must first learn the "gain" of the system before he can successfully track a target. That is he must learn the angle through which the wheel must be turned to produce movement of the pointer through a certain distance. It is our contention that this kind of learning plays a minimal role in performance of the standard pursuit-rotor task. In the argument that follows we shall demonstrate that this contention should be fairly easy to prove empirically.

The third major determinant of performance on the pursuit rotor is the man's ability to produce predetermined sequences of muscle contractions that result in the successful following of the target. To produce such predetermined sequences the movement of the target must be predictable, at least in the short term. Thus the man must first learn to predict the movement of the target and then convert this knowledge into appropriate hand movements. With learning these sequences should become longer and more accurate. The experiment by Frith (1973) already discussed demonstrated that with targets moving in a simple repetitive manner, as in the pursuit rotor, it is learning of this type that is principally responsible for the phenomenon of reminiscence. We would suggest that a rest is necessary for knowledge about the movements of the target to be converted into the appropriate and automatic sequences of movement.

Clearly the man cannot learn predetermined movement sequences if the movement of the target is irregular and unpredictable. Performance on such tracking tasks will be controlled by feedback and will depend on the rate at which the man makes detection and correction responses and on the success with which he can make corrective movements. If our contention is correct and no learning is required to make correction movements when the relation between hand and pointer movement is fairly direct, then no learning will occur when the target moves unpredictably and any changes in performance level will reflect only the build up and dissipation of inhibition. This suggests another way in which the various factors involved in pursuit tracking can be studied in isolation.

Optimum combination of these determinants of pursuit-tracking performance will depend on various properties of the task and the man performing the task. The advantage gained by a high rate of error checking responses is offset by the resultant rapid build up of inhibition. If the man has learned to produce long and accurate preprogrammed motor sequences then he can afford to make his checking responses less frequently. Inhibition, therefore, should build up more slowly in the later stages of practice. If the man, being perhaps an extravert, is particularly prone to the build up of inhibition then his optimum checking rate may be relatively slower than that of other people. To make up for this he may concentrate on predicting the movement of the target and thus building up automatic movement sequences. If this is the aspect of the task that produces learning and reminiscence then such a man will show greater reminiscence than others.

We have already pointed out that if the target moves in a random manner the man can only use feedback to control his tracking performance. If the target moves fairly slowly feedback alone will also be adequate for controlling performance. Thus people who favor control by feedback and can keep up a high rate of checking responses should perform relatively better than others when tracking targets that move slowly and irregularly.

STRATEGIES OF PERFORMANCE

From these considerations of how a man can track a target we would conclude that there should be a major dimension of performance style, or strategy that varies from control by feedback at one extreme to control by prediction and motor programs at the other. The precise strategy that the man adopts will depend on the nature of the task he is performing, the time he has spent performing the task and his degree of skill and also on his personality. It is encouraging that this conclusion agrees closely with Fleischman's factor analytic studies that were discussed in Chapter 2. The major factor that emerged in these studies distinguished between the strategy of "hunting" and the strategy of making smooth, ballistic movements. These strategies clearly correspond to control by feedback and control by motor programs. In Fleischman's studies this factor distinguished between different kinds of task and between different stages of practice within tasks.

Another study in which this dimension of strategy seems to emerge is that by Davis (1948) on stress in Pilots. Davis found that under stressful conditions in a simulated cockpit different personality groups broke down in different ways. Dysthmics (neurotic introverts) over-corrected errors whereas hysterics (neurotic extraverts) undercorrected errors. This is what we would expect if these personality groups used strategies at each extreme of the dimension we have been discussing. Excessive dependence on feedback and error correction would result in the over-correction of errors whereas excessive dependence on prediction and automatic control would result in a lack of attention to errors and hence under-correction.

SOME PHYSIOLOGICAL SPECULATIONS

The speculation in this chapter about the mechanisms by which a subject tracks a target are at an entirely different level from hypotheses about the physiological mechanisms underlying voluntary movements. By this we mean that proof or disproof of the behavioral theories would have little effect on the status of the physiological theories and vice versa. Nevertheless theories from different areas of discourse can be mutually inspiring. Recently a very detailed theory about the physiological mechanisms underlying voluntary movements has been put forward (Marr, 1969; Blomfield & Marr, 1970) which appears to have many parallels with the theory of tracking described above. Marr has considered the detailed anatomical and physiological construction of the cerebellum and proposed mechanisms by which this structure could learn and control voluntary and postural movements. The precise anatomical details of this theory need not concern us here. It is assumed that there is a dictionary of "elemental movements" (each corresponding to an olivary cell) which can represent every possible action. The "elemental movement" might take many forms; it might be a limb movement, or a fine digit movement. In the initial stages of performance the appropriate sequence of elemental movements is controlled by the cerebrum. This causes the cerebellum to learn the contexts within which these elemental movements are required. Thus the next time such a context occurs the relevant elemental movement is automatically evoked. "The cerebellum could learn to carry out any previously rehearsed action which the cerebrum chose to initiate, for as the action progressed, the context for the next part of it would form, would be recognized by the appropriate Purkinje cells, and these would turn on the next set of muscles, allowing further development of the action. In this way, each muscle would be turned on and off at the correct moment, and the action would be automatically performed."

These sequences of elemental movements controlled by the cerebellum are closely analogous to the motor programs hypothesized in the behavioral theory. Furthermore these automatic sequences have to be learned with control initially being exerted by another mechanism.

Marr also suggests, "If the contexts change slowly, a context driven system will not reproduce the timing of the stages in a movement at all accurately, and so cerebellar learning will be rather bad." This seems to correspond to the notion in the behavioral theory that fast movements will tend to be controlled by motor programs while slow movements are controlled by feedback. Marr also suggests that the cerebellar mechanisms are such that movements learned at one speed could relatively easily be performed at another. As we have seen, in the chapter on transfer and interpolated activity, pursuit-rotor learning at one speed readily transfers to performance at another.

The most interesting aspect of Marr's theory concerns how learning takes place. The cerebellum is supposed to recognize contexts with modifiable feature detectors called codons. Learning consists of the modification of these codons. In his more general theory of learning Marr (1970) suggests that when these codon cells are modified ordinary sensory information must be rigorously excluded. "The only time when this exclusion condition is satisfied is during certain phases of sleep." It is very tempting to relate this notion to the theory of consolidation in motor learning, which states that a "rest" is required before the learning of a motor skill can be manifested in performance. In this case the "rest" is a period in which no closely related activity takes place, rather than sleep. However, we are concerned with cerebellar learning which may require more circumscribed rests than the learning in the cerebral neocortex that Marr was particularly discussing.

Marr's theory suggests two areas in which further investigation of the learning of motor skills would be particularly fruitful. The first would involve the classification of tasks in terms of the sequence of elemental movements which they involve. Such study would be closely related to transfer and interference with learning and with consolidation. The second would involve the study of motor skill learning in people with known defects of the cerebellum. Frith and Frith (1974) studied pursuit-rotor learning in children suffering from Down's syndrome (mongolism). People suffering from this condition are known to have cerebellae which are relatively smaller than the rest of their brain (Crome *et al.*, 1966) and it was therefore hypothesized that they would be particularly inpaired in the learning and performance of motor skills. It was found that mongol children matched with normal and autistic children on initial pursuit-rotor performance failed to show an improvement after a five-minute rest whereas the other children showed a marked improvement. In addition the same mongol children produced very slow sequences of taps in a simple tapping task in comparison to the other children. Both these deficits would be consistent with a difficulty specific to mongolism in the development of automatic motor sequences. Other explanations would be equally plausible (e.g., low arousal), but further investigation of this syndrome might well throw more light on the mechanisms underlying the phenomenon of reminiscence.

CHAPTER 13

The Rise and Fall of Reminiscence: An Explanation Is Proposed and Some Morals Are Drawn

In writing this book we have not been concerned merely to give an account of all the investigations that have been made into reminiscence in motor skill learning. Certainly the phenomenon is interesting in its own right and worthy of such treatment. However, perhaps of more interest still is the fact that the history of research into reminiscence presents in miniature a history of experimental psychology. It is our hope therefore that from a study of the successes and failures of research into pursuit-motor learning we may learn some lessons applicable to experimental psychology as a whole.

It will have become obvious to the diligent reader of this book that there was a tremendous upsurge of interest in pursuit-rotor reminiscence during the middle years of this century resulting in the appearance of large numbers of research reports. However, by the mid sixties the flow of such studies had reduced to the merest trickle and interest in the subject of reminiscence had faded and died. Those readers less favorably disposed to the pursuit rotor may feel no surprise at the decline of interest in this task, but rather wonder how it ever came to be so popular.

There are a number of reasons for the attractiveness of studies of pursuit-rotor learning. The apparatus is simple and the learning of the task slow and steady. More important still, the various phenomena associated with pursuit-rotor learning are observed with great reliability. The effects of varying rest length, varying pre-rest practice and shifting from massed to spaced practice may all be repeatedly and reliably observed and, as shown in Figures 7-10 and 7-11, may be closely approximated by simple mathematical abstractions. Furthermore in this task better than in any other we may reliably observe the phenomenon of reminiscence, that paradoxical event that appears to demonstrate the occurrence of learning without practice. Why then did interest in this task show such a catastrophic decline?

The rise and fall in interest in reminiscence closely parallels the rise and fall in the influence of Hullian learning theory which was used to explain reminiscence. It is natural that the influence of theories should decline as newer and better rival theories are evolved. However, one would not expect an attendant decline of interest in a phenomenon unless that phenomenon had been satisfactorily explained. This was certainly not the case with pursuit-rotor reminiscence.

Our remarks above imply a rather naive view of a world in which phenomena exist inviolate and wait to be studied. In reality our view of a phenomenon is always distorted by the glass of theory. Indeed the glass may sometimes become opaque so that we do not see the phenomenon at all. For one theory a phenomenon may be of vital importance, for another it may be of no interest.

Hull's theory assumed that learning, or habit strength, was steadily incremented as a result of practice. It was thus crucial to that theory to demonstrate that reminiscence was not a manifestation of learning without practice, but a manifestation of something other than learning. It was therefore suggested that reminiscence was the result of a dissipation of reactive inhibition (Kimble, 1949). Hull's theory also assumed that the mechanisms underlying learning were essentially the same in all tasks. Therefore instead of investigating learning in many different tasks attention can be restricted to the few most convenient for study. One of these few was, of course, the pursuit rotor. (The same argument holds when we consider the choice of organism for study. Since the mechanisms of learning are assumed common to all species we may restrict our studies to the most convenient: rats, pigeons, and psychology students.) This generality of Hullian learning theory also applies to the different phenomena associated with a single task. "Inhibition" theory attempts to explain not only reminiscence, but also upswing, downswing, and the difference between massed and spaced practice. Hence all these effects may be studied in the one task. Only if the various effects were thought to reflect different mechanisms would we wish to study them in isolation and therefore analyze the task into simpler components. Finally the generality of Hullian learning theory assumes that all people learn in the same way and so individual differences are ignored. It was the study of just such individual differences, in particular motivation and introversion–extraversion, which was more than anything responsible for showing up the inadequacies of learning theory's account of reminiscence.

Thus it is clear that whereas a general theory, of which Hull's is an extreme example, would encourage the intensive study of one task such as pursuit-rotor learning, a more specific theory would encourage the study of many different tasks and also the analysis of these tasks into discrete components. Perhaps, then, it was the abandonment of a general theory in favor of a number of more specific hypotheses which lead to the decline of interest in pursuit-rotor reminiscence.

This change is illustrated in Tables 13-1, 13-2, and 13-3. These tables present brief summaries of research relating to reminiscence in three kinds of task: tapping, verbal learning, and pursuit-rotor learning. For each task we have listed which of a number of phenomena, such as reminiscence, learning and upswing, occur. We have then listed a number of theories and indicated whether they account for the various phenomena, and, if so, how.

In these tables we have labeled the explanation of reminiscence and related phenomena derived from Hull's learning theory "Inhibition theory" since the major components of the explanation are reactive indibition (I_R) and conditioned indibition $(_sI_R)$. In terms of this theory the same basic explanation is applied to all three kinds of task. The next two explanations, in terms of set and consolidation, are somewhat more specific. They are indeed complementary, for consolidation deals with a permanent facilitation of performance while set deals with a temporary facilitation of performance. Furthermore the exact details of these mechanisms are slightly different in the different tasks. Consolidation has no role in tapping since no learning is involved in this simple task. Regaining set in the tapping task involves a literal "warming up" of the muscles involved. Thus many different muscular tasks would induce the appropriate set. Set in verbal learning can also be induced by other tasks such as color naming, but clearly does not involve any muscular components. Set for pursuit-rotor performance seems to be extremely specific and no other task has yet been found that will successfully instate it. Consolidation too, although applied to both verbal learning and pursuit rotor learning operates in a slightly different way in the two tasks.

TABLE 13-1. Tapping

Phenomenon	Observation	Expectation		
		Inhibition	Consolidation	Set/muscular effects
Reminiscence	Yes (Grassi, 1968)	Yes, dissipation of I_R	—	Yes, dissipation of fatigue
Learning	No	—	Nothing to consolidate	—
Initial upswing	No	Yes, extinction of $_sI_R$ (Eysenck, 1956b)	—	No, warm-up of muscles to slow
Interserial warm-up	Yes (Wells, 1908)	No	—	Yes, warm-up of muscles (Eysenck, 1969)
Rest pauses	Yes (Spielman, 1963)	Yes, excess I_R	—	Yes, excess fatigue/insufficient force (Frith, 1973b)
Downswing	Yes (Grassi, 1968)	Yes, increasing	—	Yes, increasing fatigue
Cessation of downswing	?	Yes, equilibrium state	—	Yes, equilibrium state
Individual differences	Yes, more IRPs for low drive/extraversion (Eysenck, 1964c)	Yes, low drive/ extraversion greater proneness to I_R (Eysenck, 1964c)	—	Yes, oscillations about minimum necessary force (Frith, 1973b)

TABLE 13-2. Verbal Learning

Phenomenon	Observation	Expectation		
		Inhibition	Consolidation/set	Organization of memory
Reminiscence	?, dependent on arousal and type of material	Yes, dissipation of I_R	Yes, dependent on arousal, time needed to consolidate	Yes, for semantically organized LTM (Chapter 11)
Learning	Yes		Yes, consolidation	Storage, organization and retrieval
Initial upswing	Unobservable	Yes, extinction of $_sI_R$	Yes, regaining of set. Set reinstating tasks found (Irion & Wham, 1951)	?, acquiring organizing and retrieval strategies
Interserial warm-up	Yes (Thune, 1951)	—	Yes, acquiring set. Set reinstating tasks found (Thune, 1950)	?, acquiring organizing and retrieval strategies
Rest pauses	Unobservable	Yes, excess I_R	—	—
Downswing	Unobservable	Yes, buildup of I_R	—	—
Individual differences	Yes, arousal/extraversion in interaction with rest length and material (Howarth & Eysenck, 1968; Schwartz, 1974)	Yes, variation in proneness to I_R	Yes, arousal effects consolidation (Kleinsmith & Kaplan, 1963) different rates of set acquisition?	Yes, different strategies adopted relating to arousal and material (Schwartz, 1974)

TABLE 13-3. Pursuit-Rotor Learning

Phenomenon	Observation	Expectations		
		Inhibition	Consolidation/set	Strategies/engineering approach
Reminiscence	Yes	Yes, dissipation of I_R (Kimble, 1948)	Yes, Material consolidates during rest (Chapter 11)	Yes, laying down of motor programs (Chapter 12)
Learning	Yes	—	Yes	Yes, learning to predict and to make corrective movements (Chapter 12)
Initial upswing	Yes	Yes, extinction of $_sI_R$ (Eysenck, 1956b)	Yes, regaining set. Reinstating tasks found only for simple skills (Nacson & Schmidt, 1971)	Yes, switching in and aligning motor programs (Chapter 12)
Interserial warm-up	Unobservable	?	?	?
Rest pauses	Unobservable; movement does not cease, could be attention (Ammons et al., 1958)	Yes, excess I_R	—	?, checking responses intermittent and self paced (Chapter 12)
Downswing	Yes	Yes, increasing I_R	Yes, partially consolidated material being destroyed (Chapter 11)	Yes, slowing down in rate of checking (Chapter 12)
Cessation of downswing	Yes (Farley, 1966)	? Yes, equilibrium	Yes, all partially consolidated material destroyed (Chapter 11)	Yes, rate of checking in equilibrium (Chapter 12)
Individual differences	Yes, in reminiscence for drive/extraversion post-rest	Yes, proneness to build up of I_R related to drive/extraversion pre-rest (Eysenck, 1956b)	Yes, speed of consolidation related to arousal (Walker & Tarte, 1963), but no crossover found with long rests. Schizophrenics rapidly lose set (Chapter 10)	Yes, differences in strategies adopted (Chapter 12)

Finally in each table mechanisms for reminiscence and associated phenomena are described which are entirely specific to the tasks involved. These explanations tend to be the most recent and also the most successful. They also assume that the tasks consist of various independent components that could be studied in isolation. Thus rate of tapping is determined by a fatigue process, whereas rest pauses reflect a strategy for discovering the minimum force that needs to be applied. In verbal learning a distinction is made between the organization of material in short-term and long-term memory. In pursuit-rotor performance a distinction is made between learning to make correcting movements to match stylus and target and learning to predict the movement of the target. Clearly, if one wished to test such a theory, one would not use the standard pursuit rotor apparatus, but tasks in which the hypothetical components could be studied in isolation. Furthermore since the mechanisms underlying reminiscence seem to be different for each task, then, to "explain" reminiscence it would not be sufficient to study just one task. On these grounds we would expect a decline, not only in studies of pursuit-rotor learning, but also in explicit studies of reminiscence, since this now appears to be a blanket term applied to a number of basically different effects. Instead these specific effects should be studied.

It is obviously of great interest to speculate whether the large amount of work that went into the study of pursuit-rotor learning and the inhibiton theory of reminiscence was a waste of effort that could have been avoided, or whether it was a necessary stage in the evolution of the subject. We shall return to this problem later on in this chapter. Before that however, we shall consider in detail the merits and failings of the various theories that have been put forward to explain reminiscence in various tasks.

REMINISCENCE IN TAPPING

The principal phenomena to be explained in tapping performance are reminiscence (or rather recovery), downswing, interserial warm-up, and rest pauses. Since no learning is involved in this simple task one might expect that "inhibition" theory would explain these phenomena with reasonable success. Downswing would be expected from the gradual build up of reactive inhibition generated by each tap. When I_R eventually reached the level of drive (D) then an involuntary rest pause should occur. Tapping is indeed one of the few tasks in which such IRPs have been successfully identified (Spielman, 1963). However, the story according to inhibition theory does not finish here. The drive reduction resulting from the IRPs is rewarding and so a habit of producing IRPs develops called conditioned inhibition ($_sI_R$). This should result in permanent work decrement and in initial upswing when this negative habit extinguishes after the rest. In practice there is no evidence either for a permanent work decrement in tapping nor for an initial upswing in tapping performance immediately after a rest. The interserial warm-up that is observed in tapping tasks clearly cannot be identified as a manifestation of the extinction of conditioned inhibition. The existence of conditioned inhibition should depress performance below the level of the initial pre-rest performance, even though the rest has been long enough for all inhibition to dissipate. The extinction of this conditioned inhibition should allow performance to return to this initial prerest level. After interserial warm-up has occurred post rest practice is consistently higher than pre-rest practice and there is decreased decline in performance with continuing work. Such a general improvement in performance cannot be a result of inhibition whether conditioned or otherwise. On the other hand the improvement in performance labeled interserial warm-up cannot be a learning effect since it is temporary and dissipates after an hour or so without practice. Although it has not been directly tested with the tapping task, the most likely explanation of interserial warm up seems to be that it is a result of a literal warming up which results from the tapping movements themselves, allows a greater ease and efficiency of movement, and hence a greater resistance to the build-up of fatigue. However, it will dissipate after some time without further practice. Clearly it would be possible to warm up the muscles in other ways before commencing the tapping task and this should eliminate interserial warm-up.

If interserial warm-up is explained in this way then the source of the inhibition and hence the downswing in performance may be muscular also. This hypothesis has also not been tested for the tapping task directly, but has been shown to be true for the repeated voluntary flexion of a single muscle (Merton, 1954).

The mechanism by which I_R was supposed to produce IRPs could also apply to muscular fatigue. However, the build-up and dissipation of muscular fatigue is probably too slow to account for IRPs since they occur quite early on in a tapping task and are extremely short. (If a subject were tapping at the rate of 5 taps per sec average length of rest pauses would be 200 msec.) Frith (1973) observed that rest pauses were almost exactly double the normal intertap interval and appeared to occur when a subject attempted a tap with insufficient force for it to be recorded. He suggested that subjects attempt to perform the tapping task with minimal effort. Although there will be some fairly constant minimum force required to make contact with the morse key or whatever is being tapped, the effort to be made by the subject will vary with his physical state, level of muscular fatigue, etc. The only way he can discover the level of minimum effort is by "testing" the limits, i.e., emitting a series of progressively weaker taps until one falls below the minimum level. This will result in a rest pause. Alternatively the taps emitted by a subject may vary randomly about some mean level. The nearer this mean level is to the minimum level the more likely the subject is to produce a rest pause. The increase in effort needed as fatigue increases will increase the probability of a rest pause occurring. This mechanism would also provide an alternative explanation of the observation that extraverts and subjects with poor motivation tend to produce many rest pauses. Such subjects would be expected to be less cautious and therefore to set their mean tapping effort closer to the minimum required than would subjects motivated to do well. This is a very different explanation from that of Eysenck (1956) who proposed that extraverts and those suffering from low motivation were more prone to the build up of inhibition.

REMINISCENCE IN VERBAL LEARNING

For the experimental psychologist verbal learning tends to mean learning lists of nouns or nonsense syllables or pairs of nouns or nonsense syllables. In early experiments on the learning of this type of material "learning theory" had reasonable success in explaining the results. However, this success was related to that aspect of learning theory that assumes that learning consists of the gradual strengthening of associative bonds between a stimulus and a response. In our study of reminiscence this aspect of learning theory has been relatively unimportant. Instead we have concentrated on the hypothetical inhibition processes. There is no reason why such processes should not occur in verbal learning just as in motor skill learning. However application of this aspect of learning theory to verbal learning has been much less successful. (The inhibition processes we are discussing here are quite different from proactive and retroactive inhibition which have been successfully applied to verbal learning, but which might be better labeled "interference" rather than "inhibition" processes.) One reason for this lack of success lies in the nature of the verbal learning tasks, for they do not provide a continuous measure of performance. In general the measure of performance is derived from the complete list of words or pairs which takes several minutes to present. It is therefore impossible to observe rapid changes in performance. Such unobservable changes would include initial upswing, rest pauses, and downswing. It should be possible however to observe learning, reminiscence, and interserial warm-up. Learning and interserial warm-up certainly occur, but the latter is difficult to explain in terms of inhibition processes. Furthermore reminiscence in verbal learning is notorious for being found in some studies and not in others. It seems then that inhibition theory receives little support from studies of verbal learning.

The picture is very different for set theory, which has achieved its most notable successes in this field. Although initial upswing cannot be observed directly, its presence can be inferred from an overall lowering of performance. Set theory predicts that if some set reinstating task is carried out just before the beginning of post-rest practice then the initial depression of performance that is followed by upswing will be reduced and hence overall performance will be improved. Such set-reinstating tasks have been discovered (Irion & Wham, 1951). Set theory has also been used to explain interserial warm-up and here too appropriate set reinstating tasks have been found (Thune, 1950), other than a parallel form of the verbal learning task itself which is the standard form of the interserial warm-up paradigm. Set theory does not have the grandiose aims of inhibition and learning theories and so it makes no attempt to explain learning effects and any possible reminiscence effects.

Since Walker's (1958) theory of action decrement this deficiency has been made good by consolidation theory. This theory assumes that verbal material once learned needs to be consolidated during a rest and also that the nature of this consolidation process depends on the organism's level of arousal. At a low level of arousal the material is consolidated quickly and poorly so that it is already available for recall after a short rest, but tends to be lost as the rest length increases. At a high level of arousal the material is consolidated slowly and well so that it is not available for recall after a short rest, but becomes available and is not lost as the rest increases in length. "Arousal" in this context seems to be of a fairly general nature. It can vary with the emotional connotations of the words being learned (e.g., pond vs rape, Kleinsmith & Kaplan, 1963), it can be varied by bombarding the subjects with white noise while they are learning the words (McClean, 1969), it can be varied with drugs (Andersson, 1974), or it can vary with the personality of the subject (Howarth & Eysenck, 1968). It is clear from these results that the finding of reminiscence in a verbal learning experiment will depend on the words used, the personality of the subjects, and the length of the rest. Failure to control these variables would account for the equivocal status of reminiscence in verbal learning.

However, as we have shown in Chapter 11, although Walker's theory of action decrement correctly predicted these effects of arousal and rest length, the theoretical basis of these predictions is somewhat weak. The crucial problem is to explain why the immediate recall of material learned under conditions of high arousal is depressed. Furthermore there are certain details of the results that are not predicted by action decrement theory. For example, in a serial learning task the reminiscence effect seems to be contributed by items at the beginning of the list rather than those at the end. Just as with tapping we can go a long way towards solving these problems by considering mechanisms which are specific to the task in question. Recent work has suggested that there are two distinct mechanisms involved in the retention of verbal material which have been labelled short-term memory (STM) and long-term memory (LTM). As the names imply recall after a short rest involves STM and recall after long rest involves LTM. However, the two storage mechanisms also differ in other ways. Material is stored in STM in terms of physical characteristics such as sound (i.e., phonemes) (Conrad, 1964). There is also evidence that STM is favored by low levels of arousal (Gale et al., 1974). One might speculate that the capacity of short-term memory is related to span of attention which is thought to be narrowed with increasing arousal. Material in long-term memory, on the other hand, is stored in terms of meaning. Storage in and retrieval from this long-term store is a complex matter presumably involving some sort of filing process. It would be plausible that filing material away in LTM would take time and also that retrieval would be difficult until the filing process was complete. Such an explanation of reminiscence is clearly very specific to verbal learning and has nothing to do with the kind of inhibition processes hypothesized by Hull and little to do with the "action decrement" hypothesized by Walker.

More direct evidence that level of arousal differentially affects the two memory stores is provided by Schwartz (1974). Under high arousal semantically similar lists of words are relatively better remembered than phonemically similar lists of words (after short intervals) whereas under low arousal the reverse is the case. Interpretation of these results is difficult, but they would be consistent with the notion that in high-arousal STM was relatively impaired resulting in phonemic confusions, whereas in low-arousal LTM was impaired resulting in semantic confusions. Furthermore M. W. Eysenck (1974) has shown that arousal affects retrieval from memory independent of its effects on storage.

Even if these speculations turn out to be quite false Schwartz's results have revealed yet another variable (semantic versus phonemic confusibility of lists) which may determine whether or not reminiscence is found in verbal learning.

REMINISCENCE IN PURSUIT-ROTOR LEARNING

From our summaries of research on tapping and verbal learning it will be clear that we believe reminiscence in these tasks to be a result of mechanisms specific to these tasks. Such a conclusion denies the general applicability of Hull's theory of learning and inhibition. It is possible that the theory can nevertheless be applied to the pursuit rotor, since this is the task which has been studied most in relation to this theory. However, as we have already seen for this task too the theory breaks down and, once again due to over-generality.

In many ways inhibition theory did very well in explaining the details of pursuit-rotor performance. Reminiscence was explained by the dissipation of I_R (Kimble, 1948), initial upswing by the extinction of $_sI_R$ (Eysenck, 1956b), and downswing by increasing I_R. Even certain individual differences in reminiscence could be explained (Eysenck, 1956a) although this already involved a departure from the original generality of the theory which tended to ignore individual differences. However, although the broad outlines did indeed support inhibition theory in the details of these results, there were many problems. IRPs were clearly not associated with cessation of movement (Ammons *et al.*, 1958). It was concluded that IRPs were pauses in attention rather than movement, but such things are inherently unobservable with standard measures of pursuit-rotor performance. The explanation of upswing as the extinction of $_sI_R$ was criticized by Adams (1961) who found, contrary to the results of Eysenck, that upswing occurred under spaced practice conditions. It was found that downswing ceased after sufficiently long periods of post-rest practice (Farley, 1966). This too is difficult to explain in terms of inhibition theory unless one assumes that eventually an equilibrium state is reached in which all the additional I_R built up during practice is dissipated during the unobservable rest pauses. However, most damaging of all for inhibition theory were the details of the individual differences in reminiscence. Inhibition theory would predict that high-drive subjects should perform better than low-drive subjects during pre-rest practice, but differences are only found after rest. The greater reminiscence shown by extraverts should be due to an inferiority to introverts pre-rest, but is in fact due to a superiority post-rest (Eysenck 1956a).

As with verbal learning this inadequate inhibition theory was replaced by two slightly more specific theories which explained the various phenomena associated with pursuit-rotor learning by set and by consolidation.

Explanation of initial upswing or "warm-up" in terms of the regaining of set had been proposed early on in the study of pursuit-rotor performance. The main difficulty for this theory was that no neutral, set reinstating task could be found. Recently Schmidt and his colleagues (Schmidt & Nacson, 1971) have shown that neutral set reinstating tasks do exist for certain very simple motor skills. However, these warm-up tasks have to be very similar to the target task. As our review of transfer in Chapter 6 has shown the skill involved in pursuit-rotor learning seems to be extremely specific. To put the position in its extreme form the only appropriate warm-up task for the pursuit-rotor skill may be pursuit-rotor performance. This is obviously not a neutral task. In Chapter 10 we have seen that the pursuit-rotor performance of schizophrenic patients is consistent with the hypothesis that such people acquire set slowly and lose it rapidly. This seems to be a general feature of these patients and not specific to pursuit-rotor performance.

Having explained initial upswing in terms of the acquisition of set, the remaining pursuit-rotor phenomena (principally reminiscence and downswing) can be explained in terms of consolidation. We have given the details of this explanation in Chapter 11. There are two important features of this consolidation theory of pursuit-rotor learning which render it specific to motor skills and possibly even specific to this particular motor skill. First, we believe that reminiscence really is a manifestation of an active process during rest whereby the organism's potential for performance is improved. This is contrary to the earlier theories of inhibition and action decrement both of which suppose that the potential for performance is present before a rest begins, but cannot manifest itself because of competing processes. We hypothesize that learning about how the target moves has to be converted into appropriate and automatic sequences of hand movements. This conversion and the subsequent protection of the converted traces (which is the consolidation process) can best take place during a rest. Second, we believe that pursuit-rotor performance itself destroys partially consolidated learning (causing downswing). However, because of the extreme specificity of the pursuit-rotor skill, almost no other task performed during the rest will interfere with the partially consolidated learning. Given these two simple assumptions we can explain most of the major phenomena observed in pursuit-rotor performance. However, the gain in explanatory power is offset by a loss in generality. It is doubtful if this model applies to any tasks other than simple repetitive motor skills.

Furthermore even though consolidation theory will explain the major phenomena of pursuit-rotor performance there are still details left unexplained. In particular the observed individual differences in reminiscence do not fit in very well with this theory. What little evidence we have suggests that consolidation of learning should be better under high levels of arousal. Thus high arousal should lead to better post-rest performance. This fits in well with our observations of high-drive subjects. However, we would also predict on this basis that introverts would perform better after rest than extraverts. In fact the opposite is the case. It is possible that the enhancing effect of high arousal on consolidation can only be observed after long rests, but attempts to demonstrate such a cross-over with introverts showing more reminiscence than extraverts after long rests have only been partially successful. Also the different strategies of pursuit rotor performance observed by Frith (1973) and the changes in style of performance during post-rest upswing cannot be explained in terms of either consolidation or set theory.

The last theory of pursuit-rotor performance, discussed in Chapter 12, is the most specific of all. This theory is based on considerations of what one actually needs to do to be able to track a moving target. Two principal mechanisms would seem necessary: feedback, by which a subject detects and corrects any discrepancies between the position of the target and the position of his stylus, and motor programs, by which the subject can initiate movement sequences which anticipate the predicted movement of the target. Given these two mechanisms we can still apply some of the concepts derived from consolidation theory and inhibition theory. For example we suggest that it is the motor programs that require rest for efficient consolidation. On the other hand the detection and correction of errors involved in the feedback system must be made intermittently and hence, these corrections and detections could be the "responses" that must be identified in order to apply inhibition theory. With the build up of inhibition the rate of such responding would slow down. Such slowing down might account for downswing.

The most attractive aspect of this model of pursuit-rotor performance is that it explains certain previously inexplicable details. After a rest a subject cannot immediately switch in his motor programs since they must first be "aligned" with the movement of the target. Thus initially he will be almost entirely dependent on feedback. This switch from dependence on feedback to dependence on motor programs occurs during the period of post rest upswing and accounts for the change in style of performance observed during this period. The different strategies of performance adopted by introverts and extraverts suggest that introverts make more use of feedback and extraverts more use of motor programs. This would be consistent with their hypothesized differences in arousal. Tracking by feedback requires frequent checking and the rapid detection and correction of errors. This requires a high degree of concentration and hence would be favored by high arousal. With low levels of arousal the use of motor programs would be more appropriate since these are automatic and require less frequent checking. However, we have also supposed that it is the laying down of motor programs that underlies reminiscence and indeed improvement in pursuit-rotor performance in general. Hence those subjects who choose to rely more on motor programs, the extraverts, will show the greater reminiscence and the better post-rest performance.

We stated above that our theory of consolidation was probably specific to repetitive motor tasks. This conclusion is, however, a result of empirical observations. There is nothing in the theory itself that would prevent it from being applied to verbal learning or any other kind of learning. It is merely that observation of the learning process in these other tasks suggests that this revised consolidation theory would not apply to them. On the other hand the theory of reminiscence based on feedback and motor programs is, by its very nature, applicable only to repetitive motor skills. It would make no sense whatever to apply this theory to verbal learning.

Fifty Years of Pursuit-Rotor Studies

The perceptive reader will have noticed that after the immense amount of activity in the 1940s and 1950s the number of pursuit rotor studies per year has declined almost to zero. This decline took place in spite of the fact that many of the experimental phenomena associated with the pursuit rotor, notably reminiscence, remained largely unexplained. What was the reason for this decline? Had all those pursuit rotor studies been a time consuming and irrelevant diversion from the path that leads to a better understanding of learning? Clearly our answer to this last question must be an emphatic no. The studies of pursuit-rotor learning were vital for the further delineation of the mechanisms underlying learning.

The decline in the number of pursuit rotor studies was a direct result of advances in the understanding of the learning process. As we have shown in the previous chapter the phenomenon of reminiscence has entirely different causes in the three situations in which it has been investigated: tapping, verbal learning, and pursuit-rotor learning. Indeed the phenomenon of pursuit-rotor reminiscence is probably specific only to certain kinds of repetitive motor skills. This specificity is quite contrary to Hull's notion that learning would be essentially the same in any task. Given this view it was reasonable to limit attention to a few representative tasks of which the pursuit rotor was an ideal example. However, as a direct result of all the research that was done with this apparatus we have come to recognize that different tasks involve different learning processes. It is therefore no longer an acceptable strategy to study the pursuit rotor alone. The current requirement is for the construction of a taxonomy of motor skills (and other learning tasks) in which the pursuit rotor will represent one of many classes of task.

It has also become clear as a direct result of research into pursuit rotor learning that there are a number of independent mechanisms underlying the learning process (set, consolidation, etc.). These are now sufficiently delineated for them to be studied in isolation. For this purpose also the pursuit rotor is no longer the ideal apparatus.

However, perhaps the most exciting fact that the pursuit rotor has revealed in its long reign as the psychologists' favorite piece of apparatus is that reminiscence, learning while resting, is a real phenomenon. For repetitive motor skills at least it is clear that efficient and speedy "learning" which probably involves the building up of new connections in the nervous system can only happen while the performer is resting. In the next few years we will expect to see dramatic advances in our understanding of this learning mechanism. It will be of particular interest to discover whether it is of general importance in the nervous system, as Marr suggests, and underlies many kinds of learning. The pursuit rotor will have an extremely minor part to play in any of these future developments, but it should not be thrown on the scrap heap. In recognition of its long and honorable service it should take its place in some museum of scientific psychology alongside Kraepelin's ergograph.

On the basis of our analysis of the development of the study of reminiscence we are hopefully now in a better position to answer the two questions we posed earlier. The first question in its general form concerned the proper subject matter of psychology. This sort of question is essentially a matter of definition and therefore to some extent arbitrary, but we think most psychologists would agree that their subject matter is the behavior or possibly the mental life of the individual, the behavior of groups being the province of the sociologist. (Of course many studies lie on the border lines, but this is the basic distinction between the two disciplines.) In its specific form, i.e., was pursuit-rotor learning an appropriate subject for study, the question is more difficult to answer. Here too the answer is a matter of opinion. On the one hand considerable progress has been made towards explaining the phenomena associated with motor skill learning, new theories and techniques have been developed and interesting phenomena have been discovered. On the other hand all these results remain of purely academic interest and at present appear remote from the problems of the "real world." We, naturally, think that the study of the pursuit rotor has been worth while, believing, with Medawar (1967) that experimentation is "the art of the soluble" and therefore that it is better to investigate an "academic" problem that is probably solvable rather than a profound and important problem from "real life" that, as yet, is probably not solvable.

Our second question concerned the proper methodology for the study of psychology. This question is less a matter of arbitrary definition. Indeed we hope that our survey of research on reminiscence will lead to some answers. The first point that clearly emerged from this survey was that the early students of the pursuit rotor used experimental and statistical techniques that were applicable to the study of group behavior, but not properly applicable to the study of individual behavior. From our definition of the appropriate subject matter of psychology this was an improper methodology. What then are the proper methods for studying individual behavior? One psychologist who has long emphasized the need for the study of individual behavior is, of course B. F. Skinner. His position was, to a large extent, taken up as a response to the failure of Hull's grand scheme. However although his solution to the problem was very different from that of the more recent "humanistic" psychologists, his analysis of what was wrong with previous experimental methodology was very similar to theirs and, like theirs was faulty. For Skinner also concluded that statistical methods are applicable only to group behavior and therefore, in his studies of individual behavior, he avoided the use of statistics. This is better than abandoning experimentation altogether, but it is very limiting. Only the most stable and clear-cut aspects of behavior can be studied. Furthermore having found such rare units of behavior (bar pressing, key pecking, etc.) there is a strong temptation to study these responses to the exclusion of all others and also to use them as indices of underlying processes, such as anxiety, when they may be misleading. Skinner also concluded that it was Hull's extensive theorizing that lead to failure and therefore claims not to use theories or the intervening variables which are the apparatus of theory. In making this claim he deludes himself, for the very act of making an observation or conducting an experiment implies a hypothesis of some kind. It is better from the point of view of experimental design (for it tells us which variables are relevant and which irrelevant) to have an explicit theory clearly stated than to have an implicit theory whose existence is denied. Nevertheless, Skinner's approach has been invaluable for it has clearly demonstrated that with suitable techniques experiments can be performed on individual subjects.

However, in most cases the error of measurement associated with individual performance is too great to allow firm conclusions to be drawn. It is therefore essential either to combine data from different subjects or from the same subjects at different times. There is, at the moment, a sad lack of statistical techniques explicitly designed to combine data from different subjects, while at the same time retaining as far as possible the basic properties of the individual behavior. In our survey of reminiscence studies we have seen the beginnings of attempts to develop such techniques. Two basic and interlocking methods seem to be emerging. First, there must be continuous checking of grouped data against individual data. This permits not only the development of more appropriate techniques for grouping the data so that the basic individual processes are not disguised, but also indicates which are the most important measures to be extracted from the individual data. Second, the important individual differences must be identified, since only then can appropriate procedures be developed for combining results from different individuals without giving a distorted picture of the underlying processes.

The next step in the development of an experimental methodology appropriate to psychology must be the invention of statistical methods for handling data collected from single individuals. Although, as we have seen, data from single individuals have been presented in some of the later studies of pursuit-rotor performance they have not been subjected to sophisticated analysis and hence only the most blatantly obvious phenomena present in such data have been observed. Rather it is in clinical psychology, normally considered the most theoretically and methodologically backward area of psychology, that the most advanced methods of analysis of data from single subjects are being developed (Chassan, 1967; Shapiro, 1961; Gottman, 1973; Leitenberg, 1973; Slater, 1969). This is largely due to the involvement of clinical psychologists in the treatment of patients. Unlike their psychiatric colleagues these therapists have had a thorough grounding in experimental methods and a strong desire to use these methods in developing new and better therapies. However, unlike their colleagues in academic research they can never fall into the trap of believing that psychology can advance by studying large groups of subjects using the statistical methods appropriate for such groups. For the clinical psychologist is confronted with an individual patient and it is the behavior of this one person that he must understand. The experimental psychologists would benefit greatly if he paid more attention to the activities of his clinical colleagues.

We have outlined what we believe to be the most important current directions for the development of psychological methodology, but what of psychological theory? Firstly it is obvious that theory is vital in guiding research and suggesting experiments. The recent upsurge in research on reminiscence in motor skills was a direct result of the development of new theories based on concepts like consolidation, feedback and motor programs. However, is there any indication from our survey that some types of theory are more fruitful in generating research than others? In our introduction we contrasted the "conceptual" theory with the theory that consists of a set of mathematical equations. In fact these two theoretical approaches are usually complementary. A conceptual theory can always be converted into mathematical terms which will give a much greater precision to the predictions made. On the other hand it sometimes happens that a mathematical theory may be developed for which no corresponding concepts that are also intelligible can be found. The theories presented in this book have all been of the conceptual type. We could have converted these to mathematical theories, but have deliberately chosen not to do so. The operation would have necessitated our making further and very detailed assumptions of the kind which the data available so far would not warrant. Furthermore the precision of the resulting predictions would be far beyond the precision of the existing experimental techniques.

The quarrel between those who prefer a purely mathematical theory (e.g., Reynolds & Adams) and those who like to formulate theories in conceptual terms is not confined to psychology, of course. The theory of heat in physics furnishes us with a good example; here we have side by side the thermodynamic and the kinetic theory. Thermodynamics deals with unimaginable concepts of a purely quantitative kind; *temperature*, measured on a thermometer, *pressure*, measured as the force exerted per unit area, and *volume*, measured by the size of the container. Nothing is said in the laws of thermodynamics about the nature of heat. Bernouilli, in his famous treatise on hydraulics, postulated that all "elastic fluids," such as air, consist of small particles which are in constant irregular motion, and which constantly collide with each other and with the walls of the container. This was the foundation stone of the kinetic theory of heat, which results in a picture of events which is eminently visualizable, and which gives to many people a feeling of greater "understanding," of better and more thorough "explanation," than do the laws of thermodynamics. Consider for example the "insight" which we seem to gain in looking at Cailetet's famous experiment, which originated cryogenic research, by considering his cooling device as part of a single stroke of an expansion engine! Nevertheless, many phenomena are quite intractable to kinetic interpretations even today which yield easily to a thermodynamic solution (Eysenck, 1970).

Our theory is more closely similar to the kinetic theory, in that we postulate certain mechanisms and agents which render the process of reminiscence understandable and even "visualizable." Consider by contrast such a formulation as that given by Reynolds and Adams (1953) for the description of psychomotor acquisition data as a function of the distribution of practice:

$$P = M(1 - e^{-iT}) + bT$$

where P is a performance measure, T is the number of trials, e is the basis of natural logarithms, M is the limit for the exponential component and is assumed to increase as a negatively accelerated function of the interval between trials, i is the rate of growth for the exponential component and assumed to be a negatively accelerated decay function of the interval between trials, and b is a parameter independent of intertrial interval. At worst this is little more than curve-fitting, at best it is theory without content. At the present stage of development of psychology, we believe that "content" theories are more likely to advance understanding than overly mathematical theories.

Hull, of course, did attempt to "mathematize" his theory and this is probably the weakest part of his work, for at this point the discrepancy between theory and methodology is at its most extreme. Hull's mathematical model is supposed to describe individual behavior, but the numbers he derives for insertion into this model are derived from group curves. These numerical parameters are therefore essentially meaningless. Only when we have experimental methods sufficiently precise to be able to derive such parameters from the behavior of single individuals will the mathematization of psychology be worthwhile. Then, perhaps, the discipline of psychology will be able to scale those dizzy heights described by the leading intergalactic psychologist of the future imagined by Isaac Asimov: "The atomic physicists are too far behind the psychologists to expect them to catch up at this late date."

References and Bibliography

Ach, N. Über die Beeinflussung der Auffassungsfähigkeit durch einige Arzneimittel. *Psychol. Arb.*, 1901, **3**, 283–288.

Adams, J. A. Warm-up decrement in performance on the pursuit-rotor. *Amer. J. Psychol.*, 1952, **65**, 404–414.

Adams, J. A. The prediction of performance at advanced stages of training on a complex psychomotor task. *USAF Human Resour. Res. Cent. Res. Bull.*, 1953, 53–59.

Adams, J. A. Psychomotor performance as a function of intertrial rest interval. *J. Exp. Psychol.*, 1954, **48**, 131–133.

Adams, J. A. A source of decrement in psychomotor performance. *J. Exp. Psychol.*, 1955, **49**, 390–394.

Adams, J. A. The second facet of forgetting: a review of warm-up decrement. *Psychol. Bull.*, 1961, **58**, 257–273.

Adams, J. A. Comment on Feldman's "Reconsideration of the extinction hypothesis of warm-up in motor behaviour." *Psychol. Bull.*, 1963, **60**, 460–467.

Adams, J. A., and Reynolds, B. Effect of shift in distribution of practice conditions following interpolated rest. *J. Exp. Psychol.*, 1954, **47**, 32–36.

Albert, D. J. The effects of polarizing currents on the consolidation of learning. *Neuropsychol.*, 1966, **4**, 65–77.

Albert, T. G. Task-orientation and ego-orientation as factors in reminiscence. *J. Exp. Psychol.*, 1948, **38**, 224–238.

Amberg, E. Über die Wirkung der Theebestandtheile auf Körperliche und geistige Arbeit. *Psychol. Arb.*, 1895, **1**, 378–488.

Ammons, C. H. Task for the study of perceptual learning and performance variables. *Percept. Mot. Skills*, 1955, **5**, 11–14.

Ammons, C. H. Temporary and permanent inhibitory effects associated with acquisition of a simple perceptual motor-skill. *J. Gen. Psychol.*, 1960, **62**, 223–245.

Ammons, R. B. Acquisition of motor skill: I. Quantitive analysis and theoretical formulation. *Psychol. Rev.*, 1947a, **54**, 263–281.

Ammons, R. B. Acquisition of motor skill: II. Rotary pursuit performance with continuous practice before and after a single rest. *J. Exp. Psychol.*, 1947b, **37**, 393–411.

Ammons, R. B. Acquisition of motor skill: III. Effects of initially distributed practice on rotary pursuit performance. *J. Exp. Psychol.*, 1950, **40**, 777–787.

Ammons, R. B. Effect of distribution of practice on rotary pursuit "Hits." *J. Exp. Psychol.*, 1951a, **41**, 17–22.

Ammons, R. B. Effects of pre-practice activities on rotary pursuit performance. *J. Exp. Psychol.*, 1951b, **41**, 187–191.

Ammons, R. B. Relationship of motivation and method of testing to distribution of practice phenomena in rotary pursuit. *Quart. J. Exp. Psychol.*, 1952, **4**, 155–164.

Ammons, R. B. Rotary pursuit apparatus: 1. Survey of variables. *Psychol. Bull.*, 1955a, **52**, 69–76.

Ammons, R. B. Rotary pursuit apparatus: II. Effect of stylus length on performance. *Psychol. Rep.*, 1955b, **1**, 103.

Ammons, R. B., Adams, C., and Ammons, C. H. *Relationship of motivation and proficiency to components of simple skill performance.* Paper presented at the annual meeting of the Rocky Mountain Psychological Association, 1966.

Ammons, R. B., Adams, E., Lenthold, B., and Ammons, C. H. *Evaluation of some methods for fitting rotary pursuit performance curves for individual subjects.* Paper presented at the annual meeting of the Montana Psychological Association, 1965.

Ammons, R. B., and Ammons, C. H. *Decremental and related processes in skilled performance.* Invited paper, Symposium on Motivation and Learning, Iowa: University of Iowa, 1969.

Ammons, R. B., Ammons, C. H., and Morgan, R. Z. Subskills in rotary pursuit as affected by rate and accuracy requirements and by distribution of practice. *J. Gen. Psychol.*, 1958, **58**, 259–279.

Ammons, R. B., and Wilig, L. Acquisition of motor skill: IV. Effects of repeated periods of massed practice. *J. Exp. Psychol.*, 1956, **51**, 118–126.

Andersson, K. *Effects of cigarette smoking on learning and retention.* Psychology lab report, University of Stockholm, 415, 1974.

Archer, E. J. Effects of distribution of practice on a component skill of rotory pursuit tracking. *J. Exp. Psychol.*, 1958, **56**, 427–436.

Armstrong, H. E., Johnson, M. H., Ries, H. A., and Holmes, D. S. Extraversion–introversion and process-reactive schizophrenia. *Brit. J. Soc. Clin. Psychol.*, 1967, **6**, 69.

Aschaffenburg, G. Experimentelle Studien über Associationen. *Psychol. Arb.*, 1895, **1**, 209–299.

Asmussen, E. "Muscular exercise." In W. O. Fenn & N. Daku (eds.), *Handbook of Physiology*, Sect. 3, Respiration. Baltimore: Williams & Wilkins, 1965.

Asmussen, E., and Bøje, O. Body temperature and capacity for work. *Acta Physiol. Scand.*, 1945, **10**, 1–22.

Åstrand, I., Åstrand, P. O., Christensen, E. H., and Hedman, R. Myoglobin as an oxygen store in man. *Acta Physiol. Scand.*, 1960, **48**, 454–460.

Babcock, H. *Dementia Praecox, a psychological study.* Lancaster: Science Press, 1933.

Baddeley, A. D., and Patterson, K. The relation between long-term and short-term memory. *Brit. Med. Bull.*, 1971, 27, **3**, 237–242.

Bahrick, H. P., Fitts, P. M., and Briggs, C. E. Learning curves—facts or artifacts. *Psychol. Bull.*, 1957, **54**, 256–268.

Bakan, P., Belton, J., and Tath, J. "Extraversion–introversion and decrement in an auditory vigilance task." In D. N. Buckner & J. J. McGrath (eds.), *Vigilance: a Symposium.* New York: McGraw–Hill, 1963.

Ballard, P. B. Obliviscence and reminiscence. *Brit. J. Psychol.*, 1913, *Monogr. Suppl.*, **1**, No. 2.

Barch, A. M. Bilateral transfer of warm-up in rotary pursuit. *Percept. Mot. Skills,* 1963, **17,** 723–726.

Bartlett, M. S. The use of transformations. *Biometrics,* 1947, **3,** 29–50.

Becker, W. C. Cortical inhibition and extraversion–introversion. *J. Abnorm. Soc. Psychol.,* 1960, **61,** 52–66.

Beggs, W. D. A., and Howarth, C. I. Movement control in a repetitive motor task. *Nature,* 1970, **225,** 752–753.

Beggs, W. D. A., and Howarth, C. I. The accuracy of aiming at a target; some further evidence for a theory of intermittent control. *Acta Psychol.,* 1972, **36,** 171–177.

Bell, H. M. Rest pauses in Motor Learning as related to Snoddy's Hypothesis of Mental Growth. *Psychol. Monogr.,* 1942, **54,** No. 1.

Bending, A. W., and Eigenbrode, C. R. A factor analytic investigation of personality variables and reminiscence in motor learning. *J. Abnorm. Soc. Psychol.,* 1961, **62,** 698–700.

Bending, A. W., and Vaughan, C. J. Extraversion, Neuroticism, and motor learning. *J. Abnorm. Soc. Psychol.,* 1959, **59,** 399–403.

Berlyne, D. E., Borsa, D. M., Craw, M. A., Gelman, R. S., and Mandell, E. E. Effects of stimulus complexity and induced arousal on paired associate learning. *J. Verb. Learn. & Verb. Behav.,* 1965, **4,** 291–299.

Berlyne, D. E., Borsa, D. H., Hamacher, J. H., and Koenig, I. D. V. Paired associate learning and the timing of arousal. *J. Exp. Psychol.,* 1966, **72,** 1–6.

Berry, R. M. Skin conductance levels and verbal recall. *J. Exp. Psychol.,* 1962, **63,** 225–277.

Bills, A. G. Blocking: a new principle of mental fatigue. *Amer. J. Psychol.,* 1931, **43,** 230–275.

Bills, A. G. Fatigue, oscillations and blocks. *J. Exp. Psychol.,* 1935, **18,** 562–573.

Bills, A. G. A study of blocking and other response variables in psychotic, brain-damaged and personality-disturbed patients. *Behav. Res. Ther.,* 1964, **2,** 99–106.

Bilodeau, E. A. Decrements and recovery from decrements in a simple work task with variation in force requirements at different stages of practice. *J. Exp. Psychol.,* 1952, **44,** 96–100.

Bilodeau, E. A. *Acquisition of skill.* London: Academic Press, 1966.

Bilodeau, I. McD., and Bilodeau, E. A. Some effects of work loading in a repetitive motor task. *J. Exp. Psychol.,* 1954, **48,** 455–467.

Binet, A. Sommaire des travaux en cours à la société de psychologie de l'enfant. *Annee Psychol.,* 1904, **10,** 116–130.

Bjenner, B. Alpha depression and lowered pulse rate during delayed action in a serial reaction time test. *Acta Physiol.,* 1949, **19** (suppl.), 65, 1–93.

Bleke, R. Reward and punishment as determiners of reminiscence effects in schizophrenic and normal subjects. *J. Pers.,* 1959, **23,** 479–498.

Blomfield, S., and Marr, D. How the cerebellum may be used. *Nature,* 1970, **227,** 1224–1228.

Boring, E. G. Learning in dementia praecox. *Psychol. Rev.,* 1913, **15,** 1–101.

Boring, E. G. *A history of experimental psychology* (2nd ed.). New York: Appleton-Century-Crofts, 1950.

Bovet, D., Bovet-Nitti, F., and Oliverio, A. Memory and consolidation mechanisms in avoidance learning of inbred mice. *Brain Res.,* 1968, **10,** 168–182.

Breen, R. A., and McGaugh, J. L. Facilitation of maze learning with post-trial injections of picrotoxin. *J. Comp. Physiol. Psychol.,* 1961, **54,** 498–501.

Brengelmann, J. C., and Brengelmann, L. Deutsche validierung von Fragebogen der

Extraversion, neurotischen Tendenz und Rigidität. *Z. Exp. Psychol.*, 1960, **7**, 291–331.

Broadbent, D. E. "Neglect of the surroundings in relation to fatigue decrements in output." In W. F. Floud and A. T. Welford (eds.), *Fatigue*. London: H. K. Lewis, 1953.

Broadhurst, A., and Eysenck, H. J. Pursuit rotor reminiscence in schizophrenics and normals. *J. Mot. Behav.*, 1973a, **5**, 73–80.

Broadhurst, A., and Eysenck, H. J. Involuntary rest pauses (IRPs) in schizophrenics and normals. *J. Mot. Behav.*, 1973b, **5**, 186–192.

Broadhurst, P. L., and Broadhurst, A. An analysis of the pursuit rotor learning of chronic psychotics. *Brit. J. Psychol.*, 1964, **55**, 321–331.

Brown, W. To what extent is memory measured by a single recall? *J. Exp. Psychol.*, 1923, **49**, 191–196.

Buckner, D. N., and McGrath, J. J. (eds.). *Vigilance: a Symposium*. London: McGraw-Hill, 1963.

Bunch, M. E. The measurement of reminiscence. *Psychol. Rev.*, 1938, **45**, 525–531.

Buxton, C. E. The status of research in reminiscence. *Psychol. Bull.*, 1943a, **40**, 313–340.

Buxton, C. E. Level of mastery and reminiscence in pursuit learning. *J. Exp. Psychol.*, 1943b, **32**, 176–180.

Buxton, C. E., and Grant, D. A. Retroaction and gains in motor learning: 11. Sex differences, and a further analysis of gains. *J. Exp. Psychol.*, 1939, **25**, 198–208.

Buxton, C. E., and Henry, C. E. Retroaction and gains in motor learning: 1. Similarity of interpolated task as a factor in gains. *J. Exp. Psychol.*, 1939, **25**, 1–17.

Buxton, C. E., and Humphrey, L. G. The effects of practice upon intercorrelation of motor skills. *Science*, 1935, **81**, 441–442.

Carr, G. *Introversion-extraversion and vigilance performance*. Proceedings of the 79th annual convention of the APA, 1971.

Carr, H. A. Distribution of effort. *Psychol. Rev. Mon. Sup.*, 1920, **24**, 26–28.

Carron, A. V., and Leavitt, J. L. Individual differences in two motor learning tasks under massed practice. *Percept. Mot. Skills*, 1968, **27**, 499–504.

Catalano, J. F. Arousal as a factor in reminiscence. *Percept. Mot. Skills*, 1967, **24**, 1171–1180.

Chassan, J. B. *Research design in clinical psychology and psychiatry*. Appleton-Century-Crofts: New York, 1967.

Child, D. The relationships between introversion-extraversion, neuroticism and performance in school examinations. *Brit. J. Educ. Psychol.*, 1964, **34**, 187–196.

Child, D. Reminiscence and personality—a note on the effect of different test instructions. *Brit. J. Soc. Clin. Psychol.*, 1966, **5**, 92–94.

Christensen, E. H., and Hohndahl, J. The influence of rest pauses on mechanical efficiency. *Acta Physiol. Scand.*, 1960, **48**, 443–447.

Cicero, M. T. *Tuscularum Disputationum*. Rome, 43 B.C., London: Heinemann, 1927.

Cieutat, V. J., and Nobel, C. E. Ability vs. practice in two-hand coordination. *Percept. Mot. Skills*, 1958, **8**, 226.

Claridge, G. "The excitation-inhibition balance in neurotics." In H. J. Eysenck (ed.), *Experiments in personality*, Vol. 2, London: Routledge & Kegan Paul, 1960.

Clark, A. M. The relationship of arousal to reminiscence, attention withdrawal, and the Hunter index in chronic schizophrenia. Unpublished Ph.D. thesis, University of London, 1967.

Cochrane, R., and Duffy, J. Psychology and the scientific method. *Bull. Br. Psychol. Soc.*, 1974, **27**, 117–121.

Coghill, G. E. *Anatomy and the problem of behaviour.* London: Cambridge University Press, 1929.

Colquhoun, W. P. (ed.). *Biological rhythms and human performance.* London: Academic Press, 1971.

Cook, S., and Hilgard, E. R. Distributed practice in motor learning: progressively increasing and decreasing rests. *J. Exp. Psychol.,* 1949, **39,** 169–172.

Connolly, K. "Skill development: problems and plans." In Connolly, K. (ed.), *Mechanisms of motor skill development.* London: Academic Press, 1970.

Conrad, R. Acoustic confusions in immediate memory. *Brit. J. Psychol.,* 1964, **55,** 73–84.

Cooper, J. E., Kendell, R. E., Gurland, B. J., Sharpe, L., Copeland, J. R. M., and Simon, R. *Psychiatric diagnosis in New York and London.* London: Oxford University Press, 1972.

Corcoran, D. W. J. The relation between introversion and salivation. *Amer. J. Psychol.,* 1964, **77,** 298–300.

Corkin, S. Acquisition of motor skill after bilateral medial temporal-lobe excision. *Neuropsychologia,* 1968, **6,** 255–265.

Corteen, R. S. Basal conductance level and motor performance. *Brit. J. Psychol.,* 1967, **58,** 93–100.

Costello, C. G. "Ego involvement, success and failure: a review of the literature." In H. J. Eysenck (ed.). *Experiments in motivation.* London: Pergamon Press, 1964.

Costello, C. G. The effects of an alien stimulus on reminiscence in pursuit rotor performance. *Psychon. Sci.,* 1967, **8,** 331–332.

Costello, C. G., Brown, P. A., and Low, K. J. Some physiological concomitants of pursuit rotor performance and reminiscence. *J. Mot. Behav.,* 1969, **1,** 181–194.

Costello, C. G., and Discipio, W. An experimental test of a "frustration": theory of reminiscence. *Psychon. Sci.,* 1967, **8,** 333–334.

Costello, C. G., and Feldman, P. Unpublished data, 1962.

Costello, C. G., Feldman, M. P., and Slater, P. D. "The effect of success and failure reports on pursuit motor performance and reminiscence." In H. J. Eysenck (ed.). *Experiments in motivation,* pp. 209–222. London: Pergamon Press, 1964.

Craik, F. I. M. Primary memory. *Brit. Med. Bull.,* 1971, **27,** 232–236.

Craik, K. J. W. Theory of the human operator in control systems. II. Man as an element in a control system. *Brit. J. Psychol.,* 1948, **38,** 142–148.

Crome, L. C., Cowie, V., and Slater, E. A statistical note on cerebellar and brain stem weight in mongolism. *J. Ment. Def. Res.,* 1966, **10,** 69–72.

Cronbach, L. J., and Farley, L. How we should measure "change"—or should we? *Psychol. Bull.,* 1970, **74,** 68–80.

Cronholm, B., and Molander, L. Influence of an interpolated E.C.S. on rentention of memory material. University of Stockholm Psychology Lab Report No. 61, 1956.

Das, J. P. An experimental study of the relation between hypnosis, conditioning and reactive inhibition. Unpublished Ph.D. thesis, University of London, 1957.

Davis, D. R. *Pilot error; some laboratory experiments.* London: HMSO, 1948.

Davies, D. R., and Tune, G. S. *Human vigilance performance.* London: Staples Press, 1970.

Davol, S. H., and Breakell, S. L. Sex differences in rotary pursuit performance of young children: a follow-up. *Percept. Mot. Skills,* 1968, **26,** 1199–1202.

Denny, M. R. The shape of the post-rest performance curve for the continuous rotary pursuit task. *Mot. Skills Res. Exch.,* 1951, **3,** 103–105.

Denny, M. R., Frisbey, N., and Weaver, J. Rotary pursuit performance under alternate conditions of distributed and massed practice. *J. Exp. Psychol.,* 1955, **49,** 48–54.

Dey, M. K., and Ammons, R. B. Stimulation-maturation prediction of distribution phenomena in compensatory pursuit. *Canad. J. Psychol.,* 1956, **10,** 139–146.

Dore, L. R., and Hilgard, E. R. Spaced practice and the maturation hypothesis. *J. Psychol.*, 1937, **4,** 245–259.

Dore, L. R., and Hilgard, E. R. Spaced practice as a test of Snoddy's two processes in mental growth. *J. Exp. Psychol.*, 1938, **23,** 359–374.

Duncan, C. P. The effect of unequal amounts of practice on motor learning before and after rest. *J. Exp. Psychol.*, 1951, **42,** 257–264.

Easterbrook, J. A. The effect of emotion on cue utilisation and the organisation of behaviour. *Psychol. Rev.*, 1959, **66,** 183–201.

Ebbinghaus, H. *Über das Gedächtniss.* Leipzig: Dunker and Humbolt, 1885.

Edgerton, H. A., & Valentine, W. L. A factor analysis of learning data. *Psychol. Bull.*, 1935, **32,** 719.

Ellis, D. S., Montgomery, V., and Underwood, B. J. Reminiscence in a manipulative task as a function of work-surface height, prerest practice, and interpolated rest. *J. Exp. Psychol.*, 1952, **44,** 420–427.

Ellis, N. R., and Distefano, M. K., Jr. Effects of verbal urging and praise upon rotary pursuit performance in mental defectives. *Amer. J. Ment. Def.*, 1959, **64,** 486–490.

Essman, E. B., and Jarvik, M. E. The retrograde effect of ether anaesthesia on a conditioned avoidance response in mice. *Amer. Psychol.*, 1960, **15,** 498.

Eysenck, H. J. An experimental study of the improvement of mental and physical functions in the hypnotic state. *Brit. J. Med. Psychol.*, 1941, **18,** 304–316.

Eysenck, H. J. *The dimensions of personality.* London: Routledge & Kegan Paul, 1947.

Eysenck, H. J. Reminiscence, drive and personality theory. *J. Abnorm. Soc. Psychol.*, 1956*a*, **53,** 328–333.

Eysenck, H. J. "Warm-up" in pursuit rotor learning as a function of the extinction of conditioned inhibition. *Acta Psychol.*, 1956*b*, **12,** 349–370.

Eysenck, H. J. *The dynamics of anxiety and hysteria.* London: Routledge & Kegan Paul, 1957.

Eysenck, H. J. A short questionnaire for the measurement of the dimensions of personality. *J. Appl. Psychol.*, 1958, **92,** 13–17.

Eysenck, H. J. Reminiscence as a function of rest, practice, and personality. *Percept. Mot. Skills*, 1960*a*, **11,** 91–94.

Eysenck, H. J. Reminiscence, extraversion and neuroticism. *Percept. Mot. Skills*, 1960*b*, **11,** 21–22.

Eysenck, H. J. Reminiscence and post-rest increment after massed practice. *Percept. Mot. Skills*, 1960*c*, **11,** 221–222.

Eysenck, H. J. Psychosis, drive and inhibition: a theoretical and experimental account. *Amer. J. Psychiat.*, 1961, **118,** 198–204.

Eysenck, H. J. Reminiscence, drive and personality—revision and extension of a theory. *Brit. J. Soc. Clin. Psychol.*, 1962, **1,** 127–140.

Eysenck, H. J. (ed.). *Experiments in motivation.* London: Pergamon Press, 1964*a*.

Eysenck, H. J. An experimental test of the "inhibition" and "consolidation" theories of reminiscence. *Life Sci.*, 1964*b*, **3,** 175–188.

Eysenck, H. J. Involuntary rest pauses in tapping as a function of drive and personality. *Percept. Mot. Skills*, 1964*c*, **18,** 173–174.

Eysenck, H. J. *Crime and personality.* London: Routledge & Kegan Paul, 1964*d*.

Eysenck, H. J. Personality and reminiscence—an experimental study of the "reactive inhibition" and the "conditioned inhibition" theories. *Life Sci.*, 1964*e*, **3,** 189–198.

Eysenck, H. J. A three factor theory of reminiscence. *Brit. J. Psychol.*, 1965, **56,** 163–181.

Eysenck, H. J. On the dual function of consolidation. *Percept. Mot. Skills*, 1966, **22,** 273–274.

Eysenck, H. J. *The biological basis of personality.* Springfield: C. C. Thomas, 1967.

Eysenck, H. J. A new theory of post-rest upswing or "warm-up" in motor learning. *Percept. Mot. Skills,* 1969, **28**, 992–994.

Eysenck, H. J. "Explanation and the concept of personality." In R. Borger & F. Cioffi (eds.). *Explanations in the behavioural sciences.* Cambridge University Press, 1970a.

Eysenck, H. J. Programme research and training in research methodology. *Bull. Brit. Psychol. Soc.,* 1970b, **23**, 9–16.

Eysenck, H. J. *The structure of human personality* (3rd ed.). London: Methuen, 1970c.

Eysenck, H. J. A note on the alleged non-existence of individual differences in reminiscence. *Psychol. Bull.,* 1973a, **80**, 243–244.

Eysenck, H. J. "Personality, learning and 'anxiety'." In H. J. Eysenck (ed.), *Handbook of abnormal psychology.* London: Pitman, 1973b.

Eysenck, H. J., and Cookson, D. Unpublished manuscript, 1974.

Eysenck, H. J., and Eysenck, S. B. G. Reminiscence in the spiral after-effect as a function of length of rest and number of pre-rest trials. *Percept. Mot. Skills,* 1960, **10**, 93–94.

Eysenck, H. J., and Eysenck, S. B. G. On the unitary nature of extraversion. *Acta Psychol.,* 1967, **26**, 383–390.

Eysenck, H. J., and Gray, J. E. Reminiscence and the shape of the learning curve as a function of subjects' ability level on the pursuit rotor. *Brit. J. Psychol.,* 1971, **62**, 199–215.

Eysenck, H. J., Iseler, A., Star, K., and Willett, R. A. Post-rest upswing and downswing in pursuit rotor learning after distributed practice as a function of length of practice. *Brit. J. Psychol.,* 1969, **60**, 373–384.

Eysenck, H. J., and Maxwell, A. E. Reminiscence as function of drive. *Brit. J. Psychol.,* 1961, **52**, 43–52.

Eysenck, H. J., and Prell, D. B. The inheritance of neuroticism: an experimental study. *J. Ment. Sci.,* 1951, **97**, 441–465.

Eysenck, H. J., and Sartory, G. E. Leistung und Reminiszenz am Pursuit-rotor und beim Spiegelzeichnen in Abhängigkeit von Aktivation, Pausenlänge und Persönlichkeitsvariablen. *Ztsch. f. Exp. u. angew. Psychol.,* 1971, **18**, 525–557.

Eysenck, H. J., and Thompson, W. The effects of distraction on pursuit rotor learning, performance and reminiscence. *Brit. J. Psychol.,* 1966, **57**, 99–106.

Eysenck, H. J., and Warwick, K. M. "Situationally determined drive and the concept of 'arousal'." In H. J. Eysenck, (ed.), *Experiments in motivation.* London: Pergamon Press, 1964.

Eysenck, H. J., and Willett, R. The measurement of motivation through the use of objective indices. *J. Ment. Sci.,* 1961, **107**, 961–968.

Eysenck, H. J., and Willett, R. Cue utilisation as a function of drive: an experimental study. *Percept. Mot. Skills,* 1962a, **15**, 229–230.

Eysenck, H. J., and Willett, R. A. Performance and reminiscence on a symbol substitution task as a function of drive. *Percept. Mot. Skills,* 1962b, **15**, 389–390.

Eysenck, H. J., and Willett, R. A. "Situation-produced motivation: I. Introduction." In H. J. Eysenck (ed.). *Experiments in motivation.* London: Pergamon Press, 1964.

Eysenck, H. J., and Willett, R. A. The effect of drive on performance and reminiscence in a complex tracing task. *Brit. J. Psychol.,* 1966, **57**, 107–112.

Eysenck, M. W. Extraversion, Arousal, and Retrieval from Semantic Memory. *J. Person.,* 1974, **42**, 319–331.

Eysenck, S. B. G. Retention of a well-developed motor skill after one year. *J. Gen. Psychol.,* 1960, **63**, 267–273.

Eysenck, S. B. G., and Eysenck, H. J. *Manual of the Personality Questionnaire*. London: University of London Press, 1974.

Fahrenberg, J., and Self, H. *Das Freiburger Persönlichkeits-inventar, FPI. Handanweisung*. Gottingen: Hogrete, 1970.

Farley, F. H. Reminiscence and postrest performance as a function of length of rest, drive and personality. Unpublished Ph.D. thesis, University of London, 1966.

Farley, F. H. *Personality and reminiscence*. Paper read at the International Congress of Psychology, London, 1969.

Farley, F. H. "Reminiscence, performance and personality." In H. J. Eysenck (ed.). *Readings in extraversion-introversion*, Vol. 3. London: Staples Press, 1971.

Farmer, E. Parallelism in curves of motor performance. *Brit. J. Psychol.*, 1927, **42**, 335–342.

Feldman, M. P. A reconsideration of the extinction hypothesis of warm-up in motor behaviour. *Psychol. Bull.*, 1963, **60**, 452–459.

Feldman, M. P. "Motivation and task performance: a review of the literature." In H. J. Eysenck, (ed.), *Experiments in motivation*. London: Pergamon Press, 1964a.

Feldman, M. P. "Pursuit rotor performance and reminiscence as a function of drive level." In H. J. Eysenck, (ed.), *Experiments in motivation*. London: Pergamon Press, 1964b.

Feldman, M. P. "Drive and pursuit rotor reminiscence: the effect of an alien stimulus." In H. J. Eysenck (ed.), *Experiments in motivation*. London: Pergamon Press, 1964c.

Fenz, W. P., and Velner, J. Physiological concomitants of behavioral indices in schizophrenia. *J. Abnorm. Psychol.*, 1970, **76**, 27–35.

Fitts, P. M. Cognitive aspect of information processing: III. Set for speed versus accuracy. *J. Exp. Psychol.*, 1966, **71**, 849–957.

Fleishman, E. A. Testing for psychomotor abilities by means of apparatus tests. *Psychol. Bull.*, 1953, **50**, 241–262.

Fleishman, E. A. Dimensional analysis of psychomotor abilities. *J. Exp. Psychol.*, 1954, **48**, 437–454.

Fleishman, E. A. Predicting advanced levels of proficiency in psychomotor skills. Symposium on Human Engineering, Personnel and Training Research, National Research Council—National Academy of Sciences, Washington DC, 1956.

Fleishman, E. A. Factor structure in relation to task difficulty in psychomotor performance. *Educ. Psychol. Measmt.*, 1957, **17**, 522–532.

Fleishman, E. A. Dimensional analysis of movement reactions. *J. Exp. Psychol.*, 1958a, **55**, 438–453.

Fleishman, E. A. A relationship between incentive motivation and ability level in psychomotor performance. *J. Exp. Psychol.*, 1958b, **56**, 78–81.

Fleishman, E. A. Abilities at different stages of practice in rotary pursuit performance. *J. Exp. Psychol.*, 1960a, **60**, 162–171.

Fleishman, E. A. "Human abilities and the acquisition of skill." In E. A. Bilodeau (ed.), *Acquisition of skill*. New York: Academic Press, 1960b.

Fleishman, E. A. Performance assessment based on an empirically derived task taxonomy. *Hum. Fact.*, 1967, **9**, 349–366.

Fleishman, E. A., and Hempel, W. E. Jr. Changes in factor structure of a complex psychomotor test as a function of practice. *Psychometrika*, 1954, **19**, 239–252.

Fleishman, E. A., and Hempel, W. E. The relation between abilities and improvement with practice in a visual discrimination reaction task. *J. Exp. Psychol.*, 1955, **49**, 301–310.

Fleishman, E. A., and Hempel, W. E. Factorial analysis of complex psychomotor performance and related skills. *J. Appl. Psychol.*, 1956, **40**, 96–104.

Fleishman, E. A., and Parker, J. F. Prediction of advanced levels of proficiency in a complex tracking task. *USAFWADC Technical Rep.*, 1959, No. 59.

French, E. G. Effects of interactions of achievement, motivation, and intelligence on problem solving success. *Amer. Psychologist,* 1957, **12**, 399–400.

Frith, C. D. Strategies in rotary pursuit tracking and their relation to inhibition and personality. *Life Sci.,* 1968*a*, **7**, 65–76.

Frith, C. D. The effect of nicotine on the consolidation of pursuit rotor learning. *Life. Sci.,* 1968*b*, **7**, 77–84.

Frith, C. D. Strategies in pursuit rotor learning. Paper for the XIX International Congress of Psychology, London, 1969.

Frith, C. D. Strategies in rotary pursuit tracking. *Brit. J. Psychol.,* 1971, **62**, 187–197.

Frith, C. D. Learning rhythmic hand movements. *Quart. J. Exp. Psychol.,* 1973*a*, **25**, 253–259.

Frith, C. D. Nature of rest pauses in a simple tapping task. *Percept. Mot. Skills,* 1973*b*, **36**, 437–438.

Frith, C. D., and Tunstall, O. Changes in pursuit rotor performance underlying the period of "postrest upswing." *Percept. Mot. Skills,* 1971, **33**, 256–258.

Frith, U., and Frith, C. D. Specific motor disabilities in Down's syndrome. *J. Child Psychol. & Psychiat.,* 1974. (In press.)

Furneaux, W. O. *Manual of Nufferno speed tests.* London: National Foundation of Education Research, 1953.

Gale, A., Jones, D.M., and Smallbone, A. Short-term memory and the EEG. *Nature,* 1974. (In press.)

Gardner, G. E. The learning ability of schizophrenics. *Amer. J. Psychiat.,* 1931, **11**, 247–252.

Garg, M., and Holland, H. C. Consolidation and maze learning: a comparison of several post-trial treatments. *Life Sci.,* 1967, **6**, 1987–1997.

Garg, M., and Holland, H. C. Consolidation and maze learning: the effects of post-trial injections of a depressant drug (Pentobarbital Sodium). *Psychopharmacologia,* 1968*a*, **12**, 127–132.

Garg, M., and Holland, H. C. Consolidation and maze learning: a further study of post-trial injections of a stimulant drug (Nicotine). *Int. J. Neuropharmacol.,* 1968*b*, **7**, 55–59.

Geissner, S., and Greenhouse, S. W. An extension of Box's results on the use of the F distribution in multivariate analysis. *Ann. Math. Statist.,* 1958, **29**, 885–891.

Geldreich, G. V. Some physiological concomitants of mental work. *Psychol. Monogr.,* 1959, No. 358.

Gellhorn, E. *Autonomic imbalance and the hypothalamus.* Minneapolis: University of Minnesota Press, 1957.

Gentry, J. R. Immediate effects of interpolated rest periods on learning performance. *Teach. Coll. Contrib. Educ.,* 1940, No. 799.

Germain, J., and Pinillos, J. L. Motor reminiscence as a function of extraversion, neuroticism and massed practice. *Psychologische Beiträge,* 1962, **6**, 501–508.

Glickman, S. E. Deficits in avoidance learning produced by stimulation of the ascending reticular formation. *Canad. J. Psychol.,* 1958, **12**, 97–102.

Glickman, S. E. Perseveration, neural processes and consolidation of the memory trace. *Psychol. Bull.,* 1961, **58**, 218–233.

Gottman, J. M. N-of-one and N-of-two research in psychotherapy. *Psychol. Bull.,* 1973, **80**, 93–105.

Gottsdanker, R. Uncertainty, timekeeping, and simple reaction time. *J. Mot. Behav.,* 1970, **2**, 245–260.

Grand, S., and Segal, S. J. Recovery in the absence of recall: an investigation of color-word interference. *J. Exp. Psychol.,* 1966, **72**, 138–144.

Grassi, J. R. An experimental study of learning in brain-damaged children, with special reference to reactive inhibition. Unpublished Ph.D. thesis, University of London, 1964.

Grassi, J. R. Performance and reminiscence of brain-damaged, behaviour-disordered, and normal children on four psychomotor and perceptual tests. *J. Abnorm. Psychol.*, 1968, **73**, 492–499.

Gray, J. E. Levels of arousal and length of rest as determinants of pursuit rotor performance. Unpublished Ph.D. thesis, University of London, 1968.

Gray, S. The influence of methodology upon the measurement of reminiscence. *J. Exp. Psychol.*, 1940, **27**, 37–44.

Greene, E. B. An analysis of random and systematic changes with practice. *Psychometrika*, 1943, **8**, 37–53.

Grice, G. R., and Reynolds, B. Effect of varying amounts of rest on conventional and bilateral transfer "reminiscence." *J. Exp. Psychol.*, 1952, **44**, 247–252.

Gross, O. *Die cerebrale Sekundärfunktion.* Leipzig: 1902.

Gross, O. *Über psychopathologische Minderwertigkeiten.* Leipzig: 1908.

Grossberg, S. Some networks that can learn, remember and reproduce any number of complicated space-time patterns, I. *J. Math. & Mech.*, 1969, **19**, 53–91.

Guttman, Z. A. "A new approach to factor analysis: the radex." In P. F. Lazarsfeld (ed.), *Mathematical thinking in the social sciences*, pp. 258–348. Glencoe: Free Press, 1954.

Haenel, H. Die psychischen Wirkungen des Trionals. *Psychol. Arb.*, 1899, **2**, 326–358.

Hall, J. F. *The psychology of learning.* New York: Lippincutt, 1966.

Hammond, D. Effects of visual and thermal stimulation upon reminiscence in rotary pursuit tracking. *Irish J. Psychol.*, 1972, **3**, 177–184.

Harkins, S., and Geen, R. G. Discriminability and criterion differences between extraverts and introverts during vigilance. Unpublished Report, University of Missouri, 1974.

Hartley, T. C. Retention as a function of the temporal position of an interpolated warming-up task. Unpublished M.A. thesis, University of Illinois, 1948.

Hayes, K. J. Anoxic and convulsive amnesia in rats. *J. Comp. Physiol. Psychol.*, 1953, **46**, 216–217.

Helmick, J. S. Pursuit learning as affected by size of target and speed of rotation. *J. Exp. Psychol.*, 1951, **41**, 126–138.

Henderson, E. N. A study of memory for connected trains of thought. *Psychol. Monogr.*, 1903, **5**, No. 23.

Heron, W. T. The warming-up effect in learning nonsense syllables. *J. Genet. Psychol.*, 1928, **35**, 219–228.

Heüman, G. Über die Beziehungen zwischen Arbeitsdauer und Pausenwirkung. *Psychol. Arb.*, 1904, **4**, 538–602.

Heüman, G., and Wirsma, E. Beiträge zur speziellen Psychologie auf Grund einer Massenuntersuchung. *Ztsch. f. Psychol.*, 1909, **51**, 1–72.

Hick, W. E. Discontinuous functioning of the human operator. *Quart. J. Exp. Psychol.*, 1948, **1**, 36–51.

Hicks, L. E. Some effects of anxiety and cognitive style upon pursuit rotor learning. *Brit. J. Soc. Clin. Psychol.*, 1975, **14**, 155–168.

Higgins, J., and Mednick, S. A. Reminiscence and stage of illness in schizophrenia. *J. Abnorm. Soc. Psychol.*, 1963, **66**, 314–317.

Hilgard, E. R., and Smith, M. B. Distributed practice in motor learning: score changes within and between daily sessions. *J. Exp. Psychol.*, 1942, **30**, 136–146.

Hoch, A. On certain studies with the ergograph. *J. Nerv. Ment. Dis.*, 1901, **28**, 620–628.

Hoch, S., and Kraepelin, E. Über die Wirkung der Theebestandtheile auf körperliche und geistige Arbeit. *Psychol. Arb.*, 1895, **1**, 378–488.

Hoegberg, P., and Lundgren, O. Uppvärmninjen inver Ken på Lopprestatione. *Svensk. Tdrott.*, 1947, **40**, 480.

Holland, H. C. Massed practice and reactive inhibition, reminiscence and disinhibition in the spiral after-effect. *Brit. J. Psychol.*, 1963, **54**, 261–272.

Holland, H. C. *The spiral after-effect.* London: Pergamon Press, 1965.

Hormann, H., and Osterkamp, U. Über den Einfluss von kontinuierlichem Lärm auf die Organisation von Gedächtnisinhalten. *Z. Angew. Psychol.*, 1966, **13**, 31–38.

Horn, P. W. Evidence for the generality of reminiscence as a function of extraversion and neuroticism. *J. Psychol.*, 1975, **90**, 41–44.

House, B. J., and Zeaman, D. "The role of attention is retardate discrimination learning." Ian N. R. Ellis (ed.), *Handbook of mental deficiency.* New York: McGraw-Hill, 1963.

Hovland, C. I., and Kuntz, K. H. Experimental studies in rote learning theory: IX. Influence of work decrement factors on verbal learning. *J. Exp. Psychol.*, 1951, **42**, 265–272.

Howarth, E., and Eysenck, H. J. Extraversion, arousal, and paired-associate recall. *J. Exp. Res. in Pers.*, 1968, **3**, 114–116.

Huguenin, C. Reminiscence paradoxale. *Arch. de Psychol.*, 1914, **14**, 379–383.

Hull, C. L. The formation and retention of associations among the insane. *Amer. J. Psychol.*, 1917, **28**, 419–435.

Hull, C. L. *Principles of behaviour.* New York: Appleton-Century-Crofts, 1943.

Hull, C. L. The place of innate individual and species differences in a natural science theory of behaviour. *Psychol. Rev.*, 1945, **52**, 55–60.

Hull, C. L. *A behavior system.* New Haven: Yale University Press, 1952.

Humphrey, L. G. A factor of time in pursuit rotor learning. *J. Psychol.*, 1936, **3**, 429–436.

Humphries, M. A method of estimating "RMS error" in pursuit rotor performance. *Percept. Mot. Skills*, 1961, **13**, 211–225.

Humphries, M. The effect of interpolated activity on reminiscence in pursuit rotor performance. Privately circulated typescript.

Humphries, M., and McIntyre, J. Effect of interpolated monocular and binocular visual pursuit reaction time activity on reminiscence in pursuit rotor performance. *Percept. Mot. Skills*, 1936a, **17**, 333–334.

Humphries, M., and McIntyre, J. An attempt to find a locus of temporary work decrement in pursuit rotor performance. *Percept. Mot. Skills*, 1963b, **17**, 397–398.

Hund, F. *The history of quantum theory.* London: Harrap, 1974.

Hunter, I. A. The warming-up effect in recall performance. *Quart. J. Exp. Psychol.*, 1955, **7**, 166–175.

Huse, M. M., and Parsons, O. A. Pursuit-rotor performance in the brain-damaged. *J. Abnorm. Psychol.*, 1965, **70**, 350–359.

Huston, P. E., & Shakow, D. Learning in schizophrenia. *J. Pers.*, 1948, **17**, 52–74.

Hutt, H. Rechenversuche bei Manisch-Depressiven. *Psychol. Arb.*, 1910, **5**, 338–370.

Hylan, J. P., and Kraepelin, E. Über die Wirkung kurzer Arbeitszeiten. *Psychol. Arb.*, 1904, **4**, 454–459.

Iltis, H. *The life of Mendel.* London: Allen & Unwin, 1966.

Irion, A. L. The relation of "set" to retention. *Psychol. Rev.*, 1948, **53**, 336–341.

Irion, A. L. Reminiscence in pursuit-rotor learning as a function of length of rest and of amount of pre-rest practice. *J. Exp. Psychol.*, 1949a, **39**, 492–499.

Irion, A. L. Retention and warming-up effects in paired-associate learning. *J. Exp. Psychol.*, 1949b, 669–675.

Irion, A. L., & Gustafson, L. M. Reminiscence in bilateral transfer. *J. Exp. Psychol.*, 1952, **43**, 321–323.

Irion, A. L., and Wham, D. S. Recovery from retention loss as a function of amount of pre-recall warming-up. *J. Exp. Psychol.*, 1951, **41**, 242–246.

Iseler, A. *Einflüsse der Aktivation auf die Konsolidierung von Gedächtnisspuren. Bericht über den 26. Kongress der Deutschen Gesellschaft für Psychologie.* Göttingen: Verlag für Psychologie, 1969.

Jahnke, J. C., and Duncan, C. P. Reminiscence and forgetting in motor learning after extended rest intervals. *J. Exp. Psychol.*, 1956, **52**, 273–282.

Jensen, A. R. On the reformulation of inhibition in Hull's system. *Psychol. Bull.*, 1961, **58**, 274–298.

Jensen, A. R. Extraversion, neuroticism and serial learning. *Acta Psychol.*, 1962, **20**, 69–77.

Jones, H. G. The status of inhibition in Hull's system: a theoretical revision. *Psychol. Rev.*, 1958, **65**, 179–182.

Jones, J. The relationship between UCS intensity, varying signal, rest, and personality in eyelid conditioning. Unpublished Ph.D. thesis, University of London, 1974.

Jones, M. B. "Individual differences." In E. A. Bilodeau (ed.), *Acquisition of Skill*. London: Academic Press, 1966.

Jones, M. B. "Differential processes in acquisition." In E. A. Bilodeau (ed.), *Principles of skill acquisition*. New York: Academic Press, 1969.

Jost, S. Die Associationsfestigkeit in ihren Abhängigkeit von der Verteilung der Wieder-holungen. *Ztsch. f. Psychol.*, 1897, **14**, 436–472.

Joynson, R. B. The breakdown of modern psychology. *Bull. Brit. Psychol. Soc.*, 1970, **23**, 261–269.

Jung, R. "Co-ordination of specific and non-specific apparent impulses at single neurones of the visual cortex." In H. H. Jasper (ed.), *Reticular formation of the brain*. London: Churchill, 1957.

Kaufman, H., Smith, J., and Zeaman, D. Tests of the generality of two empirical equations for motor learning. *Percept. Mot. Skills*, 1962, **15**, 91–100.

Keele, S. W., and Posner, M. I. Processing of visual feedback in rapid movements. *J. Exp. Psychol.*, 1968, **71**, 155–158.

Kendig, I., and Richmond, W. V. *Psychological studies in dementia praecox.* Ann Arbor: Edwards Bros., 1940.

Kendrick, D. C. Inhibition with reinforcement (conditioned inhibition). *J. Exp. Psychol.*, 1958, **56**, 313–318.

Kendrick, D. C. "The theory of "conditioned inhibition" as an explanation of negative practice effects: an experimental analysis." In H. J. Eysenck (ed.), *Behaviour therapy and the neuroses*. London: Pergamon Press, 1960.

Kent, G. H. Experiments on habit formation in dementia praecox. *Psychol. Rev.*, 1911, **18**, 375–410.

Kessell, R. An investigation into the factors affecting speed of response in psychiatric patients with special reference to distraction. Unpublished Ph.D. thesis, London University, 1955.

Kientzle, M. J. Properties of learning curves under varied distributions of practice. *J. Exp. Psychol.*, 1946, **36**, 187–211.

Kimble, G. A. An experimental test of a two-factor theory of inhibition. *J. Exp. Psychol.*, 1949a, **39**, 15–23.

Kimble, G. A. A further analysis of the variables in cyclical motor learning. *J. Exp. Psychol.*, 1949b, **39**, 332–337.

Kimble, G. A. Performance and reminiscence in motor learning as a function of the degree of distribution of practice. *J. Exp. Psychol.,* 1949c, **39,** 500–510.

Kimble, G. A. Evidence for the role of motivation in determining the amount of reminiscence in pursuit rotor learning. *J. Exp. Psychol.,* 1950, **40,** 248–253.

Kimble, G. A. Transfer of work inhibition in motor learning. *J. Exp. Psychol.,* 1952, **43,** 391–392.

Kimble, G. A., and Bilodeau, E. A. Work and rest as variables in cyclical motor learning. *J. Exp. Psychol.,* 1949, **39,** 150–157.

Kimble, G. A., and Horenstein, B. R. Reminiscence in motor learning as a function of length of interpolated rest. *J. Exp. Psychol.,* 1948, **38,** 239–244.

Kimble, G. A., and Shatel, R. B. The relationship between two kinds of inhibition and the amount of practice. *J. Exp. Psychol.,* 1952, **44,** 355–359.

King, H. E. *Psychomotor Aspects of mental disease.* Cambridge: Harvard University Press, 1954.

Kleinsmith, L. J., and Kaplan, S. Paired-associate learning as a function of arousal and interpolated interval. *J. Exp. Psychol.,* 1963, **65,** 190–193.

Kleinsmith, L. J., Kaplan, S., and Tarte, R. D. The relationship of arousal to short and long term recall. *Canad. J. Psychol.,* 1963, **17,** 393–397.

Kleinsmith, L. J., and Kaplan, S. Interaction of arousal and recall interval in nonsense-syllable paired-associate learning. *J. Exp. Psychol.,* 1964, **67,** 124–126.

Kling, J. W., Williams, J. P., and Schlosberg, H. Patterns of skin conductance during rotary pursuit. *Percept. Mot. Skills,* 1959, **9,** 303–312.

Kling, J. W., and Schlosberg, H. Relation of skin conductance and rotary pursuit during extended practice. *Percept. Mot. Skills,* 1961a, **12,** 270.

Kling, J. W., and Schlosberg, H. The uniqueness of patterns of skin conductance. *Amer. J. Psychol.,* 1961b, **74,** 74–79.

Koerth, W. A pursuit apparatus: eye-hand coordination. *Psychol. Monogr.,* 1922, **31,** 288–292.

Koch, S. Psychological science versus the science-humanism antimony: intimation of a significant science of man. *Am. Psychol.,* 1961, **16,** 629–639.

Kokubun, O., and Iizuka, A. Bilateral Reminiscence in pursuit-rotor learning. *"Tohoju Psychologica Folia,"* 1969, **27,** 113–121.

Koonce, J. M., Chambliss, D. J., and Irion, A. K. Long-term reminiscence in the pursuit-rotor habit. *J. Exp. Psychol.,* 1964, **67,** 498–500.

Kopell, B. S., Noble, E. P., and Silverman, J. The effect of thiamylal and methamphetamine on the two flash threshold. *Life Sci.,* 1965, **4,** 2211–2214.

Kraepelin, E. Der psychologische Versuch in der Psychiatrie. *Psychol. Arb.,* 1895, **1,** 1–91.

Kraepelin, G. *Psychiatrie,* Vol. 3. Leipzig: Barth, 1913.

Krantz, D. L. Research activities in "normal" and "anomalous" areas. *J. Hist. Behav. Sci.,* 1965, **1,** 39–42.

Kuhn, T. *The structure of scientific revolutions.* Chicago: University of Chicago Press, 1962.

Kurz, E., and Kraepelin, E. Über die Beeinflussung psychischer Vorgänge durch regelmässigen Alkoholgenuss. *Psychol. Arb.,* 1901, **3,** 417–457.

Lacey, J. I., and Lacey, B. C. Verification and extension of the principle of autonomic response-stereotypy. *Amer. J. Psychol.,* 1958, **71,** 50–73.

Lakatos, I., and Musgrave, A. *Criticism and the growth of knowledge.* Cambridge: University Press, 1970.

Laszlo, J. I., and Pritchard, D. A. Transfer variables in tracking skills. *J. Mot. Behav.,* 1969, **1,** 319–330.

Leavitt, H. The relation of speed of learning to amount retained and to reminiscence. *J. Exp. Psychol.*, 1945, **35,** 134–140.

Leavitt, H. J., and Schlosberg, H. The retention of verbal and of motor skills. *J. Exp. Psychol.*, 1944, **34,** 404–417.

Lefman, G. Über psychomotorische Störungen in Depressionszuständen. *Psychol. Arb.*, 1904, **4,** 603–668.

Leitenburg, H. The use of single-case methodology in psychotherapy research. *J. Abnorm. Psychol.*, 1973, **82,** 87–101.

Lenthold, D. L. Effects of motivation on rotary pursuit performance. Unpublished M.A. thesis, University of Montana, 1965.

Leonard, D. S., Karnes, E. W., Oxendine, J., and Hesson, J. Effects of task difficulty on transfer performance on rotary pursuit. *Percept. Mot. Skills,* 1970, **30,** 731–736.

Lersten, K. C. The effect of remoteness on intertrial correlations in pursuit rotor performance. *J. Mot. Behav.,* 1970, **2,** 79–87.

Leukel, F. P. The effect of ECS and pentathol anaesthesia on maze learning and retention. *J. Comp. Physiol. Psychol.,* 1957, **50,** 300–306.

Levine, J. M., Romashko, T., and Fleischman, E. A. Evaluation of an abilities classification system for integrating and generalising human performance research findings: an application to vigilance tasks. *J. Appl. Psychol.,* 1973, **58,** 149–157.

Lewis, A. Problems presented by the ambiguous word "anxiety" as used in psychopathology. *Israel Ann. Psychiat.,* 1967, **5,** 105–121.

Lindley, E. H. Uber Arbeit und Ruhe. *Psychol. Arb.,* 1901, **3,** 482–534.

Lindquist, E. F. (ed.). *Educational Measurement.* Washington: American Council on Education, 1951.

Lindsley, D. B. "The reticular system and perceptual discrimination." In H. H. Hasper (ed.), *Reticular formation of the brain.* London: Churchill, 1957.

Lobsien, M. Aussage und Wirklichkeit bei Schulkindern. *Beitr. z. Psychol. der Aussage,* 1904, **1,** 26–89.

Locke, E. A. Interaction of ability and motivation in performance. *Percept. Mot. Skills,* 1965, **21,** 719–725.

Loewald, A. Über die psychischen Wirkungen der Broms. *Psychol. Arb.,* 1895, **1,** 489–565.

London, P., Ogle, M. E., and Unikel, I. P. Effects of hypnosis and motivation on resistance to heat stress. *J. Abnorm. Psychol.,* 1968, **73,** 532–541.

Lord, F. M. The measurement of growth. *Educ. psychol. Measmt.,* 1956, **16,** 421–437.

Lorge, I. Influence of regularly interpolated time intervals upon subsequent learning. *Teach. Coll. Contrib. Educ.,* 1930, No. 438, 57.

Ludwig, S. M., Ward, B. S., and Davis, M. P. Auditory studies in schizophrenia. *Amer. J. Psychiat.,* 1962, **119,** 122–127.

Lykken, P. T., and Maley, M. Autonomic versus cortical arousal in schizophrenics and non-psychotics. *J. Psychiat. Res.,* 1968, **6,** 21–32.

Lynn, R. Extraversion, reminiscence and satiation effects. *Brit. J. Psychol.,* 1960, **51,** 319–324.

Lynn, R. Unpublished data, 1961.

Lynn, R. Russian theory and research on schizophrenia. *Psychol. Bull.,* 1963, **60,** 486–498.

Mackworth, J. F. Performance decrement in vigilance, threshold and high-speed perceptual motor tasks. *Canad. J. Psychol.,* 1964, **18,** 209–223.

Mailloux, N. M., & Neuburger, M. The work norms of psychotic individuals. *J. Abnorm. Soc. Psychol.,* 1941, **36,** 110–114.

Marr, D. A theory of cerebellar cortex. *J. Physiol.,* 1969, **202,** 437–470.

Marr, D. A theory for cerebral neocortex. *Proc. Roy. Soc. Lond. B.*, 1970, **176**, 161–234.

Martens, R., and Landers, D. M. Motor performance under stress: a test of the inverted-U hypothesis. *J. Pers. Soc. Psychol.*, 1970, **16**, 29–37.

Mather, K., and Jinks, J. L. *Biometrical genetics*. London: Chapman & Hall, 1971.

Matsui, M., and Kobayashi, T. The warming-up effect. *Jap. J. Psychol.*, 1935, **10**, 173–194.

Medawar, P. B. *The art of the soluble*. Methuen: London, 1967.

Medawar, P. B. *The hope of progress*. London: Methuen, 1972.

Mednick, S. G. A learning theory approach to research in schizophrenia. *Psychol. Bull.*, 1958, **55**, 316–327.

Meier, M. J. Inter-relationships among personality variables, kinesthetic figural after-effect, and reminiscence in motor learning. *J. Abnorm. Soc. Psychol.*, 1961, **63**, 87–94.

Meier, M. J. Reminiscence in inverted alphabet printing as a function of degree of EEG abnormality. *Percept. Mot. Skills*, 1964, **19**, 219–225.

Melton, A. W. (ed.). *Apparatus tests*. Washington: U.S. Gov't. Printing Office, 1947.

Melton, A. W. The effect of rest pauses on the acquisition of the pursuitmeter habit. *Psychol. Bull.*, 1941, **38**, 719.

Merton, P. A. Voluntary strength and fatigue. *J. Physiol.*, 1956, **123**, 557–564.

Miesemer, K. Über psychische Wirkungen körperlicher und geistiger Arbeit. *Psychol. Arb.*, 1904, **4**, 375–434.

Miles, W. R. A pursuit pendulum. *Psychol. Rev.*, 1920, **27**, 361–376.

Miller, N. E., and Coons, E. R. Conflict versus consolidation of memory to explain "retrograde amensia" produced by ECS. *Amer. Psychol.*, 1955, **10**, 394–395.

Mohan, J. An experimental study of determinants of reminiscence and post-rest extinction of conditioned inhibition. Unpublished Ph.D. thesis, Punjab University, Chandigarh, India, 1966.

Mohan, J. Personality and Reminiscence. *Indian J. Exp. Psychol.*, 1968a, **2**, 56–58.

Mohan, J. Disinhibition and Reminiscence. *Brit. J. Psychol.*, 1968b, **59**, 277–279.

Mohan, J., and Neelam. Reminiscence as a function of personality and motivation. *J. Psychol. Res.* (Madras), 1964, **13**, 89–94.

Mohan, J., and Shashi. Performance and reminiscence as functions of personality and drive. *Indian J. Exp. Psychol.*, 1972, **6**, 15–20.

Müller, E. A. Physiological methods of increasing human physical work capacity. *Ergonomics*, 1965, **8**, 409–424.

Müller, G. E., and Pilzecker, A. Experimentelle Beiträge zur Lehre vom Gedächtniss. *Z. Psychol.*, 1900, **1**, 1–300.

Munido, L. The influence of body temperature on performance in swimming. *Acta physiol. Scand.*, 1947, **12**, 102–109.

McClearn, G. E. "Genetic determination of behavior (animal)." In L. Ehrman, G. S. Omenn, and G. Caspari (eds.), *Genetics, environment and behaviour*. London: Academic Press, 1972.

McClelland, D. C., and Apicella, F. S. Reminiscence following experimentally induced failure. *J. Exp. Psychol.*, 1947, **37**, 159–169.

McGaugh, J. L., and Cole, J. M. Age and strain differences in the effect of distribution of practice on maze learning. *Psychonom. Sci.*, 1965, **2**, 253–254.

McGaugh, J. L., Jennings, R. D., and Thompson, C. W. Effect of distribution of practice on the maze learning of descendants of the Tryon maze bright and maze dull strains. *Psychol. Rep.*, 1962, **10**, 147–150.

McGaugh, J. L., and Petrinovich, L. The effect of strychnine sulphate on maze-learning. *Amer. J. Psychol.*, 1959, **72**, 99–102.

McGaugh, J. L., Westbrook, W. H., and Thompson, C. W. Facilitation of maze learning with post-trial injections of 5, 7-diphenyl—1, 3-diazadamanton—6-d (1757 I.S.). *J. Comp. Physiol. Psychol.*, 1962, **55**, 710–713.

McGeoch, G. O. The conditions of reminiscence. *Amer. J. Psychol.*, 1935, **47**, 63–89.

McGeoch, J. A., and Irion, A. L. *The psychology of human learning* (2nd ed.). New York: R. McKay, 1952.

McGhie, A., Chapman, J., and Lawson, J. S. The effect of distraction on schizophrenic performance. (I) Perception and immediate memory. *Brit. J. Psychiat.*, 1965, **111**, 383–390.

McLaughlin, R. J., & Eysenck, H. J. Extraversion, neuroticism and paired-associate learning. *J. Exp. Res. in Pers.*, 1967, **2**, 128–132.

McLean, P. D. Paired-associate learning as a function of recall interval, personality and arousal. Unpublished Ph.D. thesis, University of London, 1968.

McLean, P. D. Induced arousal and time of recall as determinants of paired-associate recall. *Brit. J. Psychol.*, 1969, **60**, 57–62.

McNemar, Q. Twin resemblances in motor skills, and the effect of practice thereon. *J. Genet. Psychol.*, 1933, **42**, 71–99.

Nacson, J., and Schmidt, R. A. The activity-set hypothesis for warm-up decrement. *J. Mot. Behav.*, 1971, **3**, 1–15.

Noble, C. E. An attempt to manipulate incentive-motivation in a continuous tracking task. *Percept. Mot. Skills*, 1955, **5**, 65–69.

Noble, C. E. Acquisition of pursuit tracking skill under extended training as a function of sex and initial ability. *J. Exp. Psychol.*, 1970, **86**, 360–373.

Noble, C. E., Fuchs, J. E., Rubel, D. P., and Chambers, R. W. Individual vs. social performance on two perceptual motor tasks. *Percept. Mot. Skills*, 1958, **8**, 131–134.

Noble, M., Fitts, P. M., and Warren, C. E. The frequency response of skilled subjects in a pursuit tracking task. *J. Exp. Psychol.*, 1955, **49**, 249–256.

Noltie, H. R. The effect of limbering-up on oxygen usage during track running. *J. Physiol.*, 1950, **111**, 15.

Nunney, D. N. Fatigue, impairment, and psycho-motor learning. *Percept. Mot. Skills*, 1963, **16**, 369–375.

O'Connor, N. Reminiscence and work decrement in catatonic and paranoid schizophrenics. *Brit. J. Med. Psychol.*, 1957, **30**, 188–193.

Oehrn, A. Experimentelle Studien zurn Individualpsychologie. *Psychol. Arb.*, 1895, **1**, 92–151.

Oseretzkowski, A., and Kraepelin, E. Über die Beeinflussung der Muskelleistung durch verschiedene Arbeitsbechingungen. *Psychol. Arb.*, 1901, **3**, 587–690.

Osgood, C. E. The similarity paradox in human learning. *Psychol. Rev.*, 1949, **56**, 132–143.

Osgood, C. E. Method and theory in experimental psychology. New York: Oxford University Press, 1953.

Pascal, C., and Svensen, G. Learning in mentally ill patients under unusual motivation. *J. Pers.*, 1952, **21**, 240–249.

Pauli, R. Untersuchungen zur Methodes des fortlaufenden Addierens. *Ztsch. angew. Psychol.*, Beiheft **29**, 1921.

Pauli, R. Beiträge zur Kentniss der Arbeitskurve. *Arch. f. d. ozen. Psychol.*, 1936, **97**, 465–532.

Pauli, R., and Arnold, W. *Der Pauli-Test.* München: J. A. Barth, 1951.

Pearlman, C. A. Jr., Sharpless, D. K., and Jarvik, M. E. Retrograde amnesia produced by anaesthetic and convulsant agents. *J. Comp. Physiol. Psychol.*, 1961, **54**, 109–112.

Perl, R. E. An application of Thurstone's method of factor analysis to practice series. *J. Gen. Psychol.*, 1939, **11**, 209–212.

Peters, E. N. Non-existent individual differences in reminiscence. *Psychol. Bull.*, 1972, **78**, 375–378.

Quarrington, B., and White, O. The differential substitutive learning ability of alcoholics, neurotics and normals. Toronto Psychiatric Hospital Technical Report, 1958.

Rachman, S. Disinhibition and the reminiscence effect in a motor learning task. *Brit. J. Psychol.*, 1962, **53**, 149–157.

Rachman, S. Inhibition and disinhibition in schizophrenics. *Arch. Gen. Psychiat.* 1963, **8**, 102–114.

Rachman, S., and Grassi, J. Reminiscence, inhibition and consolidation. *Brit. J. Psychol.*, 1965, **56**, 157–162.

Rappaport, M. Attention to competing noise message by non-acute schizophrenic patients. *J. Nerv. Ment. Dis.*, 1968, **140**, 404–411.

Rauschburg, P. Über Hemmung gleichzeitiger Reizwirkungen. *Ztsch. f. Psychol.*, 1902, **30**, 39–85.

Rauschburg, P. Über die Bedeutung der Ähnlichkeit beim Erlernen, Behalten, und bei der Reproduktion. *J. Psychol. Neurol.*, 1905, **5**, 113–288.

Ray, O. S. Personality factors in motor learning and reminiscence. *J. Abnorm. Soc. Psychol.*, 1959, **59**, 199–203.

Rechtschaffen, A. Neural satiation, reactive inhibition, and introversion-extraversion. *J. Abnorm. Soc. Psychol.*, 1958, **57**, 283–291.

Renshaw, S. An experimental test of the serial character of a case of pursuit. *J. Gen. Psychol.*, 1928, **1**, 520–533.

Renshaw, S., and Postle, D. K. Pursuit learning under three types of instruction. *J. Gen. Psychol.*, 1928, **1**, 360–367.

Renshaw, S., and Schwarzbek, W. C. The dependence of the form of the pursuit meter learning function on the length of the inter-practice rests: 1. Experimental. *J. Gen. Psychol.*, 1938a, **18**, 3–16.

Renshaw, S., and Schwarzbek, W. C. The dependence of the form of the pursuitmeter learning function on the length of the inter-practice rests: II. Theoretical. *J. Gen. Psychol.*, 1938b, **18**, 17–29.

Renshaw, S., Wallace, R. F., and Schwarzbek, W. C. Motion-picture analysis of the stages of acquisition of skill in pursuitmeter learning. Ohio State University, unpublished 800 ft. film, 1930. Quoted in S. Renshaw & W. C. Schwarzbek (1938a).

Renshaw, S., and Weiss, A. P. Apparatus for measuring changes in bodily posture. *Amer. J. Psychol.*, 1926, **28**, 261–267.

Reuning, H. The Pauli-Test: new findings from factor-analysis. *J. Nat. Inst. Personnel Res.*, 1957, **7**, 3–27.

Reyna, L. J. An experimental study of work inhibition in motor learning. Unpublished Master's thesis, State University of Iowa, 1944.

Reynolds, B. Extinction of trace conditioned responses as a function of the spacing of trials during the acquisition and extinction series. *J. Exp. Psychol.*, 1945, **35**, 81–85.

Reynolds, B. Correlation between two psychomotor tasks as a function of distribution of practice on the first. *J. Exp. Psychol.*, 1952a, **43**, 341–348.

Reynolds, B. The effect of learning on the predictability of psychomotor performance. *J. Exp. Psychol.*, 1952b, **44**, 189–198.

Reynolds, B., and Adams, J. A. Effect of distribution and shift in distribution of practice within a single training session. *J. Exp. Psychol.*, 1953, **46**, 137–145.

Reynolds, B., and Adams, J. Psychomotor performance as a function of initial level of ability. *Amer. J. Psychol.*, 1954, **67**, 268–277.

Rivers, W. H. R., and Kraepelin, E. Über Ermüdung und Erhulung. *Psychol. Arb.*, 1895, **1**, 627–678.

Rock, I. The role of repetition in associative learning. *Am. J. Psychol.*, 1957.

Rockway, M. R. Bilateral reminiscence in pursuit-rotor learning as a function of amount of first-hand practice and length of rest. *J. Exp. Psychol.*, 1953, **46**, 337–344.

Rockway, M. R., and Duncan, C. P. Pre-recall warming-up in verbal retention. *J. Exp. Psychol.*, 1952, **43**, 305–312.

Rodnick, E. H., and Shakow, D. Set in the schizophrenic as measured by a composite reaction time index. *Amer. J. Psychiat.*, 1940, **97**, 214–225.

Rohment, W. Ermittlung von Erholungspausen für statische Arbeit der Menschen. *Intern. z. angew Physiol.*, 1960, **18**, 123–164.

Rosenquist, H. S. The visual response component of rotary pursuit tracking. *Percept. Mot. Skills*, 1965, **21**, 555–560.

Rüdin, E. Über die Dauer der psychischen Alkoholwirkung. *Psychol. Arb.*, 1904, **4**, 1–44.

Russell, W. R., and Nathan, P. W. Traumatic amnesia. *Brain*, 1946, **69**, 280–300.

Salsinger, K. *Schizophrenia: behavioral aspects*. London: Wiley, 1973.

Sarasan, S. B. "The measurement of anxiety in children: some questions and problems." In C. D. Spielberger (ed.), *Anxiety and behavior*. New York: Academic Press, 1966.

Schmidt, R. A., and Nacson, J. Further tests of the activity-set hypothesis for warm-up decrement. *J. Exp. Psychol.*, 1971, **90**, 56–64.

Schmidt, R. A., and Wrisberg, C. A. The activity-set hypothesis for warm-up decrement in a movement-speed task. *J. Mot. Behav.*, 1971, **3**, 318–325.

Schmidtke, H. *Die Ermüdung*. Bern: Hans Huber, 1965.

Schwartz, S. Individual differences in cognition: some relationships between personality and memory. Personal communication, 1974.

Seashore, R. H. Stanford motor skills unit. *Psychol. Monogr.*, 1928, **39**, 51–66.

Seashore, R. H. Individual differences in motor skills. *J. Gen. Psychol.*, 1930, **3**, 38–66.

Seashore, R. H. "Work and motor performance." In S. S. Stevens (ed.), *Handbook of experimental psychology*. New York: Wiley, 1951.

Seunath, O. H. M. Strategy and consolidation in pursuit rotor performance. Unpublished Ph.D. thesis, London University, 1973.

Shakow, D. The nature of deterioration in schizophrenic conditions. *Nerv. ment. dis. Monogr.* No. 70, New York: Coolidge Foundation, 1946.

Shakow, D. Sequential set: a theory of the formal psychological deficit in schizophrenia. *Arch. gen. Psychiat.*, 1962, **6**, 1–17.

Shakow, D. Psychological deficit in schizophrenia. *Behav. Sci.*, 1963, **8**, 275–305.

Shakow, D. "Some psychophysiological aspects of schizophrenia." In J. Romano (ed.), *The origins of schizophrenia*. Amsterdam: Excerpta Medica Foundation, 1967.

Shapiro, M. B. The single case in fundamental clinical psychological research. *Brit. J. Med. Psychol.*, 1961, **34**, 255–262.

Slater, P. Theory and Technique of the repertory grid. *Brit. J. Psychiat.*, 1969, **118**, 1287–1296.

Snoddy, G. S. An experimental analysis of a case of trial and error learning in the human subject. *Psychol. Monogr.*, 1920, **28**, No. 124.

Snoddy, G. S. Learning and stability. *J. Appl. Psychol.*, 1926, **10**, 1–36.

Snoddy, G. S. *Evidence for two opposed processes in mental growth*. Lancaster: Science Press, 1935.

Snoddy, G. S. A reply to Doré and Hilgard. *J. Exp. Psychol.*, 1938, **23**, 375–383.

Sorgatz, H. Motorisches Lernen und Aktivierung. Unpublished Ph.D. thesis, Ruhr-Universitat Bochum, 1974.

Spain, B. Eyelid conditioning and arousal in schizophrenic and normal subjects. *J. Abnorm. Psychol.*, 1966, **71**, 260–266.

Spearman, C. *The abilities of man.* London: Macmillan, 1927.

Spence, W., Buxton, E., and Melton, A. W. The effect of massing and distribution of practice on rotary pursuit test scores. *Civil Aeronautics Admin. Report,* (Washington, D.C.), 1945, **44**, 9–38.

Spielberger, C. D., Gorsuch, R. L., and Lushene, R. E. *Manual for the state-trait anxiety inventory.* Palo Alto, Calif: Consulting Psychologists Press, 1970.

Spielman, I. The relation between personality and the frequency and duration of involuntary rest pauses during massed practice. Unpublished Ph.D. thesis, London University, 1963.

Stanley, J. C. "Reliability." In R. L. Thorndike (ed.), *Educational Measurement.* Washington: American Council on Education, 1971.

Star, K. W. An experimental study of "reactive inhibition" and its relation to certain personality traits. Unpublished Ph.D. thesis, University of London, 1957.

Star, K. H. Reminiscence, drive and personality theory: replication. *Percept. Mot. Skills,* 1963, **17**, 337–378.

Stetsan, R. H., and Bouman, H. D. The coordination of simple skilled movements. *Arch. néerl. Physiol.*, 1935, **22**, 177–254.

Stilson, D. W., and Kopell, B. G. The recognition of visual signals in the presence of visual noise by psychiatric patients. *J. Nerv. Ment. Dis.*, 1964, **139**, 209–221.

Stilson, D. W., Kopell, B. S., Vandenbergh, R., and Davies, M. P. Perceptual recognition in the presence of noise by psychiatric patients. *J. Nerv. Ment. Dis.*, 1966, **172**, 235–247.

Stork, C. M. *Vigilance: the problem of sustained attention.* London: Pergamon Press, 1972.

Strickland, B. R., and Jenkins, O. Simple motor performance under positive and negative approval motivation. *Percept. Mot. Skills,* 1964, **19**, 599–605.

Taylor, A. B., and Irion, A. L. Continuity hypothesis and transfer of training in paired-associate learning. *J. Exp. Psychol.*, 1964, **68**, 573–577.

Taylor, F. W. *The principles of scientific management.* New York: Harper, 1915.

Thayer, J., and Silber, D. E. Relationships between levels of arousal and responsiveness among schizophrenics and normal subjects. *J. Abnorm. Psychol.*, 1971, **77**, 162–173.

Thompson, G. G., and Hunnicutt, C. W. The effect of reprated praise or blame on the work achievement of "introverts" and "extraverts." *J. Educ. Psychol.*, 1944, **35**, 257–266.

Thompson, R. The effect of intracranial stimulation on memory in cats. *J. Comp. Physiol. Psychol.*, 1958, **51**, 421–426.

Thompson, R., and Pryer, R. S. The effect of anoxia on the retention of a discrimination habit. *J. Comp. Physiol. Psychol.*, 1956, **49**, 297–300.

Thorndike, E. L. *The psychology of learning.* New York: Teacher's College, 1913.

Thorndike, E. L. The psychology of learning. *Educ. Psychol.*, 1914a, **2**, 194–206.

Thorndike, E. L. Mental work and fatigue. *Educ. Psychol.*, 1914b, **3**, 66–68.

Thune, L. E. The effects of different types of preliminary activities on subsequent learning of paired-associate learning. *J. Exp. Psychol.*, 1950, **40**, 423–438.

Thune, L. E. Warm-up effect as a function of level of practice in verbal learning. *J. Exp. Psychol.*, 1951, **42**, 250–256.

Tizard, J., and Venables, P. The influence of extraneous stimulation on the RT of schizophrenics. *Brit. J. Psychol.*, 1957, **48**, 299–305.

Travis, R. C. Practice and rest periods in motor learning. *J. Psychol.,* 1936, **3,** 183–187.

Travis, R. C. The effect of the length of the rest-period on motor learning. *J. Psychol.,* 1937, **3,** 189–194.

Trayer, M. E. Influence of the lengths of intercyclic interval on pursuitmeter learning. Unpublished Master's thesis, Ohio State University, 1930.

Treadwell, E. Motor reminiscence and individual personality differences. Unpublished B.A. thesis, Queen's University, Belfast, 1956.

Tulving, E. Subjective organisation in free recall of "unrelated" words. *Psychol. Rev.,* 1962, **69,** 344–354.

Underwood, B. J. "Motor-skills learning and verbal learning: some observations." In, E. A. Bilodeau (ed.), *Acquisition of skill,* pp. 489–516. London: Academic Press, 1966.

Vandenberg, S. G. The hereditary abilities study: hereditary components in a psychological test battery. *Amer. J. Human Genet.,* 1962, **14,** 220–237.

Venables, P. H. A short scale for rating "activity-withdrawal" in schizophrenics. *J. Mental Sci.,* 1957, **103,** 197–199.

Venables, P. H. Factors in the motor behaviour of functional psychotics. *J. Abnorm. Soc. Psychol.,* 1959, **58,** 153–156.

Venables, P. H. The effect of auditory and visual stimulation on skin potential response of schizophrenics. *Brain,* 1960, **83,** 77–92.

Venables, P. H. Changes due to noise in the threshold of fusion of paired light flashes in schizophrenics and normals. *Brit. J. Soc. Clin. Psychol.,* 1963a, **2,** 94–99.

Venables, P. H. The relationship between level of skin potential and fusion of paired light flashes in schizophrenics and normal subjects. *J. Psychiatric Res.* 1963b, **1,** 279–286.

Venables, P. H. Selectivity of attention, withdrawal, and cortical activation. *Arch. Gen. Psychiat.,* 1963c, **9,** 74–78.

Venables, P. H. A comparison of two flash and two click thresholds in schizophrenic and normal subjects. *Q. J. Exp. Psychol.,* 1966, **18,** 371–373.

Venables, P. H., and O'Connor, N. A short scale for rating paranoid schizophrenics. *J. Mental Sci.,* 1959, **105,** 815–818.

Venables, P. H., and Tizard, J. Performance of functional psychotics on a repetitive task. *J. Abnorm. Soc. Psychol.,* 1956, **53,** 23–26.

Venables, P. H., and Wing, J. K. Level of arousal and subclassification of schizophrenics. *Arch. Gen. Psychiatry,* 1962, **7,** 114–119.

Verma, R. M., and Eysenck, H. J. Severity and type of psychotic illness as a function of personality. *Brit. J. Psychiatry,* 1973, **122,** 573–585.

Vince, M. Corrective movements in a pursuit task. *Q. J. Exp. Psychol.,* 1948, **1,** 85–105.

Viteles, M. S. The influence of training on motor test performance. *J. Exp. Psychol.,* 1933, **16,** 556–564.

Voss, G. von. Über die Schwankungen der geistigen Arbeitsleistung. *Psychol. Arb.,* 1899, **2,** 399–449.

Wade, T. Some effects of shifts of rotation speeds under massed practice in a pursuit rotor task. *J. Child Develop.,* 1970, **6,** 63–77.

Walker, E. L. The course and duration of the reaction decrement and the influence of reward. *J. Comp. Physiol. Psychol.,* 1956, **49,** 167–176.

Walker, E. L. Action decrement and its relation to learning. *Psychol. Res.,* 1958, **65,** 129–172.

Walker, E. L., and Paradise, N. A positive correlation between action decrement and learning. *J. Exp. Psychol.,* 1958, **56,** 45–47.

Walker, E. L., and Tarte, R. D. Memory storage as a function of arousal time with homogeneous and heterogeneous lists. *J. Verbal Learning and Verbal Behavior,* 1963, **2,** 113–119.

Ward, L. B. Reminiscence and rote learning. *Psychol. Monogr.*, 1937, **49**, No. 220.

Wasserman, H. N. The effect of motivation and amount of pre-rest practice upon inhibitory potential in motor learning. *J. Exp. Psychol.*, 1951, **42**, 162–172.

Wasserman, H. N. A unifying theoretical approach to motor learning. *Psychol. Rev.*, 1952, **59**, 278–284.

Webb, W. W. Massed versus distributed practice in pursuitmeter learning. *J. Gen. Psychol.*, 1933, **8**, 272–278.

Weiler, K. Untersuchungen über die Muskelarbeit der Menschen. *Psychologische Arb.*, 1910, 528–582.

Wells, F. L. Normal performance in the tapping test. *Amer. J. Psychol.*, 1908, **19**, 437–483.

Weygandt, W. Über den Einfluss des Arbeitswechsels auf fortlaufende, geistige Arbeit. *Psychologische Arb.*, 1899, **8**, 118–202.

Wheeler, R. H. *The science of psychology.* New York: Crowell 1929.

Wheeler, R. H., and Perkins, F. T. *Principles of mental development.* New York: Crowell 1932.

Willett, R. A., and Eysenck, H. J. An experimental study of human motivation. *Life Sciences*, 1962, **4**, 119–127.

Williams, H. L., Lubin, A., and Goodman, J. J. Impaired performance with acute sleep loss. *Psychol. Monogr.*, 1959, No. 484.

Wilson, C. D., Tunstall, O. A., and Eysenck, H. J. Individual differences in tapping performance as a function of time on the task. *Percep. Mot. Skills*, 1971, **33**, 375–378.

Wimer, R., Symington, L., Farmer, H., and Schwartzbrain, T. Differences in memory processes between inbred mouse strains C57 BL/6Z and DBA/2Z. *J. Comp. Physiol. Psychol.*, 1968, **65**, 126–131.

Wishart, G. M. A new type of pursuit-meter. *Brit. J. Psychol.*, 1923, **14**, 94–98.

Withey, S., Buxton, C. E., and Elkin, A. Control of rest interval activities in serial verbal learning. *J. Exp. Psychol.*, 1949, **39**, 173–176.

Wright, S. T. H., and Taylor, D. V. Distributed practice in verbal learning and the motivation hypothesis. *J. Exp. Psychol.*, 1949, **39**, 527–531.

Yates, A. J., and Laszlo, I. Learning and performance of extraverts and introverts in the pursuit rotor. *J. Pers. Soc. Psychol.*, 1965, **1**, 79–84.

Zacks, R. T. Invariance of total learning time under different conditions of practice. *J. Exp. Psychol.*, 1969, **82**, 441–447.

Zeaman, D., and Kaufman, H. Individual differences and theory in a motor learning task. *Psychol. Monogr.*, 1955, **69**, No. 6.

Reference Index

Subject Index